CONDUCTOR BOOK 3

ESSENTIAL TECHNIQUE for Band

INTERMEDIATE TO ADVANCED STUDIES

TIM LAUTZENHEISER • JOHN HIGGINS • CHARLES MENGHINI
PAUL LAVENDER • TOM C. RHODES • DON BIERSCHENK

Percussion consultant and editor
WILL RAPP

To create an account, visit:
www.essentialelementsinteractive.com

Activation Code
E3BD-5057-7084-8283

ISBN 979-835013663-0

TABLE OF CONTENTS

SEQUENCE OF

Director Page	1	12–17	18–24	25–27	28–34	35–41	42–47	48–51	52–56	57–63	64–67	68–71
Student Page	**1**	**2**	**3**	**4**	**5**	**6**	**7**	**8**	**9**	**10**	**11**	**12**
Rhythms				Rhythm Rap			Rhythm Rap	Rhythm Rap			Rhythm Rap	Rhythm Rap, Sixteenth Notes and Rests
Theory				$\frac{3}{8}$, $\frac{9}{8}$	Minor Keys			$\frac{12}{8}$			Triplets with Rests	
History			Handel, Baroque Period				Johann Strauss Jr.		Native American Music		Claude Debussy	
Terms		*div.*, *a2*	Maestoso				Tempo di Valse, Operetta	Lento, molto	Lento Mysterioso		Giocoso	
Special Features	Title Page	Concert B♭ Major, Chorale, Chromatic Scale			Concert A Minor, EE Quiz	Concert E♭ Major, Chorale, Chromatic Scale			Concert C Minor, EE Quiz	Concert F Major, Chorale, Chromatic Scale		EE Quiz
Note Sequence												
Flute												
Oboe												
Bassoon		*Enharmonic*										
B♭ Clarinet									*Enharm.*			
E♭ Alto Clar.												
B♭ Bass Clar.					*Enharm.*	*Enharm.*						
E♭ Alto Sax.						*Enharm.*						
B♭ T. Sax.												
E♭ Bar. Sax.			*Enharm.*			Alt.						
B♭ Trumpet Bar. T.C.										Tpt.		
F Horn												
Trombone Bar. B.C. E. Bass						(- Bass)						
Tuba												
Kybd. Perc.												
Percussion Techniques			16th Note Rhythm Review				Five Stroke Roll Nine Stroke Roll	Flam Accent No. 2		Reverse Paradiddle		
New Perc. Instruments			Tam-Tam (Gong)		Concert Tom-Toms Anvil (Brake Drum)							

ESSENTIAL TECHNIQUE

Director Page	72–77	78–84	85–89	90–93	94–99	100–105	106–109	110–113	114–120	121–127	128–132	133–137
Student Page	**13**	**14**	**15**	**16**	**17**	**18**	**19**	**20**	**21**	**22**	**23**	**24**
Rhythms				Rhythm Rap				Rhythm Rap			Rhythm Rap	
Theory				Grace Note				Quarter Note Triplets	Meter Changes		$\frac{5}{4}$	
History			Star Spangled Banner				African American Spirituals	African Folk Music	Late 19th Cent. French Composers			Handel, Baroque Period
Terms	Allegro Vivo		*ff* *pp*	Andante Grazioso	Agitato						Espressivo	
Special Features	Concert D Minor, EE Quiz	Concert A♭ Major, Chorale, Chromatic Scale			Concert F Minor, EE Quiz	Concert C Major, Chorale, Chromatic Scale	Duet		Concert A Minor	Concert D♭ Major, Chorale, Chromatic Scale		EE Quiz
Note Sequence												
Flute												
Oboe										*Enharm.*		
Bassoon										Alt.	Alt.	
B♭ Clarinet	*Enharm.*											
E♭ Alto Clar.												
B♭ Bass Clar.		*Enharm.*										
E♭ Alto Sax.	*Enharm.*	Alt. *Enharm.*				Alt.				*Enharm.*		
B♭ T. Sax.	*Enharm.*	*Enharm.*										
E♭ Bar. Sax.		Alt. *Enharm.*				Alt.				*Enharm.*		
B♭ Trumpet Bar. T.C.		*Enharm.*										
F Horn												
Trombone Bar. B.C. E. Bass		(- Bass) *Enharm.*										
Tuba		Bass										
Kybd. Perc.												
Percussion Techniques		Four Stroke Ruff				Inward Paradiddle				Ex. 1 R R R R L L L L Ex. 2 Four Stroke Ruff		
New Perc. Instruments					Brushes			Agogo Bells	Finger Cymbals			

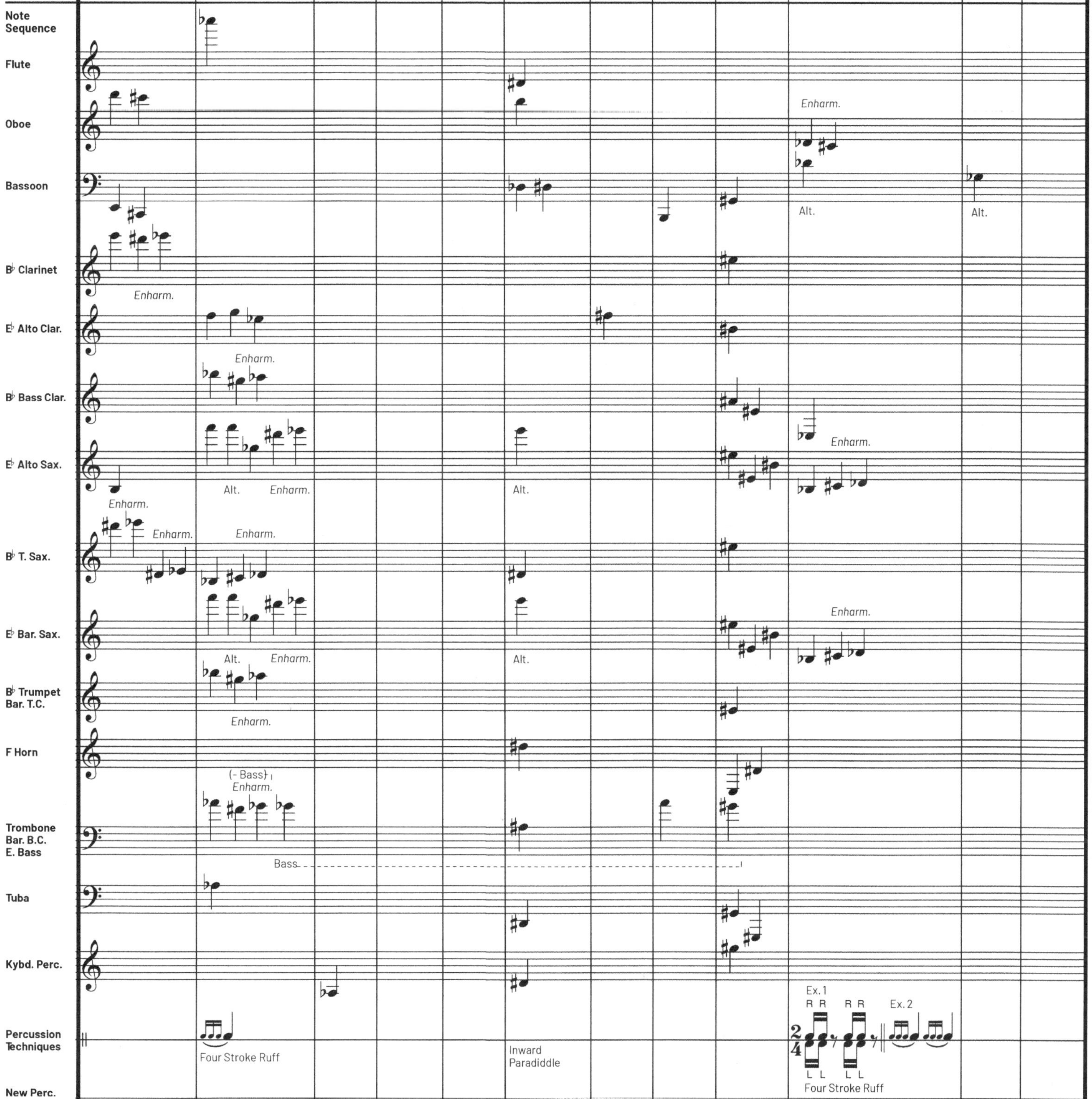

SEQUENCE OF

Director Page	138–142	143–149	150–155	156–161	162–167	168–173	174–179	180–189	180–189	190–196	197–201	202–209
Student Page	**25**	**26**	**27**	**28**	**29**	**30**	**31**	**32**	**33**	**34**	**35**	**36**
Rhythms												
Theory	Ostinato			D.C. al Coda/ D.S. al Coda								
History	Gustav Holst		Nationalism/ Composers, Renaissance Period	Native Japanese Instruments		Latin American Music, Romantic Period						
Terms			Marziale, Animato									
Special Features	Concert B♭ Minor, Duet/Trio	Concert G Major, Chorale, Chromatic Scale		Concert E Minor	Concert D Major, Chorale, Chromatic Scale, Concert B Minor		Concert G♭ Major, Chorale, Chromatic Scale, Concert E♭ Major	Individual Studies	Individual Studies	Reading Skill Builders	Reading Skill Builders	Chorales
Note Sequence												
Flute		Alt.										
Oboe												
Bassoon												
B♭ Clarinet												
E♭ Alto Clar.												
B♭ Bass Clar.												
E♭ Alto Sax.												
B♭ T. Sax.												
E♭ Bar. Sax.												
B♭ Trumpet Bar. T.C.				Bar.								
F Horn												
Trombone Bar. B.C. E. Bass		(- Bass)			(- Bass)							
Tuba												
Kybd. Perc.												
Percussion Techniques		Delayed Paradiddle	or or Crushed Ruff		Thirteen Stroke Roll Seventeen Stroke Roll		Seven Stroke Roll		Drag Paradiddle No. 1 Drag Paradiddle No. 2 Lesson 25 Single Ratamacue Triple Ratamacue			
New Perc. Instruments												

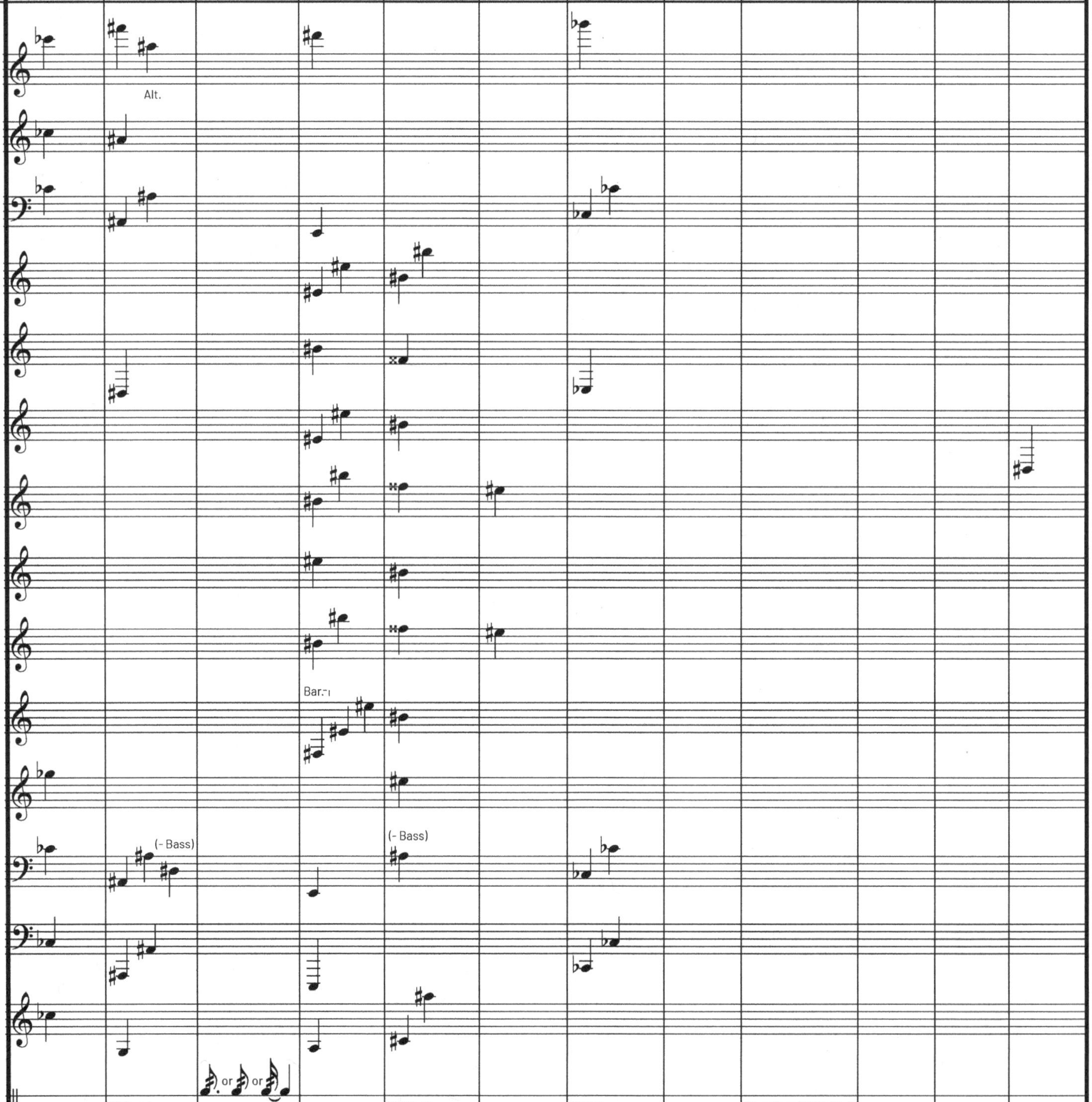

ESSENTIAL TECHNIQUE

Director Page	210-217	218	219	220-223	224-229	230-234	235-240	241-244	245-261	262-299	262-299	300-301
Student Page	**37**	**38**	**39**	**40**	**41**	**42**	**43**	**44**	**45**	**46**	**47**	**48**
Rhythms												
Theory												
History												
Terms												
Special Features	Chorales	Rhythm Studies	Rhythm Studies	Basics of Jazz Style	Basics of Jazz Style	Major Scales	Major Scales	Minor Scales	Woodwinds: Trill Chart, Brass: Special Exercises, Bass: Bass Tips	Fingering Chart, Percussion Rudiment Chart	Fingering Chart, Percussion Rudiment Chart	Reference Index

STUDENT BOOKS

00870335	FLUTE
00870336	OBOE
00870337	BASSOON
00870338	B♭ CLARINET
00870339	E♭ ALTO CLARINET
00870340	B♭ BASS CLARINET
00870341	E♭ ALTO SAXOPHONE
00870342	B♭ TENOR SAXOPHONE
00870343	E♭ BARITONE SAXOPHONE
00870344	B♭ TRUMPET
00870345	F HORN
00870346	TROMBONE
00870347	BARITONE (B.C.)
00870348	BARITONE (T.C.)
00870349	TUBA
00870350	ELECTRIC BASS
00870351	PERCUSSION (incl. Keyboard)

USING ESSENTIAL TECHNIQUE

Essential Technique is a multipurpose book for band musicians that can be used with full band, like-instrument classes, or by individuals. It can serve as a technique-building tool for any band program or function as Book 3 of the *Essential Elements* comprehensive method. Concepts, new notes, and musical terms introduced in *Essential Technique* follow the pedagogy of *Essential Elements* Books 1 and 2.

The Conductor Book includes all music and text from the students' books. As in the student books, the introduction of a new concept is always highlighted by a **color** box.

KEY CENTERED SYSTEM

Essential Technique is organized with sections featuring **9 major keys** and their **related minor keys**. Each major key is introduced with a scale exercise, short etudes, and also includes a chromatic scale.

The **Balance Builder** is designed to teach balance within triadic chord structures and is best suited to small like-instrument lessons or small mixed ensembles.

The full band **Chorale** found at the bottom of each major key page (in the student books) is written to develop the full band sonority in the featured key. Each instrument part is written to included ALL scale degrees of the key, i.e., all players play every note of the major scale within the chorale.

The **related minor key** follows each major key, with scales introducing the natural and harmonic versions.

Each key section has **music examples** to build technique, reinforce the key center, and introduce new notes, rhythms, and concepts. Carefully selected excerpts from classical, folk, and cultural music provide a wide variety of styles throughout the book.

RHYTHM RAPS

Like *Essential Elements* Books 1 and 2, new rhythms and meters are presented as clapping exercises in the innovative **Rhythm Rap** format. After each Rhythm Rap, the identical rhythms are played on simple pitches in the next exercise. Finally, in subsequent exercises they appear in appropriate melodic settings.

SPECIAL STUDIES SECTION

Starting on page 32 of each student book, the **Special Studies** section includes several categories for individual and group use:

Individual Studies – Student pages 32-33

Specially designed individual instrument studies explore useful techniques that are commonly associated with each instrument, such as alternate fingerings, lip slurs, etc. They also provide an opportunity to develop the concepts of expression, articulation, ornamentation, and tonguing. Each Play-along track features a professional player demonstrating the etudes. (Not included on the Conductor CD.)

Reading Skill Builders – Student pages 34-35

These etudes are carefully written to improve reading skills, or may be used to assess sight-reading ability. They incorporate various rhythms, keys, and musical styles to further strengthen the student's musical aptitude. These skill builders can be used with full band or individuals. The Play-along tracks include a piano accompaniment without a melody cue.

Chorales – Student pages 36-37

Seven full-length chorales arranged by John Higgins can work as a warm-up, for balance and intonation study, or for a performance.

Rhythm Studies – Student pages 38-39

These supplementary rhythm studies become sequentially more advanced and can be used in any length of measure groupings. Simply choose the beginning and ending measures, plus any repetition desired.

Start by using a single pitch throughout the measure(s) selected. Then, change pitch only at the beginnings of measures. By specifying different times to change pitch, the rhythms can be very challenging.

The accompaniments include background tracks at both slow and fast tempo for each metered section.

Basics Of Jazz Style – Student pages 40–41

Taken from *Essential Elements for Jazz Ensemble* by Mike Steinel, these pages introduce the basics of jazz style and improvisation.

The included exercises have been selected for use with full concert band, small ensembles, or individuals. Demonstration and accompaniment tracks are included on the Play-along tracks.

Scales And Arpeggios – Student pages 42–44

Two-octave scales and arpeggios for 10 major keys and 5 minor keys, including melodic minor, provide study for extended range development. The Play-along tracks have demonstration and accompaniment tracks for each exercise.

MUSIC THEORY, HISTORY, AND CROSS-CURRICULAR ACTIVITIES

All the necessary materials to relate music to history, world cultures or other subjects are woven into the learning program—right in the student books. These Theory and History features are highlighted by **color** boxes and appear throughout the book.

As a result, teachers can efficiently meet and exceed the ***National Standards for Arts Education***, while still having the time to focus on music performance skills.

Online audio includes:

- Individual Studies (for each instrument)
- Reading Skill Builders (accompaniment only)
- Chorales (full band recordings)
- Rhythm Studies (accompaniment tracks at slow and fast tempos)
- Basics of Jazz Style (full band demonstration and accompaniment tracks)
- Scales and Arpeggios (full band demonstration and accompaniment tracks)

B♭ MAJOR

1. SCALE AND ARPEGGIO *Practice both upper and lower octaves.**

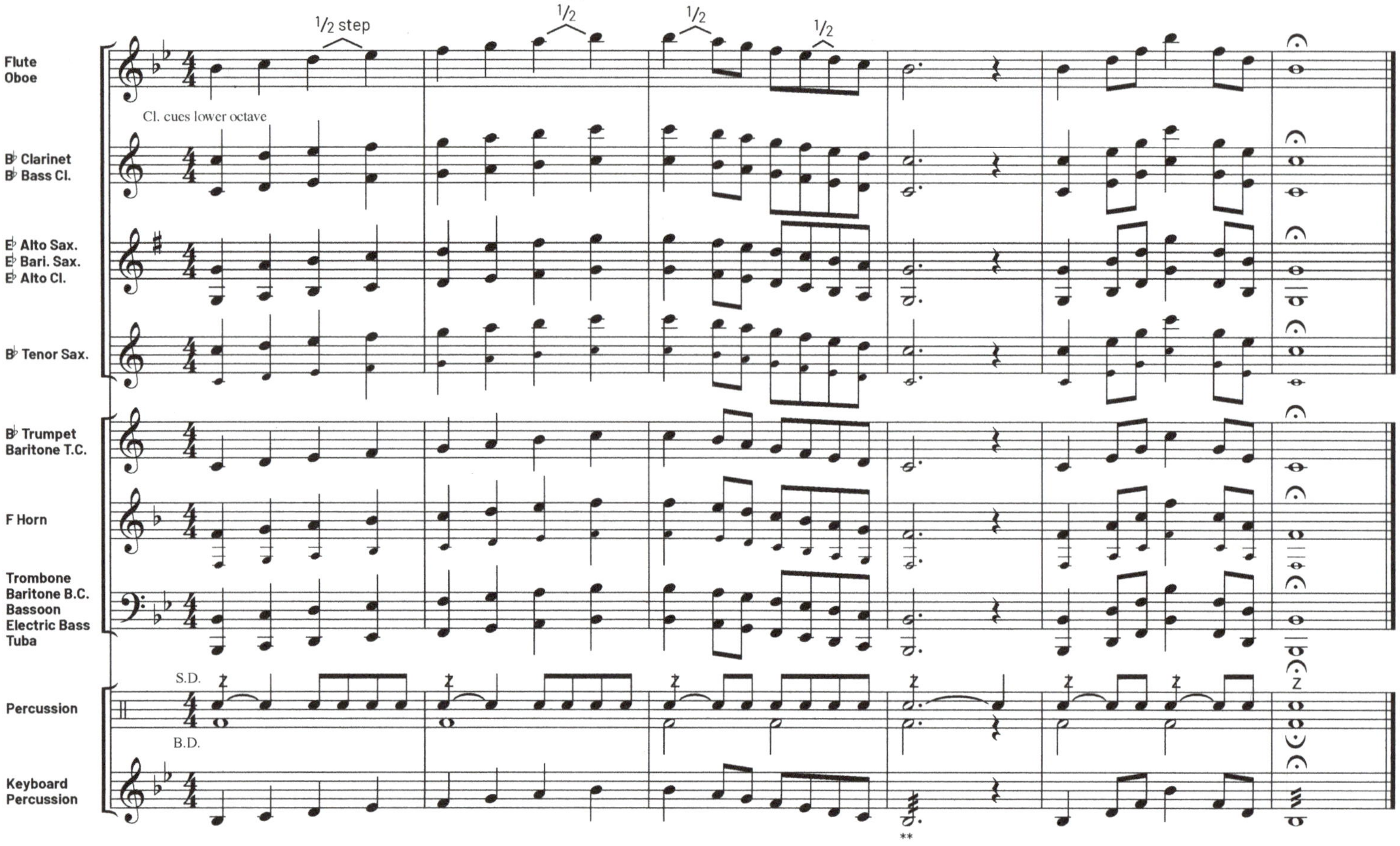

1/2 step
1/2
1/2
1/2
Flute
Oboe
Cl. cues lower octave
B♭ Clarinet
B♭ Bass Cl.
E♭ Alto Sax.
E♭ Bari. Sax.
E♭ Alto Cl.
B♭ Tenor Sax.
B♭ Trumpet
Baritone T.C.
F Horn
Trombone
Baritone B.C.
Bassoon
Electric Bass
Tuba
S.D.
Percussion
B.D.
Keyboard
Percussion
**

Tenor Saxophone
B
F Horn
G
T

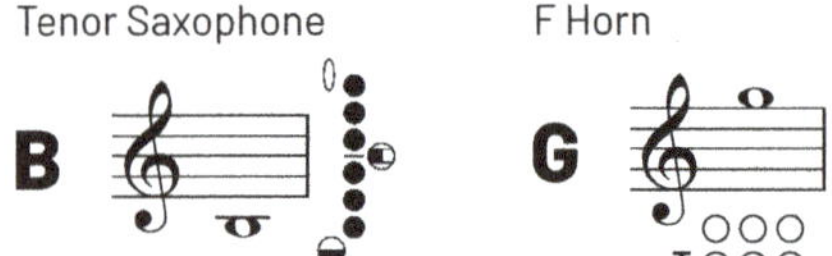

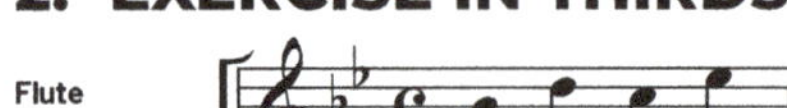

2. EXERCISE IN THIRDS

Flute
Oboe
B♭ Clarinet
B♭ Bass Cl.
E♭ Alto Sax.
E♭ Bari. Sax.
E♭ Alto Cl.
B♭ Tenor Sax.
B♭ Trumpet
Baritone T.C.
F Horn
Trombone
Baritone B.C.
Bassoon
Electric Bass
Tuba
L R R R L L L R R R L
L R L R L L R R R L
S.D.
Percussion
B.D.
Keyboard
Percussion

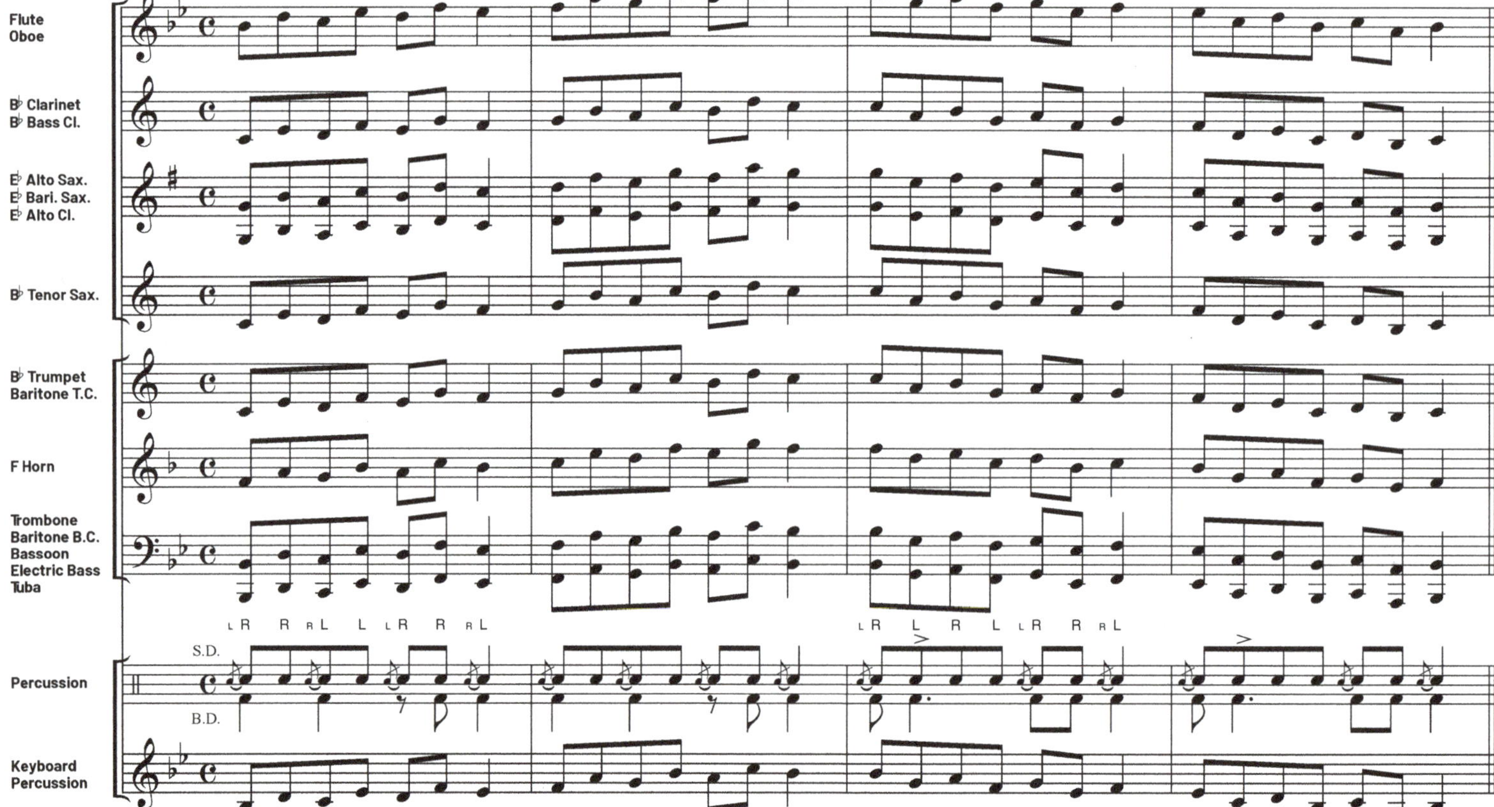

*Student books have two octaves at times throughout.
**Throughout this book, rolls are for xylophone and marimba only.

3. ARPEGGIO STUDY

*A. Cl.: For smoother technique, try using "right" B (R) when not in combination with C.

Bassoon

4. TWO-PART ETUDE

Fl. cues lower octave

Flute
Oboe

a2

B♭ Clarinet
B♭ Bass Cl.

E♭ Alto Sax.
E♭ Bari. Sax.
E♭ Alto Cl.

B♭ Tenor Sax.

B♭ Trumpet
Baritone T.C.

F Horn

Trombone
Baritone B.C.
Bassoon
Electric Bass

Bsn. 8vb

Tuba

L R L R R R L R L L L R L R R R L R L L R L R L R R L R L R L L R L R L R L R L R L R L

S.D.

B.D.

Percussion

Keyboard
Percussion

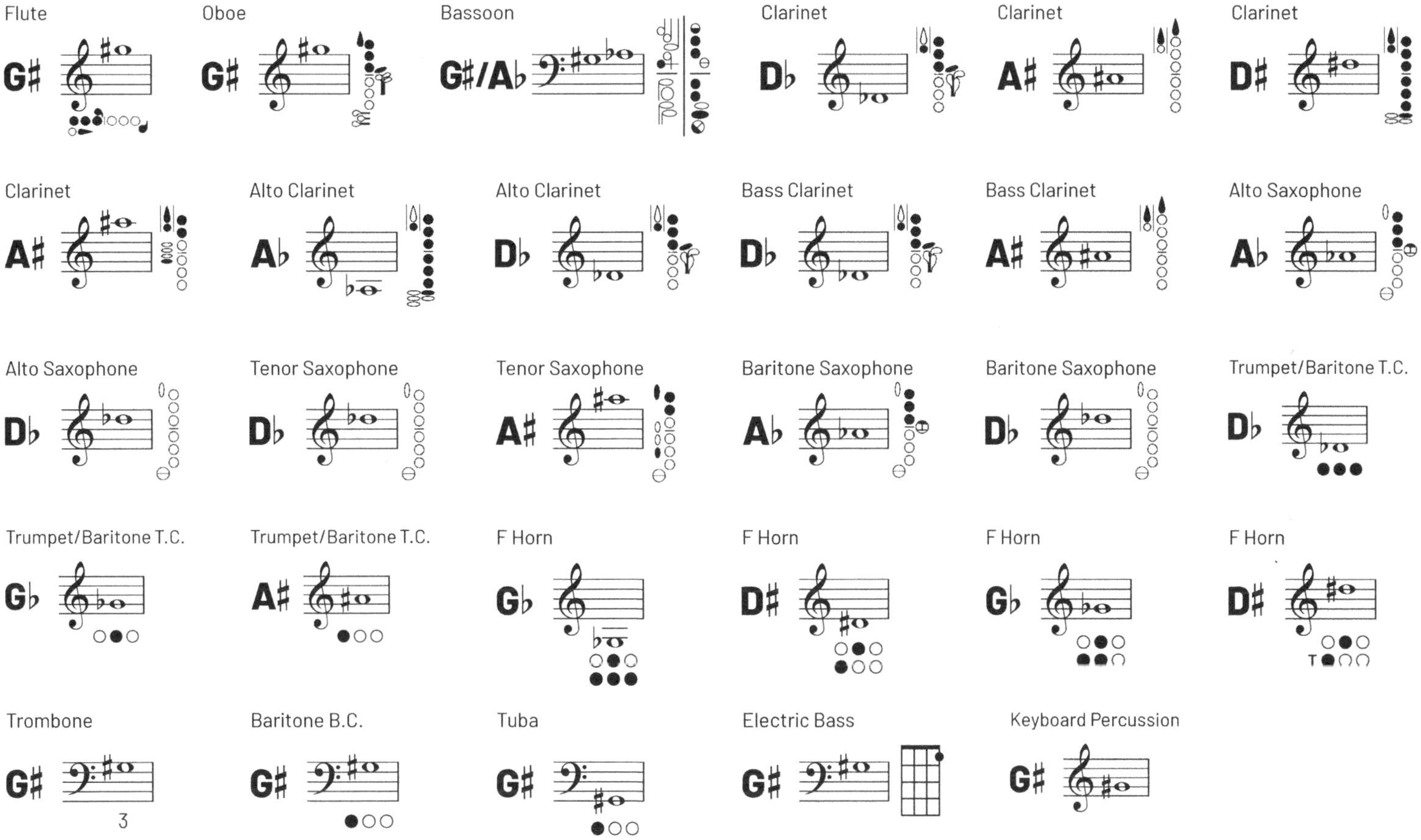

Flute G♯

Oboe G♯

Bassoon G♯/A♭

Clarinet D♭

Clarinet A♯

Clarinet D♯

Clarinet A♯

Alto Clarinet A♭

Alto Clarinet D♭

Bass Clarinet D♭

Bass Clarinet A♯

Alto Saxophone A♭

Alto Saxophone D♭

Tenor Saxophone D♭

Tenor Saxophone A♯

Baritone Saxophone A♭

Baritone Saxophone D♭

Trumpet/Baritone T.C. D♭

Trumpet/Baritone T.C. G♭

Trumpet/Baritone T.C. A♯

F Horn G♭

F Horn D♯

F Horn G♭

F Horn D♯ T

Trombone G♯ 3

Baritone B.C. G♯

Tuba G♯

Electric Bass G♯

Keyboard Percussion G♯

5. CHROMATIC SCALE

*All Saxes: Remember to use Alternate F♯(G♭) whenever F♯ follows or precedes F♮.

6. BALANCE BUILDER

*Parts are separated in student books.

divisi or *div.*	Divide the written parts among players, usually into two parts, with equal numbers playing each part.
unison or *a2*	All players play the same part (usually found after a *divisi* section).

7. CHORALE

An additional Chorale in the key of concert B♭ major, 167. (Prelude from Hansel and Gretel), can be found on p. 202.

Student Book Page 3

Tenor Saxophone

8. GREAT GATE OF KIEV

Modeste Mussorgsky

Maestoso ◄ *Bold, stately*

1. 2.

Flute
Oboe

B♭ Clarinet
B♭ Bass Cl.

E♭ Alto Sax.
E♭ Bari. Sax.
E♭ Alto Cl.

B♭ Tenor Sax.

B♭ Trumpet
Baritone T.C.

F Horn

Trombone
Baritone B.C.
Bassoon
Electric Bass

Tuba

Percussion

Tam-Tam (Gong)

B.D.

Keyboard
Percussion

Timpani

f

Percussion

Tam-Tam (Gong)

Tam-Tam is the name given to a large, flat gong with no definite pitch. While the Gong has a rich history dating back to the early sixth century in China, the Tam-Tam is the specific type of gong that has traditionally been used in western band and orchestra music. Use a heavy mallet designed for this instrument; a concert bass drum mallet is not heavy enough to bring out the low, fundamental sound.

Experiment to find the "sweet spot" on the instrument, typically near the center, where the fundamental sound is best. Until a Tam-Tam starts vibrating, the initial sound is often late. You can compensate for this by "priming" the instrument; that is, lightly tapping the instrument with the mallet two or three times prior to playing your first note.

9. CHILDREN'S SHOES

African American Spiritual

1. 2.

Flute
Oboe

B♭ Clarinet
B♭ Bass Cl.

E♭ Alto Sax.
E♭ Bari. Sax.
E♭ Alto Cl.

B♭ Tenor Sax.

B♭ Trumpet
Baritone T.C.

F Horn

Trombone
Baritone B.C.
Bassoon
Electric Bass

Tuba

Percussion

Keyboard
Percussion

Percussion

16th Note Rhythm

This is an excellent review of the eighth-sixteenth note rhythms learned in EE Book 2. Count carefully to ensure rhythmic accuracy.

HISTORY

English composer **George Frideric Handel** (1685–1759) is among the best known composers of the **Baroque Period (1600–1750)**. *Sound an Alarm* (from *Judas Maccabaeus*) and his most famous work, the *Hallelujah Chorus* (from *Messiah*), are two well-known melodies from his **oratorios** – large scale works for solo voices, chorus, and orchestra.

Bassoon

D

Baritone Saxophone

C♯/D♭

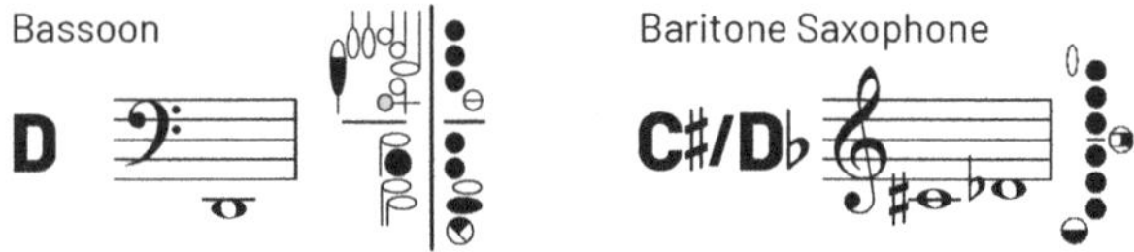

10. SOUND AN ALARM

George Frideric Handel

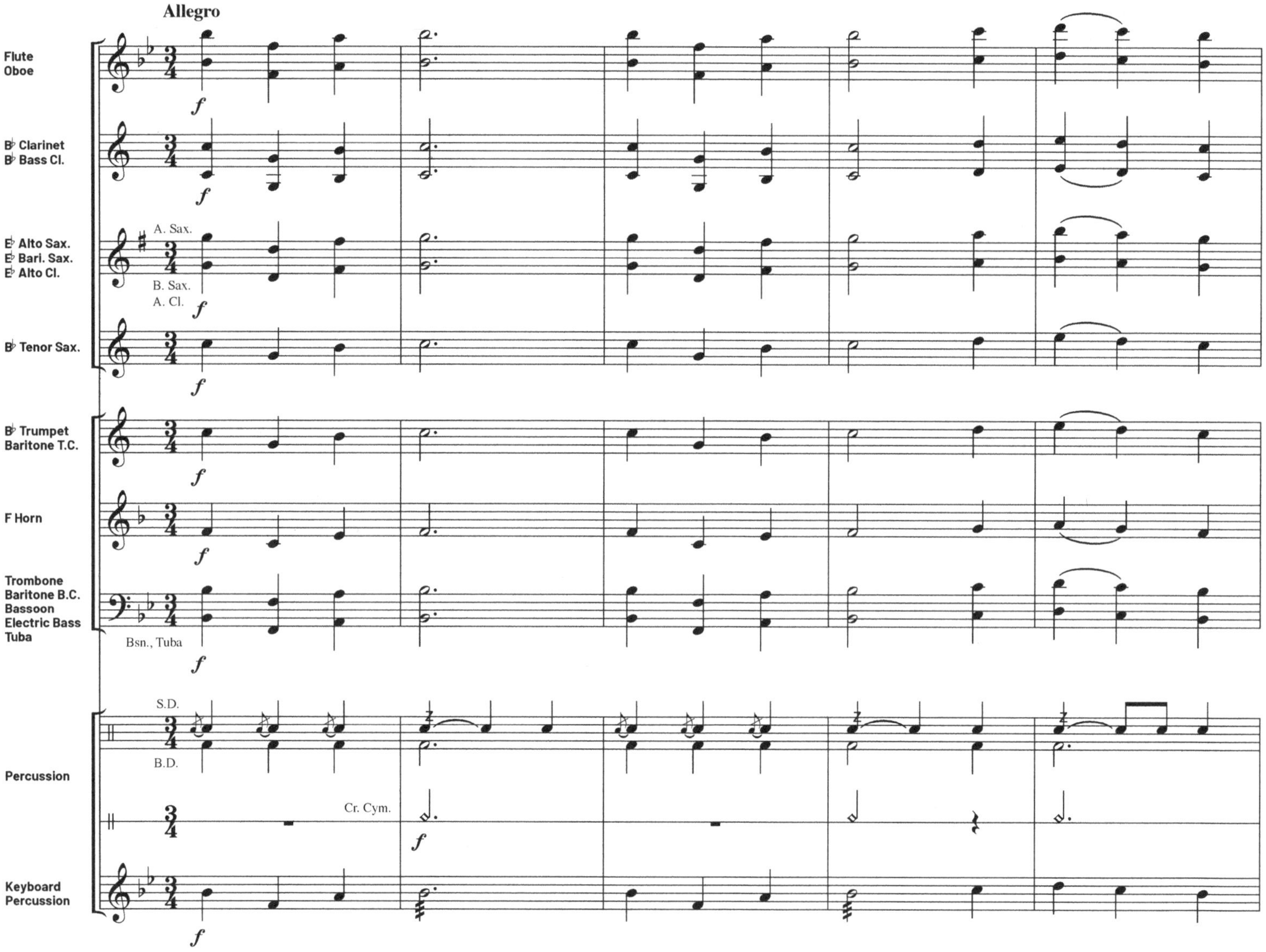
Allegro
Flute
Oboe
B♭ Clarinet
B♭ Bass Cl.
E♭ Alto Sax.
E♭ Bari. Sax.
E♭ Alto Cl.
A. Sax.
B. Sax.
A. Cl.
B♭ Tenor Sax.
B♭ Trumpet
Baritone T.C.
F Horn
Trombone
Baritone B.C.
Bassoon
Electric Bass
Tuba
Bsn., Tuba
S.D.
B.D.
Percussion
Cr. Cym.
Keyboard
Percussion

Flute
Oboe
B♭ Clarinet
B♭ Bass Cl.
E♭ Alto Sax.
E♭ Bari. Sax.
E♭ Alto Cl.
B♭ Tenor Sax.
B♭ Trumpet
Baritone T.C.
F Horn
Trombone
Baritone B.C.
Bassoon
Electric Bass
Tuba
Percussion
Keyboard
Percussion
mf
cresc.
f

11. HALLELUJAH CHORUS

George Frideric Handel

12. RHYTHM RAP *Clap the rhythm while counting and tapping.*

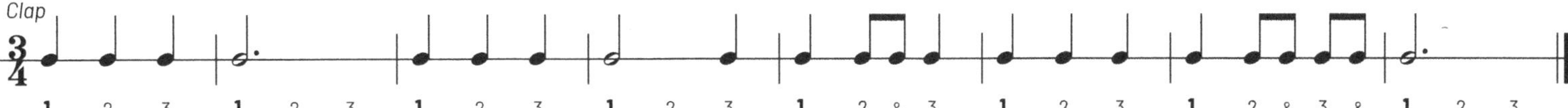

Clap
1 2 3 1 2 3 1 2 3 1 2 3 1 2 & 3 1 2 3 1 2 & 3 & 1 2 3

$\frac{3}{8}$ Time Signature

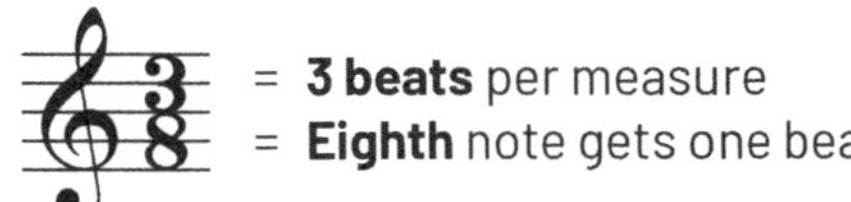

= **3 beats** per measure
= **Eighth** note gets one beat

♪ = 1 beat ♩ = 2 beats ♩. = 3 beats

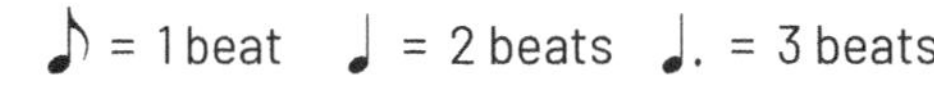

THEORY

3/8 time is usually played with a slight emphasis on the 1st beat of each measure. In faster music, this primary beat will make the music feel like it's counted "in 1."

13. RHYTHM RAP *Compare this exercise with No. 12.*

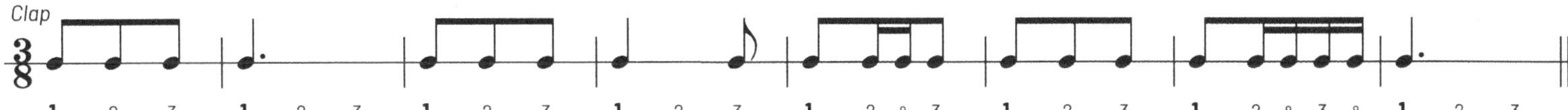

Clap
1 2 3 1 2 3 1 2 3 1 2 3 1 2 & 3 1 2 3 1 2 & 3 & 1 2 3

14. WALTZ PETITE

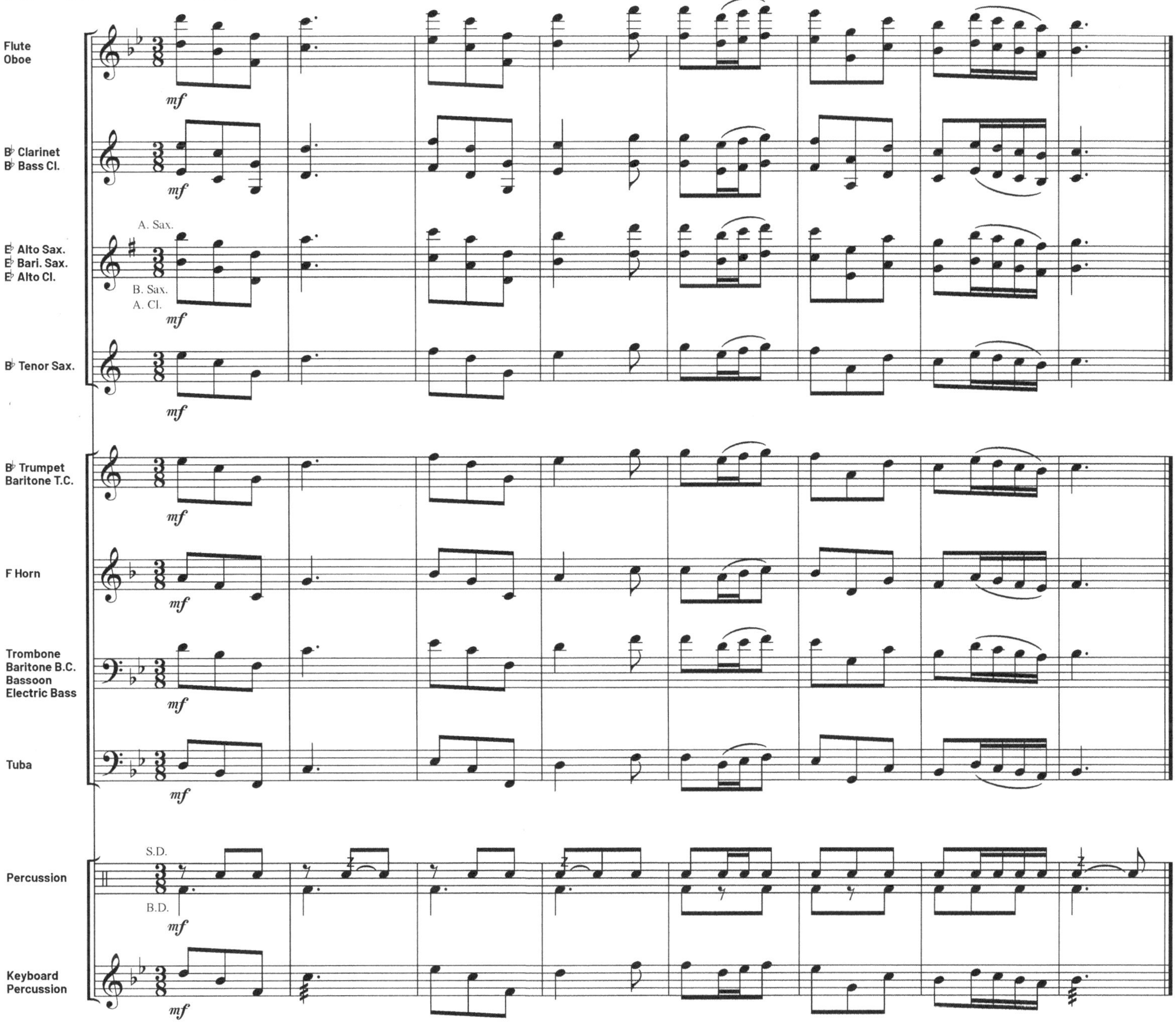

Flute
Oboe
B♭ Clarinet
B♭ Bass Cl.
A. Sax.
E♭ Alto Sax.
E♭ Bari. Sax.
E♭ Alto Cl.
B. Sax.
A. Cl.
B♭ Tenor Sax.
B♭ Trumpet
Baritone T.C.
F Horn
Trombone
Baritone B.C.
Bassoon
Electric Bass
Tuba
S.D.
Percussion
B.D.
Keyboard
Percussion
mf

Bassoon

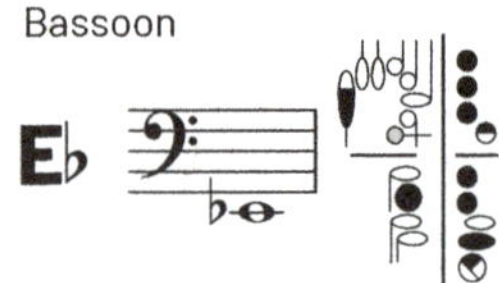

15. MOLLY BANN

English Folksong

Flute
Oboe

mf 3 1 2 3 & 1 2 3 f

B♭ Clarinet
B♭ Bass Cl.

mf f

E♭ Alto Sax.
E♭ Bari. Sax.
E♭ Alto Cl.

A. Sax. B. Sax. A. Cl. mf f

B♭ Tenor Sax.

mf f

B♭ Trumpet
Baritone T.C.

mf f

F Horn

mf f

Trombone
Baritone B.C.
Bassoon
Electric Bass

Bsn. 8vb mf f

Tuba

mf f

Percussion

S.D. B.D. mf f

Keyboard
Percussion

mf f

THEORY

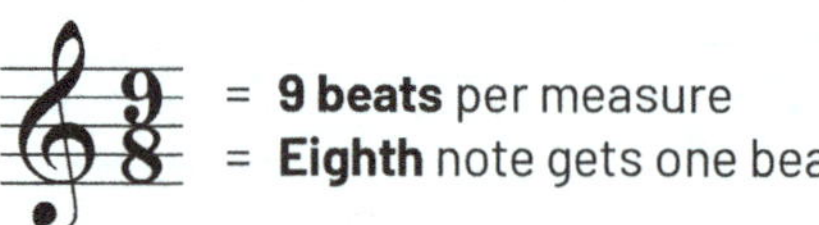

= **9 beats** per measure
= **Eighth** note gets one beat

♪ = 1 beat ♩. = 3 beats
♩ = 2 beats 𝅗𝅥. = 6 beats

9/8 time is usually played with a slight emphasis on the **1st**, **4th**, and **7th** beats of each measure. This divides the measure into 3 groups of 3 beats each. In faster music, these three primary beats will make the music feel like it's counted "in 3."

16. RHYTHM RAP *Clap the rhythm while counting and tapping.*

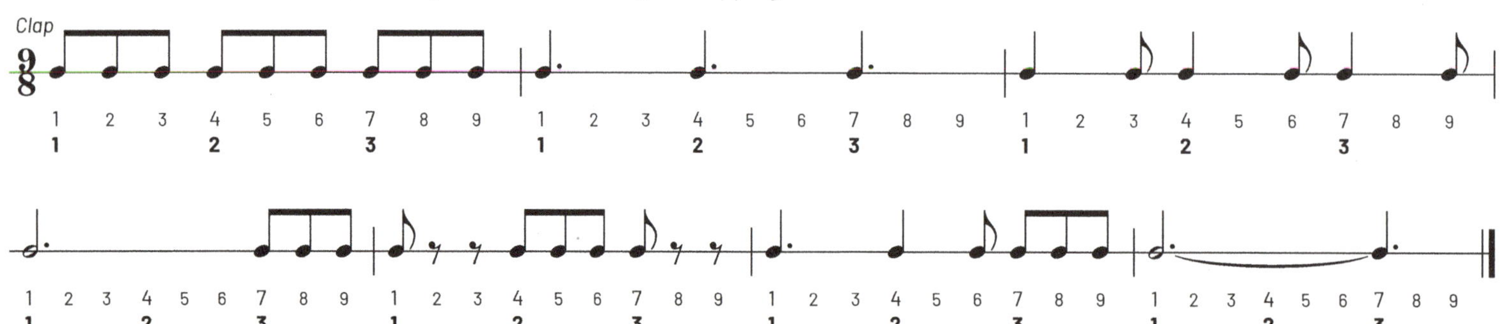

17. SUNDAY AT NINE

G MINOR

THEORY

Minor Keys

Minor keys and their scales sound different from major keys because of their different pattern of whole and half steps. Each minor key is *relative* or "related" to the major key with the same key signature.

The simplest form of a minor key is called **natural minor**. Two other types are **harmonic minor** and **melodic minor**, each of which have certain altered tones.

Alto Clarinet
E
Bass Clarinet
A
Alto Saxophone
E
Baritone Saxophone
E
Trumpet
A
Trombone
G
-2
Baritone B.C.
G
Baritone T.C.
A
Tuba
G
Electric Bass
G
12fr

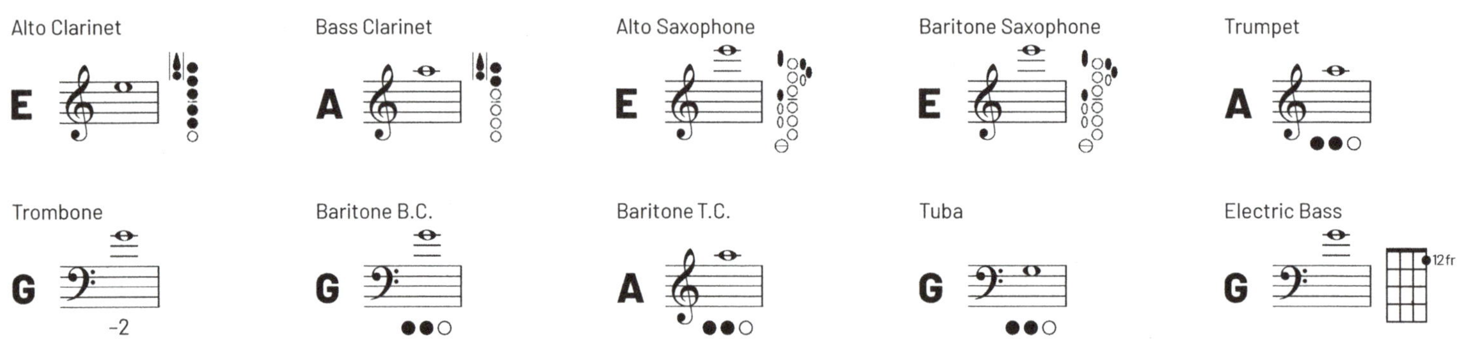

18. NATURAL MINOR

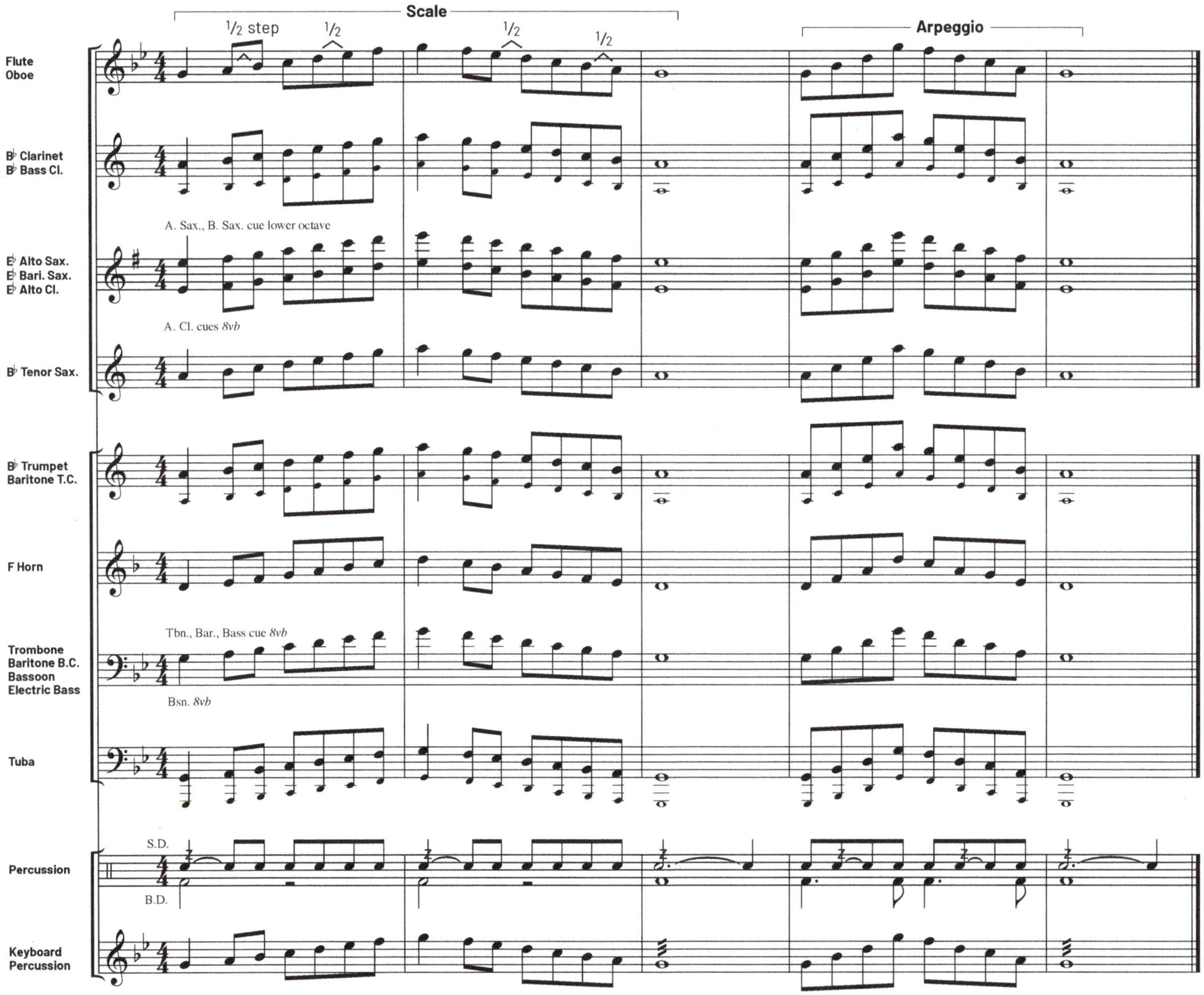

Scale
1/2 step
1/2
1/2
1/2
Arpeggio
Flute Oboe
B♭ Clarinet B♭ Bass Cl.
A. Sax., B. Sax. cue lower octave
E♭ Alto Sax. E♭ Bari. Sax. E♭ Alto Cl.
A. Cl. cues 8vb
B♭ Tenor Sax.
B♭ Trumpet Baritone T.C.
F Horn
Tbn., Bar., Bass cue 8vb
Trombone Baritone B.C. Bassoon Electric Bass
Bsn. 8vb
Tuba
S.D.
B.D.
Percussion
Keyboard Percussion

Alto Clarinet
D♯
Bass Clarinet
G♯/A♭
Alto Saxophone
D♯
Baritone Saxophone
D♯
Trumpet
G♯
Trombone
F♯
-3
Baritone B.C.
F♯
Baritone T.C.
G♯
Tuba
F♯
Electric Bass
F♯
11fr

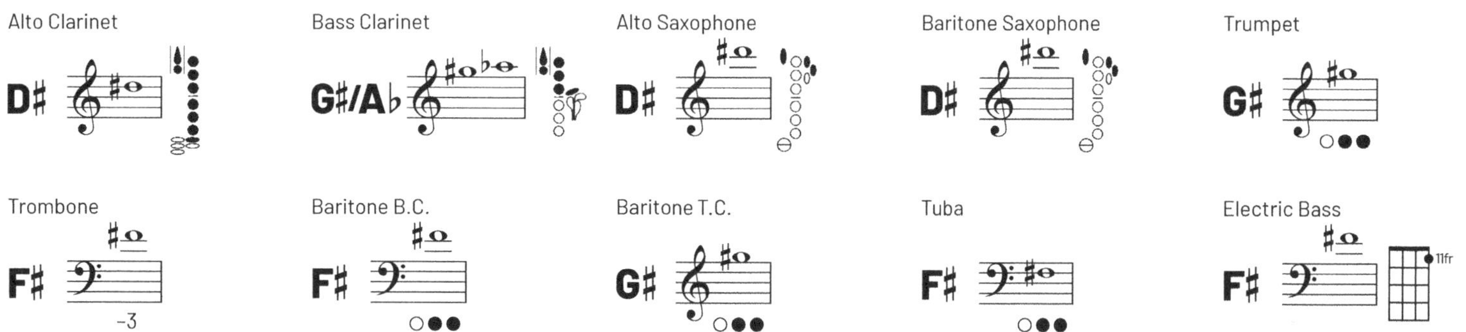

19. HARMONIC MINOR *Practice both upper and lower octaves.*

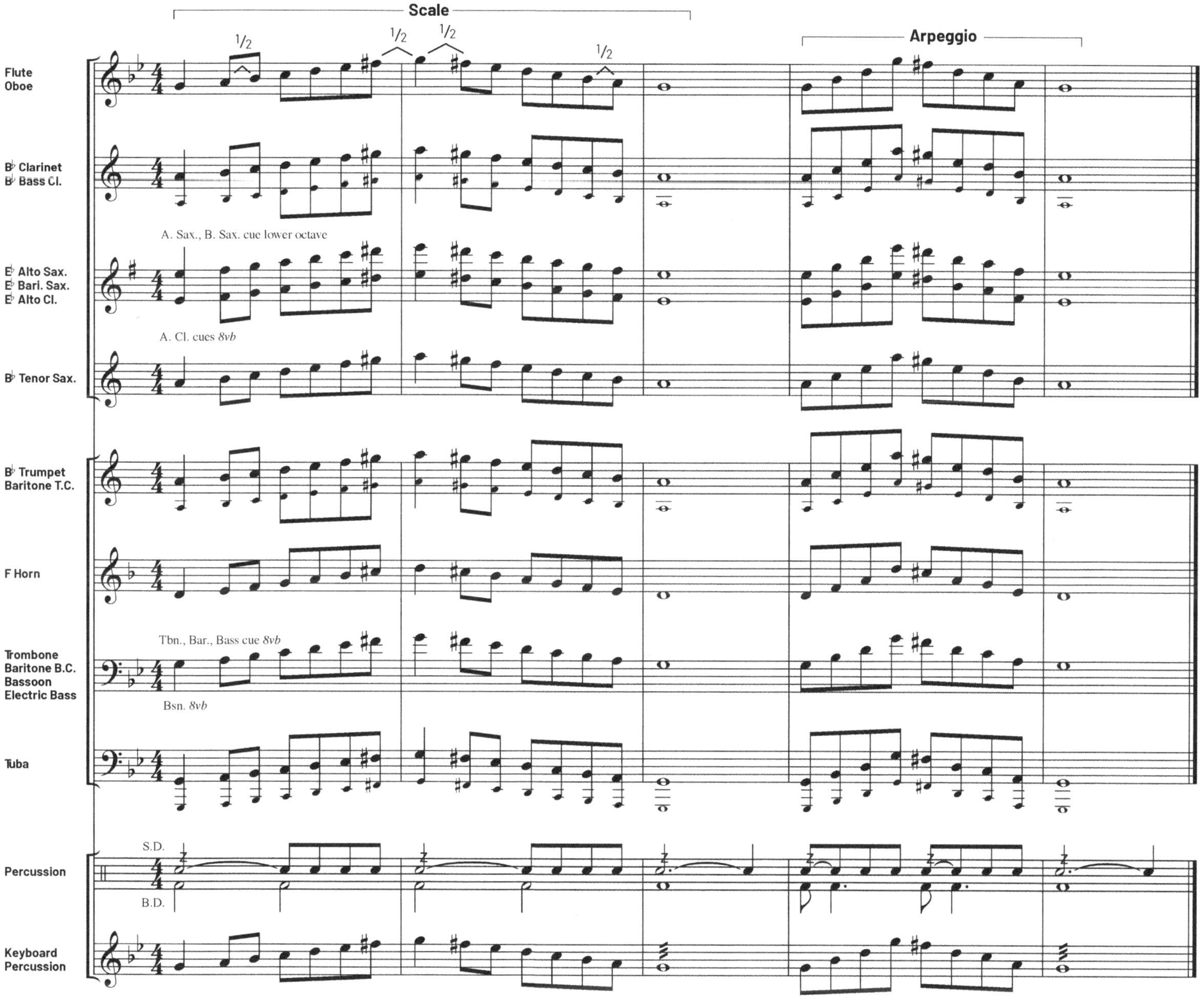
Scale
Arpeggio
1/2
1/2
1/2
1/2
Flute
Oboe
B♭ Clarinet
B♭ Bass Cl.
A. Sax., B. Sax. cue lower octave
E♭ Alto Sax.
E♭ Bari. Sax.
E♭ Alto Cl.
A. Cl. cues 8vb
B♭ Tenor Sax.
B♭ Trumpet
Baritone T.C.
F Horn
Tbn., Bar., Bass cue 8vb
Trombone
Baritone B.C.
Bassoon
Electric Bass
Bsn. 8vb
Tuba
S.D.
Percussion
B.D.
Keyboard
Percussion

(Ex. 20)
Percussion

Concert Tom-Toms

Concert Tom-Toms are usually single headed, graduated in size, and mounted on a stand. Hard felt mallets are recommended. The most resonant sound is achieved by playing toward the edge of the head.

20. PAT-A-PAN

French

Flute
Oboe
B♭ Clarinet
B♭ Bass Cl.
E♭ Alto Sax.
E♭ Bari. Sax.
E♭ Alto Cl.
B♭ Tenor Sax.
B♭ Trumpet
Baritone T.C.
F Horn
Trombone
Baritone B.C.
Bassoon
Electric Bass
Tuba
Percussion
Keyboard
Percussion

21. THE SLEDGEHAMMER SONG

Russian

Percussion

Anvil (Brake Drum)

The metallic sound of a hammer on an anvil (metal block) can be heard in several famous Opera scores of Verdi and Wagner. The most common substitution is the use of an automobile brake drum, which has been used by modern American composers such as John Cage and Lou Harrison. Use a small ball-type hammer or hard bell mallet.

Flute
Oboe
B♭ Clarinet
B♭ Bass Cl.
E♭ Alto Sax.
E♭ Bari. Sax.
E♭ Alto Cl.
B♭ Tenor Sax.
B♭ Trumpet
Baritone T.C.
F Horn
Trombone
Baritone B.C.
Bassoon
Electric Bass
Tuba
Percussion
Keyboard
Percussion
f

22. ESSENTIAL ELEMENTS QUIZ – AUSTRALIAN FOLK SONG

Australian

A Chorale, 173. (Prelude) in the key of concert G minor, can be found on p. 216.

E♭ MAJOR

Tenor Saxophone

F

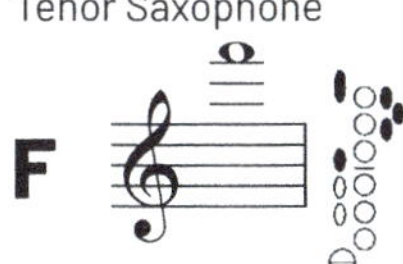

23. SCALE AND ARPEGGIO

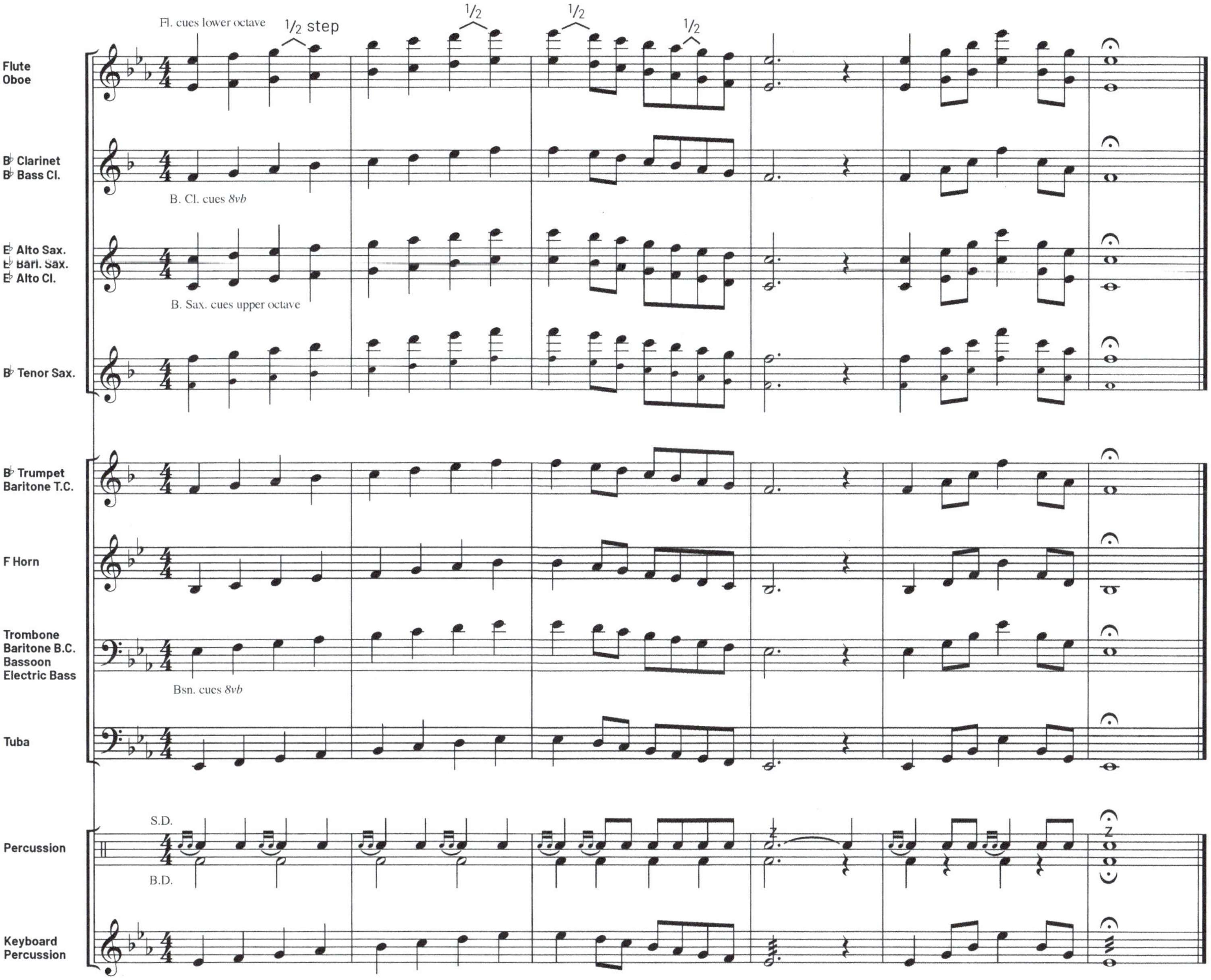
Fl. cues lower octave
1/2 step
1/2
1/2
1/2
Flute
Oboe
B♭ Clarinet
B♭ Bass Cl.
B. Cl. cues 8vb
E♭ Alto Sax.
E♭ Bari. Sax.
E♭ Alto Cl.
B. Sax. cues upper octave
B♭ Tenor Sax.
B♭ Trumpet
Baritone T.C.
F Horn
Trombone
Baritone B.C.
Bassoon
Electric Bass
Bsn. cues 8vb
Tuba
S.D.
Percussion
B.D.
Keyboard
Percussion

Student Book Page 6

Baritone Saxophone

24. EXERCISE IN THIRDS

Flute
Oboe

B♭ Clarinet
B♭ Bass Cl.

E♭ Alto Sax.
E♭ Bari. Sax.
E♭ Alto Cl.

B. Sax. cues upper octave

B♭ Tenor Sax.

B♭ Trumpet
Baritone T.C.

F Horn

Trombone
Baritone B.C.
Bassoon
Electric Bass

Bsn. cues *8vb*

Tuba

Percussion

S.D.

B.D.

Keyboard
Percussion

Tenor Saxophone

F

Alternate fingering

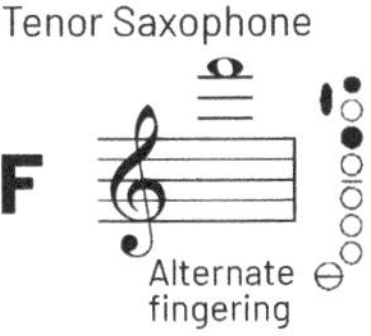

25. ARPEGGIO STUDY

Flute
Oboe
Cl. cues lower octave
B♭ Clarinet
B♭ Bass Cl.
E♭ Alto Sax.
E♭ Bari. Sax.
E♭ Alto Cl.
Alt.
Alt.
B♭ Tenor Sax.
B♭ Trumpet
Baritone T.C.
F Horn
Trombone
Baritone B.C.
Bassoon
Electric Bass
Tuba
S.D.
B.D.
Percussion
Keyboard
Percussion
a2
Flute
Oboe
a2
B♭ Clarinet
B♭ Bass Cl.
E♭ Alto Sax.
E♭ Bari. Sax.
E♭ Alto Cl.
R
Alt.
B♭ Tenor Sax.
B♭ Trumpet
Baritone T.C.
F Horn
Trombone
Baritone B.C.
Bassoon
Electric Bass
Tuba
Percussion
Keyboard
Percussion

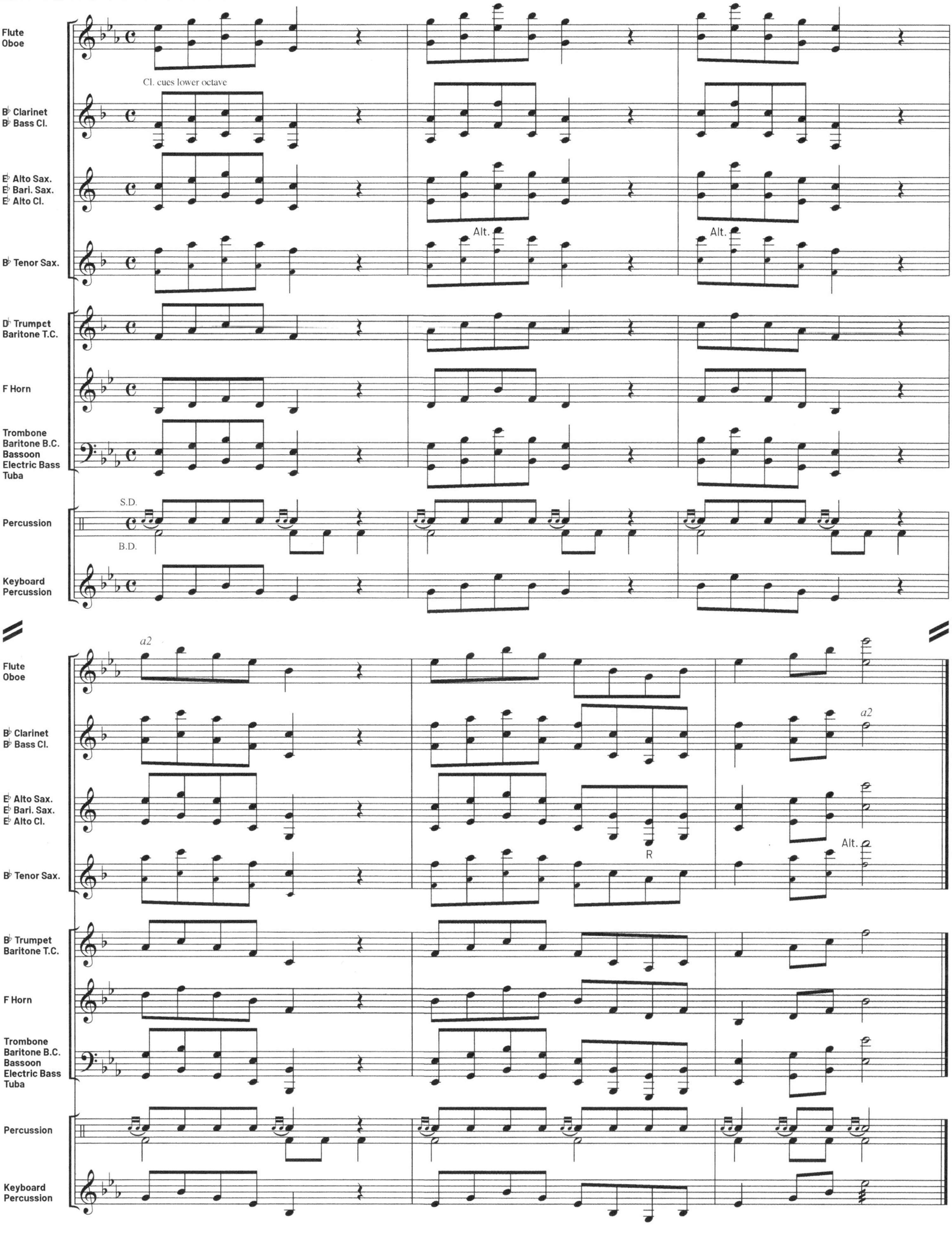

26. TWO-PART ETUDE

Flute
C♯
Alto Clarinet
G♭
Chr.
Alto Clarinet
A♭
Alto Clarinet
A♯
Bass Clarinet
D♯/E♭
Alto Saxophone
C♯/D♭
Alto Saxophone
G♭
Alt.
Alto Saxophone
G♭
Alt.
Alto Saxophone
A♭
Alto Saxophone
A♯
Tenor Saxophone
G♭
Alt.
Tenor Saxophone
D♭
Baritone Saxophone
G♭
Alt.
Baritone Saxophone
G♭
Alt.
Baritone Saxophone
A♭
Baritone Saxophone
A♯
Trumpet/Baritone T.C.
D♭
Trumpet/Baritone T.C.
D♯
Trombone
C♯
2
Baritone B.C.
C♯

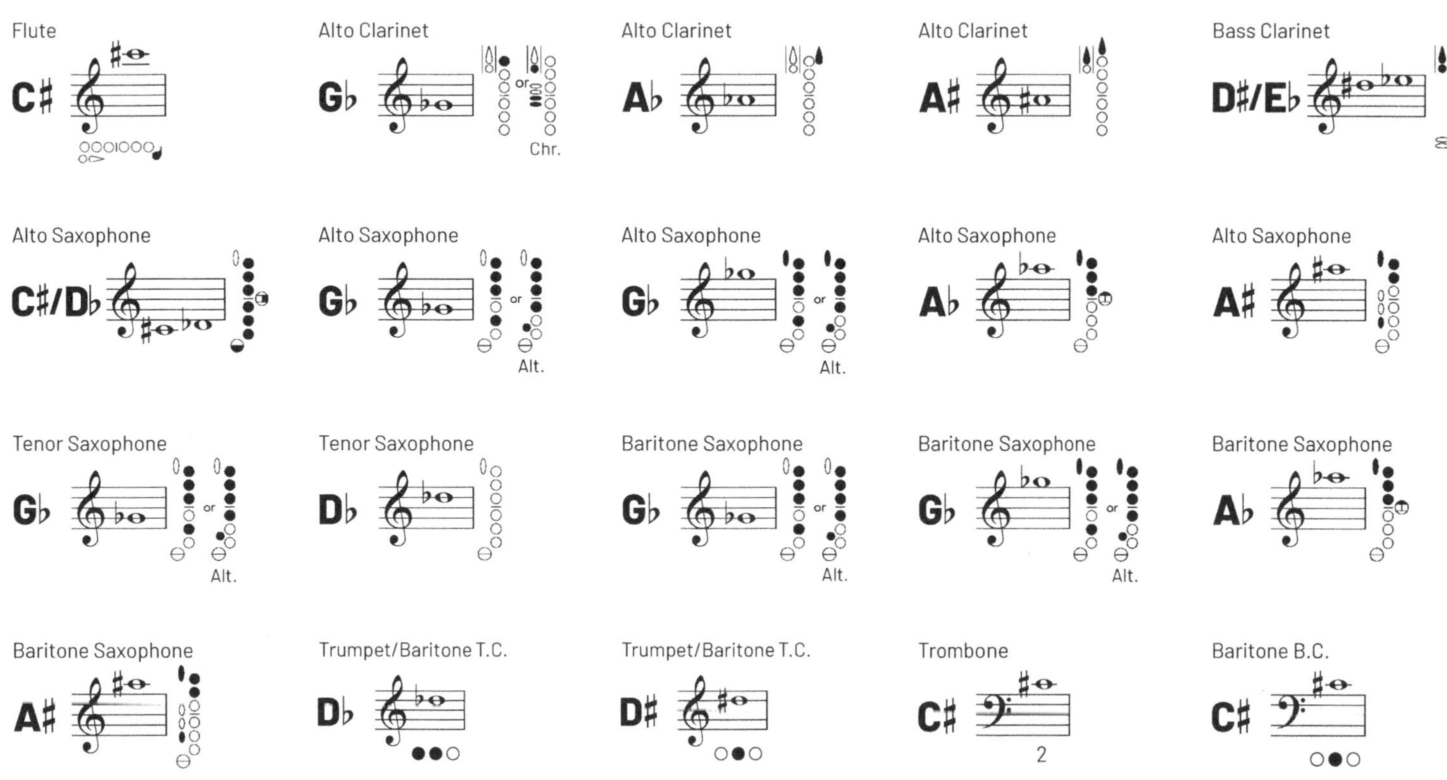

27. CHROMATIC SCALE

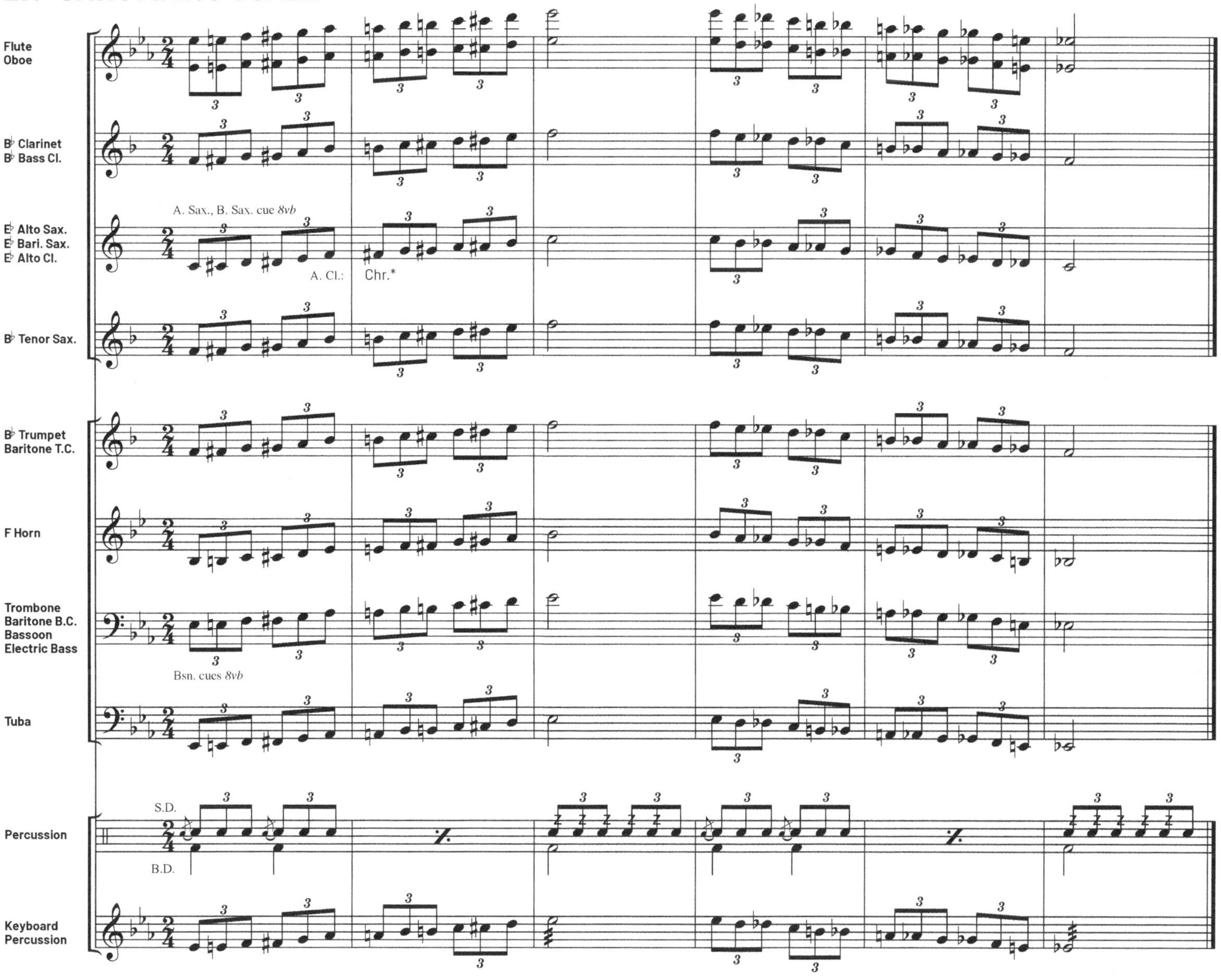

Flute
Oboe
B♭ Clarinet
B♭ Bass Cl.
E♭ Alto Sax.
E♭ Bari. Sax.
E♭ Alto Cl.
A. Sax., B. Sax. cue 8vb
A. Cl.:
Chr.*
B♭ Tenor Sax.
B♭ Trumpet
Baritone T.C.
F Horn
Trombone
Baritone B.C.
Bassoon
Electric Bass
Bsn. cues 8vb
Tuba
Percussion
S.D.
B.D.
Keyboard
Percussion

*A. Cl.: Use chromatic (Chr.) F♯(G♭) in chromatic passages.

28. BALANCE BUILDER

29. CHORALE

An additional Chorale in the key of concert E♭ major, 168. (Based on a Theme by Palestrina), can be found on p. 205.

Student Book Page 7

HISTORY

Austrian composer **Johann Strauss Jr.** (1825–1899) is also known as "The Waltz King." He wrote some of the world's most famous waltzes (dances in 3/4 meter). This waltz is from *Die Fledermaus* ("The Bat"), Strauss' most famous **operetta**. Operettas were the forerunners of today's musicals, such as *Oklahoma*, *The Sound of Music*, *The Phantom of the Opera*, *Wicked* and *Hamilton*.

30. ADELE'S SONG

Johann Strauss Jr.

2.
Flute
Oboe
B♭ Clarinet
B♭ Bass Cl.
E♭ Alto Sax.
E♭ Bari. Sax.
E♭ Alto Cl.
B♭ Tenor Sax.
B♭ Trumpet
Baritone T.C.
F Horn
Trombone
Baritone B.C.
Bassoon
Electric Bass
Tuba
Percussion
Keyboard
Percussion
f

31. MARINE'S HYMN

Flute
Oboe
B♭ Clarinet
B♭ Bass Cl.
E♭ Alto Sax.
E♭ Bari. Sax.
E♭ Alto Cl.
B♭ Tenor Sax.
B♭ Trumpet
Baritone T.C.
F Horn
Trombone
Baritone B.C.
Bassoon
Electric Bass
Tuba
Percussion
Keyboard
Percussion

Student Book Page 7

32. RHYTHM RAP

Percussion

Rudiment

Five Stroke Roll

Use open, double bounces to play five evenly divided notes in order to form this measured roll. Remember that the hands will be moving at the speed of sixteenth notes. The Five Stroke Roll used in the exercise starts on the beat and ends on the upbeat.

33. KEEPIN' SECRETS

Moderato

Appalachian Folk Song

Flute
Oboe

B♭ Clarinet
B♭ Bass Cl.

E♭ Alto Sax.
E♭ Bari. Sax.
E♭ Alto Cl.

B♭ Tenor Sax.

B♭ Trumpet
Baritone T.C.

F Horn

Trombone
Baritone B.C.
Bassoon
Electric Bass

Tuba

Percussion (S.D., B.D.) — RRLLR, LLRRL, LLRRL, RRLLR

Keyboard Percussion

mf

(Ex. 34)
Percussion

Rudiment

Nine Stroke Roll

Use open, double bounces to play nine evenly divided notes in order to form this measured roll. Remember that the hands will be moving at the speed of sixteenth notes. The Nine Stroke Roll starts on the beat and ends on the beat.

34. THE KEEL ROW

Sea Song

35. JACK'S THE MAN

Percussion

Rudiment

Flam Accent No. 2

This rudiment is a variation of the Flam Accent. Notice that when the rest appears, you omit the sticking that would normally occur if you played at that spot, which produces the double sticking you see in the exercise.

Flute
Oboe

B♭ Clarinet
B♭ Bass Cl.

Cl. *div.*
Cl. *a2*

E♭ Alto Sax.
E♭ Bari. Sax.
E♭ Alto Cl.

B♭ Tenor Sax.

B♭ Trumpet
Baritone T.C.

F Horn

Trombone
Baritone B.C.
Bassoon
Electric Bass

Tuba

Percussion

L R L R R L L L R L R R L L L R R L L L R L R R L

Keyboard
Percussion

12/8 Time Signature

12/8 = **12 beats** per measure = **Eighth** note gets one beat

♪ = 1 beat; ♩. = 3 beats; 𝅗𝅥.‿♩. = 9 beats; ♩ = 2 beats; 𝅗𝅥. = 6 beats; 𝅝. = 12 beats

THEORY

12/8 time is usually played with a slight emphasis on the **1st**, **4th**, **7th,** and **10th** beats of each measure. This divides the measure into 4 groups of 3 beats each. These four primary beats will make the music feel like it's counted "in 4."

36. RHYTHM RAP *Clap the rhythm while counting and tapping.*

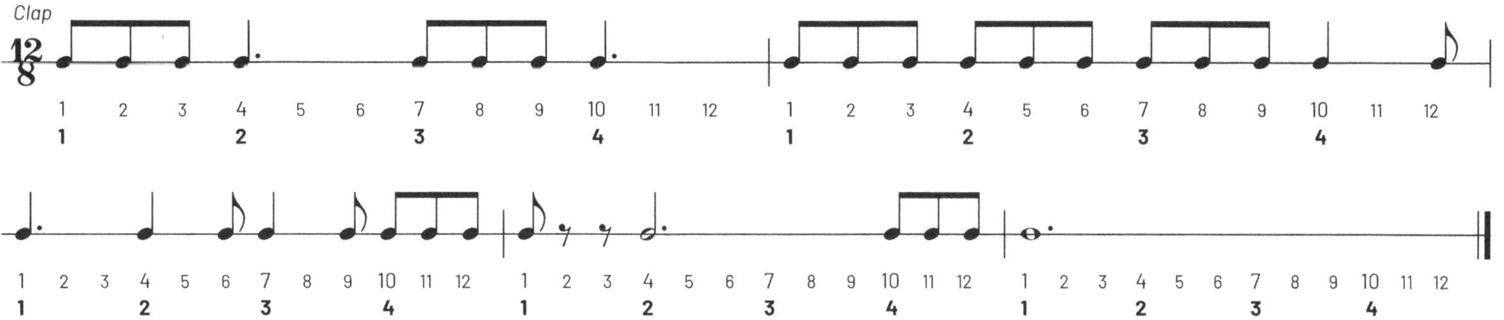

Bassoon

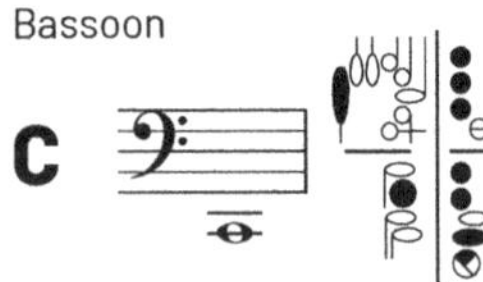

37. SERENADE

Flute
Oboe

B♭ Clarinet
B♭ Bass Cl.

E♭ Alto Sax.
E♭ Bari. Sax.
E♭ Alto Cl.

B♭ Tenor Sax.

B♭ Trumpet
Baritone T.C.

F Horn

Trombone
Baritone B.C.
Bassoon
Electric Bass
Tuba

Percussion

Keyboard
Percussion

p *a2* Bsn. Tuba S.D. B.D.

38. WITH THINE EYES

C MINOR

Clarinet

39. NATURAL MINOR

Scale

1/2 step

1/2

1/2

1/2

Arpeggio

Flute
Oboe

Ob. cues *8vb*

Cl. cues lower octave

B♭ Clarinet
B♭ Bass Cl.

E♭ Alto Sax.
E♭ Bari. Sax.
E♭ Alto Cl.

B♭ Tenor Sax.

B♭ Trumpet
Baritone T.C.

F Horn

Trombone
Baritone B.C.
Bassoon
Electric Bass

Bsn. cues *8vb*

Tuba

L R R L L L R L R L L R R L L L R L R L L R

L R L R R L L R L R R L L R

S.D.

B.D.

Percussion

Keyboard
Percussion

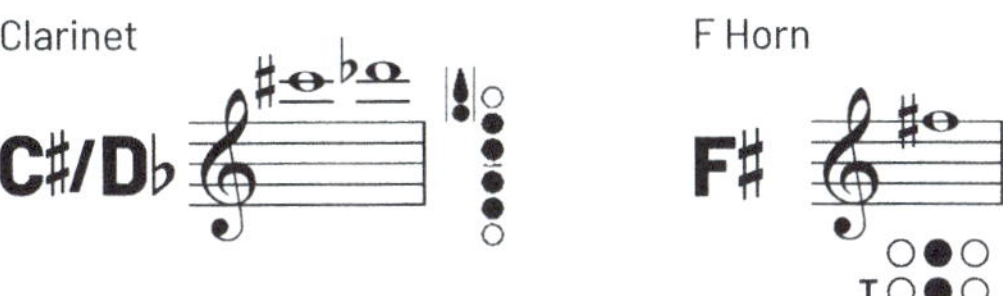

40. HARMONIC MINOR

Scale

1/2 1/2 1/2 1/2

Arpeggio

Flute
Oboe

Ob. cues 8vb

Cl. cues lower octave

B♭ Clarinet
B♭ Bass Cl.

E♭ Alto Sax.
E♭ Bari. Sax.
E♭ Alto Cl.

B♭ Tenor Sax.

B♭ Trumpet
Baritone T.C.

F Horn

Trombone
Baritone B.C.
Bassoon
Electric Bass

Bsn. cues 8vb

Tuba

Percussion

S.D.

B.D.

L R R L L L R L R R L L R R L L L R L R R L L R R R L L L R R R L L L R L R R R L R L L L R L R R L R L L R

Keyboard
Percussion

(Ex. 41)

Even today, **Native American Indian music** continues to be an important part of tribal dancing ceremonies, using Apache fiddles, rattles, flutes, and log drums to accompany simple songs. American composer **Charles Wakefield Cadman** (1881–1946) wrote this song in 1914 based on Indian melodies he researched throughout his lifetime.

HISTORY

41. SONG OF THE WEEPING SPIRIT

Native American Indian Melody
Adapt. Charles Wakefield Cadman

Amy Marcy Beach

42. SCOTTISH LEGEND

43. ESSENTIAL ELEMENTS QUIZ *Which measures sound major and which ones minor?*

*Ob.: The left (L) E♭ fingering should be used when E♭ precedes or follows low C, low D♭, or middle D♭.

F MAJOR

44. SCALE AND ARPEGGIO

1/2 1/2 1/2 1/2

Fl. cues lower octave

Flute
Oboe

B♭ Clarinet
B♭ Bass Cl.

A. Sax. cues lower octave

E♭ Alto Sax.
E♭ Bari. Sax.
E♭ Alto Cl.

A. Cl.
B. Sax. cues upper octave

B♭ Tenor Sax.

Bar. cues lower octave

B♭ Trumpet
Baritone T.C.

Tpt. cues upper octave

F Horn

Tbn., Bar., Bsn. cue lower octave

Trombone
Baritone B.C.
Bassoon
Electric Bass

Bass cues upper octave

Tuba

S.D.
Percussion
B.D.

Keyboard
Percussion

Flute

G

Bassoon

G

Trumpet

F♯

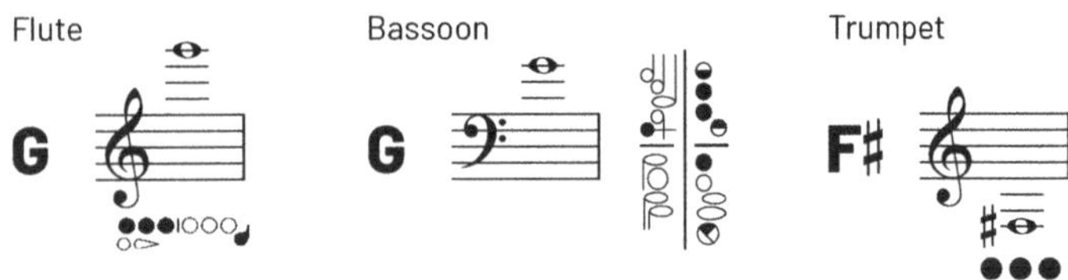

45. EXERCISE IN THIRDS

Fl. cues lower octave
Flute
Oboe
B♭ Clarinet
B♭ Bass Cl.
E♭ Alto Sax.
E♭ Bari. Sax.
E♭ Alto Cl.
B♭ Tenor Sax.
Bar. cues lower octave
B♭ Trumpet
Baritone T.C.
Tpt. cues upper octave
F Horn
Tbn. cues 8vb
Trombone
Baritone B.C.
Bassoon
Electric Bass
Bar. cues 8vb
Tuba
S.D.
Percussion
B.D.
Keyboard
Percussion

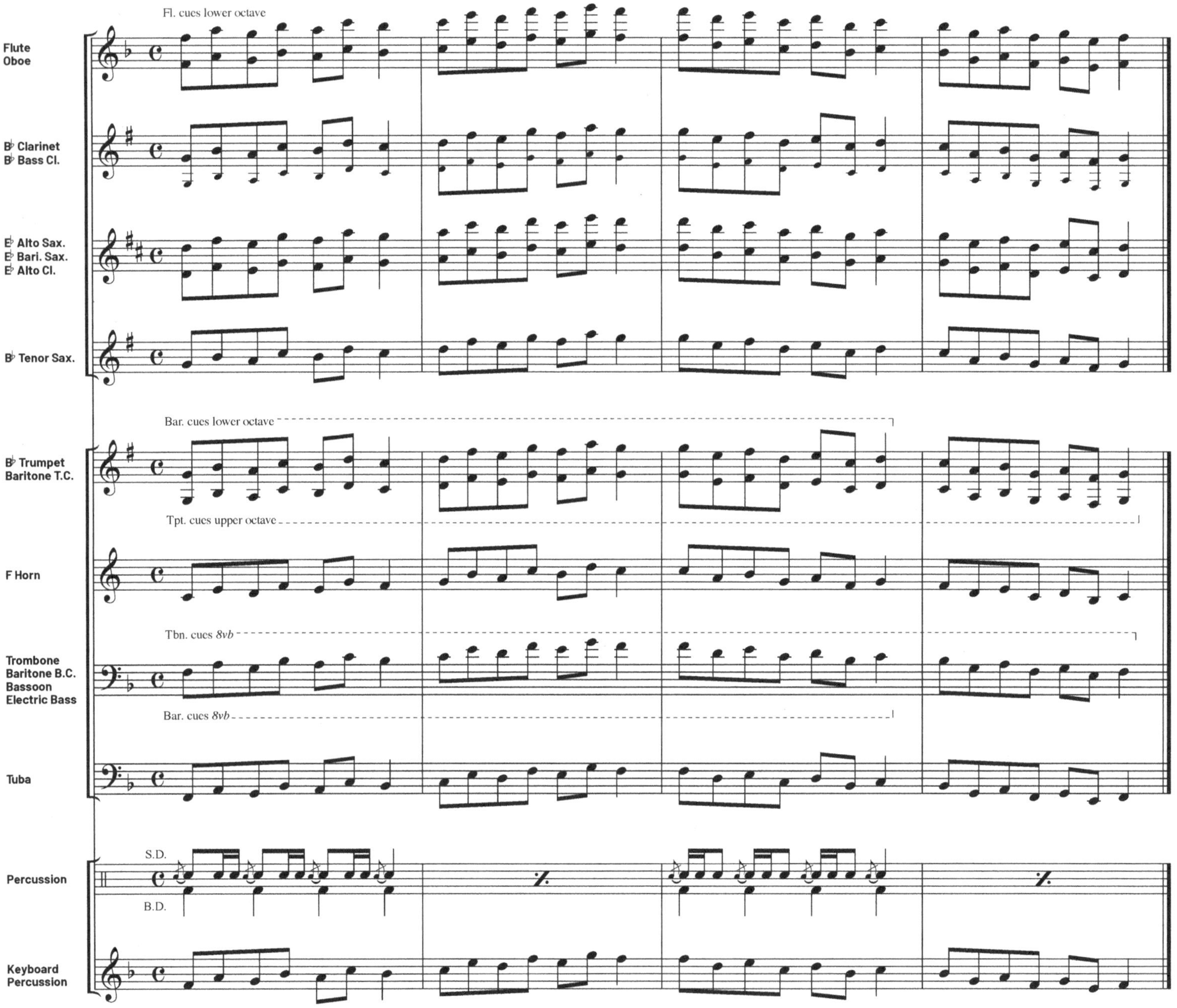

(Ex. 46)
Percussion

Rudiment

Reverse Paradiddle

This is one of three variations of the Paradiddle. Notice that the sticking is identical to the Paradiddle, but the accent has been shifted to the third note of each group. This reverses both the feel and sound of the rudiment.

46. ARPEGGIO STUDY

*Cls.: For smoother technique, try using the right (R) fingering for middle B when it is *not* preceded or followed by middle C.

47. TWO-PART ETUDE

Flute
D♯
Oboe
G♯
Oboe
D♯
or
L
R
(left)
Bassoon
D♯
Clarinet
A♯
Clarinet
G♭
or
Chr.
Alto Clarinet
D♭
Bass Clarinet
A♯
Bass Clarinet
G♭
or
Chr.
Alto Saxophone
D♭
Tenor Saxophone
A♯
Baritone Saxophone
D♭
Trumpet/Bar. T.C.
A♯
Trumpet/Bar. T.C.
G♭
F Horn
A♯
T
Trombone
G♯
3
Trombone
D♯
3
Baritone B.C.
G♯
Baritone B.C.
D♯
Tuba
D♯
Electric Bass
G♯
Electric Bass
D♯
8fr
Keyboard Percussion
D♯
48. CHROMATIC SCALE
Flute
Oboe
B♭ Clarinet
B♭ Bass Cl.
B. Cl. cues upper octave
A. Sax. cues lower octave
E♭ Alto Sax.
E♭ Bari. Sax.
E♭ Alto Cl.
B. Sax. cues upper octave
B♭ Tenor Sax.
B♭ Trumpet
Baritone T.C.
F Horn
Trombone
Baritone B.C.
Bassoon
Electric Bass
Tuba
S.D.
Percussion
B.D.
Keyboard
Percussion

49. BALANCE BUILDER

50. CHORALE

An additional Chorale in the key of concert F major, 169. (Based on a Theme by J. S. Bach), can be found on p. 208.

51. REST ALERT

52. RHYTHM RAP

1 & 2 & 1 e & a 2 & 1 & 2 & 1 e & a 2 & 1 & 2 e & a 1 & 2 e & a 1 e & a 2 & 1 e & a 2 &

53. ISLAND SONG

Flute
Oboe

B♭ Clarinet
B♭ Bass Cl.

E♭ Alto Sax.
E♭ Bari. Sax.
E♭ Alto Cl.

B♭ Tenor Sax.

B♭ Trumpet
Baritone T.C.

F Horn

Trombone
Baritone B.C.
Bassoon
Electric Bass

Tuba

Percussion
S.D.
B.D.

Keyboard
Percussion

f

(Ex. 54)

French composer **Claude Debussy** (1862–1918) created moods and "impressions" with his music. While earlier composers used music to describe events (such as Tchaikovsky's *1812 Overture*), Debussy's new ideas helped shape today's music. The style of art and music created in this time is called "impressionism." The first automobile was produced during Debussy's lifetime. He died the same year that World War I ended.

HISTORY

54. THE LITTLE CHILD

Claude Debussy

Triplets with Rests

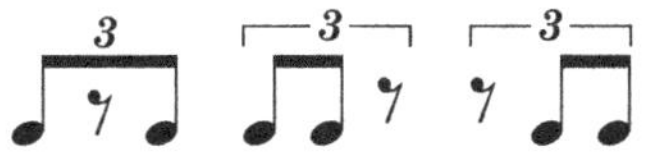

Triplets that start or end with a rest are usually marked with a bracket

55. TRIPLET AND REST VARIATIONS

Flute
Oboe

B♭ Clarinet
B♭ Bass Cl.

E♭ Alto Sax.
E♭ Bari. Sax.
E♭ Alto Cl.

A. Sax.
B. Sax.
A. Cl.

B♭ Tenor Sax.

B♭ Trumpet
Baritone T.C.

F Horn

Trombone
Baritone B.C.
Bassoon
Electric Bass
Tuba

Percussion

S.D.
B.D.

Keyboard
Percussion

Flute
Oboe

B♭ Clarinet
B♭ Bass Cl.

E♭ Alto Sax.
E♭ Bari. Sax.
E♭ Alto Cl.

B♭ Tenor Sax.

B♭ Trumpet
Baritone T.C.

F Horn

Trombone
Baritone B.C.
Bassoon
Electric Bass
Tuba

Percussion

Keyboard
Percussion

Student Book Page 12

56. TURKEY IN THE STRAW

American Folk Song

Flute
Oboe
B♭ Clarinet
B♭ Bass Cl.
E♭ Alto Sax.
E♭ Bari. Sax.
E♭ Alto Cl.
B♭ Tenor Sax.
B♭ Trumpet
Baritone T.C.
F Horn
Trombone
Baritone B.C.
Bassoon
Electric Bass
Tuba
Percussion
Keyboard
Percussion
f

57. ESSENTIAL ELEMENTS QUIZ *Write the first 2 lines of exercise 56 in cut time.*

Flute
Oboe

B♭ Clarinet
B♭ Bass Cl.

E♭ Alto Sax.
E♭ Bari. Sax.
E♭ Alto Cl.

B♭ Tenor Sax.

B♭ Trumpet
Baritone T.C.

F Horn

Trombone
Baritone B.C.
Bassoon
Electric Bass

Tuba

Percussion

Keyboard
Percussion

Flute
Oboe

B♭ Clarinet
B♭ Bass Cl.

E♭ Alto Sax.
E♭ Bari. Sax.
E♭ Alto Cl.

B♭ Tenor Sax.

B♭ Trumpet
Baritone T.C.

F Horn

Trombone
Baritone B.C.
Bassoon
Electric Bass

Tuba

Percussion

Keyboard
Percussion

Sixteenth Notes and Rests in 6/8, 3/8, 9/8, 12/8

𝅘𝅥𝅯 = 1/2 beat 𝄿 = 1/2 beat 𝅘𝅥 = 2 beats 𝄽 = 2 beats

𝅘𝅥𝅮 = 1 beat 𝄾 = 1 beat 𝅘𝅥. = 3 beats 𝄽. = 3 beats

58. RHYTHM RAP

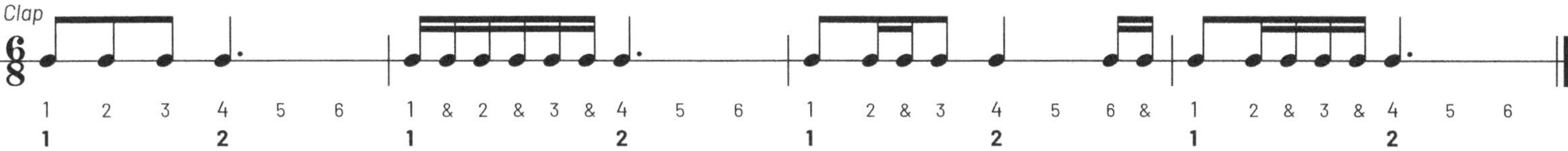

Clap
1 2 3 4 5 6
1 2
1 & 2 & 3 & 4 5 6
1 2
1 2 & 3 4 5 6 &
1 2
1 2 & 3 & 4 5 6
1 2

59. SONATINA

Flute
Oboe
B♭ Clarinet
B♭ Bass Cl.
E♭ Alto Sax.
E♭ Bari. Sax.
E♭ Alto Cl.
B♭ Tenor Sax.
B♭ Trumpet
Baritone T.C.
F Horn
Trombone
Baritone B.C.
Bassoon
Electric Bass
Tuba
Percussion
S.D.
B.D.
Keyboard
Percussion
a2

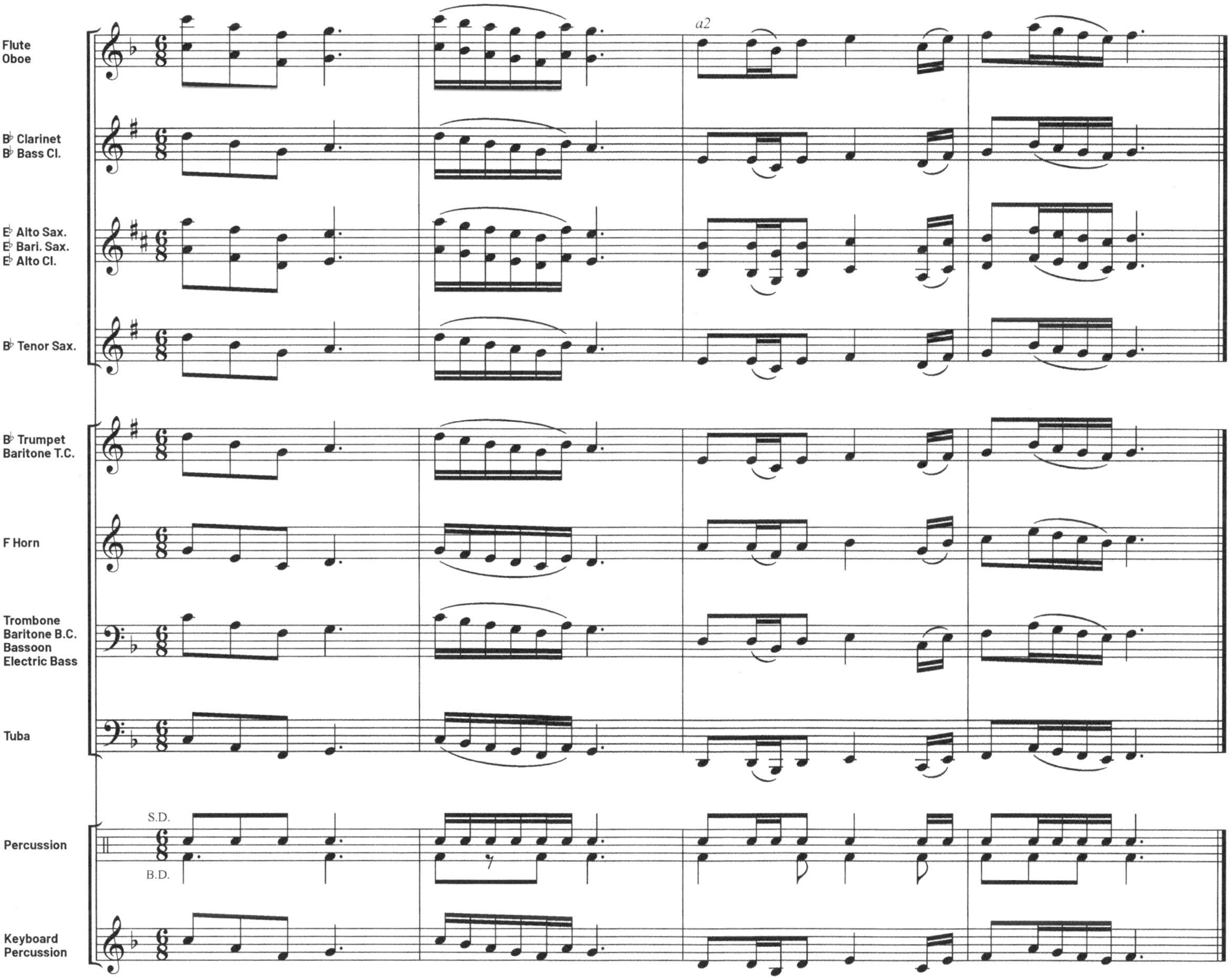

D MINOR

Oboe
D

Bassoon
E

Clarinet
E

Alto Saxophone
B

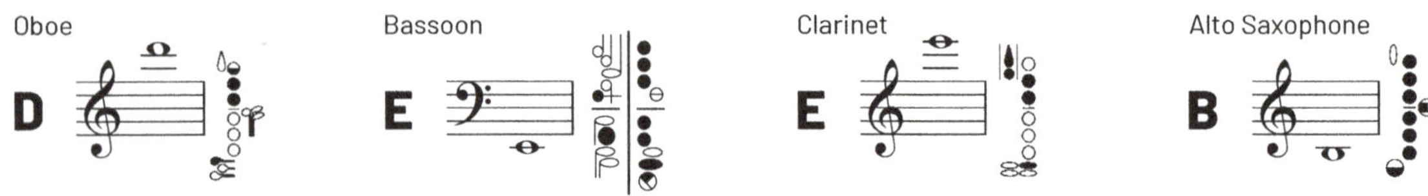

60. NATURAL MINOR

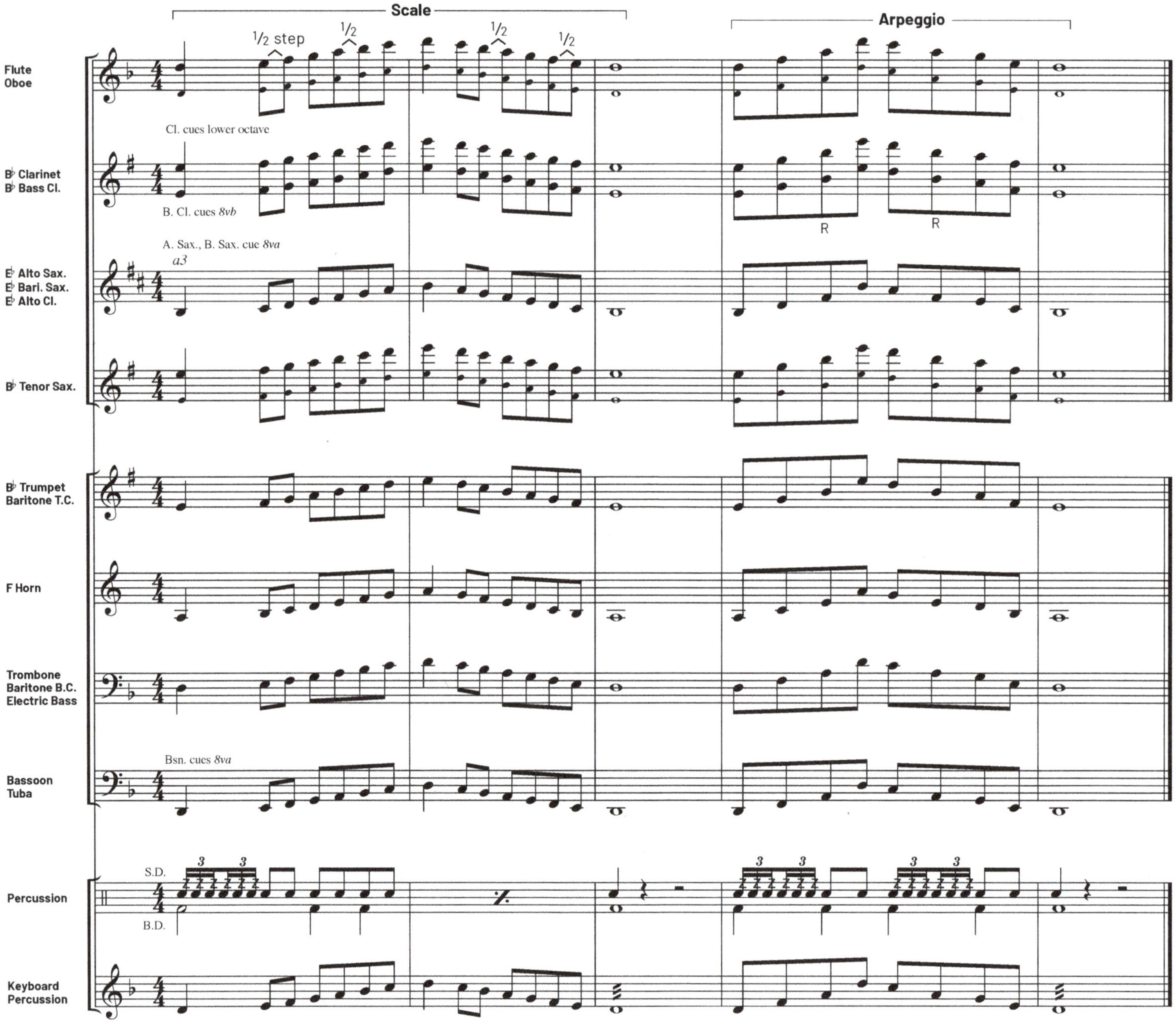
Scale
1/2 step
1/2
1/2
1/2
Arpeggio
Flute
Oboe
Cl. cues lower octave
B♭ Clarinet
B♭ Bass Cl.
B. Cl. cues 8vb
R
R
A. Sax., B. Sax. cue 8va
a3
E♭ Alto Sax.
E♭ Bari. Sax.
E♭ Alto Cl.
B♭ Tenor Sax.
B♭ Trumpet
Baritone T.C.
F Horn
Trombone
Baritone B.C.
Electric Bass
Bsn. cues 8va
Bassoon
Tuba
S.D.
B.D.
Percussion
Keyboard
Percussion

61. HARMONIC MINOR

Scale
1/2 1/2 1/2 1/2
Arpeggio

Flute
Oboe

Cl. cues lower octave
B♭ Clarinet
B♭ Bass Cl.
B. Cl. cues 8vb
R L L R

A. Sax., B. Sax. cue 8va
a3
E♭ Alto Sax.
E♭ Bari. Sax.
E♭ Alto Cl.

B♭ Tenor Sax.

B♭ Trumpet
Baritone T.C.

F Horn

Trombone
Baritone B.C.
Electric Bass

Bsn. cues 8va
Bassoon
Tuba

S.D.
B.D.
Percussion

Keyboard
Percussion

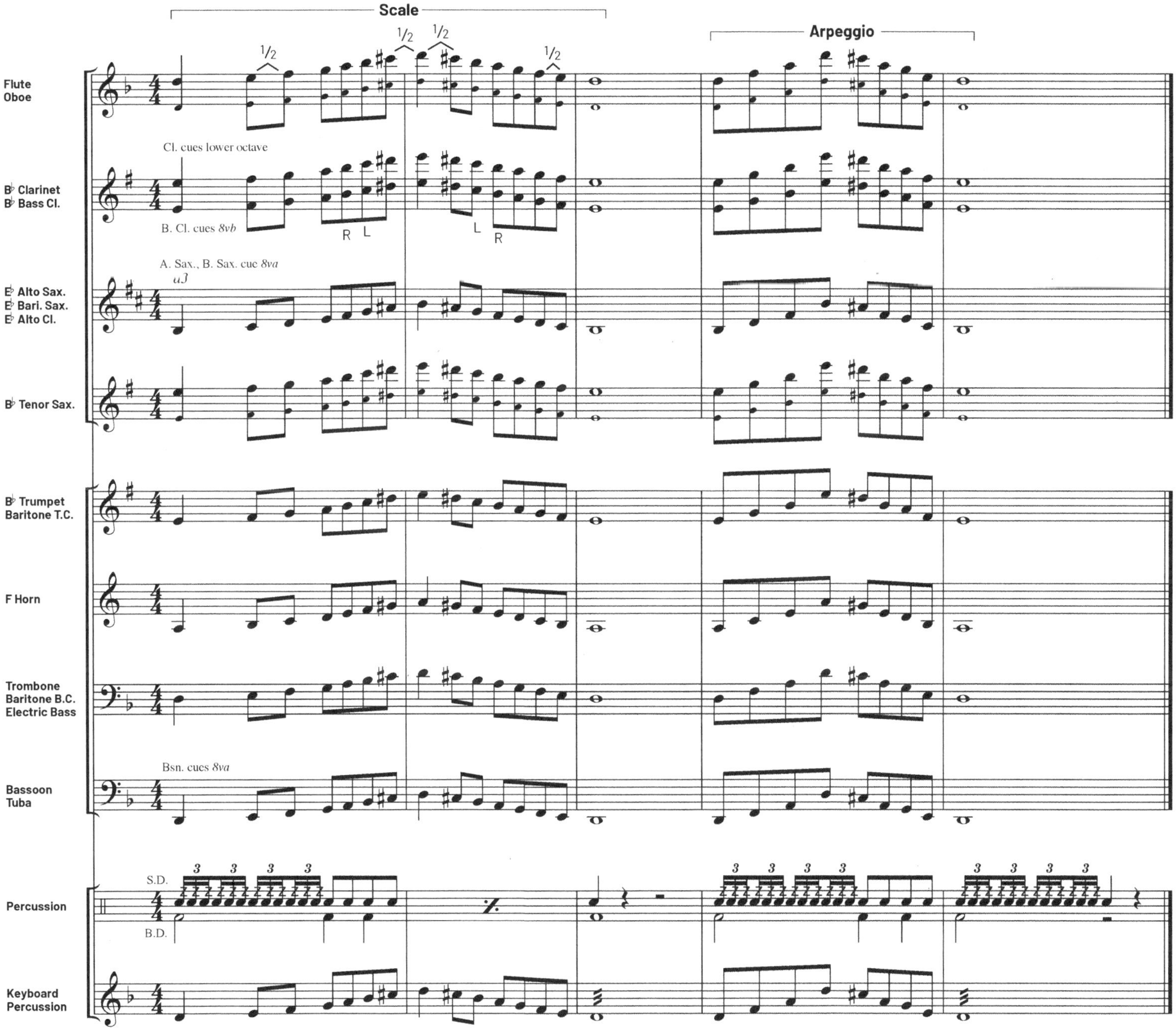

62. COSSACK MARCH

*A. Cl.: Use chromatic (Chr.) B in combination with B♭ (A♯).

63. SLAVONIC DANCE NO. 2

64. ESSENTIAL ELEMENTS QUIZ – THE PRETTY GIRL

A Chorale, 170. (Based on a Theme by Tchaikovsky) in the key of concert D minor, can be found on p. 210.

Student Book Page 14

A♭ MAJOR

(Ex. 65)
Percussion

Rudiment

Four Stroke Ruff

This is the traditional name given to the rudiment now called the Single Stroke Four (see Snare Drum International Rudiments section, courtesy of the Percussive Arts Society page 45). While the Single Stroke Four best describes how this rudiment is used in marching percussion applications, the Four Stroke Ruff (traditional name) is the term when the rudiment is used in a concert or orchestral application.

The same alternate sticking R L R L (or L R L R) should be used to learn this rudiment. Care should be taken to play all of the grace notes ahead of the beat to keep all rhythms accurate.

Alto Clarinet

66. EXERCISE IN THIRDS

Flute
Oboe

Ob.: L

L

L

B♭ Clarinet
B♭ Bass Cl.

E♭ Alto Sax.
E♭ Bari. Sax.
E♭ Alto Cl.

a3

A. Cl. cues 8vb

B♭ Tenor Sax.

B♭ Trumpet
Baritone T.C.

F Horn

Trombone
Baritone B.C.
Bassoon
Electric Bass

Tuba

Percussion

S.D.

B.D.

Keyboard
Percussion

Alto Saxophone

F
Alternate fingering

Baritone Saxophone

F
Alternate fingering

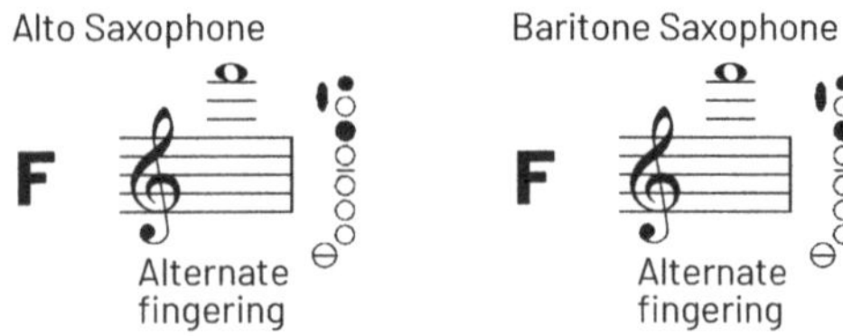

67. ARPEGGIO STUDY

Fl. cues lower octave
Flute
Oboe
Ob.: L L
B♭ Clarinet
B♭ Bass Cl.
B. Cl. cues 8vb
B. Cl.:
B. Sax. cues lower octave
Alt.
Alt.
Alt.
B. Sax.:
E♭ Alto Sax.
E♭ Bari. Sax.
E♭ Alto Cl.
A. Cl. cues 8vb
A. Cl.:
B♭ Tenor Sax.
*F
F
F
F
F
F
F
B♭ Trumpet
Baritone T.C.
F Horn
Tbn., Bar. cue lower octave
Tbn., Bar.:
Tbn., Bar.:
a4
Trombone
Baritone B.C.
Bassoon
Electric Bass
Bsn.
Bsn. cues 8vb
Tuba
S.D.
B.D.
Percussion
Keyboard
Percussion

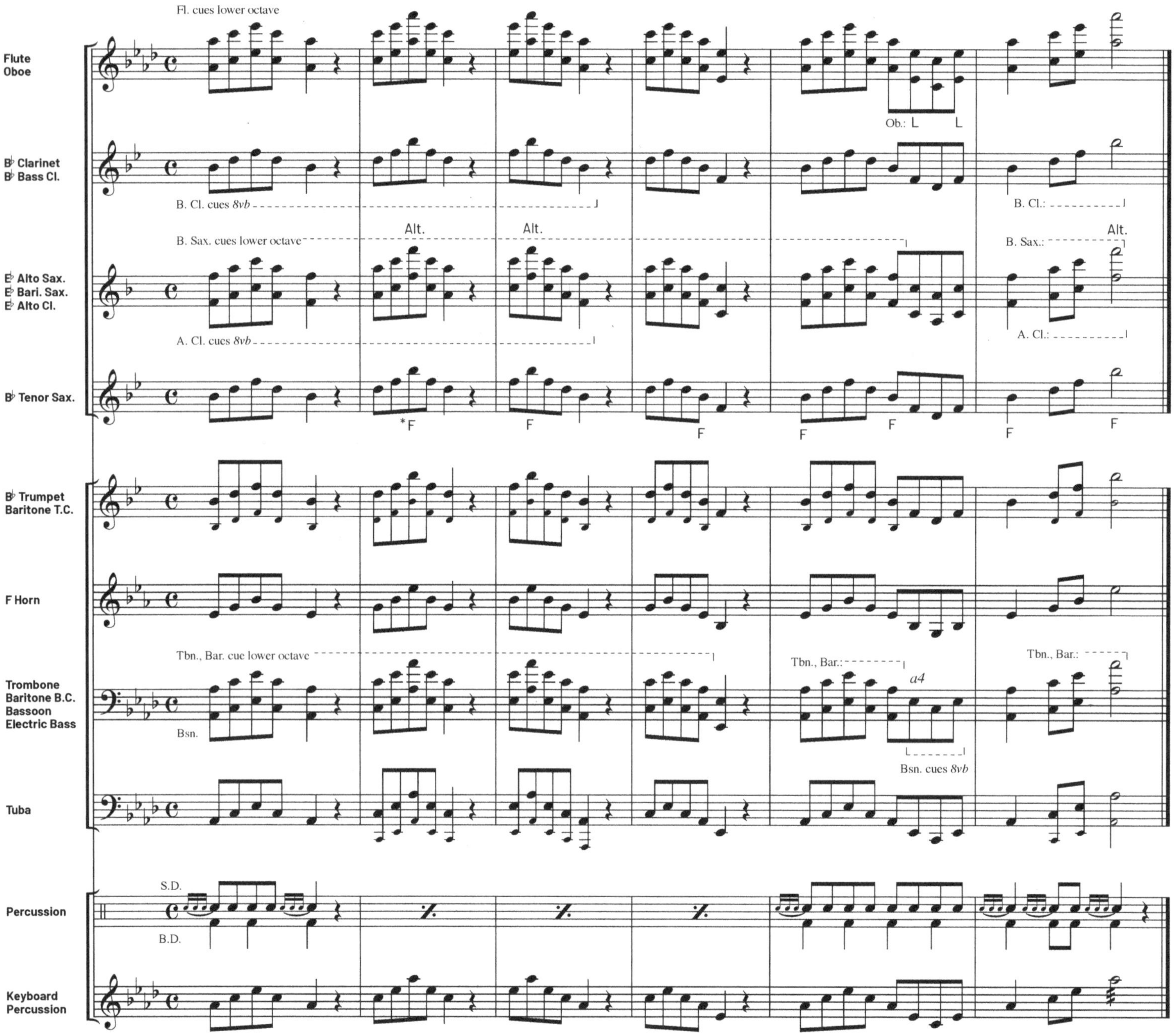

*T. Sax.: Forked B♭ (F) is convenient to use in a B♭ major arpeggio.

68. TWO-PART ETUDE

Flute
Oboe

Ob: L L L L

a2

B♭ Clarinet
B♭ Bass Cl.

a2

E♭ Alto Sax.
E♭ Bari. Sax.
E♭ Alto Cl.

A. Sax.: Alt.
B. Sax. *8vb*
Alt.
A. Cl. cues *8vb*

B♭ Tenor Sax.

B♭ Trumpet
Baritone T.C.

F Horn

Trombone
Baritone B.C.
Bassoon
Electric Bass

Bsn. cues *8vb*
Tbn., Bar. cues lower octave
Bsn., Bass

Tuba

Percussion

S.D.
B.D.

Keyboard
Percussion

Alto Clarinet

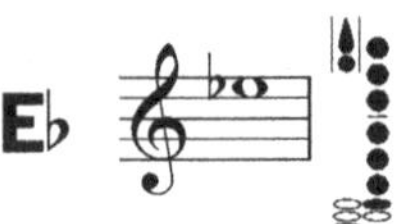

E♭

Bass Clarinet

G♯/A♭

Alto Saxophone

G♭

Alto Saxophone

D♯/E♭

Tenor Saxophone

C♯/D♭

Baritone Saxophone

G♭

Baritone Saxophone

D♯/E♭

Trumpet

G♯/A♭

Trombone

F♯/G♭

Baritone B.C.

F♯/G♭

Baritone T.C.

G♯/A♭

Electric Bass

G♭

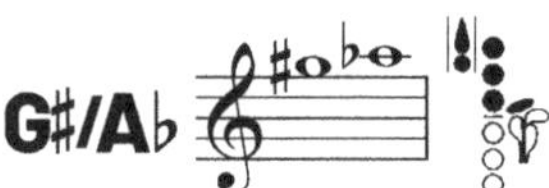

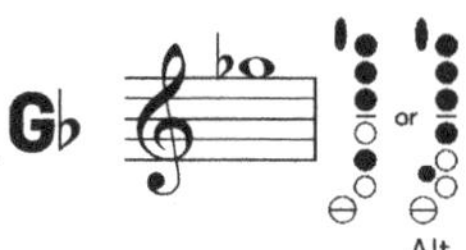

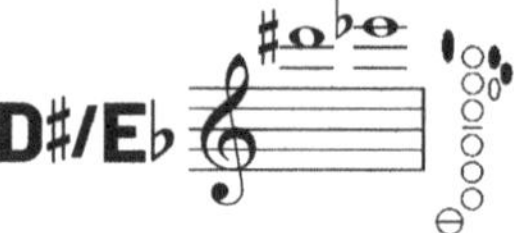

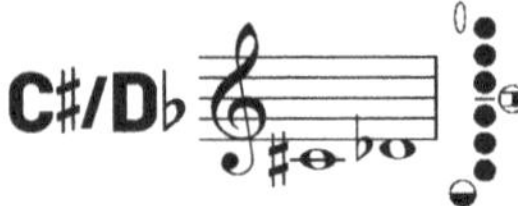

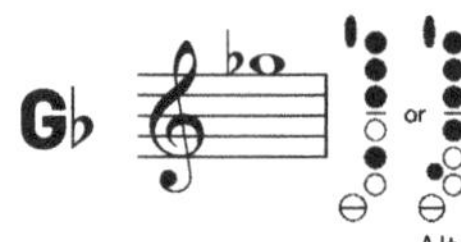

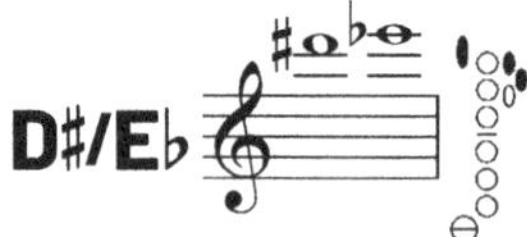

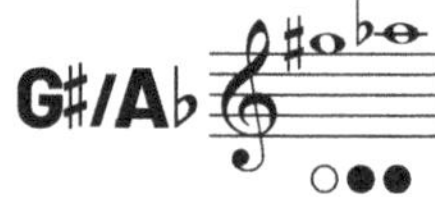

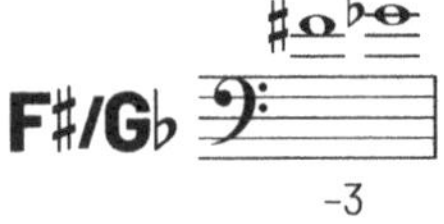

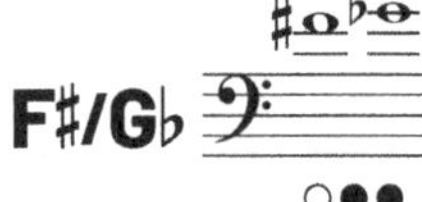

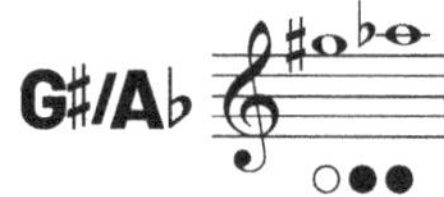

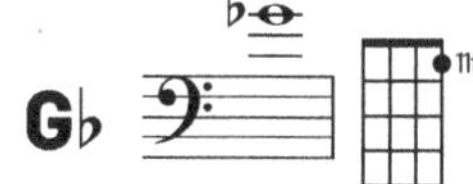

69. CHROMATIC SCALE

Flute
Oboe
B♭ Clarinet
B♭ Bass Cl.
A Sax., B. Sax. cue lower octave
E♭ Alto Sax.
E♭ Bari. Sax.
E♭ Alto Cl.
B♭ Tenor Sax.
B♭ Trumpet
Baritone T.C.
F Horn
Tbn., Bar., Bass cue 8vb
Trombone
Baritone B.C.
Bassoon
Electric Bass
Bsn. 8vb
Tuba
S.D.
B.D.
Percussion
2
Keyboard
Percussion

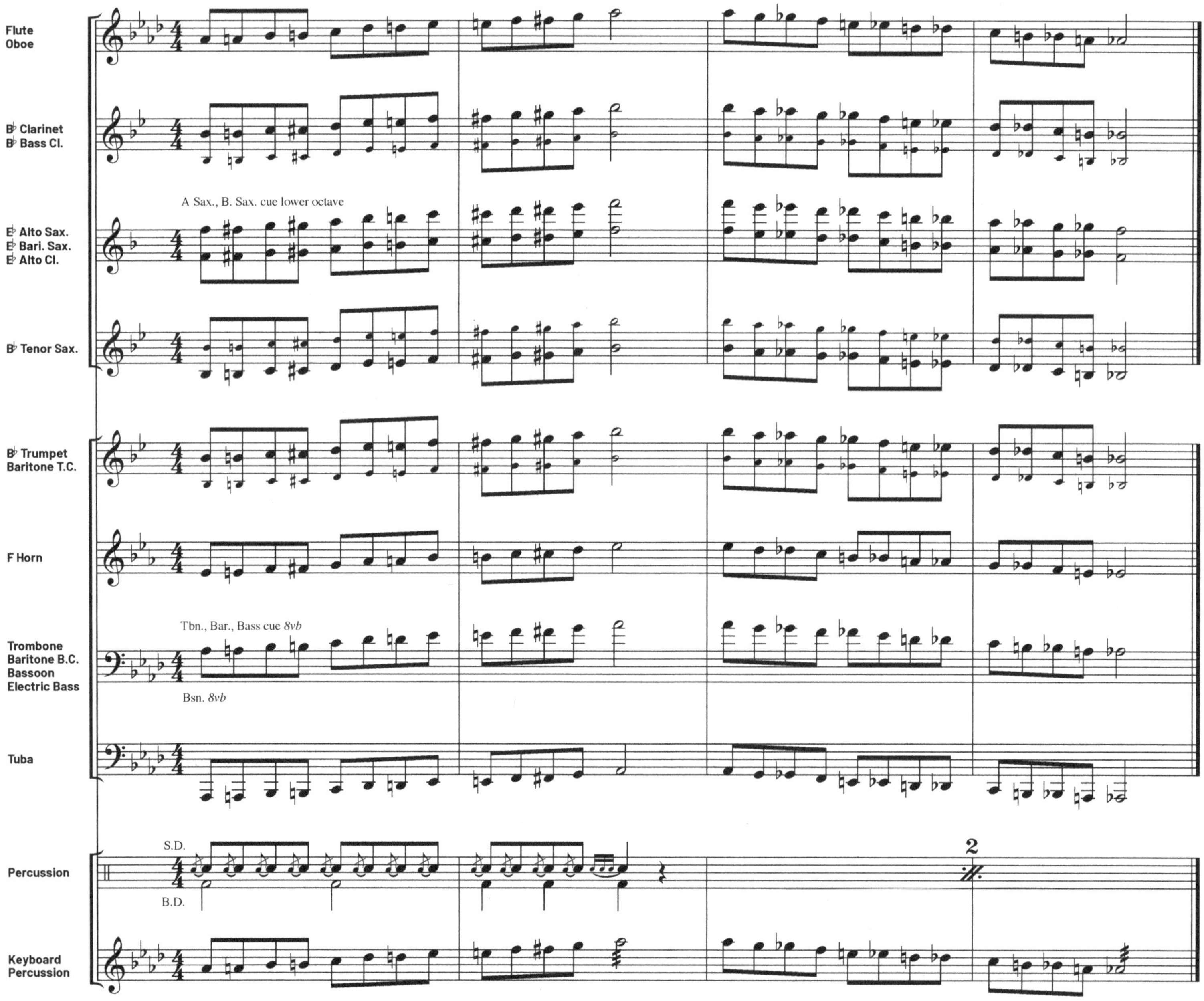

70. BALANCE BUILDER

71. CHORALE

An additional Chorale in the key of concert A♭ major, 171. (Erhalt Uns In Der Wahrheit), can be found on p. 212.

HISTORY

The Star Spangled Banner is the national anthem of the United States of America. Francis Scott Key wrote the words during the 1814 battle at Fort McHenry. He listened to the sounds of the fighting throughout the night while being detained on a ship. At dawn, he saw the American flag still flying over the fort. He was inspired to write these words, which were later set to the melody of a popular English song.

Keyboard Percussion

72. THE STAR SPANGLED BANNER

Words by Francis Scott Key
Music by John Stafford Smith

Allegro maestoso

Flute / Oboe

Oh say can you see, by the dawn's ear - ly light, what so proud - ly we hailed at the

B♭ Clarinet / B♭ Bass Cl.

E♭ Alto Sax. / E♭ Bari. Sax. / E♭ Alto Cl.

B♭ Tenor Sax.

B♭ Trumpet / Baritone T.C.

F Horn

Trombone / Baritone B.C. / Bassoon / Electric Bass

Tuba

Percussion

Use Sixteenth Note Triplet Multiple Bounce Rolls

S.D.

Keyboard Percussion

Flute
Oboe
twi - light's last gleam - ing? Whose broad stripes and bright stars, through the per - il - ous fight, o'er the
B♭ Clarinet
B♭ Bass Cl.
E♭ Alto Sax.
E♭ Bari. Sax.
E♭ Alto Cl.
B♭ Tenor Sax.
B♭ Trumpet
Baritone T.C.
F Horn
Trombone
Baritone B.C.
Bassoon
Electric Bass
Tuba
Percussion
Keyboard
Percussion
ram - parts we watched were so gal - lant - ly stream - ing. And the rock - et's red glare, the bombs
Ob.: L
L
mf

Flute
Oboe
burst - ing in air, gave proof through the night that our flag was still there. Oh say does that
B♭ Clarinet
B♭ Bass Cl.
E♭ Alto Sax.
E♭ Bari. Sax.
E♭ Alto Cl.
B♭ Tenor Sax.
B♭ Trumpet
Baritone T.C.
F Horn
Trombone
Baritone B.C.
Bassoon
Electric Bass
Tuba
Percussion
Keyboard
Percussion
Star Span - gled Ban - ner yet wave o'er the land of the free and the home of the brave?

Student Book Page 15

THEORY

Dynamics

pp - *pianissimo* (play very softly) *ff* - *fortissimo* (play very loudly)
Remember to use full breath support to produce the best possible tone and intonation.

73. INTERMEZZO

Flute
Oboe
B♭ Clarinet
B♭ Bass Cl.
E♭ Alto Sax.
E♭ Bari. Sax.
E♭ Alto Cl.
B♭ Tenor Sax.
B♭ Trumpet
Baritone T.C.
F Horn
Trombone
Baritone B.C.
Bassoon
Electric Bass
Tuba
Percussion
Keyboard
Percussion
2.
pp
f
ff

74. RHYTHM RAP

75. MORNING STAR

Moderato

Flute
Oboe

mf

B♭ Clarinet
B♭ Bass Cl.

mf

L

E♭ Alto Sax.
E♭ Bari. Sax.
E♭ Alto Cl.

mf

B♭ Tenor Sax.

mf

B♭ Trumpet
Baritone T.C.

mf

F Horn

mf

Trombone
Baritone B.C.
Bassoon
Electric Bass

mf

Tuba

mf

Percussion

S.D.
B.D.

mf

Keyboard
Percussion

mf

76. SONATA

Wolfgang Amadeus Mozart

77. RONDEAU

Jean-Joseph Mouret

Grace Note 

A small note (or notes) which is played on, or slightly before the beat.

78. JULIET'S WALTZ

Charles Gounod

Tempo di valse

Flute / Oboe — *mf* — Ob.: L

B♭ Clarinet / B♭ Bass Cl. — *mf*

E♭ Alto Sax. / E♭ Bari. Sax. / E♭ Alto Cl. — a3 — *mf*

B♭ Tenor Sax. — *mf*

B♭ Trumpet / Baritone T.C. — Bar. 8va — *mf*

F Horn — *mf*

Trombone / Baritone B.C. / Bassoon / Electric Bass — Tbn., Bar. 8va — *mf*

Tuba — *mf*

Percussion — S.D. / B.D. — *mf*

Keyboard Percussion — *mf*

Flute / Oboe — *f*

B♭ Clarinet / B♭ Bass Cl. — *f*

E♭ Alto Sax. / E♭ Bari. Sax. / E♭ Alto Cl. — *f*

B♭ Tenor Sax. — *f*

B♭ Trumpet / Baritone T.C. — Bar. *loco* — *f*

F Horn — *f*

Trombone / Baritone B.C. / Bassoon / Electric Bass — Tbn., Bar. *loco* — *f*

Tuba — *f*

Percussion — *f*

Keyboard Percussion — *f*

F MINOR

79. NATURAL MINOR

80. HARMONIC MINOR

Student Book Page 17

81. SORCERER'S APPRENTICE

Paul Dukas

82. I WALK THE ROAD AGAIN

American

Percussion
Brushes

Brushes with wire strands are recommended for the exercises in this book. Using a counterclockwise motion, the left hand should make a complete circle on each beat (stems down), while the right hand plays the rhythm (stems up).

83. ESSENTIAL ELEMENTS QUIZ – GREENSLEEVES

English Folk Song

Flute
Oboe
B♭ Clarinet
B♭ Bass Cl.
E♭ Alto Sax.
E♭ Bari. Sax.
E♭ Alto Cl.
B♭ Tenor Sax.
B♭ Trumpet
Baritone T.C.
F Horn
Trombone
Baritone B.C.
Bassoon
Electric Bass
Tuba
Percussion
Keyboard
Percussion
mp
mf
rit.
p

Student Book Page 18

C MAJOR

Oboe

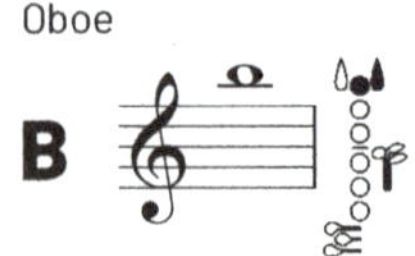

84. SCALE AND ARPEGGIO

1/2 step

1/2

1/2

1/2

Flute
Oboe

Ob. cues *8vb*
Cl. cues lower octave

B♭ Clarinet
B♭ Bass Cl.

E♭ Alto Sax.
E♭ Bari. Sax.
E♭ Alto Cl.

B♭ Tenor Sax.

B♭ Trumpet
Baritone T.C.

F Horn

Bsn. cues lower octave

Trombone
Baritone B.C.
Bassoon
Electric Bass
Tuba

S.D.
B.D.

Percussion

Keyboard
Percussion

85. EXERCISE IN THIRDS

Flute
Oboe

Ob. cues *8vb*

B♭ Clarinet
B♭ Bass Cl.

E♭ Alto Sax.
E♭ Bari. Sax.
E♭ Alto Cl.

B♭ Tenor Sax.

B♭ Trumpet
Baritone T.C.

F Horn

Trombone
Baritone B.C.
Bassoon
Electric Bass
Tuba

S.D.
B.D.

Percussion

Keyboard
Percussion

Alto Saxophone E Alternate fingering

Baritone Saxophone E Alternate fingering

Percussion

Rudiment

Inward Paradiddle

This is one of three variations of the Paradiddle. Notice that the sticking is identical to the Paradiddle, but the accent has been shifted to the fourth sixteenth note of each group, placing this paradiddle variation on the inside of the beat.

86. ARPEGGIO STUDY

Student Book Page 18

87. TWO-PART ETUDE

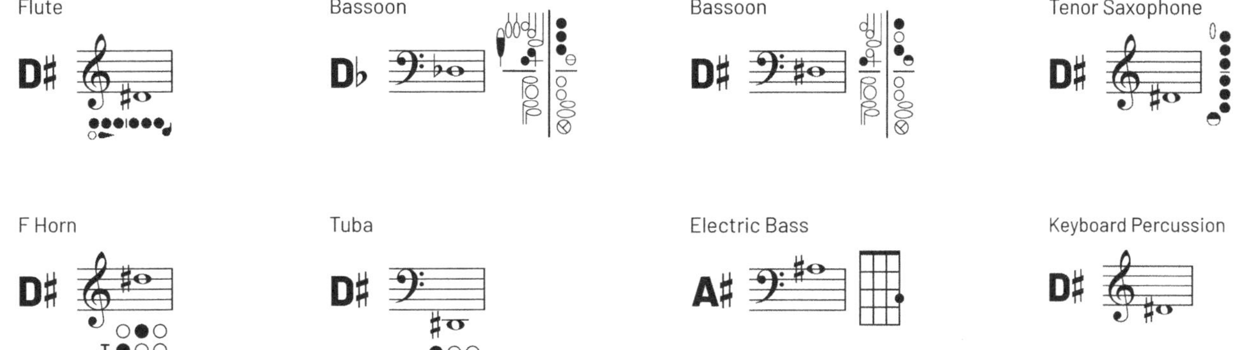

88. CHROMATIC SCALE

Fl. cues 8vb

Flute
Oboe

B♭ Clarinet
B♭ Bass Cl.

E♭ Alto Sax.
E♭ Bari. Sax.
E♭ Alto Cl.

B♭ Tenor Sax.

B♭ Trumpet
Baritone T.C.

F Horn

Trombone
Baritone B.C.
Bassoon
Electric Bass

Tuba

L R L R L L R L R L L R L R L L R
L R L R L L R L R L L R L R L L R

S.D.
B.D.

Percussion

Keyboard
Percussion

Student Book Page 18

89. BALANCE BUILDER

90. CHORALE

An additional Chorale in the key of concert C major, 172. (Navy Hymn), can be found on p. 214.

Student Book Page 19

HISTORY

African American spirituals originated in the 1700's. As one of the largest categories of true American folk music, these melodies were sung and passed on for generations without being written down. Black and white people worked together to publish the first spiritual collection in 1867, four years after *The Emancipation Proclamation* was signed into law.

91. SIT DOWN, SISTER

African American Spiritual

Fine
a2
Flute
Oboe
B♭ Clarinet
B♭ Bass Cl.
E♭ Alto Sax.
E♭ Bari. Sax.
E♭ Alto Cl.
B♭ Tenor Sax.
B♭ Trumpet
Baritone T.C.
F Horn
Trombone
Baritone B.C.
Bassoon
Electric Bass
Tuba
Percussion
Keyboard
Percussion
mp
f
D.S. al Fine
2

Student Book Page 19

F♯

92. SPINNING SONG – Duet

Johann Ellmenreich

Moderato

Flute
Oboe

B♭ Clarinet
B♭ Bass Cl.

E♭ Alto Sax.
E♭ Bari. Sax.
E♭ Alto Cl.

B♭ Tenor Sax.

B♭ Trumpet
Baritone T.C.

F Horn

Keyboard
Percussion

Tri.
B.D.
Tamb. (use thumb rolls)
Xylophone
Bells

Fine
D.S. al Fine
Flute
Oboe
B♭ Clarinet
B♭ Bass Cl.
E♭ Alto Sax.
E♭ Bari. Sax.
E♭ Alto Cl.
B♭ Tenor Sax.
B♭ Trumpet
Baritone T.C.
F Horn
Trombone
Baritone B.C.
Bassoon
Electric Bass
Tuba
Percussion
Keyboard
Percussion
a2
a3
p
cresc.
mf
mp
f

THEORY

Quarter Note Triplets

Similar to eighth note triplets where 1 beat is divided into 3 equal notes,

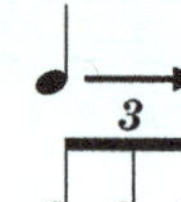

quarter note triplets divide 2 beats into 3 equal notes.

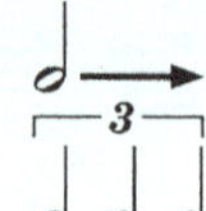

93. RHYTHM RAP

▼ *1 beat divided into 3 notes.*

▼ *2 beats divided into 3 notes.*

Clap
3
3
1 2 3 4 1 2 trip - let 3 4 1 2 3 4 1 trip - let 3 4
(2)

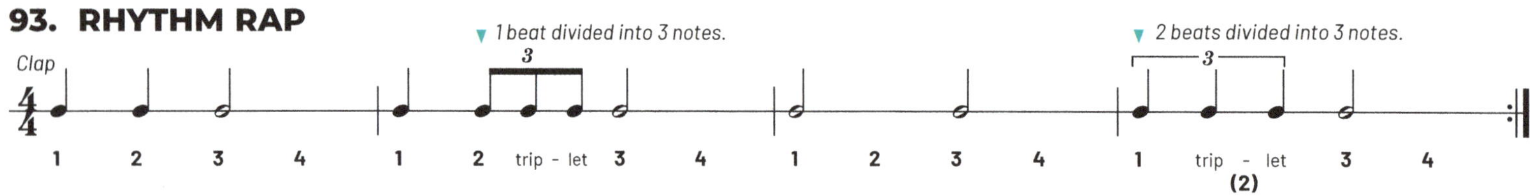

Bassoon

B

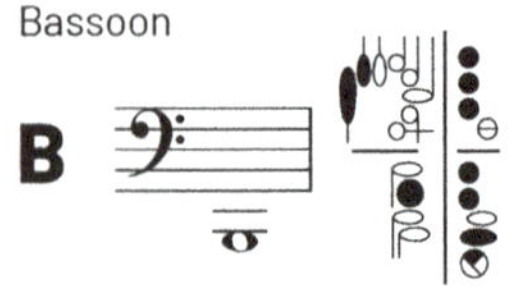

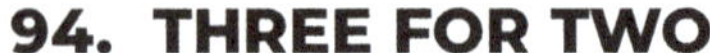

94. THREE FOR TWO

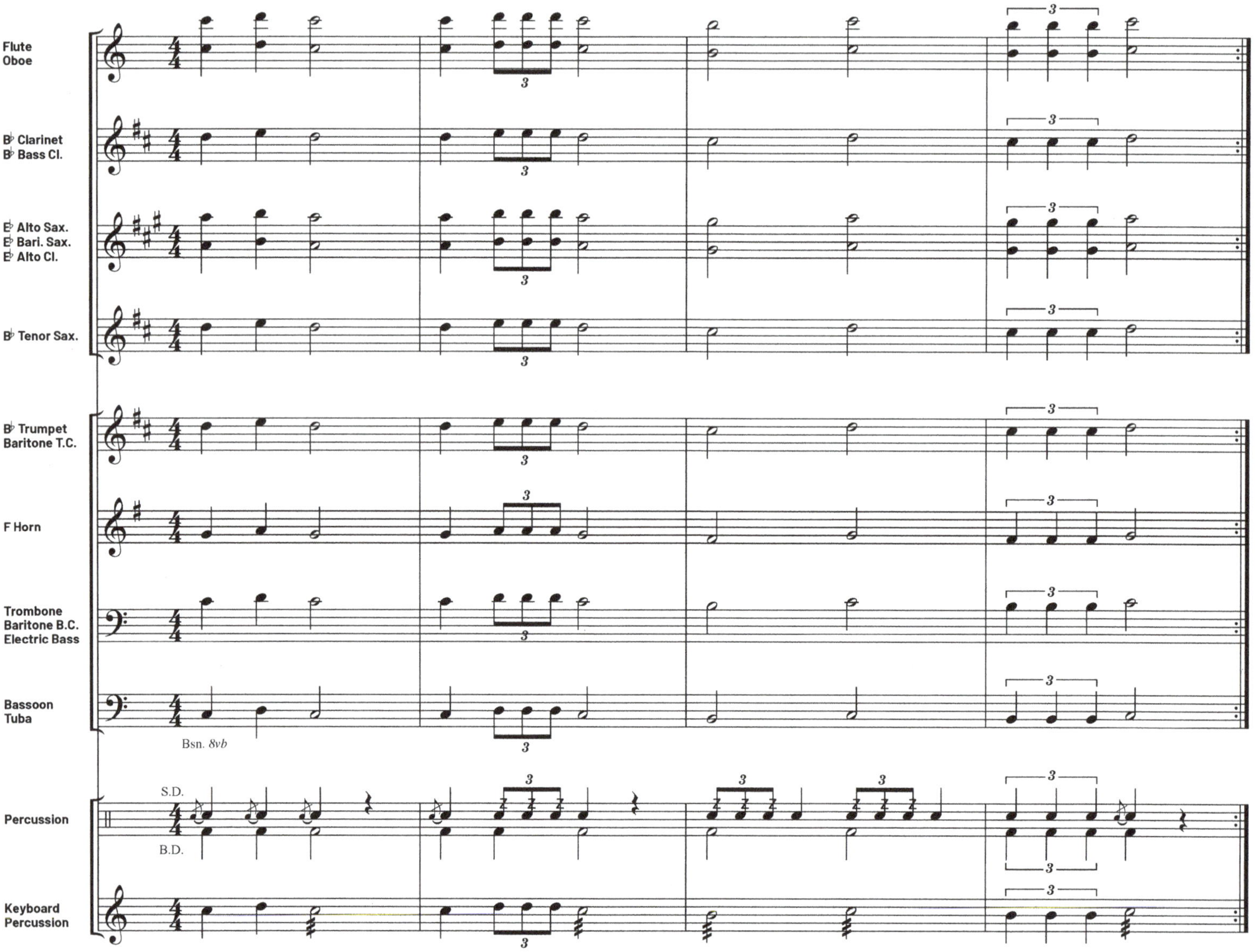

Flute
Oboe
B♭ Clarinet
B♭ Bass Cl.
E♭ Alto Sax.
E♭ Bari. Sax.
E♭ Alto Cl.
B♭ Tenor Sax.
B♭ Trumpet
Baritone T.C.
F Horn
Trombone
Baritone B.C.
Electric Bass
Bassoon
Tuba
Bsn. 8vb
Percussion
S.D.
B.D.
Keyboard
Percussion

95. SURIRAM'S SONG

Malaysian Folk Song

Student Book Page 20

HISTORY

Africa is a large continent that is made up of many nations, and **African folk music** is as diverse as its many cultures. Folk songs from any country are expressions of work, love, war, sadness, and joy. This song is from Tanzania. The words describe a rabbit hopping and running through a field. Listen to the percussion section play African-sounding drums and rhythms.

Electric Bass

96. JIBULI (The Rabbit's Song)

Adapted Tanzanian Folk Song

Allegro

Flute
Oboe

B♭ Clarinet
B♭ Bass Cl.

E♭ Alto Sax.
E♭ Bari. Sax.
E♭ Alto Cl.

B♭ Tenor Sax.

B♭ Trumpet
Baritone T.C.

F Horn

Trombone
Baritone B.C.
Bassoon
Electric Bass

Tuba

Percussion

Keyboard Percussion

a3 · Bsn. 8vb · Congas and Agogo Bells · a2 · *mf*

Percussion

Agogo Bells

Traditionally an Iron Double Bell of African origin (with two pitches), the modern Agogo Bell is from Brazil, somewhat smaller in size, and made of steel. Use a stick and play toward the open end of each bell. If not available, substitute two different size cowbells.

Flute
Oboe
B♭ Clarinet
B♭ Bass Cl.
E♭ Alto Sax.
E♭ Bari. Sax.
E♭ Alto Cl.
B♭ Tenor Sax.
B♭ Trumpet
Baritone T.C.
F Horn
Trombone
Baritone B.C.
Bassoon
Electric Bass
Tuba
Percussion
Keyboard
Percussion
Tpt. 8vb
Tbn., Bar. 8vb
p
mf
f
3

A MINOR

F Horn

E
T

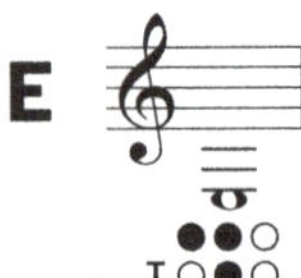

97. NATURAL MINOR

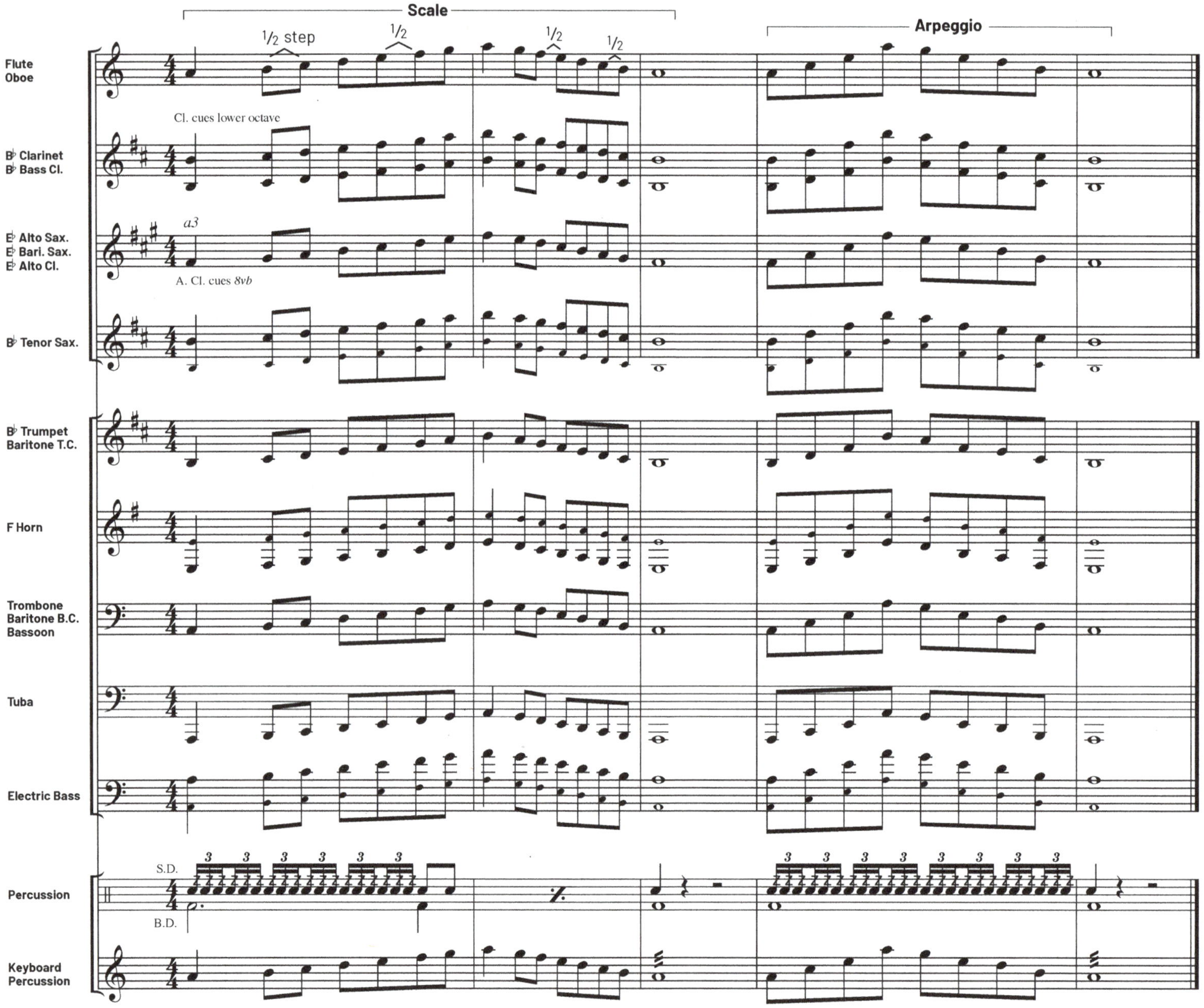
Scale
1/2 step
1/2
1/2
1/2
Arpeggio
Flute
Oboe
Cl. cues lower octave
B♭ Clarinet
B♭ Bass Cl.
a3
E♭ Alto Sax.
E♭ Bari. Sax.
E♭ Alto Cl.
A. Cl. cues 8vb
B♭ Tenor Sax.
B♭ Trumpet
Baritone T.C.
F Horn
Trombone
Baritone B.C.
Bassoon
Tuba
Electric Bass
S.D.
B.D.
Percussion
Keyboard
Percussion

(Ex. 98)

Bass Clarinet

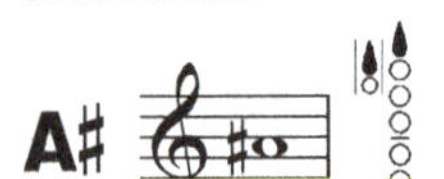

A♯

Alto Saxophone

E♯

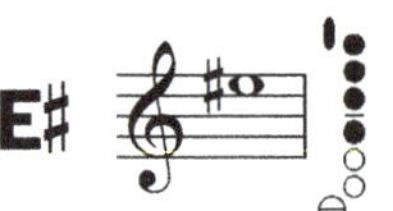

Baritone Saxophone

E♯

F Horn

D♯

Tuba

G♯

Electric Bass

G♯
13fr

Keyboard Percussion

G♯

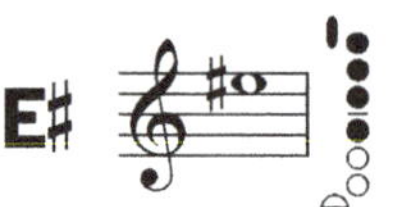

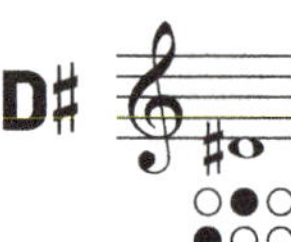

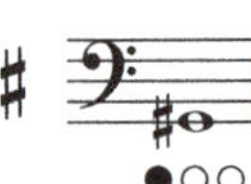

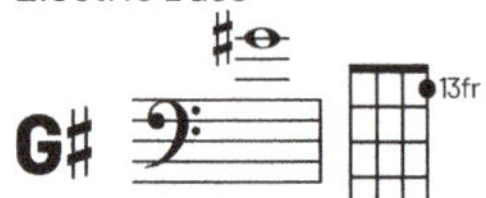

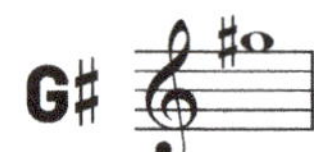

98. HARMONIC MINOR

THEORY

Meter Changes

Meter changes, or changing time signatures within a section of music, are commonly found in contemporary music. Composers use this technique to create a unique rhythm, pulse, or musical style.

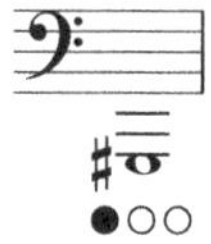

99. TIME ZONES

Allegro

Flute
Oboe

B♭ Clarinet
B♭ Bass Cl.

E♭ Alto Sax.
E♭ Bari. Sax.
E♭ Alto Cl.

B♭ Tenor Sax.

B♭ Trumpet
Baritone T.C.

F Horn

Trombone
Baritone B.C.
Bassoon
Electric Bass

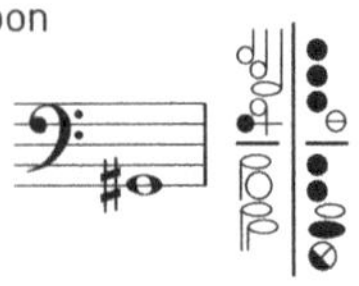

Bsn. 8vb

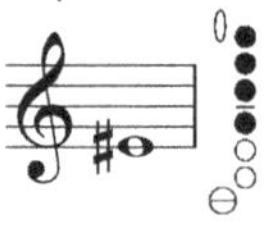

Tbn., Bar. 8vb

Tuba

Percussion

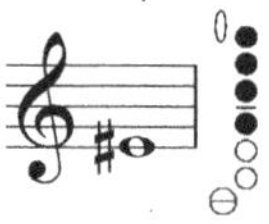

S.D.

B.D.

Keyboard
Percussion

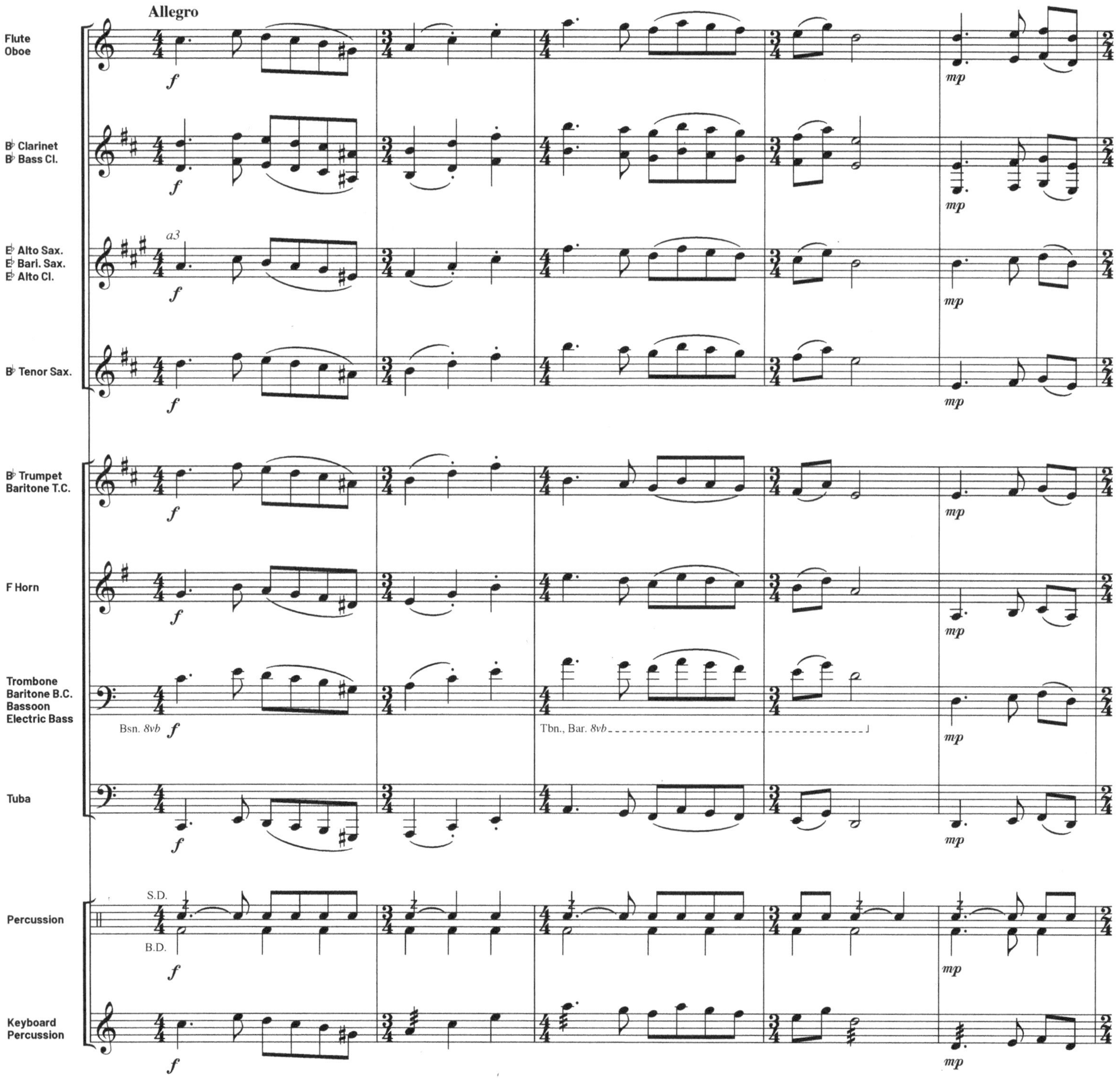

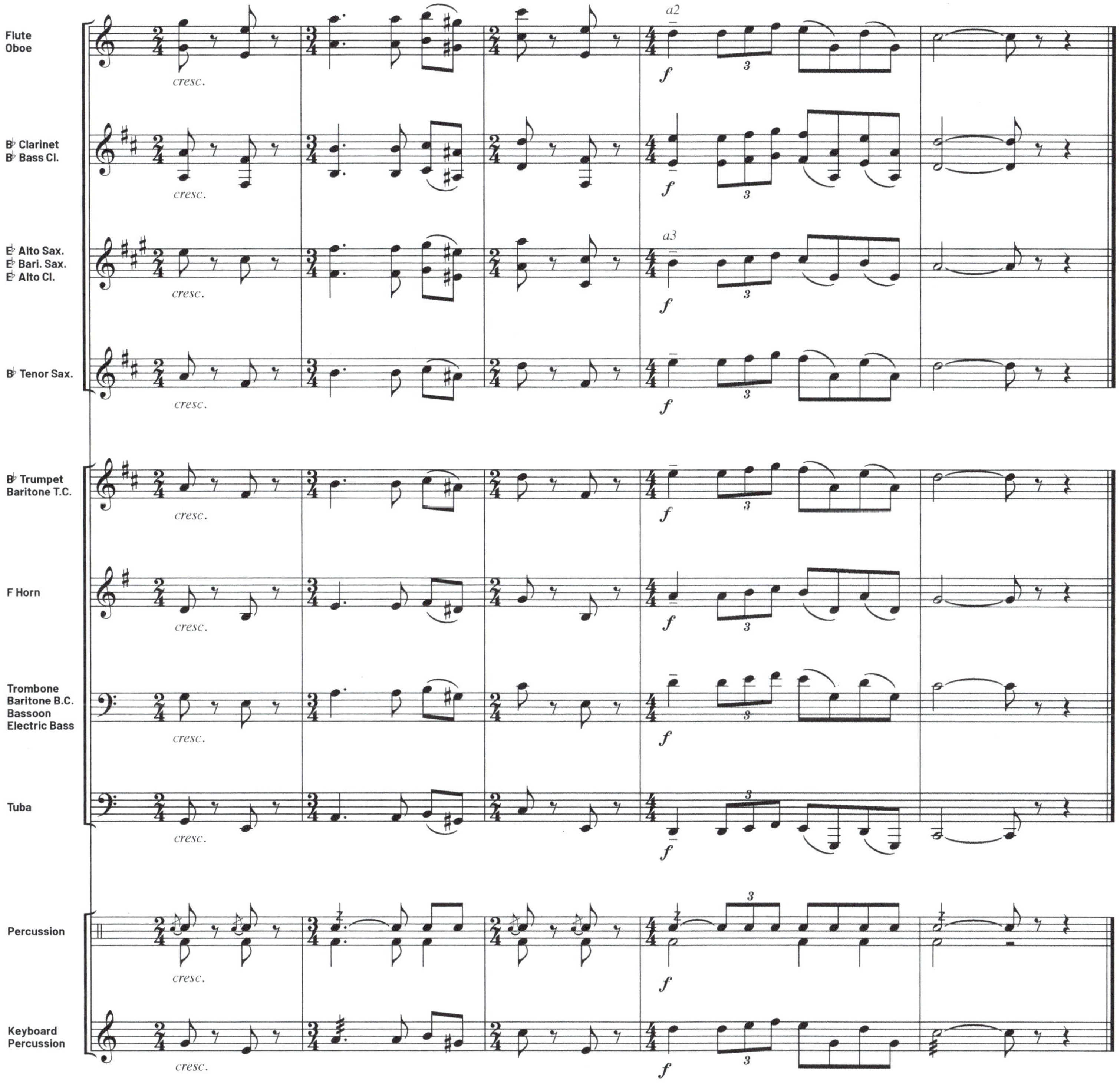

Flute
Oboe
B♭ Clarinet
B♭ Bass Cl.
E♭ Alto Sax.
E♭ Bari. Sax.
E♭ Alto Cl.
B♭ Tenor Sax.
B♭ Trumpet
Baritone T.C.
F Horn
Trombone
Baritone B.C.
Bassoon
Electric Bass
Tuba
Percussion
Keyboard
Percussion
cresc.
a2
a3
f
3

HISTORY

Important French composers of the late 19th century include **Claude Debussy** (1862–1918), **Gabriel Fauré** (1845–1924), **Erik Satie** (1866–1925), **César Franck** (1822–1890), **Camille Saint-Saëns** (1835–1921), and **Paul Dukas** (1865–1935). Their works continue to have influence on the music of modern day composers. Gabriel Fauré wrote *Pavanne* (originally for orchestra) in 1887, two years before the Eiffel Tower was completed in Paris.

Clarinet

E♯

Alto Clarinet

B♯

Bass Clarinet

E♯

Alto Saxophone

B♯

Tenor Saxophone

E♯

Baritone Saxophone

B♯

Trumpet

E♯

Baritone T.C.

E♯

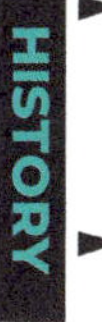

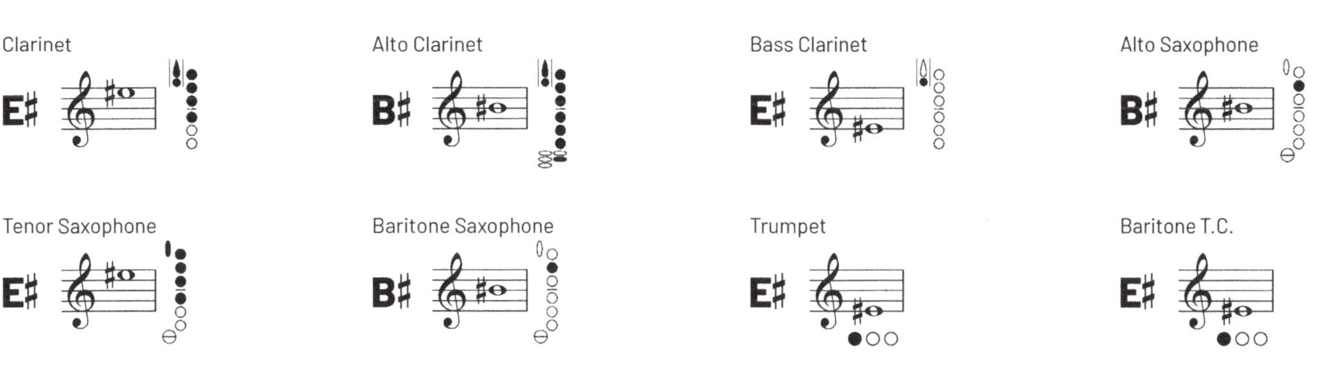

100. PAVANNE

Gabriel Fauré

Percussion

Finger Cymbals

These small brass cymbals should be played by holding the edges perpendicular (at a right angle) to one another, then lightly striking the edges together. In the case of the heavier cast cymbals, some performers prefer to allow both cymbals to hang, then drop one past the other, allowing the edges to come in contact. Experiment to achieve the best sound.

Flute
Oboe
Bassoon
B♭ Clarinet
E♭ Alto Cl.
B♭ Bass Cl.
E♭ Alto Sax.
B♭ Tenor Sax.
E♭ Bari. Sax.
B♭ Trumpet
F Horn
Trombone
Baritone
Tuba
Electric Bass
Percussion
Keyboard
Percussion
a2
p
mf

Flute
Oboe
Bassoon
B♭ Clarinet
E♭ Alto Cl.
B♭ Bass Cl.
E♭ Alto Sax.
B♭ Tenor Sax.
E♭ Bari. Sax.
B♭ Trumpet
F Horn
Trombone Baritone
Tuba
Electric Bass
Percussion
Keyboard Percussion
div.
a2
rit.
pp
p
mf
Xylo.
Bells

D♭ MAJOR

Oboe

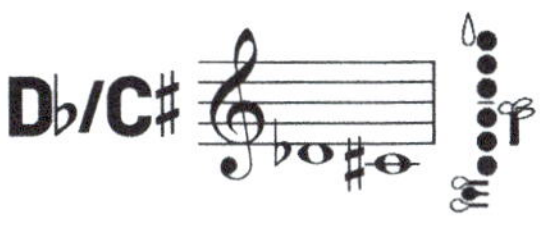
D♭/C♯

Bass Clarinet

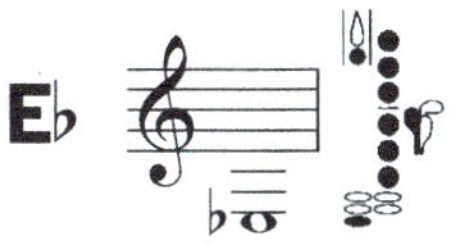
E♭

Alto Saxophone

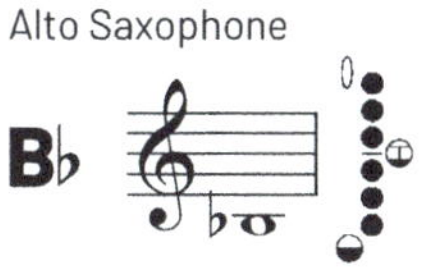
B♭

Baritone Saxophone

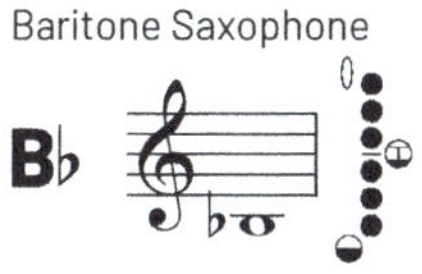
B♭

101. SCALE AND ARPEGGIO

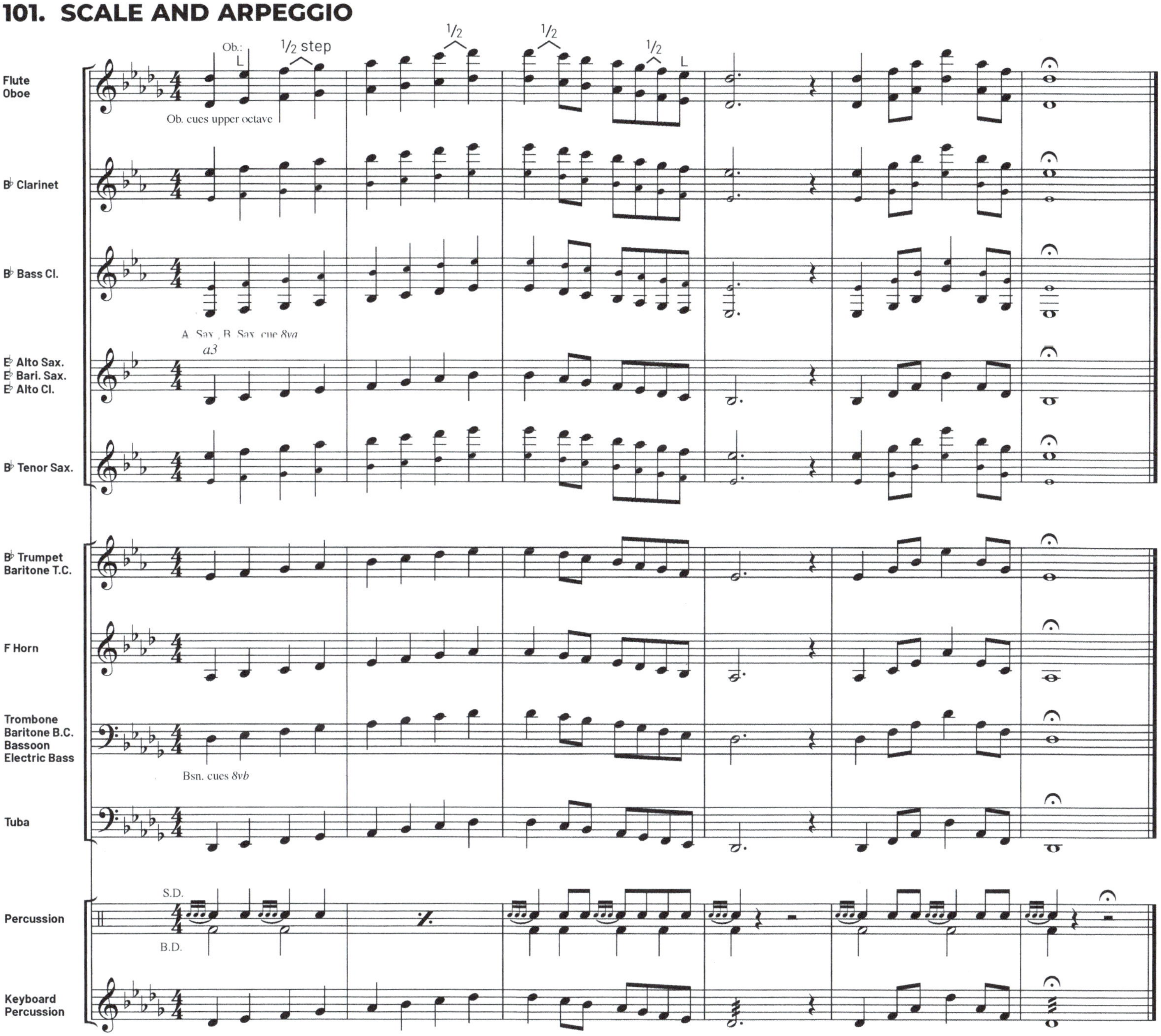
Flute
Oboe
Ob.:
L
1/2 step
1/2
1/2
1/2
L
Ob. cues upper octave
B♭ Clarinet
B♭ Bass Cl.
A. Sax., B. Sax. cue 8va
a3
E♭ Alto Sax.
E♭ Bari. Sax.
E♭ Alto Cl.
B♭ Tenor Sax.
B♭ Trumpet
Baritone T.C.
F Horn
Trombone
Baritone B.C.
Bassoon
Electric Bass
Bsn. cues 8vb
Tuba
S.D.
Percussion
B.D.
Keyboard
Percussion

Percussion

Rudiment

Four Stroke Ruff

Now that you have established the alternate sticking pattern used to play the grace notes ahead of the beat, begin to practice controlled bounces with **both hands together** (Example 1). Once you gain a level of comfort, begin to move one hand just slightly ahead of the other each time you begin a set of controlled bounces. As soon as you get one hand to move slightly ahead of the other, you will immediately hear the four notes articulated clearly (Example 2). This is an alternative approach to using four fast single strokes when playing the Four Stroke Ruff.

Example 1
Example 2
R R
R R
L L
L L

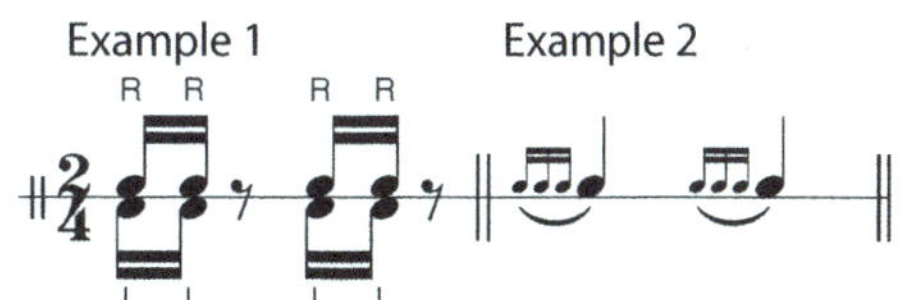

102. EXERCISE IN THIRDS

Bassoon

D♭
Alternate fingering

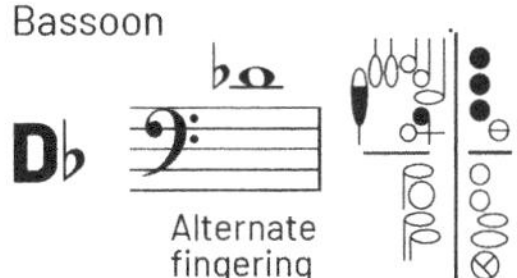

103. ARPEGGIO STUDY

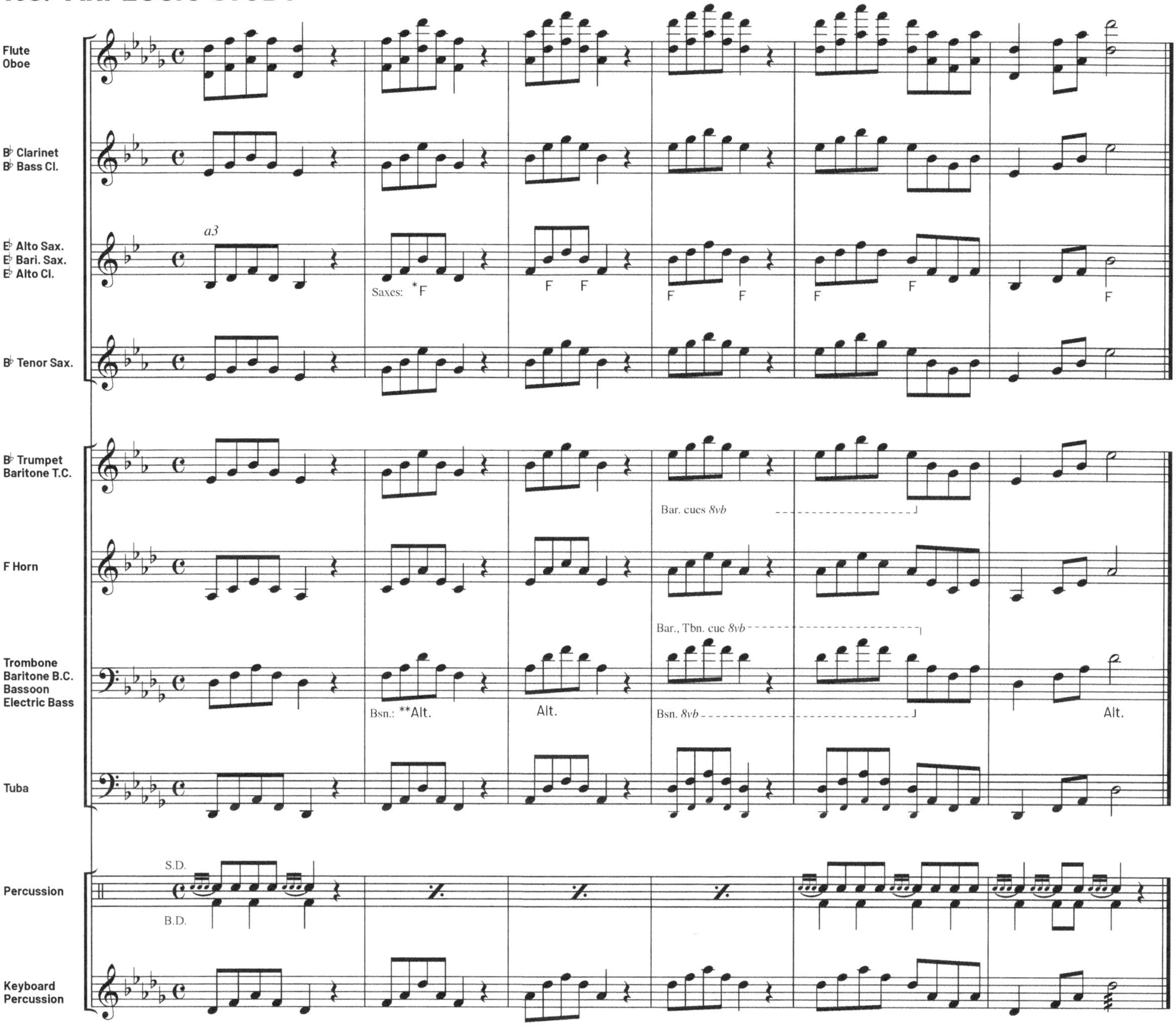

Flute
Oboe
B♭ Clarinet
B♭ Bass Cl.
E♭ Alto Sax.
E♭ Bari. Sax.
E♭ Alto Cl.
a3
Saxes: *F
F F
F F
F F
F
B♭ Tenor Sax.
B♭ Trumpet
Baritone T.C.
Bar. cues 8vb
F Horn
Bar., Tbn. cue 8vb
Trombone
Baritone B.C.
Bassoon
Electric Bass
Bsn.: **Alt.
Alt.
Bsn. 8vb
Alt.
Tuba
S.D.
Percussion
B.D.
Keyboard
Percussion

*Saxes: Forked B♭ (F) is convenient to use when playing a B♭ major arpeggio.

**Bsn.: When moving to or from middle A♭, use alternate D♭ fingering.

104. TWO-PART ETUDE

Alto Saxophone

Baritone Saxophone

105. CHROMATIC SCALE

Flute
Oboe

Ob. cues 8vb

B♭ Clarinet
B♭ Bass Cl.

B. Cl. cues upper octave

A. Sax., B. Sax. cue 8va

a3

E♭ Alto Sax.
E♭ Bari. Sax.
E♭ Alto Cl.

B♭ Tenor Sax.

B♭ Trumpet
Baritone T.C.

F Horn

Trombone
Baritone B.C.
Bassoon
Electric Bass

Bsn. cues 8vb

Tuba

Percussion

S.D.

B.D.

2

Keyboard
Percussion

Student Book Page 22

106. BALANCE BUILDER

107. CHORALE

Andante
Flute
Oboe
Bassoon
div.
B♭ Clarinet
E♭ Alto Cl.
B♭ Bass Cl.
E♭ Alto Sax.
B♭ Tenor Sax.
E♭ Bari. Sax.
Andante
div.
B♭ Trumpet
F Horn
Trombone
Baritone
Tuba (Electric Bass)
Percussion
Triangle
Keyboard Percussion
mf
rit.
L
F

Bassoon

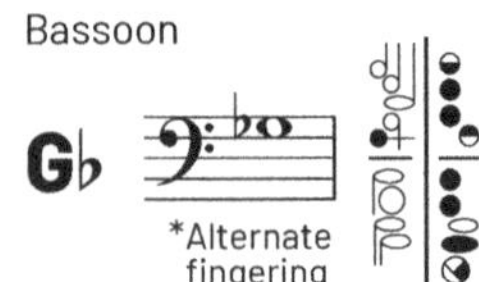

108. GERMAN NATIONAL ANTHEM

Franz Josef Haydn

*Alternate G♭ (F♯) should be used when moving to or from B♭ or D♭.

Flute
Oboe

B♭ Clarinet
B♭ Bass Cl.

E♭ Alto Sax.
E♭ Bari. Sax.
E♭ Alto Cl.

B♭ Tenor Sax.

B♭ Trumpet
Baritone T.C.

F Horn

Trombone
Baritone B.C.
Bassoon
Electric Bass

Tuba

Percussion

Keyboard
Percussion

Flute
Oboe

B♭ Clarinet
B♭ Bass Cl.

E♭ Alto Sax.
E♭ Bari. Sax.
E♭ Alto Cl.

B♭ Tenor Sax.

B♭ Trumpet
Baritone T.C.

F Horn

Trombone
Baritone B.C.
Bassoon
Electric Bass

Bsn.: Alt.

Tuba

Percussion

Keyboard
Percussion

*Bsn.: Alternate G♭(F♯) should be used when moving to or from B♭ or D♭.

109. JOY

Johann Sebastian Bach

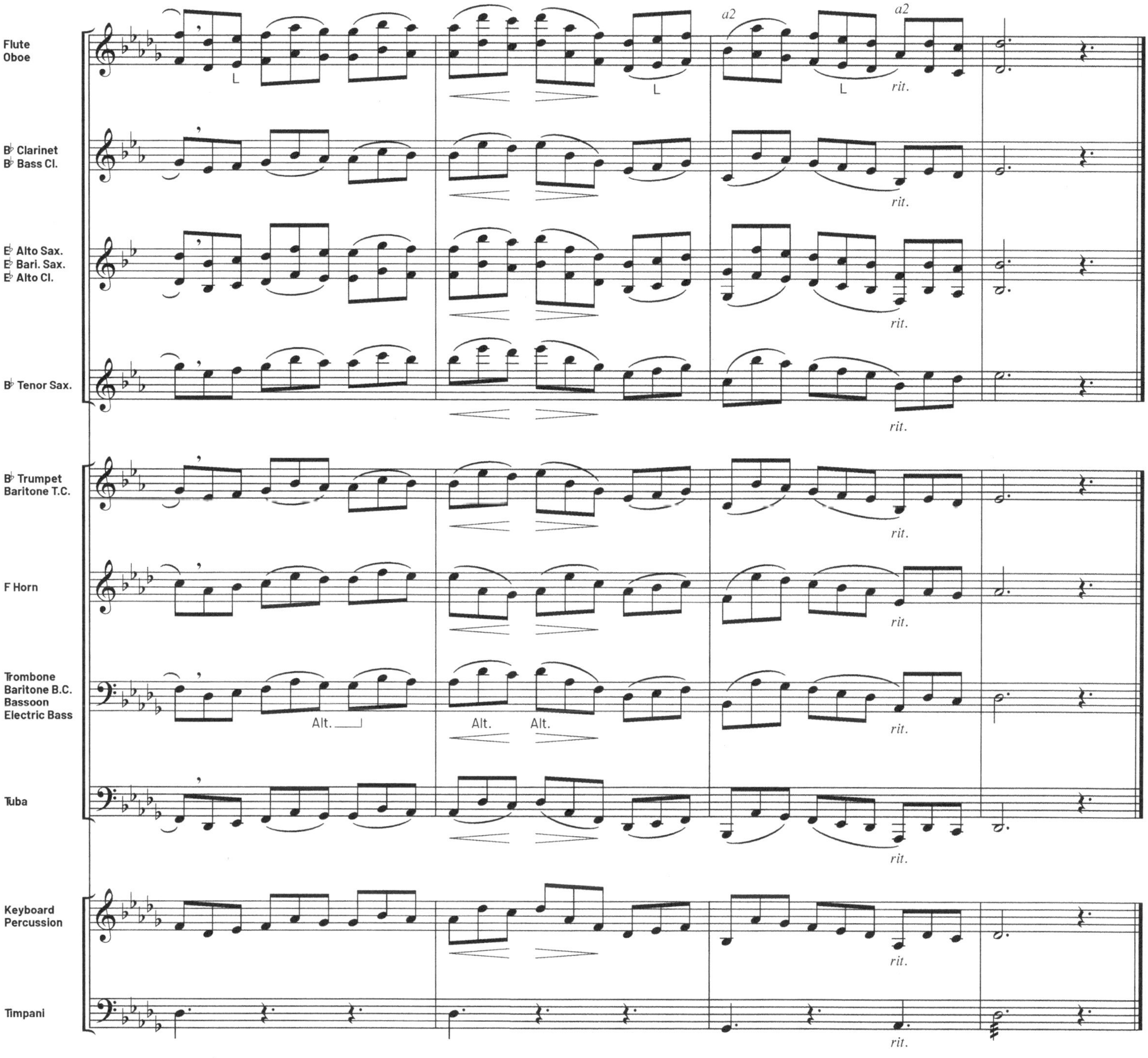

Flute
Oboe

B♭ Clarinet
B♭ Bass Cl.

E♭ Alto Sax.
E♭ Bari. Sax.
E♭ Alto Cl.

B♭ Tenor Sax.

B♭ Trumpet
Baritone T.C.

F Horn

Trombone
Baritone B.C.
Bassoon
Electric Bass

Tuba

Keyboard
Percussion

Timpani

a2 *a2* L L L *rit.* Alt. Alt. Alt.

$\frac{5}{4}$ Time Signature

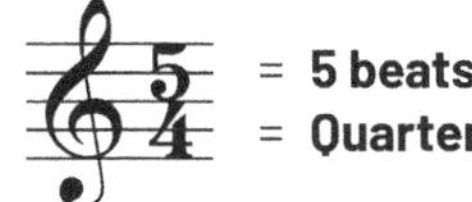

= **5 beats** per measure
= **Quarter** note gets one beat

Conducting

Practice conducting these five-beat patterns.

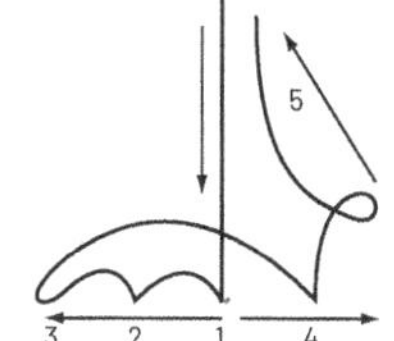

or

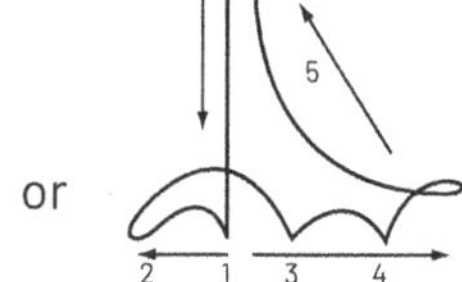

110. RHYTHM RAP

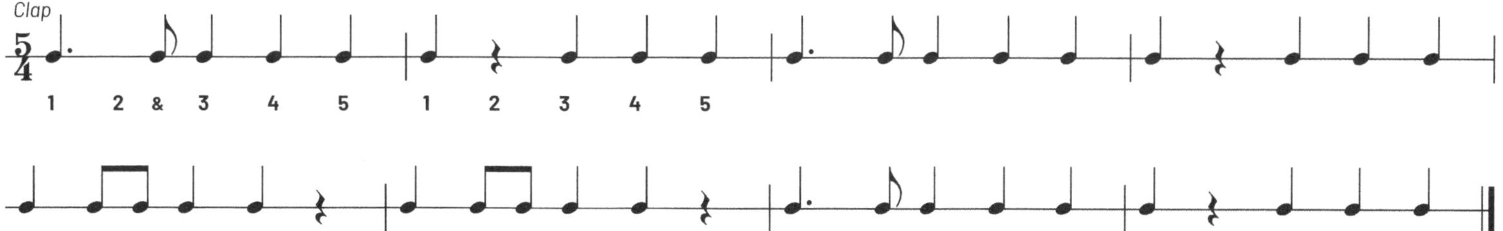

111. LET'S COUNT FIVE

112. SUKURU ITO

African Folk Song

HISTORY

English composer **George Frideric Handel** (1685–1759) lived during the **Baroque Period (1600–1750)**. *Water Music* was written in honor of England's King George I. The first performance took place on the Thames River on July 17, 1717. Fifty musicians performed the work while floating on a barge. Handel lived during the same time as Johann Sebastian Bach, perhaps the most famous Baroque composer.

113. WATER MUSIC

George Frideric Handel

Flute
Oboe
B♭ Clarinet
B♭ Bass Cl.
E♭ Alto Sax.
E♭ Bari. Sax.
E♭ Alto Cl.
B♭ Tenor Sax.
B♭ Trumpet
Baritone T.C.
F Horn
Trombone
Baritone B.C.
Bassoon
Tuba
Electric Bass
Percussion
Keyboard
Percussion
Timpani
div.
Bsn. 8va
a2
(Tpt. only)
(Bsn. only)
Xylo.
Bells
f

114. ESSENTIAL TECHNIQUE QUIZ – PICTURES AT AN EXHIBITION

Modeste Mussorgsky

Flute
Oboe
B♭ Clarinet
B♭ Bass Cl.
E♭ Alto Sax.
E♭ Bari. Sax.
E♭ Alto Cl.
B♭ Tenor Sax.
B♭ Trumpet
Baritone T.C.
F Horn
Trombone
Baritone B.C.
Bassoon
Electric Bass
Tuba
Percussion
Keyboard
Percussion

B♭ MINOR

115. NATURAL MINOR

Scale

Arpeggio

½ step ½ ½ ½

Flute
Oboe

Ob.: L

Cl. cues lower octave

B♭ Clarinet
B♭ Bass Cl.

E♭ Alto Sax.
E♭ Bari. Sax.
E♭ Alto Cl.

A. Cl. cues upper octave

B♭ Tenor Sax.

B♭ Trumpet
Baritone T.C.

F Horn

Bsn. cues lower octave

Trombone
Baritone B.C.
Bassoon
Electric Bass
Tuba

S.D.
B.D.

Percussion

Keyboard
Percussion

116. HARMONIC MINOR

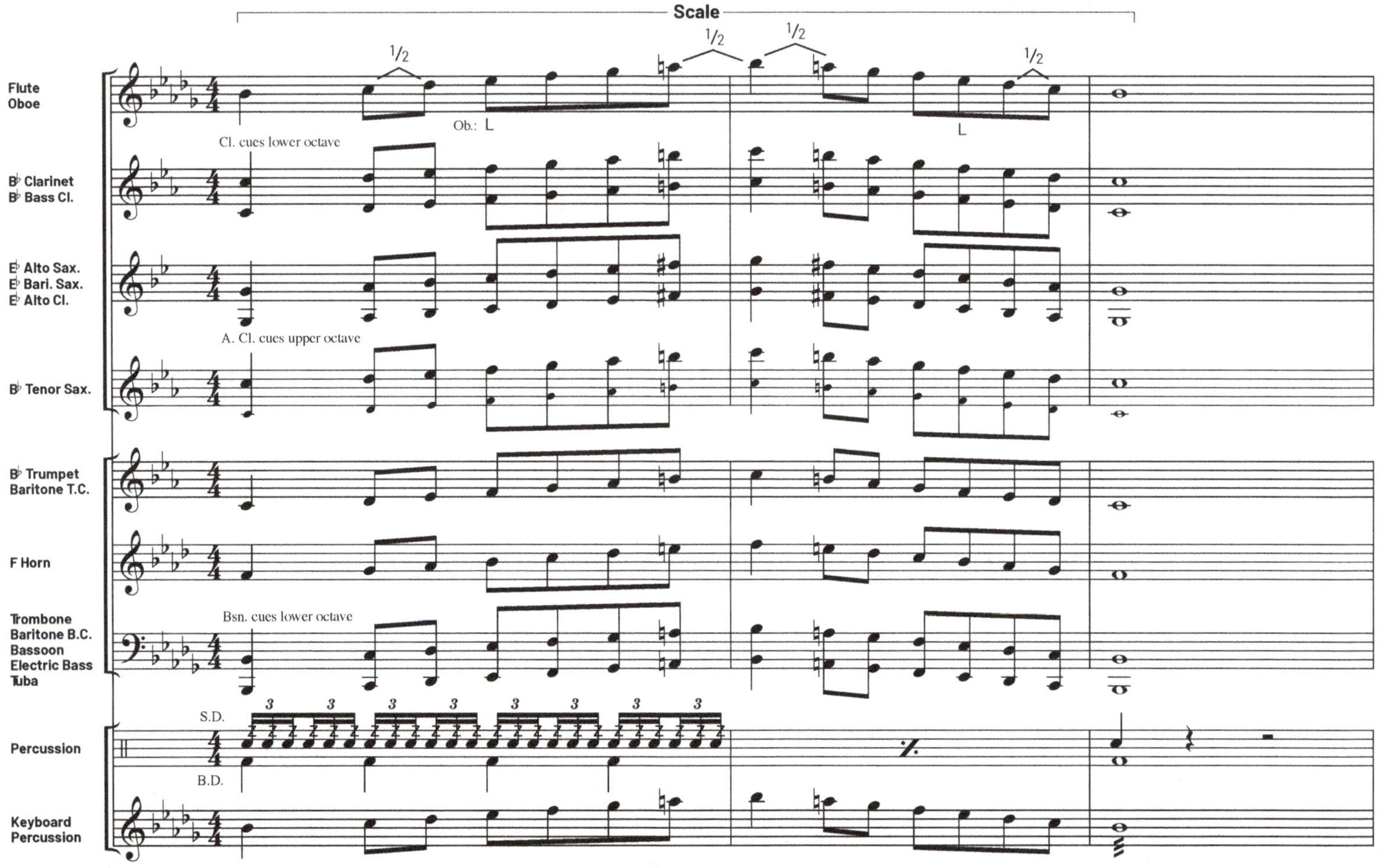

Scale

½ ½ ½ ½

Flute
Oboe

Ob.: L

Cl. cues lower octave

B♭ Clarinet
B♭ Bass Cl.

E♭ Alto Sax.
E♭ Bari. Sax.
E♭ Alto Cl.

A. Cl. cues upper octave

B♭ Tenor Sax.

B♭ Trumpet
Baritone T.C.

F Horn

Bsn. cues lower octave

Trombone
Baritone B.C.
Bassoon
Electric Bass
Tuba

S.D.
B.D.

Percussion

Keyboard
Percussion

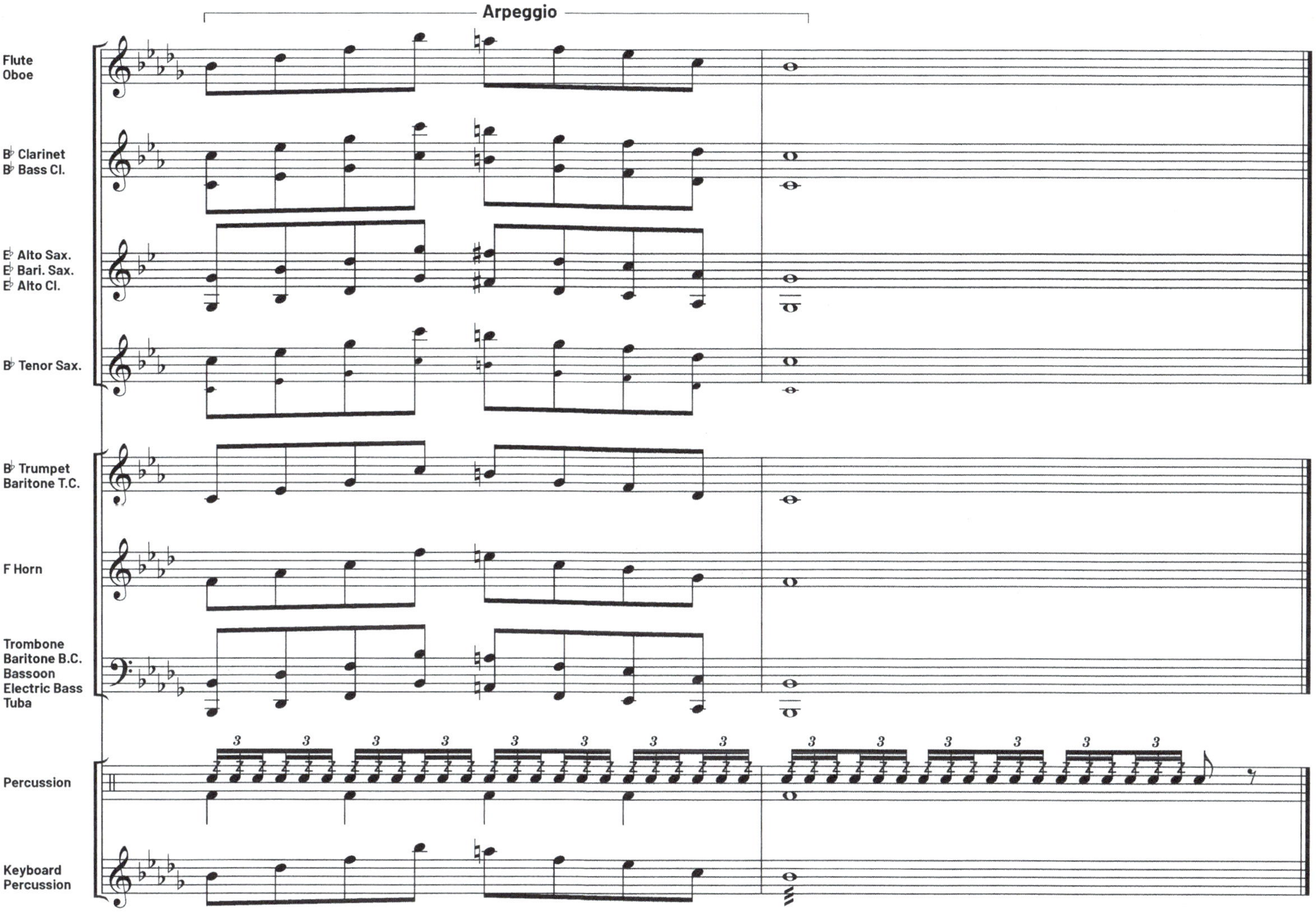

Arpeggio
Flute
Oboe
B♭ Clarinet
B♭ Bass Cl.
E♭ Alto Sax.
E♭ Bari. Sax.
E♭ Alto Cl.
B♭ Tenor Sax.
B♭ Trumpet
Baritone T.C.
F Horn
Trombone
Baritone B.C.
Bassoon
Electric Bass
Tuba
Percussion
Keyboard Percussion

(Ex. 117)

Ostinato

A clear and distinct musical phrase that is repeated persistently.

THEORY

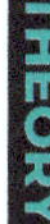

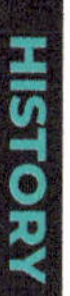

British composer **Gustav Holst** (1874–1934) is one of the most widely played composers for concert band today. Many of his compositions, including his familiar military suites, are based on tuneful English folk songs. His most famous work for orchestra, *The Planets* (1916), has seven movements—one written for each known planet, excluding Earth.

HISTORY

Flute
C♭
Oboe
C♭
Bassoon
C♭
F Horn
G♭
T
Trombone
C♭
4
Baritone B.C.
C♭
Tuba
C♭
Electric Bass
C♭
Keyboard Percussion
C♭

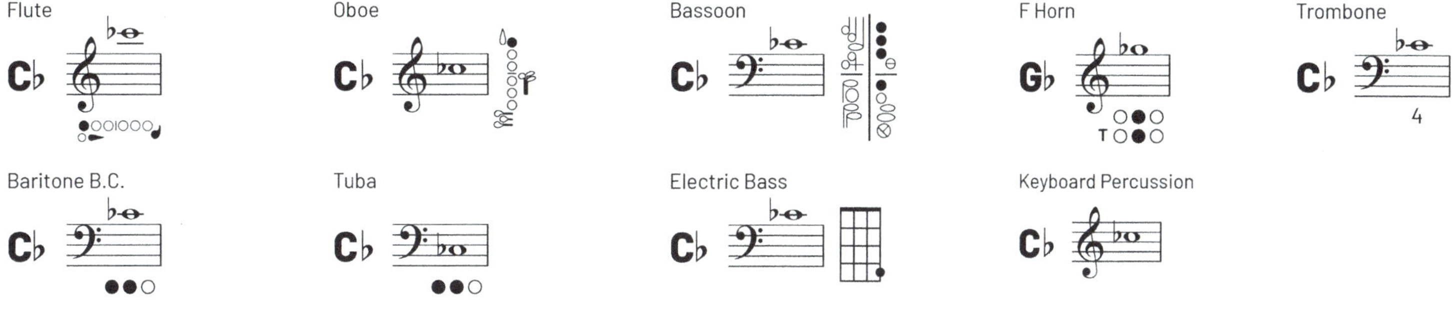

Student Book Page 25

117. MARS – Duet/Trio

Gustav Holst

Flute
Oboe
Opt. div.
B♭ Clarinet
B♭ Bass Cl.
E♭ Alto Sax.
E♭ Bari. Sax.
E♭ Alto Cl.
B♭ Tenor Sax.
B♭ Trumpet
Baritone T.C.
F Horn
Trombone
Baritone B.C.
Bassoon
Electric Bass
Tuba
Percussion
S.D.
mf
Keyboard
Percussion
Timpani

Flute
Oboe
B♭ Clarinet
B♭ Bass Cl.
E♭ Alto Sax.
E♭ Bari. Sax.
E♭ Alto Cl.
B♭ Tenor Sax.
B♭ Trumpet
Baritone T.C.
F Horn
Trombone
Baritone B.C.
Bassoon
Electric Bass
Tuba
Percussion
Keyboard Percussion
Timpani
a2
f
rit.
ff
Bsn. 8vb
(no roll)

G MAJOR

Flute

118. SCALE AND ARPEGGIO

Fl. cues lower octave

½ ½ ½ ½

Flute Oboe

B♭ Clarinet B♭ Bass Cl.

R L L R R R

E♭ Alto Cl.

R L L R L L

A. Sax. cues lower octave

E♭ Alto Sax. E♭ Bari. Sax.

B. Sax. cues upper octave

B♭ Tenor Sax.

B♭ Trumpet Baritone T.C.

F Horn

Trombone Baritone B.C. Bassoon Electric Bass

Tuba

S.D.

Percussion

B.D.

Keyboard Percussion

Alto Clarinet

119. EXERCISE IN THIRDS

Flute
Oboe

B♭ Clarinet
B♭ Bass Cl.

E♭ Alto Sax.
E♭ Bari. Sax.
E♭ Alto Cl.

A. Cl.: L

L L L L
(slide)

B♭ Tenor Sax.

B♭ Trumpet
Baritone T.C.

F Horn

Trombone
Baritone B.C.
Bassoon
Electric Bass

Tuba

Percussion

R R L L L R R R L L R

S.D.

B.D.

Keyboard
Percussion

(Ex. 120)
Percussion

Rudiment

Delayed Paradiddle

This is one of three variations of the Paradiddle. Notice that the sticking is identical to the Paradiddle, but the accent has been shifted (or delayed) to the second sixteenth note of each group.

Keyboard Percussion

120. ARPEGGIO STUDY

Student Book Page 26

121. TWO-PART ETUDE

Oboe
A♯
Bassoon
A♯
Bassoon
A♯
Trombone
A♯
1
Trombone
D♯
3
Trombone
A♯
1 or 5
Baritone B.C.
A♯
Baritone B.C.
D♯
Baritone B.C.
A♯
Tuba
A♯
Tuba
A♯
Electric Bass
A♯
Electric Bass
A♯
122. CHROMATIC SCALE
Fl. cues lower octave
Fl.: A♯(B♭ enharmonic)
Flute
Oboe
B♭ Clarinet
B♭ Bass Cl.
E♭ Alto Cl.
A. Sax. cues lower octave
E♭ Alto Sax.
E♭ Bari. Sax.
B. Sax. cues upper octave
B♭ Tenor Sax.
B♭ Trumpet
Baritone T.C.
Bar. cues 8vb
F Horn
Trombone
Baritone B.C.
Bassoon
Electric Bass
Tuba
Pataflafla Review
L R L R R L L R L R R L
S.D.
B.D.
2
Percussion
Keyboard
Percussion

Student Book Page 26

123. BALANCE BUILDER

124. CHORALE

Andante
Flute
Oboe
Bassoon
B♭ Clarinet
E♭ Alto Cl.
B♭ Bass Cl.
E♭ Alto Sax.
B♭ Tenor Sax.
E♭ Bari. Sax.
Andante
B♭ Trumpet
F Horn
Trombone
Baritone
Tuba (Electric Bass)
Percussion
Triangle
Keyboard Percussion
mf
div.
rit.

Student Book Page 27

HISTORY

Norwegian composer **Edvard Grieg** (1843–1907) based much of his music on the folk songs and dances of Norway. During the late 19th century, composers often used melodies from their native land. This trend is called **nationalism**. Russian **Modeste Mussorgsky** (1839–1881), Czech **Antonin Dvořák** (1841–1904), and Englishman **Sir Edward Elgar** (1857–1934) are other famous composers whose music was influenced by nationalism.

125. NORWEGIAN DANCE

Edvard Grieg

Percussion

Rudiment Crushed Ruff

Essentially, the Crushed Ruff is one of the easiest drum rudiments to master. Simply play a multiple bounce stroke with both hands at the same time.

Flute Oboe

B♭ Clarinet B♭ Bass Cl.

E♭ Alto Sax. E♭ Bari. Sax. E♭ Alto Cl.

B♭ Tenor Sax.

B♭ Trumpet Baritone T.C.

F Horn

Trombone Baritone B.C. Bassoon Electric Bass

Tuba

Percussion

Keyboard Percussion

126. FRENCH NATIONAL ANTHEM (LA MARSEILLAISE)

Rouget De L'Isle

Flute
Oboe
B♭ Clarinet
B♭ Bass Cl.
E♭ Alto Sax.
E♭ Bari. Sax.
E♭ Alto Cl.
B♭ Tenor Sax.
B♭ Trumpet
Baritone T.C.
F Horn
Trombone
Baritone B.C.
Bassoon
Electric Bass
Tuba
Percussion
f
Keyboard
Percussion

Student Book Page 27

HISTORY

Music written during the **Renaissance Period (1430–1600)** was often upbeat and dance-like. *Wolsey's Wilde* was originally written for the lute, an ancestor to the guitar and the most popular instrument of the Renaissance era. Modern day concert band composer Gordon Jacob used this popular song in his *William Byrd Suite*, written as a tribute to English composer William Byrd (1543–1623).

127. WOLSEY'S WILDE

Flute
Oboe
B♭ Clarinet
B♭ Bass Cl.
E♭ Alto Sax.
E♭ Bari. Sax.
E♭ Alto Cl.
B♭ Tenor Sax.
B♭ Trumpet
Baritone T.C.
F Horn
Trombone
Baritone B.C.
Bassoon
Electric Bass
Tuba
Percussion
S.D.
B.D.
Cr. Cym.
Keyboard
Percussion

E MINOR

Bassoon
E
Trombone
E
7
Baritone B.C.
E
Baritone T.C.
F♯
Tuba
E
Electric Bass
E

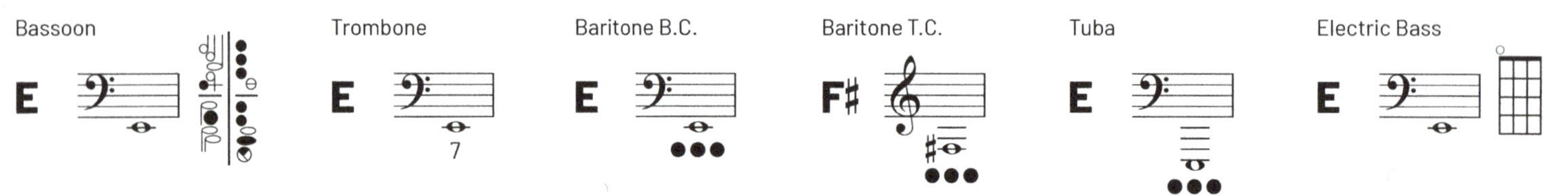

128. NATURAL MINOR

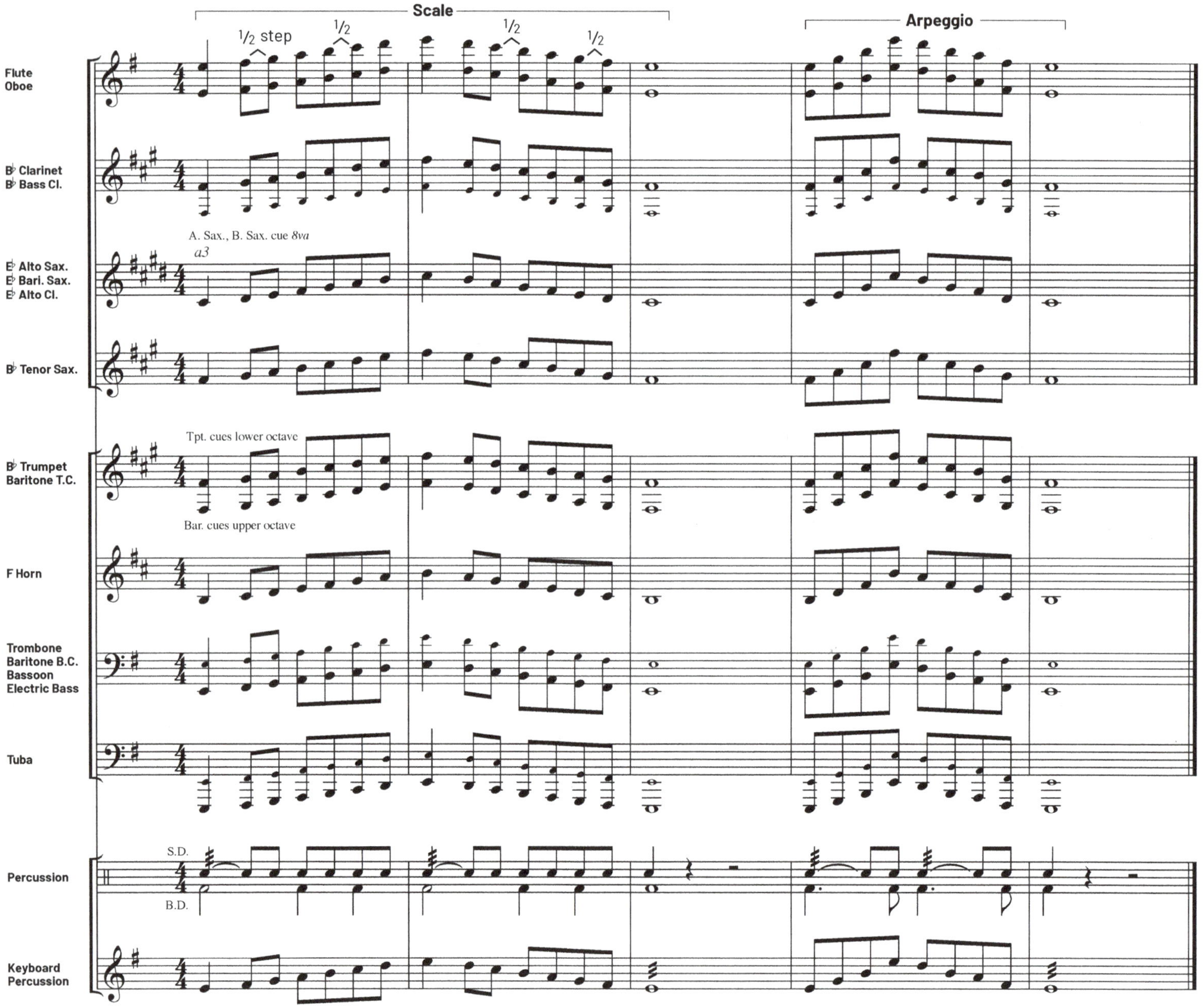

Scale
1/2 step
1/2
1/2
1/2
Arpeggio
Flute
Oboe
B♭ Clarinet
B♭ Bass Cl.
A. Sax., B. Sax. cue 8va
a3
E♭ Alto Sax.
E♭ Bari. Sax.
E♭ Alto Cl.
B♭ Tenor Sax.
Tpt. cues lower octave
B♭ Trumpet
Baritone T.C.
Bar. cues upper octave
F Horn
Trombone
Baritone B.C.
Bassoon
Electric Bass
Tuba
S.D.
B.D.
Percussion
Keyboard
Percussion

Flute
D♯
Clarinet
E♯
Clarinet
E♯
Alto Clarinet
B♯
Bass Clarinet
E♯
Bass Clarinet
E♯
Alto Saxophone
B♯
Alto Saxophone
B♯
Tenor Saxophone
E♯
Baritone Saxophone
B♯
Baritone Saxophone
B♯
Trumpet
E♯
Trumpet
E♯
Baritone T.C.
E♯
Baritone T.C.
E♯

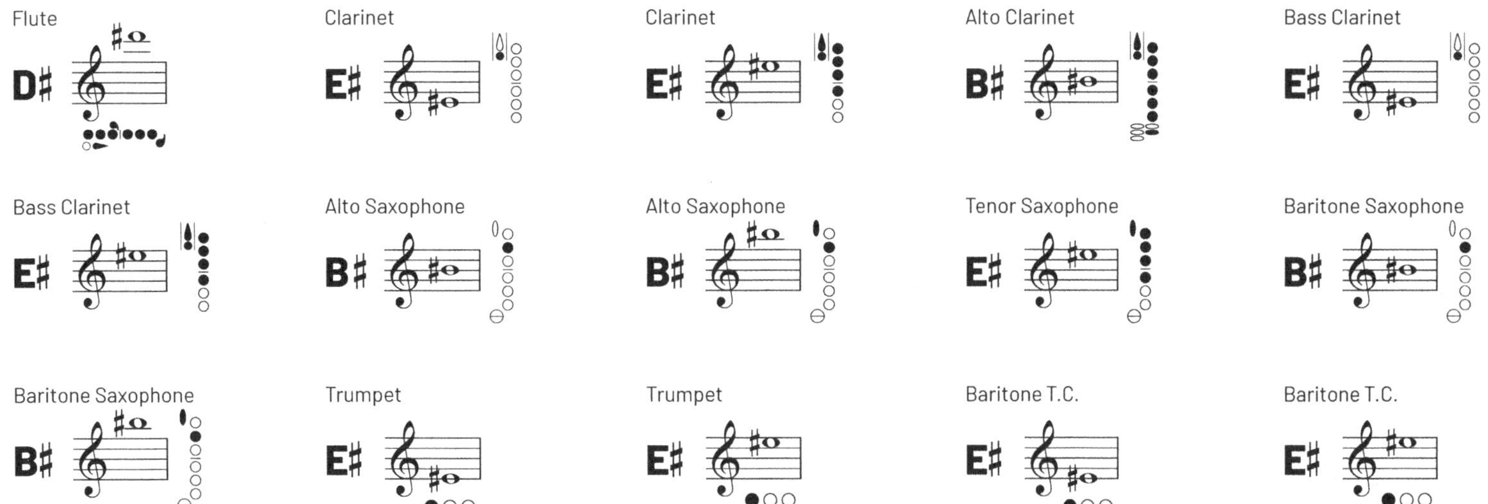

129. HARMONIC MINOR

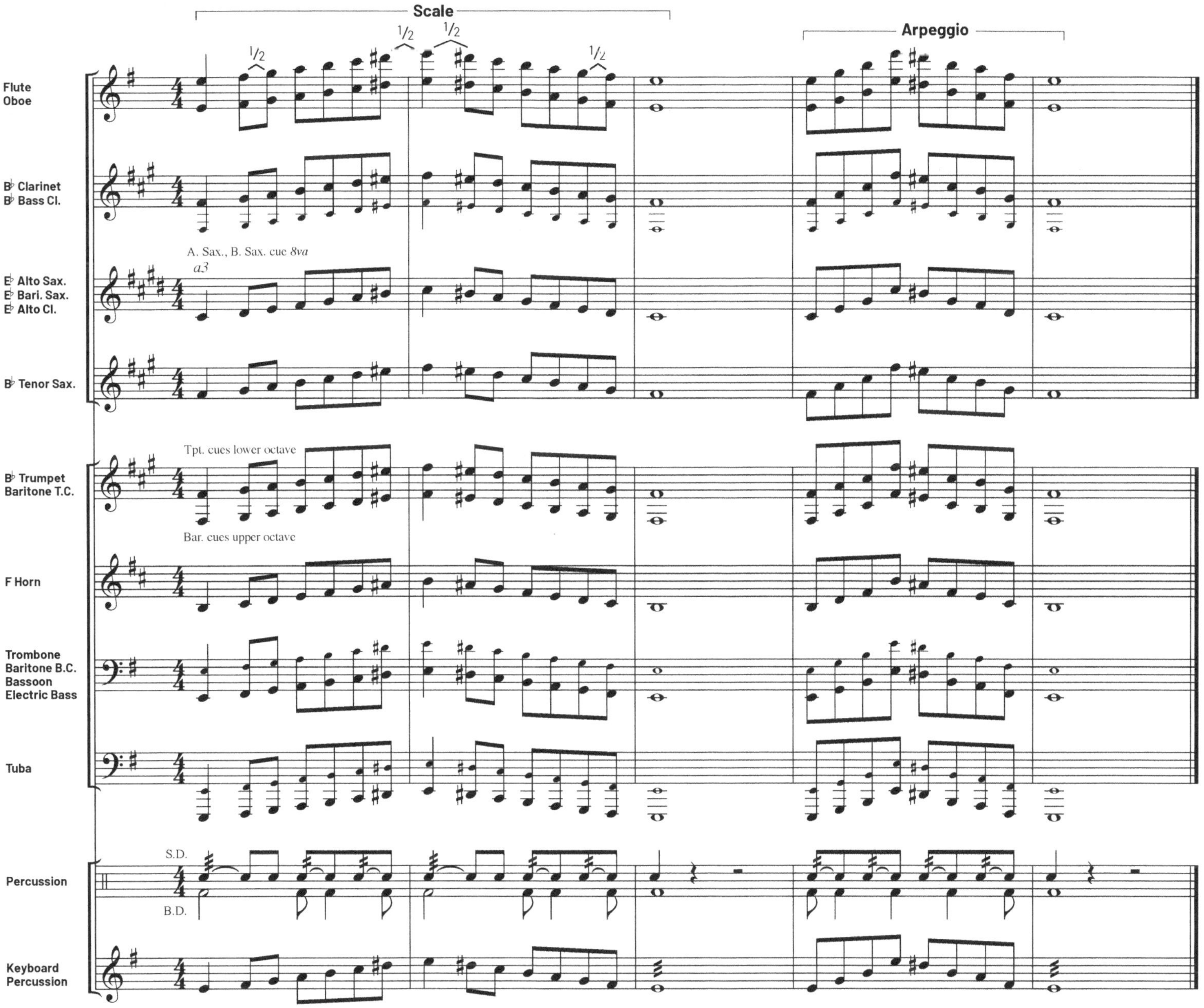

Scale
Arpeggio
1/2
Flute
Oboe
B♭ Clarinet
B♭ Bass Cl.
A. Sax., B. Sax. cue 8va
a3
E♭ Alto Sax.
E♭ Bari. Sax.
E♭ Alto Cl.
B♭ Tenor Sax.
Tpt. cues lower octave
B♭ Trumpet
Baritone T.C.
Bar. cues upper octave
F Horn
Trombone
Baritone B.C.
Bassoon
Electric Bass
Tuba
S.D.
B.D.
Percussion
Keyboard
Percussion

HISTORY

Native Japanese instruments include the *shakuhachi*, a bamboo flute played pointing downward; the *koto*, a long zither with movable frets played sitting down; and the *gakubiwa*, a pear-shaped lute with strings that are plucked. These instruments have been an important part of Japanese culture since the 8th century. *Kabuki*, a Japanese theatrical form that originated in 1603, remains popular in Japan. Performers play native Japanese instruments during Kabuki performances.

Keyboard Percussion

130. SONG OF THE SHAKUHACHI

Japanese Folk Song

Andante

Flute
Oboe

B♭ Clarinet
B♭ Bass Cl.

E♭ Alto Sax.
E♭ Bari. Sax.
E♭ Alto Cl.

B♭ Tenor Sax.

B♭ Trumpet
Baritone T.C.

F Horn

Trombone
Baritone B.C.
Bassoon
Electric Bass

Tuba

Temple Blocks

Percussion

Bongos

Keyboard Percussion

mp mf mp mf

Flute
Oboe

B♭ Clarinet
B♭ Bass Cl.

E♭ Alto Sax.
E♭ Bari. Sax.
E♭ Alto Cl.

B♭ Tenor Sax.

B♭ Trumpet
Baritone T.C.

F Horn

Trombone
Baritone B.C.
Bassoon
Electric Bass

Tuba

Percussion

Keyboard
Percussion

mp mf mp mf p

(Ex. 131)

D.C. al Coda At the **D.C. al Coda**, play again from the beginning to the indication **To Coda** ⊕, then skip to the section marked ⊕ **Coda**, meaning "ending section."

D.S. al Coda Similar to **D.C. al Coda**, but return to the sign 𝄋.

THEORY

Looking for some more fun music to play?
See the inside front cover for instructions on accessing recent popular Bonus Songs.

131. POLOVETZIAN DANCES

Alexander Borodin

D.C. al Coda
Flute
Oboe
B♭ Clarinet
B♭ Bass Cl.
E♭ Alto Sax.
E♭ Bari. Sax.
E♭ Alto Cl.
B♭ Tenor Sax.
B♭ Trumpet
Baritone T.C.
F Horn
Trombone
Baritone B.C.
Bassoon
Electric Bass
Tuba
Percussion
p
mf
Keyboard
Percussion
Coda
a2
A. Cl.: L
L
L
R
p
mf
p

Student Book Page 29

D MAJOR

132. SCALE AND ARPEGGIO

1/2 step
1/2
1/2
1/2

Flute
Oboe

Ob. cues 8vb

B♭ Clarinet
B♭ Bass Cl.

R L L R

A. Sax. cues lower octave

E♭ Alto Sax.
E♭ Bari. Sax.
E♭ Alto Cl.

A. Cl.
B. Sax. cues upper octave

B♭ Tenor Sax.

B♭ Trumpet
Baritone T.C.

F Horn

Bsn. cues lower octave

Trombone
Baritone B.C.
Bassoon
Electric Bass
Tuba

S.D.
Percussion
B.D.

Keyboard
Percussion

Keyboard Percussion

133. EXERCISE IN THIRDS

Flute
Oboe

B♭ Clarinet
B♭ Bass Cl.

A. Sax. cues lower octave

E♭ Alto Sax.
E♭ Bari. Sax.
E♭ Alto Cl.

B♭ Tenor Sax.

B♭ Trumpet
Baritone T.C.

F Horn

Bsn. cues lower octave

Trombone
Baritone B.C.
Bassoon
Electric Bass
Tuba

S.D.
Percussion
B.D.

Keyboard
Percussion

134. ARPEGGIO STUDY

Percussion

Rudiment

Thirteen Stroke Roll

Use open, double bounces to play thirteen evenly divided notes in order to form this measured roll. Remember that the hands will be moving at the speed of sixteenth notes. The Thirteen Stroke Roll starts on the beat and ends on the next upbeat.

135. TWO-PART ETUDE

(Ex. 135)
Percussion

Rudiment

Seventeen Stroke Roll

Use open, double bounces to play seventeen evenly divided notes in order to form this measured roll. Remember that the hands will be moving at the speed of sixteenth notes; the double bounces will sound the correct thirty-second note rhythm.

136. CHORALE

B MINOR

137. NATURAL MINOR

(Ex. 139)

Latin American music combines the folk music from South and Central America, the Caribbean Islands, American Indian, Spanish, and Portuguese cultures. Melodies are often accompanied by drums, maracas, and claves. Latin American music continues to influence jazz, classical, and popular styles of music. *Cielito Lindo* is a Latin American love song.

HISTORY

139. CIELITO LINDO

C. Fernandez

*Saxes: Alternate fingering "Bis" for B♭ (A♯) is commonly used, but *never* in chromatic passages.

Flute
Oboe
B♭ Clarinet
B♭ Bass Cl.
E♭ Alto Sax.
E♭ Bari. Sax.
E♭ Alto Cl.
A. Cl.:
L
R
R
R
L
L
B♭ Tenor Sax.
B♭ Trumpet
Baritone T.C.
F Horn
Trombone
Baritone B.C.
Bassoon
Electric Bass
Tuba
Percussion
Keyboard
Percussion
f

HISTORY

Tchaikovsky, along with Wagner, Brahms, Mendelssohn, and Chopin, helped define the musical era known as the **Romantic Period (1825–1900)**. The "symphonic tone poem" from this period continues to be one of the most popular musical forms performed by orchestras and bands today.

140. WALTZ IN FIVE (from SYMPHONY NO. 6)

Peter I. Tchaikovsky

Flute
Oboe
B♭ Clarinet
B♭ Bass Cl.
E♭ Alto Sax.
E♭ Bari. Sax.
E♭ Alto Cl.
L
R
B♭ Tenor Sax.
B♭ Trumpet
Baritone T.C.
F Horn
Trombone
Baritone B.C.
Bassoon
Electric Bass
(Bsn. 8vb)
Bass 8va
Tuba
Percussion
Keyboard
Percussion
Flute
Oboe
B♭ Clarinet
B♭ Bass Cl.
E♭ Alto Sax.
E♭ Bari. Sax.
E♭ Alto Cl.
a3
B♭ Tenor Sax.
B♭ Trumpet
Baritone T.C.
F Horn
Trombone
Baritone B.C.
Bassoon
Electric Bass
(Bass 8va)
Bsn., Bass 8vb
Tuba
Percussion
Keyboard
Percussion

Alto Saxophone

E♯

Baritone Saxophone

E♯

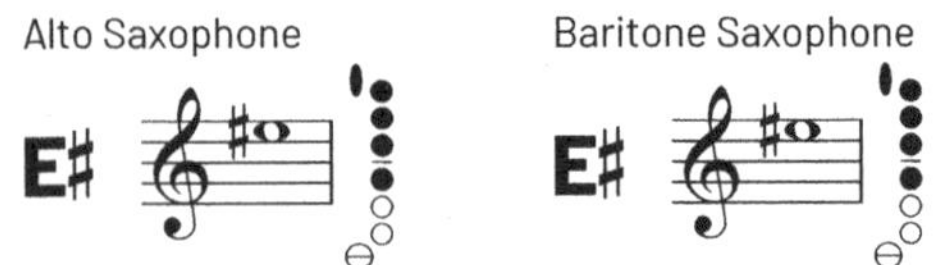

141. THE YOUNG CHEVALIER

Scottish

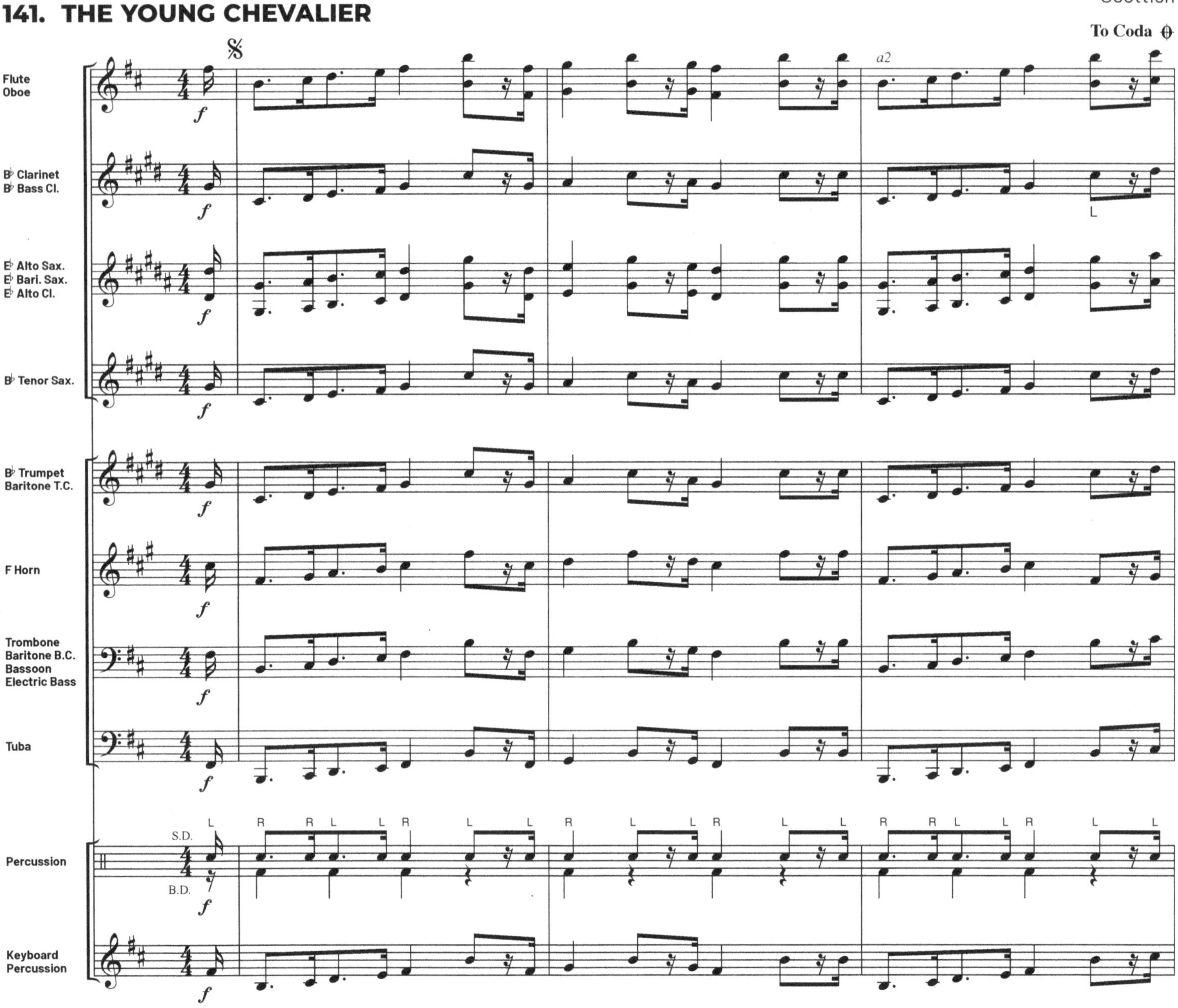
To Coda
a2
Flute
Oboe
B♭ Clarinet
B♭ Bass Cl.
E♭ Alto Sax.
E♭ Bari. Sax.
E♭ Alto Cl.
B♭ Tenor Sax.
B♭ Trumpet
Baritone T.C.
F Horn
Trombone
Baritone B.C.
Bassoon
Electric Bass
Tuba
Percussion
S.D.
B.D.
Keyboard
Percussion

Flute
Oboe
B♭ Clarinet
B♭ Bass Cl.
E♭ Alto Sax.
E♭ Bari. Sax.
E♭ Alto Cl.
B♭ Tenor Sax.
B♭ Trumpet
Baritone T.C.
F Horn
Trombone
Baritone B.C.
Bassoon
Electric Bass
Bsn.: Alt.
Alt.
Tuba
Percussion
Keyboard
Percussion
D.S. al Coda
Coda
a2

G♭ MAJOR

Flute
G♭
Bassoon
C♭
Bassoon
C♭
Alto Clarinet
E♭
Trombone
C♭
7
Trombone
C♭
4
Baritone B.C.
C♭
Baritone B.C.
C♭
Tuba
C♭
Tuba
C♭
Electric Bass
C♭
Electric Bass
C♭
Keyboard Percussion
C♭

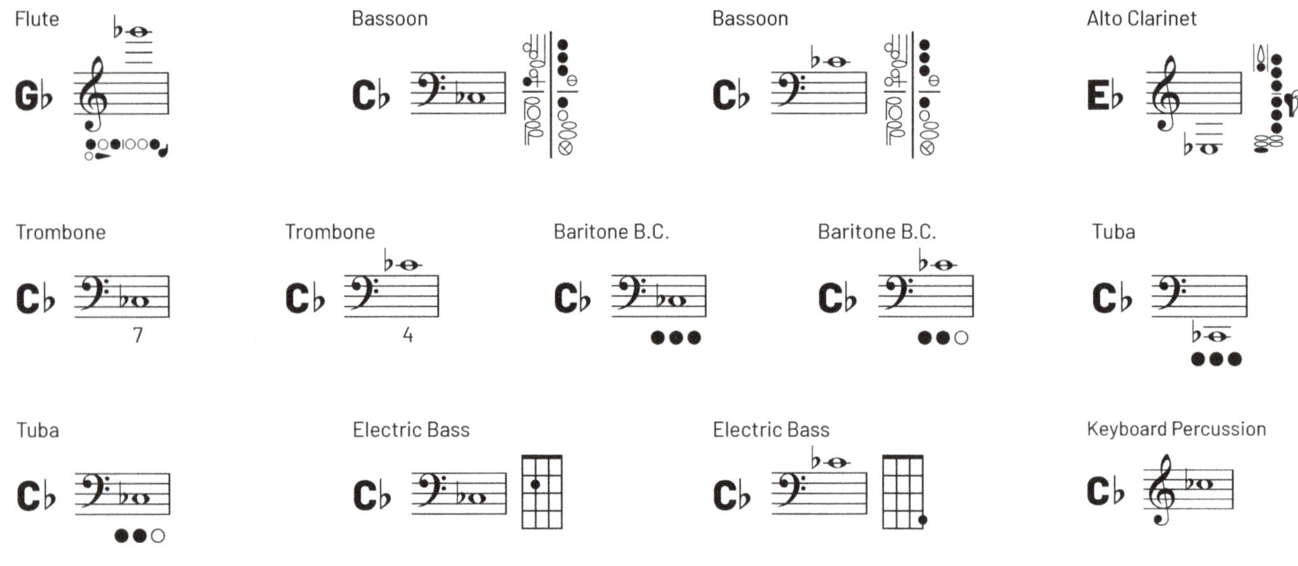

142. SCALE AND ARPEGGIO.

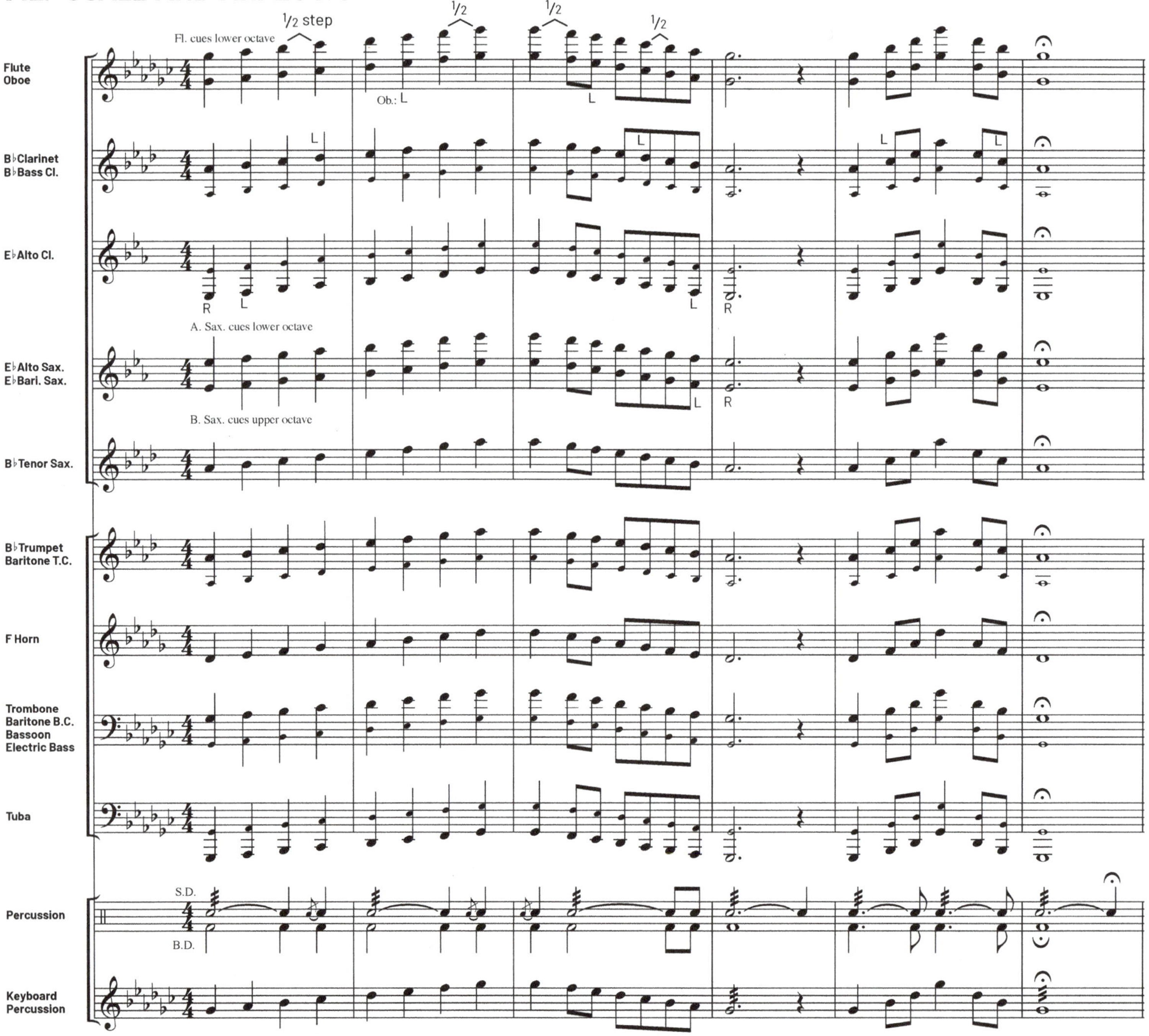

Flute
Oboe
B♭Clarinet
B♭Bass Cl.
E♭Alto Cl.
E♭Alto Sax.
E♭Bari. Sax.
B♭Tenor Sax.
B♭Trumpet
Baritone T.C.
F Horn
Trombone
Baritone B.C.
Bassoon
Electric Bass
Tuba
Percussion
Keyboard Percussion
Fl. cues lower octave
1/2 step
1/2
1/2
1/2
Ob.: L
A. Sax. cues lower octave
B. Sax. cues upper octave
S.D.
B.D.

Percussion

Seven Stroke Roll

Use open, double bounces to play seven evenly divided notes in order to form this measured roll. Remember that the hands will be moving at the speed of sixteenth notes. The Seven Stroke Roll in this exercise starts on the beat and ends on the sixteenth note preceding the next beat. The exact notation for this roll can be found in the Snare Drum International Drum Rudiments section of the book.

143. EXERCISE IN THIRDS

Student Book Page 31

144. ARPEGGIO STUDY

145. TWO-PART ETUDE

146. CHORALE

Andante
Flute
Oboe
Bassoon
B♭ Clarinet
E♭ Alto Cl.
B♭ Bass Cl.
E♭ Alto Sax.
B♭ Tenor Sax.
E♭ Bari. Sax.
Andante
B♭ Trumpet
F Horn
Trombone
Baritone
Tuba
(Electric Bass)
Percussion
Sus. Cym.
Keyboard
Percussion
div.
mf
p
rit.

E♭ MINOR

147. NATURAL MINOR

148. HARMONIC MINOR

Flute

32
INDIVIDUAL STUDY – Flute
149. RANGE AND ARPEGGIO ETUDE
150. LOW RANGE EXPRESSION STUDY
151. TRILL EXERCISE
152. ORNAMENTATION STUDY
153. CHROMATIC CHALLENGE

33
INDIVIDUAL STUDY – Flute
154. STUDY IN D♭ MAJOR
155. ARTICULATION STUDY
Allegretto
Fine
D.C. al Fine
156. EXERCISE IN F MINOR
157. TRIPLET ETUDE

Oboe

32
INDIVIDUAL STUDY – Oboe
149. STUDY IN A♭ MAJOR
150. LOW RANGE EXPRESSION STUDY
151. C MINOR ETUDE
a tempo (last time)
rit. (last time)
Fine
D.C. al Fine (no repeat)
molto rit.
152. TRILL EXERCISE

33
INDIVIDUAL STUDY – Oboe
153. ORNAMENTATION STUDY
154. CHROMATIC CHALLENGE
155. LEGATO STUDY IN D♭ MAJOR
156. EXERCISE IN F MINOR
157. TRIPLET ETUDE

Bassoon

Clarinet

Alto Clarinet

Bass Clarinet

Alto Saxophone

Tenor Saxophone

Baritone Saxophone

Trumpet

F Horn

Trombone

Baritone B.C.

Baritone T.C.

Tuba

Electric Bass

Percussion

32-A

INDIVIDUAL STUDY – Percussion

149. SINGLE PARADIDDLE VARIATIONS

150. SINGLE PARADIDDLE/REVERSE PARADIDDLE EXERCISE

151. TRIPLE/DOUBLE/SINGLE PARADIDDLE COMBINATION

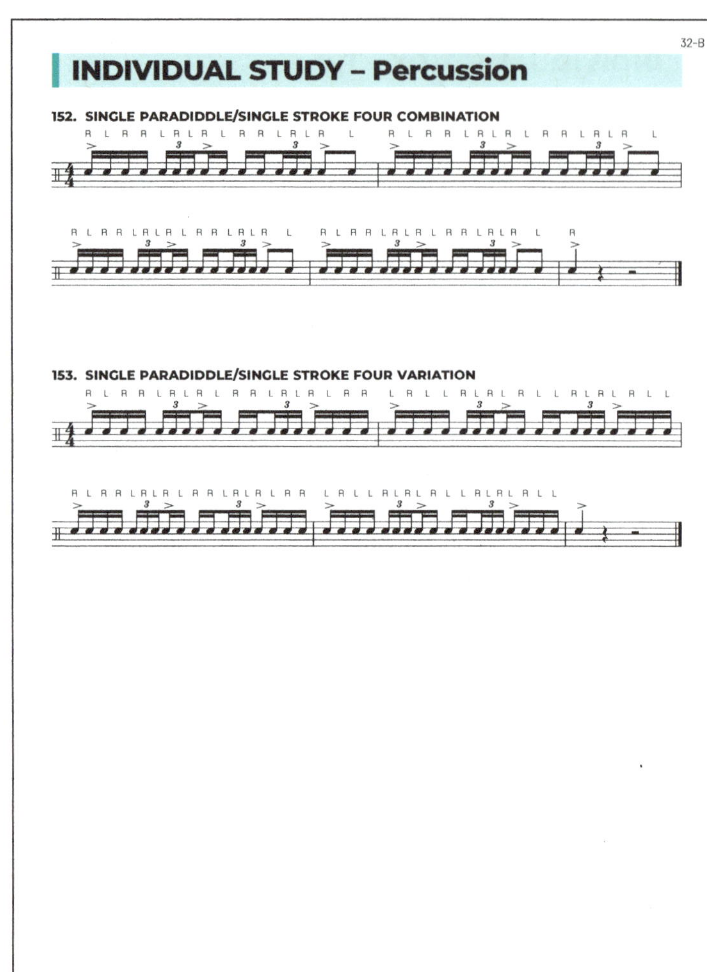
32-B

INDIVIDUAL STUDY – Percussion

152. SINGLE PARADIDDLE/SINGLE STROKE FOUR COMBINATION

153. SINGLE PARADIDDLE/SINGLE STROKE FOUR VARIATION

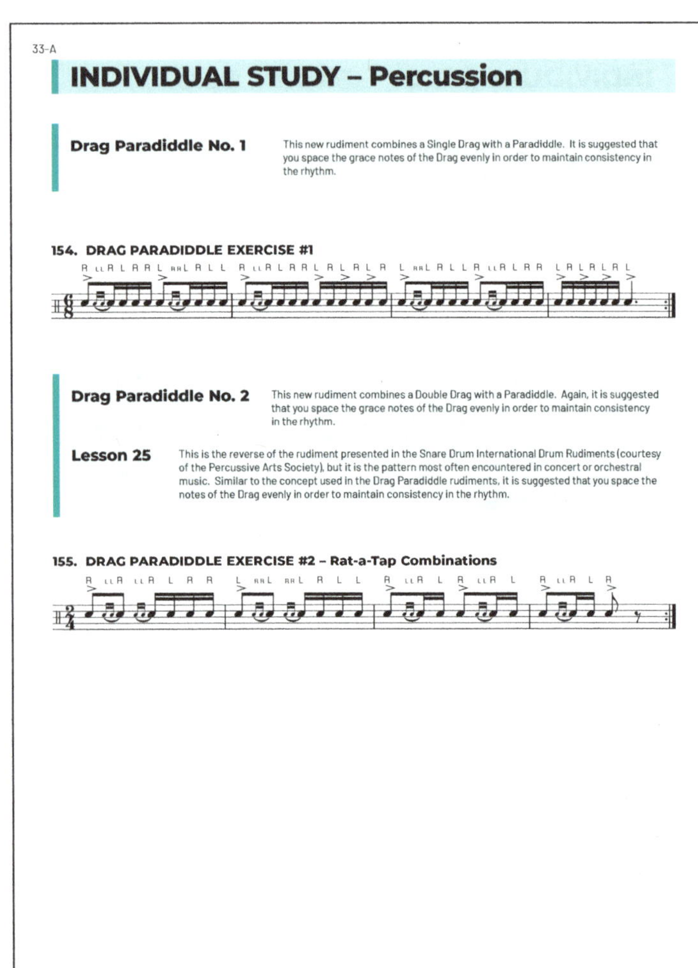
33-A

INDIVIDUAL STUDY – Percussion

Drag Paradiddle No. 1 This new rudiment combines a Single Drag with a Paradiddle. It is suggested that you space the grace notes of the Drag evenly in order to maintain consistency in the rhythm.

154. DRAG PARADIDDLE EXERCISE #1

Drag Paradiddle No. 2 This new rudiment combines a Double Drag with a Paradiddle. Again, it is suggested that you space the grace notes of the Drag evenly in order to maintain consistency in the rhythm.

Lesson 25 This is the reverse of the rudiment presented in the Snare Drum International Drum Rudiments (courtesy of the Percussive Arts Society), but it is the pattern most often encountered in concert or orchestral music. Similar to the concept used in the Drag Paradiddle rudiments, it is suggested that you space the notes of the Drag evenly in order to maintain consistency in the rhythm.

155. DRAG PARADIDDLE EXERCISE #2 – Rat-a-Tap Combinations

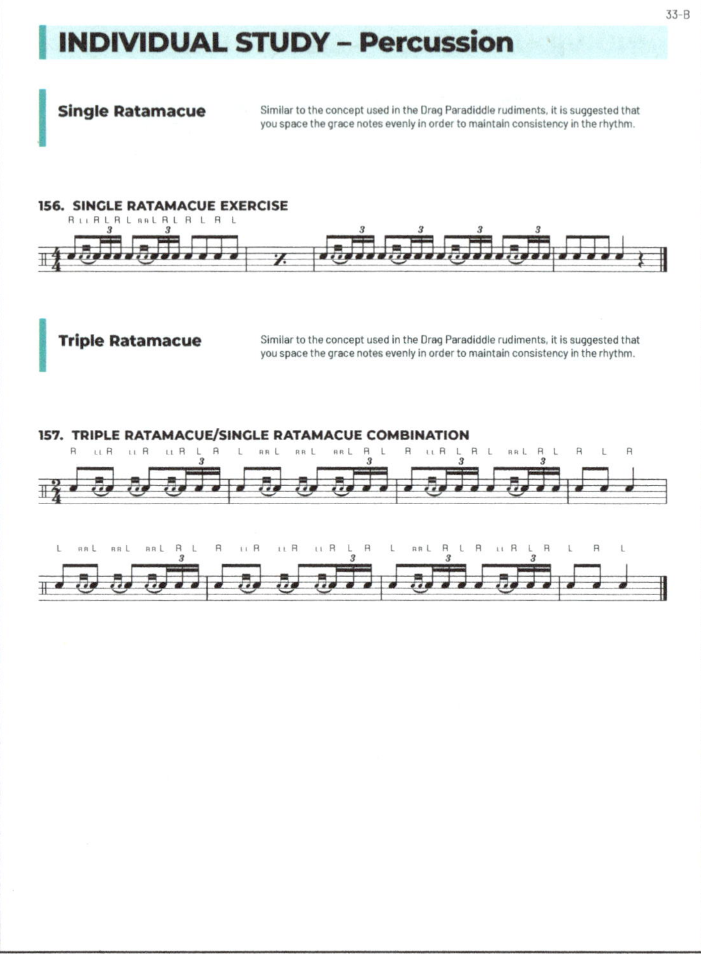
33-B

INDIVIDUAL STUDY – Percussion

Single Ratamacue Similar to the concept used in the Drag Paradiddle rudiments, it is suggested that you space the grace notes evenly in order to maintain consistency in the rhythm.

156. SINGLE RATAMACUE EXERCISE

Triple Ratamacue Similar to the concept used in the Drag Paradiddle rudiments, it is suggested that you space the grace notes evenly in order to maintain consistency in the rhythm.

157. TRIPLE RATAMACUE/SINGLE RATAMACUE COMBINATION

Keyboard Percussion

33-A

INDIVIDUAL STUDY – Keyboard Percussion

154.

155.

156.

33-B

INDIVIDUAL STUDY – Keyboard Percussion

157.

Student Book Page 34

READING SKILL BUILDERS

158. READING SKILL BUILDER NO. 1

Flute
Oboe
B♭ Clarinet
B♭ Bass Cl.
E♭ Alto Sax.
E♭ Bari. Sax.
E♭ Alto Cl.
B♭ Tenor Sax.
B♭ Trumpet
Baritone T.C.
F Horn
Trombone
Baritone B.C.
Bassoon
Electric Bass
Tuba
Percussion
Keyboard
Percussion

159. READING SKILL BUILDER NO. 2

Flute
Oboe
B♭ Clarinet
B♭ Bass Cl.
E♭ Alto Sax.
E♭ Bari. Sax.
E♭ Alto Cl.
B♭ Tenor Sax.
B♭ Trumpet
Baritone T.C.
F Horn
Trombone
Baritone B.C.
Bassoon
Electric Bass
Tuba
Percussion
Keyboard
Percussion
a2
mf
B. Sax.
(Bsn. 8vb)
f

Student Book Page 34

160. READING SKILL BUILDER NO. 3

161. READING SKILL BUILDER NO. 4

162. READING SKILL BUILDER NO. 5

163. READING SKILL BUILDER NO. 6

164. READING SKILL BUILDER NO. 7

165. READING SKILL BUILDER NO. 8

166. READING SKILL BUILDER NO. 9

Flute
Oboe
B♭ Clarinet
B♭ Bass Cl.
E♭ Alto Sax.
E♭ Bari. Sax.
E♭ Alto Cl.
B♭ Tenor Sax.
B♭ Trumpet
Baritone T.C.
F Horn
Trombone
Baritone B.C.
Bassoon
Electric Bass
Tuba
Percussion
mp legato
Keyboard
Percussion
f marcato
B. Sax.
Bsn. 8vb

167. CHORALE (Prelude from Hansel and Gretel)

Engelbert Humperdinck
Arr. by John Higgins

9
13
Flute
Oboe
Bassoon
B♭ Clarinet
E♭ Alto Cl.
B♭ Bass Cl.
E♭ Alto Sax.
B♭ Tenor Sax.
E♭ Bari. Sax.
B♭ Trumpet
F Horn
Trombone
Baritone
Tuba (Electric Bass)
Percussion
Keyboard Percussion
Timpani
cresc.
f
mp
S.D.
B.D.
Cr. Cym.
mp cresc.
mf
f

Flute
Oboe
Bassoon
B♭ Clarinet
E♭ Alto Cl.
B♭ Bass Cl.
E♭ Alto Sax.
B♭ Tenor Sax.
E♭ Bari. Sax.
B♭ Trumpet
F Horn
Trombone
Baritone
Tuba
(Electric Bass)
Percussion
Keyboard
Percussion
Timpani
17
rit.
mp

168. CHORALE (Based on a Theme by Palestrina)

Arr. by John Higgins

9
Flute
mf
Oboe
mf
Bassoon
mf
B♭ Clarinet
mf
E♭ Alto Cl.
mf
B♭ Bass Cl.
mf
E♭ Alto Sax.
mf
B♭ Tenor Sax.
mf
E♭ Bari. Sax.
mf
9
B♭ Trumpet
mf
F Horn
mf
Trombone
mf
Baritone
mf
Tuba (Electric Bass)
mf
Percussion
Tri.
mf
Keyboard Percussion
mf
Timpani
mf

17
21
Flute
Oboe
Bassoon
B♭ Clarinet
E♭ Alto Cl.
B♭ Bass Cl.
E♭ Alto Sax.
B♭ Tenor Sax.
E♭ Bari. Sax.
B♭ Trumpet
F Horn
Trombone
Baritone
Tuba
(Electric Bass)
Percussion
Keyboard
Percussion
Timpani
p-f
pp rall.
F
Play 2nd time only
S.D.
B.D.
f
rall.

169. CHORALE (Based on a Theme by J. S. Bach)

Arr. by John Higgins

Flute
Oboe
Bassoon
B♭ Clarinet
E♭ Alto Cl.
B♭ Bass Cl.
E♭ Alto Sax.
B♭ Tenor Sax.
E♭ Bari. Sax.
B♭ Trumpet
F Horn
Trombone
Baritone
Tuba
(Electric Bass)
Percussion
Keyboard
Percussion
Timpani
9
rit.
S.D.
B.D.
p

Student Book Page 37

Bass Clarinet

D♯

170. CHORALE (Based on a Theme by Tchaikovsky)

Arr. by John Higgins

Flute
Oboe
Bassoon
B♭ Clarinet
E♭ Alto Cl.
B♭ Bass Cl.
E♭ Alto Sax.
B♭ Tenor Sax.
E♭ Bari. Sax.
B♭ Trumpet
F Horn
Trombone
Baritone
Tuba (Electric Bass)
Percussion
Keyboard Percussion
Timpani
10
R
L
rall.
pp
mf

171. CHORALE (Erhalt Uns In Der Wahrheit)

Johann Sebastian Bach
Arr. by John Higgins

9
13
Flute
Oboe
Bassoon
B♭ Clarinet
E♭ Alto Cl.
B♭ Bass Cl.
E♭ Alto Sax.
B♭ Tenor Sax.
E♭ Bari. Sax.
B♭ Trumpet
F Horn
Trombone
Baritone
Tuba
(Electric Bass)
Percussion
Keyboard
Percussion
Timpani
rit.
Alt.
pp
mf

172. CHORALE (Navy Hymn)

John Dykes
Arr. by John Higgins

9
Flute
Oboe
Bassoon
B♭ Clarinet
E♭ Alto Cl.
B♭ Bass Cl.
E♭ Alto Sax.
B♭ Tenor Sax.
E♭ Bari. Sax.
B♭ Trumpet
F Horn
Trombone
Baritone
Tuba
(Electric Bass)
Percussion
Keyboard
Percussion
Timpani
cresc.
mf rall.
Sus. Cym.
pp cresc.
mf
mp

Student Book Page 37

173. CHORALE (Prelude)

Frederic Chopin
Arr. by John Higgins

Flute
Oboe
Bassoon
B♭ Clarinet
E♭ Alto Cl.
B♭ Bass Cl.
E♭ Alto Sax.
B♭ Tenor Sax.
E♭ Bari. Sax.
Alt.
B♭ Trumpet
F Horn
Trombone
Baritone
Tuba (Electric Bass)
Tri.
Sus. Cym.
Percussion
Keyboard Percussion
Timpani

RHYTHM STUDIES

RHYTHM STUDIES

THE BASICS OF JAZZ STYLE from Essential Elements for Jazz Ensemble

Accenting "2 and 4"

For most traditional music the important beats in 4/4 time are 1 and 3. In jazz, however, the emphasis is usually on beats 2 and 4. Emphasizing "2 and 4" gives the music a jazz feeling.

Traditional
1 2 3 4
Jazz
1 2 3 4

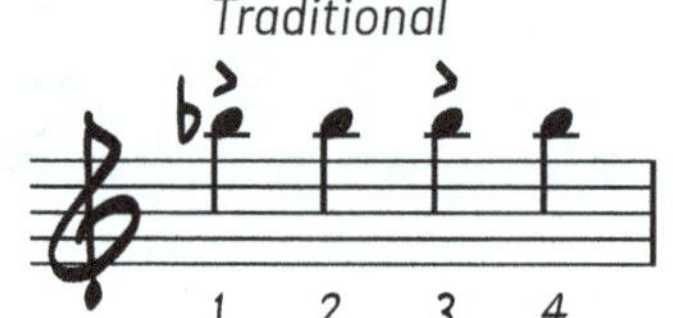

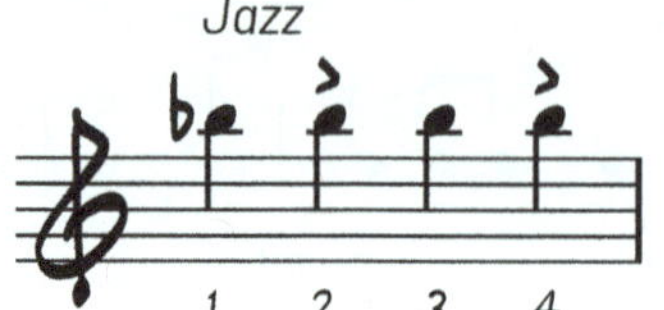

174. ACCENTING 2 AND 4

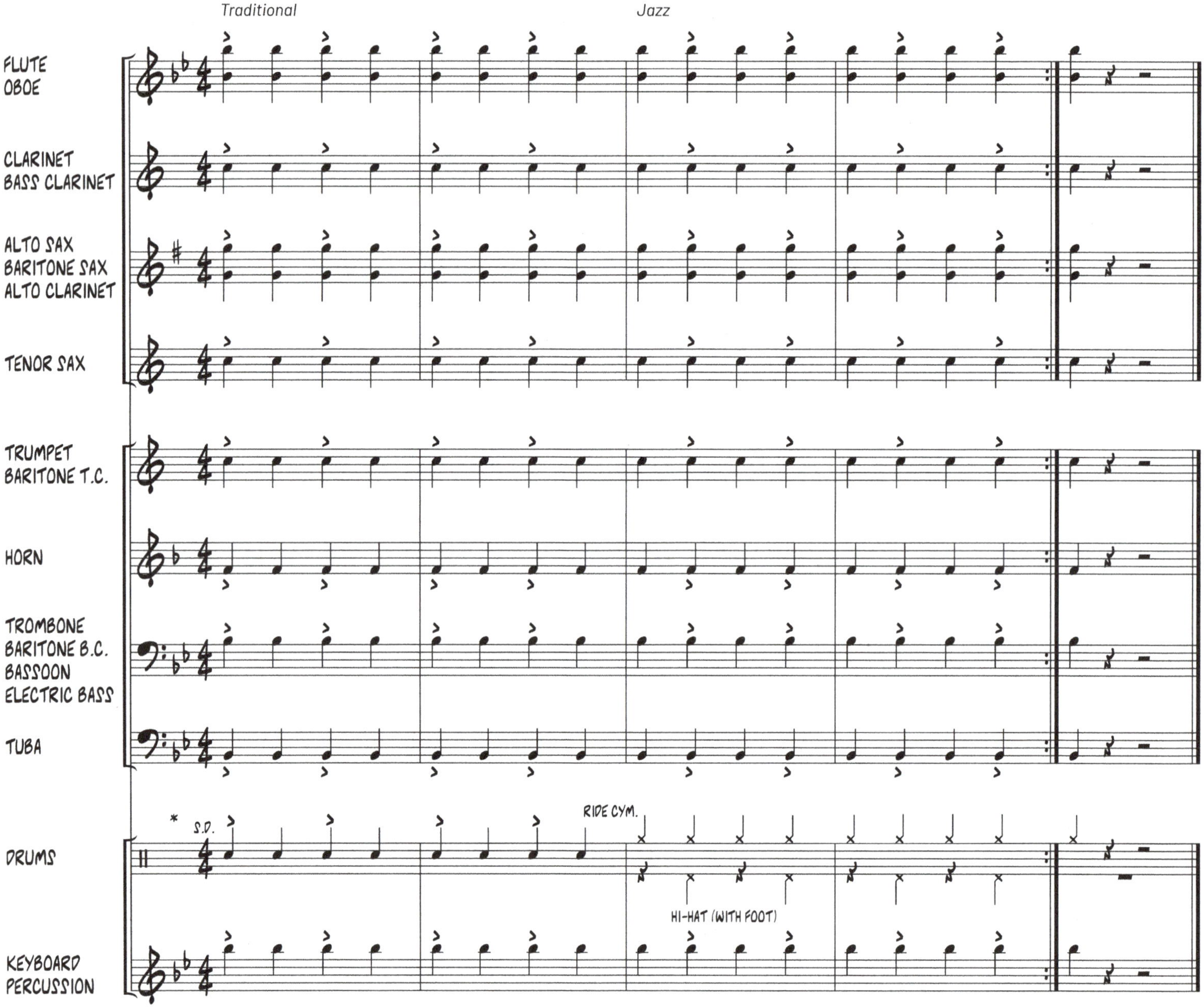
Traditional
Jazz
FLUTE
OBOE
CLARINET
BASS CLARINET
ALTO SAX
BARITONE SAX
ALTO CLARINET
TENOR SAX
TRUMPET
BARITONE T.C.
HORN
TROMBONE
BARITONE B.C.
BASSOON
ELECTRIC BASS
TUBA
DRUMS
*
S.D.
RIDE CYM.
HI-HAT (WITH FOOT)
KEYBOARD
PERCUSSION

*Note: In jazz drumming, accents on 2 and 4 are achieved by adding the hi-hat and/or snare drum.

Jazz Articulations

There are four basic articulations in jazz.

Tenuto
(full value)

Staccato
(short, unaccented)

Long Accent
(full value, accented)

Roof Top Accent
(short, accented)

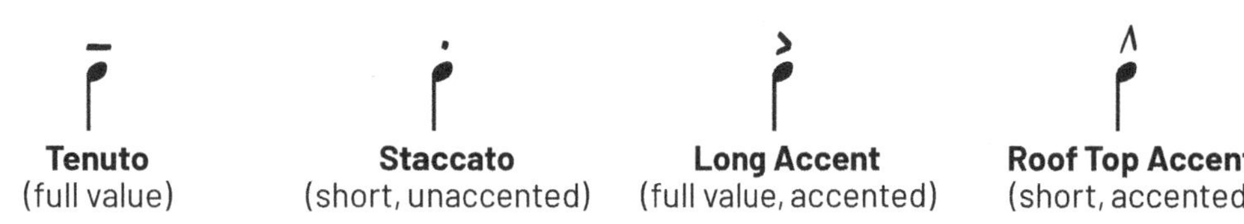

Swing 8th Notes Sound Different Than They Look

In swing, the 2nd 8th note of each beat is actually played like the last third of a triplet, and slightly accented. 8th notes in swing style are usually played *legato*.

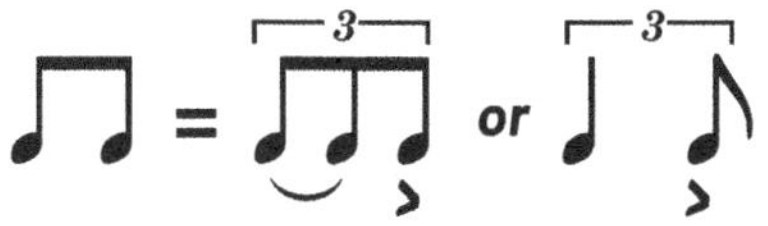

=
3
or
3

175. SWING 8TH NOTES

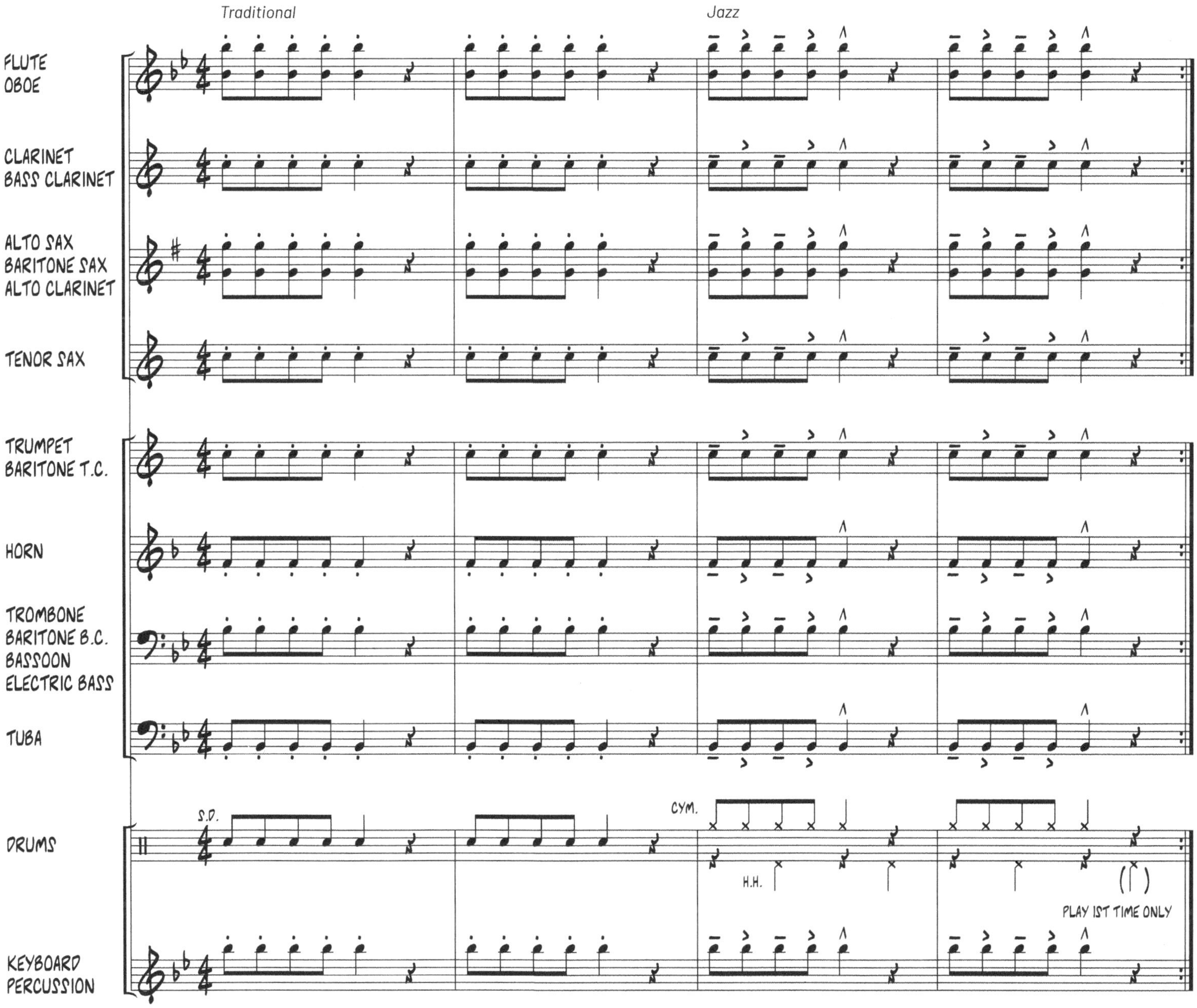

Traditional
Jazz
FLUTE
OBOE
CLARINET
BASS CLARINET
ALTO SAX
BARITONE SAX
ALTO CLARINET
TENOR SAX
TRUMPET
BARITONE T.C.
HORN
TROMBONE
BARITONE B.C.
BASSOON
ELECTRIC BASS
TUBA
DRUMS
S.D.
CYM.
H.H.
PLAY 1ST TIME ONLY
KEYBOARD
PERCUSSION

Quarter Notes

Quarter notes in swing style are usually played detached (*staccato*) with accents on beats 2 and 4.

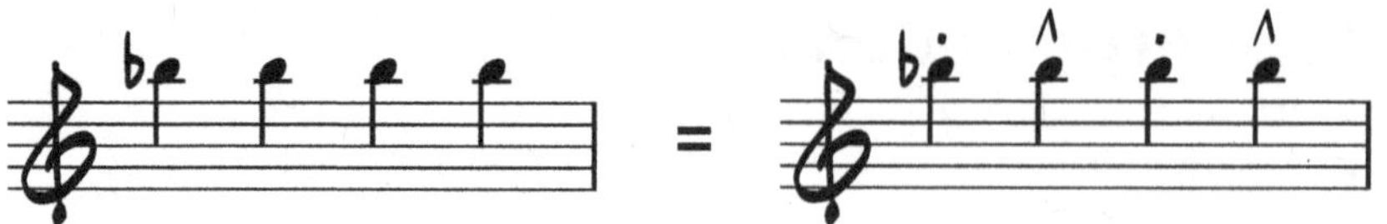

176. QUARTERS AND 8THS

FLUTE
OBOE

CLARINET
BASS CLARINET

ALTO SAX
BARITONE SAX
ALTO CLARINET

TENOR SAX

TRUMPET
BARITONE T.C.

HORN

TROMBONE
BARITONE B.C.
BASSOON
ELECTRIC BASS

TUBA

DRUMS

PLAY 1ST TIME ONLY

VIBES

KEYBOARD
PERCUSSION

177. RUNNIN' AROUND

Student Book Page 41

Syncopation in Jazz

When beats are played early (anticipated) or played late (delayed), the music becomes syncopated. Syncopation makes the music sound "jazzy."

178. WHEN THE SAINTS GO MARCHING IN – Without Syncopation

James Black and Katherine Purvis

179. WHEN THE SAINTS GO MARCHING IN – With Syncopation

"Jazzin' Up" the Melody by Adding Rhythms

Adding rhythms to a melody is another easy way to improvise in a jazz style. Start by filling out long notes with repeated 8th and quarter notes. Remember to swing the 8th notes (play *legato* and give the upbeats an accent).

180. "JAZZIN' UP" JINGLE BELLS

J. Pierpont

Jazzed Up Melody (rhythms added)
FL.
OB.
CL.
B. CL.
A. SAX
B. SAX
A. CL.
T. SAX
TPT.
BAR. T.C.
HN.
TBN.
BAR. B.C.
BSN.
TUBA
Walking Bass Line for Jazzed Up Melody
BASS
DRS.
KYBD.
PERC.

Student Book Page 41

MAKE UP YOUR OWN (IMPROVISE)

181. LONDON BRIDGE

Complete the melody in your own "jazzed up" way. Use only the notes shown in parentheses. Slashes on the staff indicate when to improvise.

Band
Solo
Band
Solo
FL.
OB.
CL.
B. CL.
A. SAX
B. SAX
A. CL.
T. SAX
TPT.
BAR. T.C.
HN.
TBN.
BAR. B.C.
BSN.
TUBA
BASS
DRS.
KYBD.
PERC.
Band
Solo – complete the melody

Student Book Page 42

THEORY

Major Scales

Play major scales as part of your daily practice routine. Play all octaves, keys, and arpeggios at various dynamic levels and tempos. Keep a steady pulse. Try different articulation patterns, such as:

182. B♭ MAJOR

Flute
Oboe

B♭ Clarinet
B♭ Bass Cl.

E♭ Alto Sax.
E♭ Bari. Sax.
E♭ Alto Cl.

A. Cl. 8vb

B♭ Tenor Sax.

B♭ Trumpet
Baritone T.C.

F Horn

Trombone
Baritone B.C.
Bassoon
Electric Bass
Tuba

Bsn., Tuba
Bsn.

Paradiddle Review
R L R R L R L R L R L R L L R L R L R L
R L R R L R L L R L R R L

Percussion
S.D.
B.D.
2

Keyboard
Percussion

a2

B. Cl. cues 8vb

All cue 8vb

R L R R L R L L R L R L
R L R R L R L L R L R R L

183. E♭ MAJOR

Flute
Oboe
a2
Cl. cues lower octave
B♭ Clarinet
B♭ Bass Cl.
E♭ Alto Sax.
E♭ Bari. Sax.
E♭ Alto Cl.
a3
B♭ Tenor Sax.
B♭ Trumpet
Baritone T.C.
F Horn
Trombone
Baritone B.C.
Bassoon
Electric Bass
Bsn. 8vb
Tuba
Triple Paradiddle Review
R L R L R L R R L R L R
L R L R L R L L R L R L
R L R L R L R L
S.D.
B.D.
2
Percussion
Keyboard
Percussion
Ob. cues 8vb
Alt.
Bsn.
R L R L R L R L R L R R
L R L R L R L R L R L L
R L R L R L R L L R

184. F MAJOR

Flute
Oboe
a2
B♭ Clarinet
B♭ Bass Cl.
Cl. cues upper octave
E♭ Alto Sax.
E♭ Bari. Sax.
E♭ Alto Cl.
a3
B♭ Tenor Sax.
B♭ Trumpet
Baritone T.C.
F Horn
Trombone
Baritone B.C.
Bassoon
Electric Bass
Tuba
Double Paradiddle Review
R L R L R R L R L R L L R L
S.D.
B.D.
Percussion
Keyboard
Percussion

185. C MAJOR

Fl. cues 8va
Fl. cues 8va
Flute
Oboe
B♭ Clarinet
B♭ Bass Cl.
Cl. cues lower octave
a2
E♭ Alto Sax.
E♭ Bari. Sax.
E♭ Alto Cl.
A. Cl. cues upper octave
B♭ Tenor Sax.
B♭ Trumpet
Baritone T.C.
F Horn
Trombone
Baritone B.C.
Electric Bass
Bassoon
Tuba
a2
Flamacue Review
R L L LR L R L
S.D.
B.D.
Percussion
Keyboard
Percussion
Flute
Oboe
a2
B♭ Clarinet
B♭ Bass Cl.
B. Cl. cues 8vb
a3
E♭ Alto Sax.
E♭ Bari. Sax.
E♭ Alto Cl.
A. Cl. cues 8vb
B♭ Tenor Sax.
B♭ Trumpet
Baritone T.C.
F Horn
Trombone
Baritone B.C.
Electric Bass
Bassoon
Tuba
a2
LR L R L LR L R L
Percussion
Keyboard
Percussion

186. A♭ MAJOR

Fl. cues lower octave
a2
Ob.:
Flute
Oboe
B♭ Clarinet
B♭ Bass Cl.
A. Sax., B. Sax. cue lower octave
E♭ Alto Sax.
E♭ Bari. Sax.
E♭ Alto Cl.
B♭ Tenor Sax.
B♭ Trumpet
Baritone T.C.
F Horn
Trombone
Baritone B.C.
Bassoon
Electric Bass
Tuba
Flam Tap Review
S.D.
B.D.
Percussion
Keyboard
Percussion
Saxes: Alt.
Bsn. cues 8vb

187. D♭ MAJOR

Flute
Oboe
Ob.: L
Ob. cues 8vb
Cl. cues lower octave
B♭ Clarinet
B♭ Bass Cl.
E♭ Alto Sax.
E♭ Bari. Sax.
E♭ Alto Cl.
A. Cl. cues upper octave
B♭ Tenor Sax.
B♭ Trumpet
Baritone T.C.
F Horn
Trombone
Baritone B.C.
Bassoon
Electric Bass
Bsn. 8vb
Tuba
Flam Paradiddle Review
S.D.
B.D.
Percussion
Keyboard
Percussion
Saxes: F
F A. Cl. cues 8vb
a2
Bsn.

188. G MAJOR

Flute
Oboe
B♭ Clarinet
B♭ Bass Cl.
E♭ Alto Sax.
E♭ Bari. Sax.
E♭ Alto Cl.
B♭ Tenor Sax.
B♭ Trumpet
Baritone T.C.
F Horn
Trombone
Baritone B.C.
Bassoon
Electric Bass
Tuba
Percussion
Keyboard
Percussion
a2
A. Sax., B. Sax. cue lower octave
A. Cl.: R
Bar. cues 8vb
Flam Accent Review
S.D.
B.D.
Bsn. cues 8vb

Flute
Oboe
a2
B♭ Clarinet
B♭ Bass Cl.
E♭ Alto Sax.
E♭ Bari. Sax.
E♭ Alto Cl.
L
B♭ Tenor Sax.
B♭ Trumpet
Baritone T.C.
F Horn
Trombone
Baritone B.C.
Bassoon
Electric Bass
(Bsn. cues 8vb)
Tuba
Percussion
Keyboard
Percussion

189. D MAJOR

Flute
Oboe
B♭ Clarinet
B♭ Bass Cl.
E♭ Alto Sax.
E♭ Bari. Sax.
E♭ Alto Cl.
B♭ Tenor Sax.
B♭ Trumpet
Baritone T.C.
F Horn
Trombone
Baritone B.C.
Bassoon
Electric Bass
Tuba
Percussion
Keyboard
Percussion
Ob. cues 8vb
Cl. cues lower octave
B. Cl. cues upper octave
a3
A. Cl. cues upper octave
Bsn. 8vb
Nine Stroke Roll/Flam Exercise
S.D.
B.D.
R
L
Bsn.
a2

190. A MAJOR

Fl. cues lower octave
a2
Flute
Oboe
B♭ Clarinet
B♭ Bass Cl.
R
L
E♭ Alto Sax.
E♭ Bari. Sax.
E♭ Alto Cl.
a3
A. Cl.: L
B♭ Tenor Sax.
B♭ Trumpet
Baritone T.C.
F Horn
Tbn., Bar., Bass cue 8vb
Trombone
Baritone B.C.
Bassoon
Electric Bass
Bsn. 8vb
Tuba
Nine Stroke Roll/Flam Tap Exercise
S.D.
B.D.
Percussion
Keyboard
Percussion
B. Cl. cues 8vb
Bsn. cues 8vb

191. G♭ MAJOR

Flute
Oboe
Ob.: L
L
L
L
a2
B♭ Clarinet
B♭ Bass Cl.
A. Sax., B. Sax. cue lower octave
E♭ Alto Sax.
E♭ Bari. Sax.
E♭ Alto Cl.
B♭ Tenor Sax.
B♭ Trumpet
Baritone T.C.
Bar. cues 8vb
F Horn
Trombone
Baritone B.C.
Bassoon
Electric Bass
Tuba
Seventeen Stroke Roll/Flam Exercise
S.D.
B.D.
Percussion
Keyboard
Percussion
Ob.
L
L
L
L
Bsn.: Alt.
Alt.
Alt.
Alt.
Alt.
Alt.
Alt.
Alt.
Alt.
Alt.
Alt.

Minor Scales

Play minor scales as part of your daily practice routine. Play all octaves, all three forms, and the arpeggios at various dynamic levels and tempos. Keep a steady pulse. Try different articulation patterns, such as:

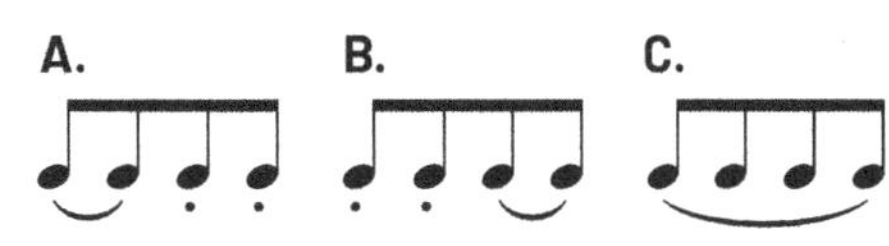

192. D MINOR SCALE

Natural — Melodic

Flute
Oboe

Cl. cues 8va

B♭ Clarinet
B♭ Bass Cl.

A. Sax. cues lower octave

R L

E♭ Alto Sax.
E♭ Bari. Sax.
E♭ Alto Cl.

A. Cl.
B. Sax. cues upper octave

B♭ Tenor Sax.

B♭ Trumpet
Baritone T.C.

F Horn

Bsn. cues lower octave

Trombone
Baritone B.C.
Bassoon
Electric Bass
Tuba

Six Stroke Roll Development Exercise

R R L R L R L R L R L

R R L R L L R R L R L L R R L

S.D.
B.D.

Percussion

Keyboard
Percussion

Harmonic — Arpeggio

Flute
Oboe

B♭ Clarinet
B♭ Bass Cl.

R L — L R

E♭ Alto Sax.
E♭ Bari. Sax.
E♭ Alto Cl.

B♭ Tenor Sax.

B♭ Trumpet
Baritone T.C.

F Horn

Trombone
Baritone B.C.
Bassoon
Electric Bass
Tuba

Percussion

Keyboard
Percussion

193. G MINOR SCALE

194. C MINOR SCALE

Student Book Page 44

195. F MINOR SCALE

TRILL CHART

FLUTE

Here are some common trill fingerings. Trill the **red** key(s).

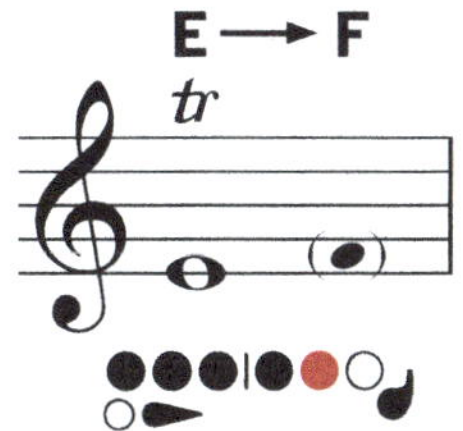

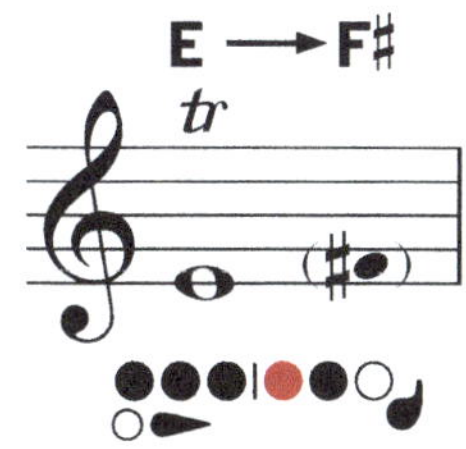

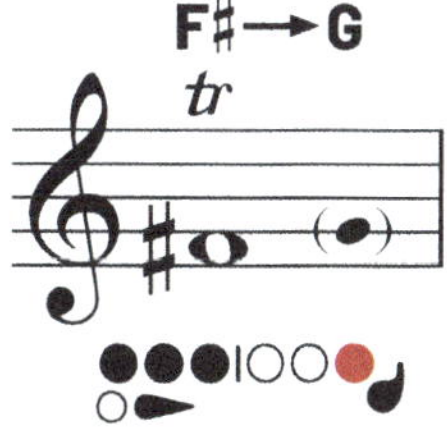

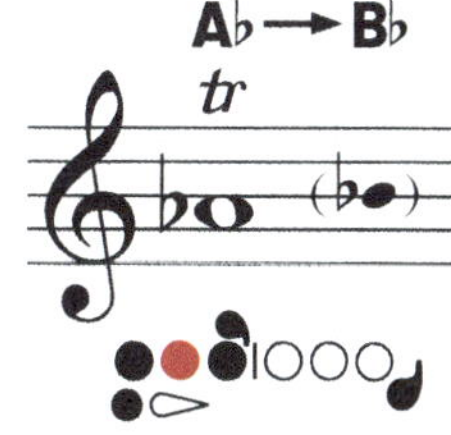

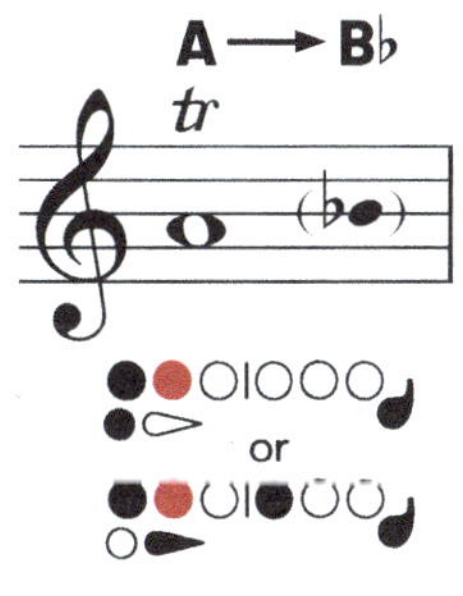

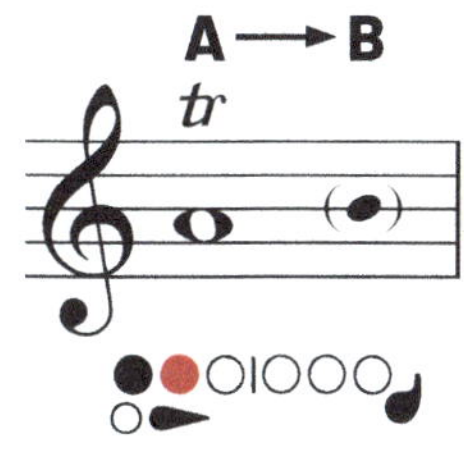

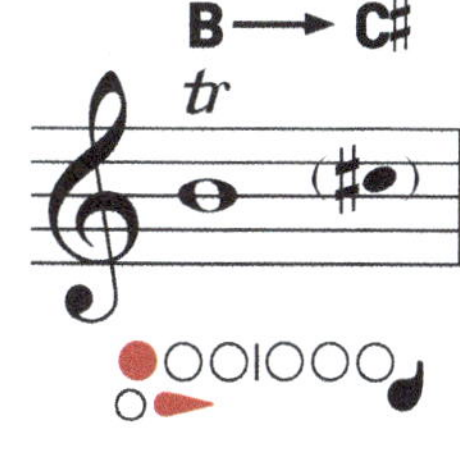

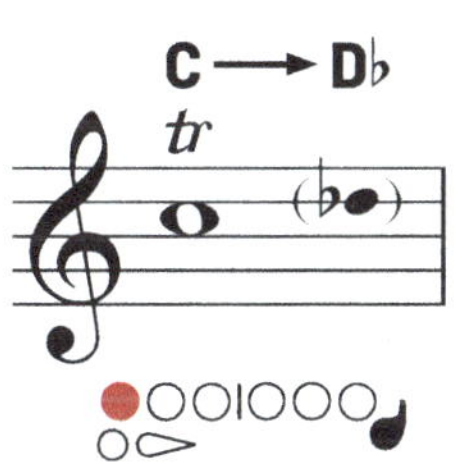

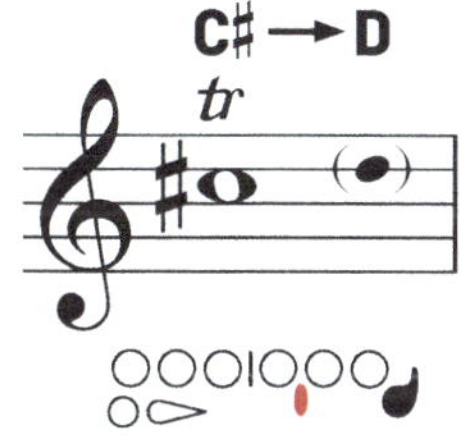

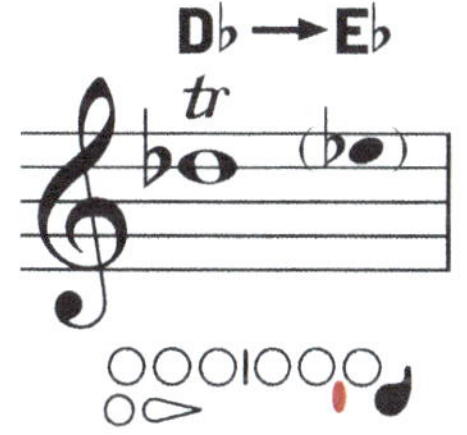

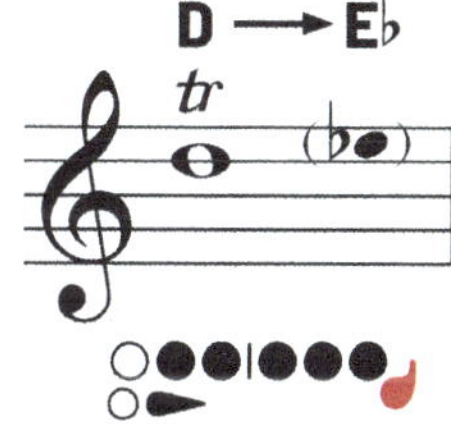

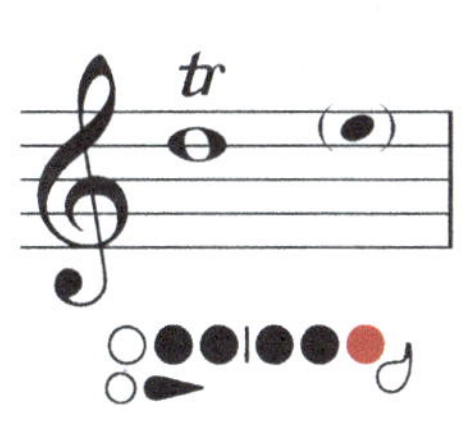

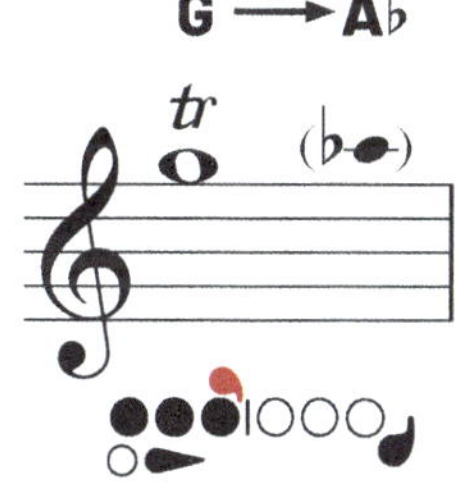

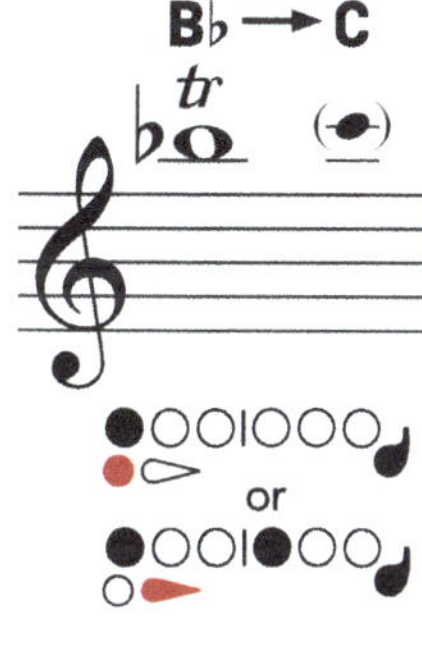

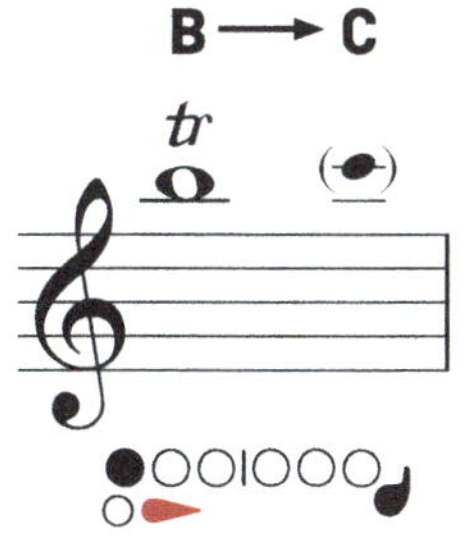

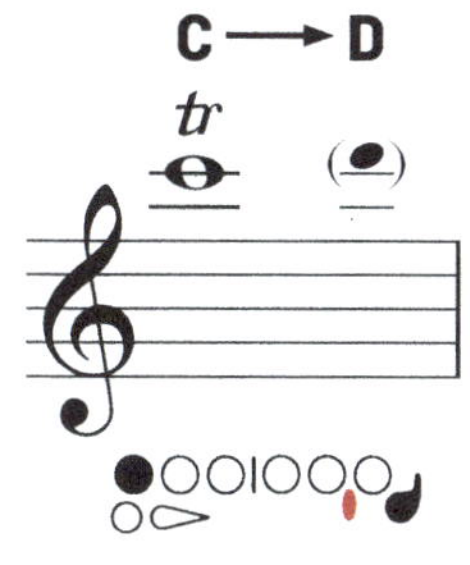

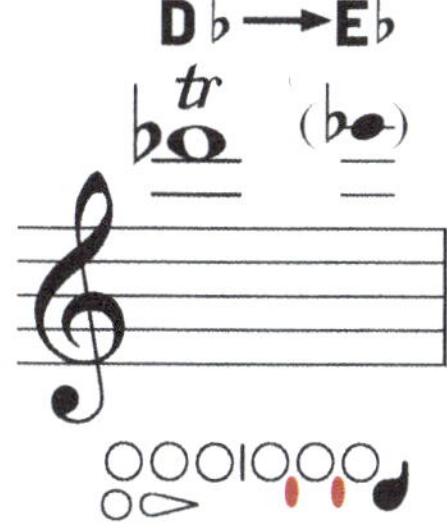

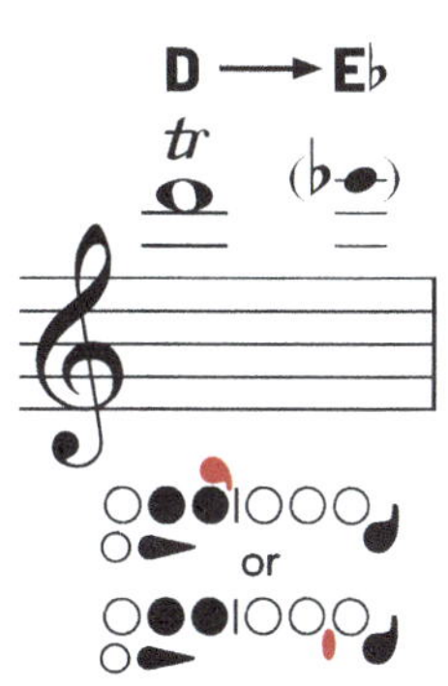

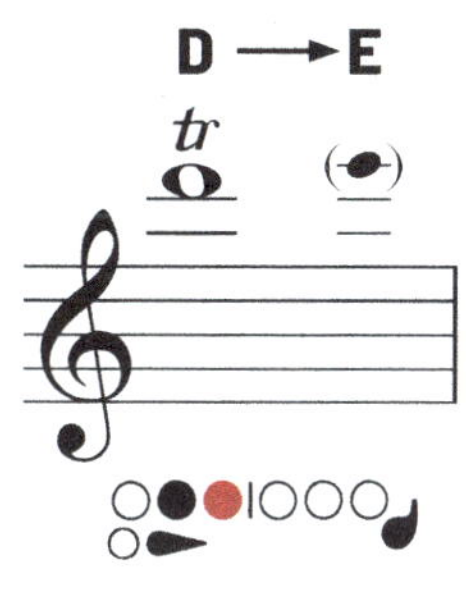

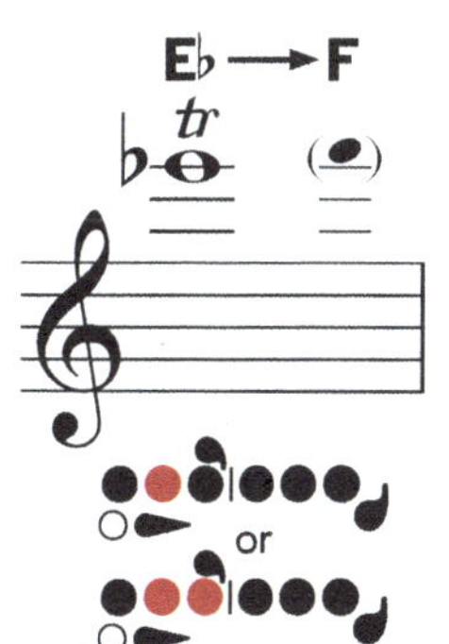

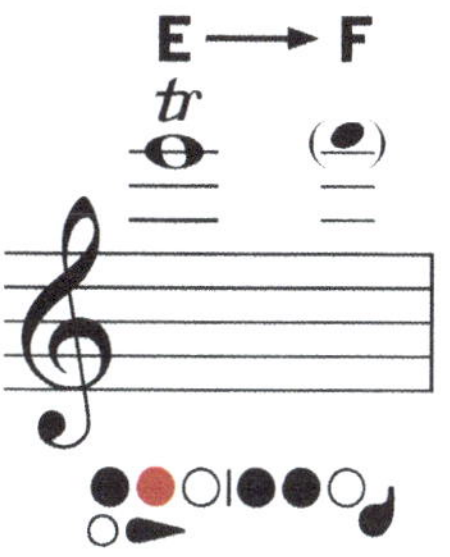

TRILL CHART

OBOE

Here are some common trill fingerings. Trill the **red** key(s).

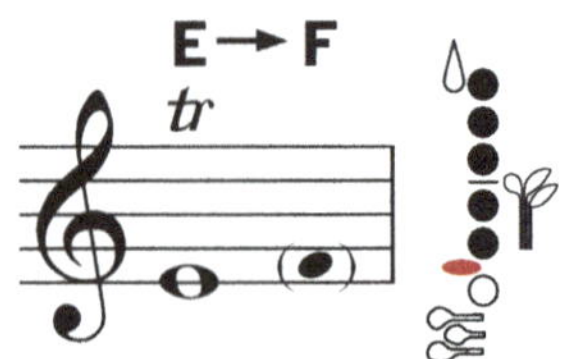

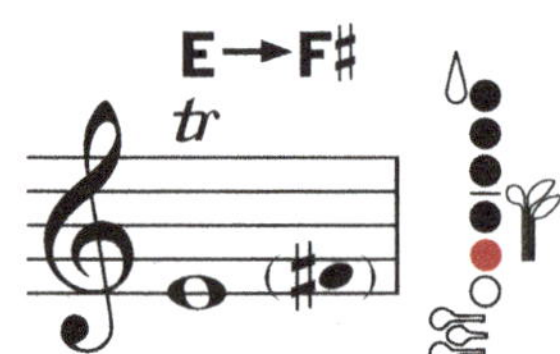

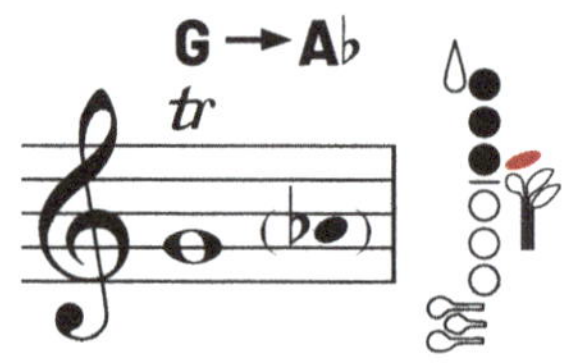

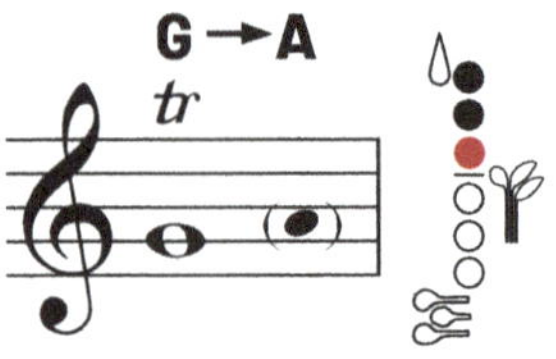

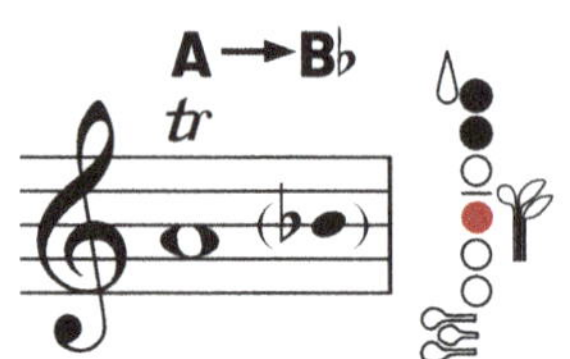

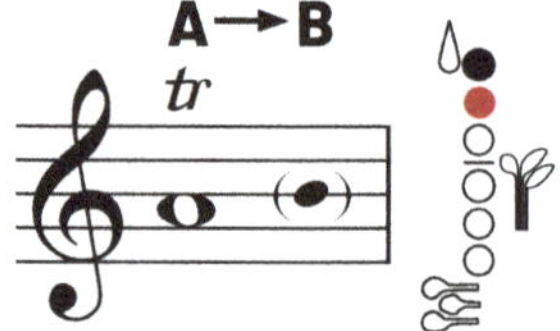

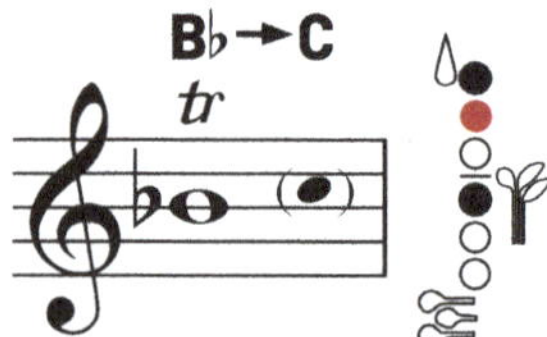

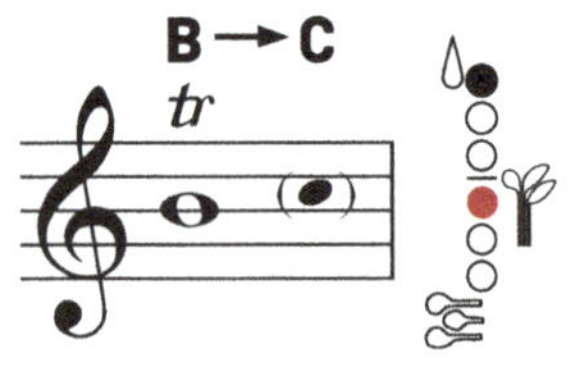

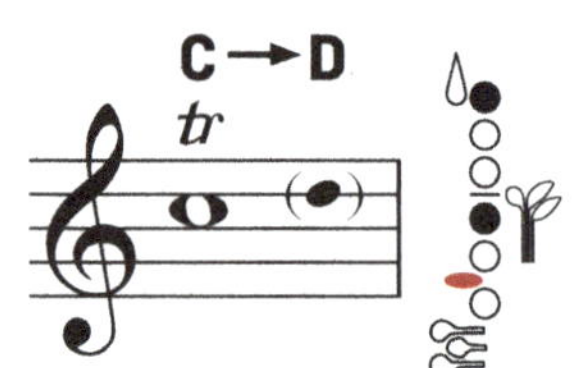

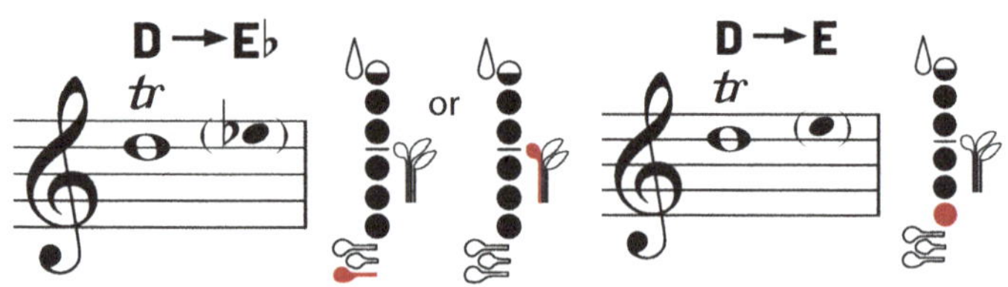

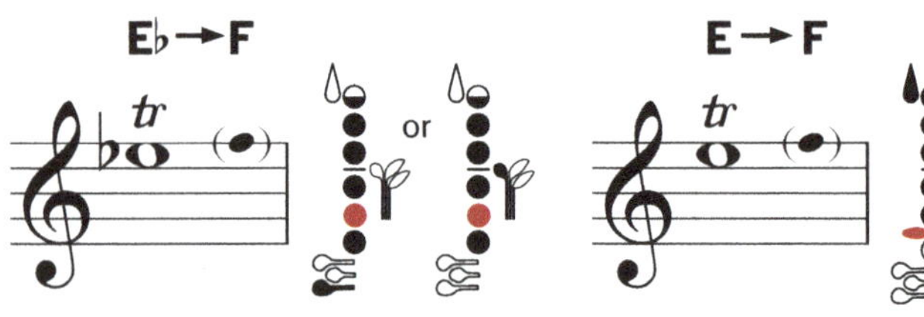

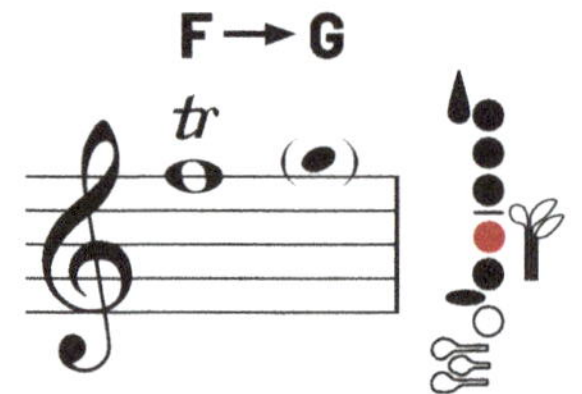

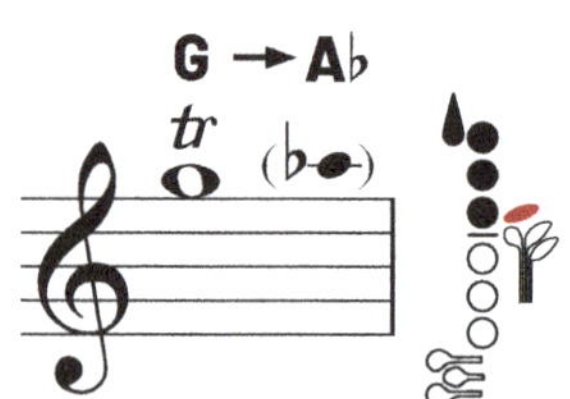

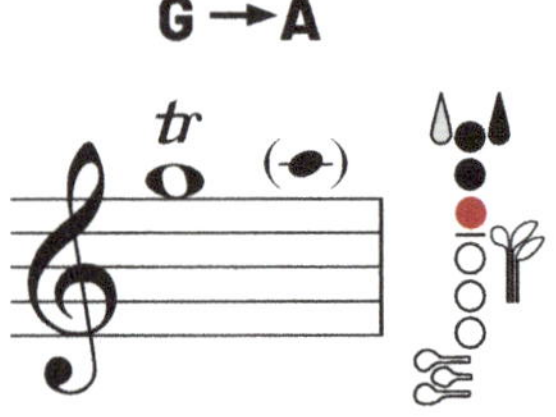

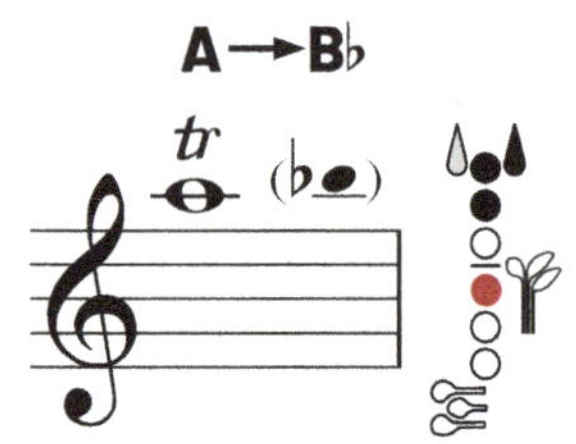

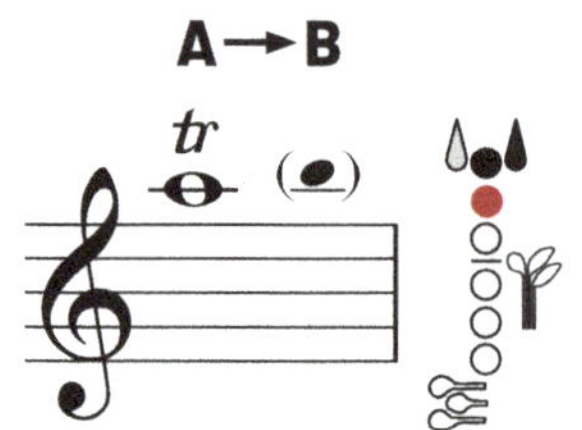

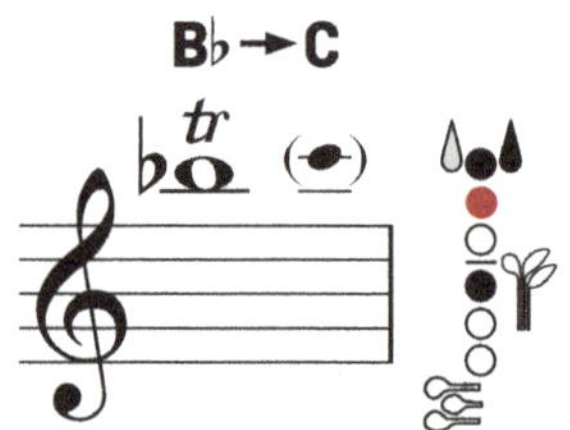

TRILL CHART

BASSOON

Here are some common trill fingerings. Trill the **red** key(s).

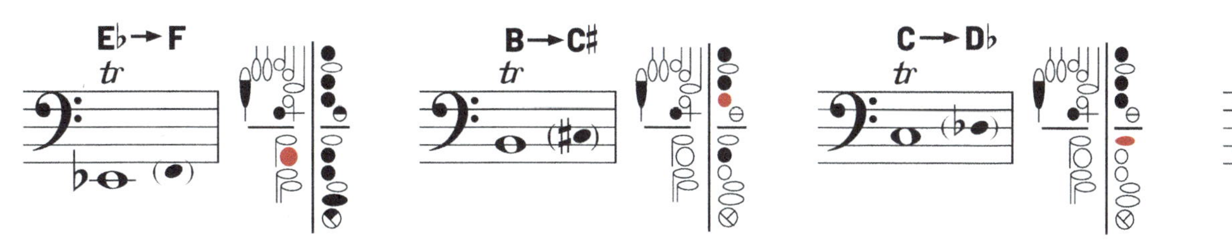

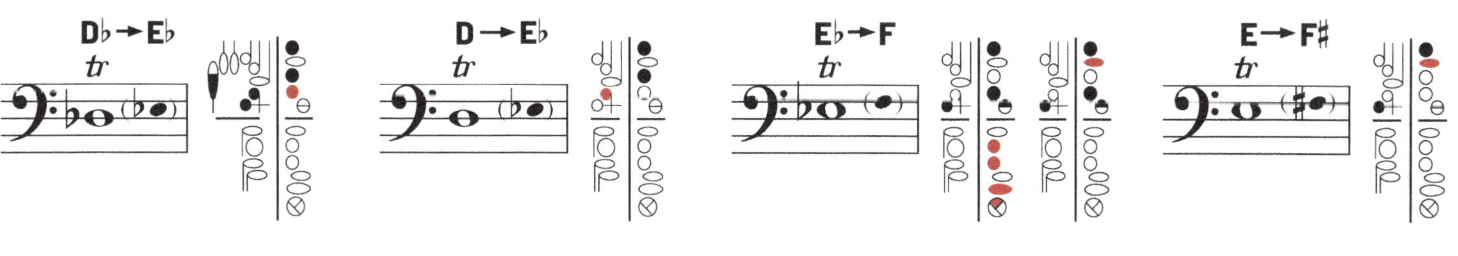

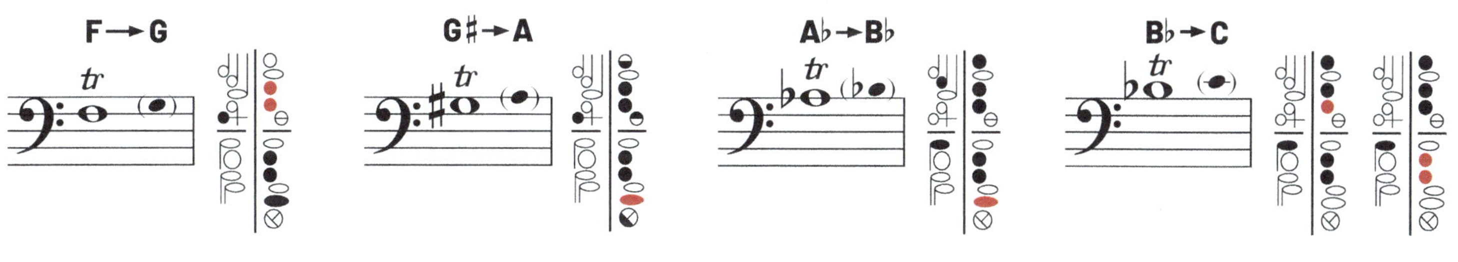

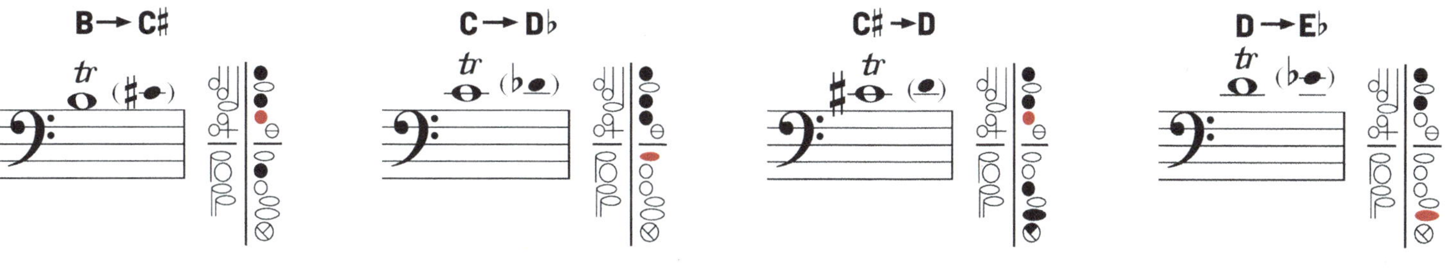

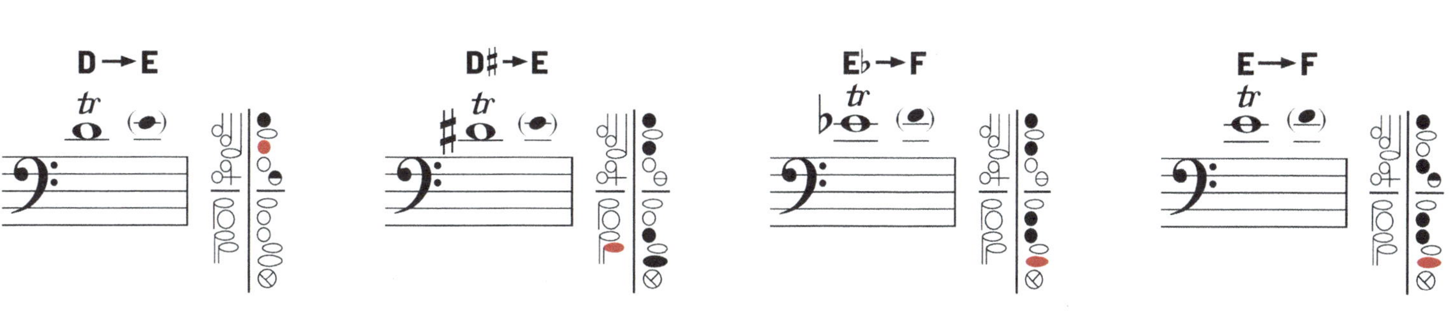

TRILL CHART

B♭ CLARINET

Here are some common trill fingerings. Trill the **red** key(s).

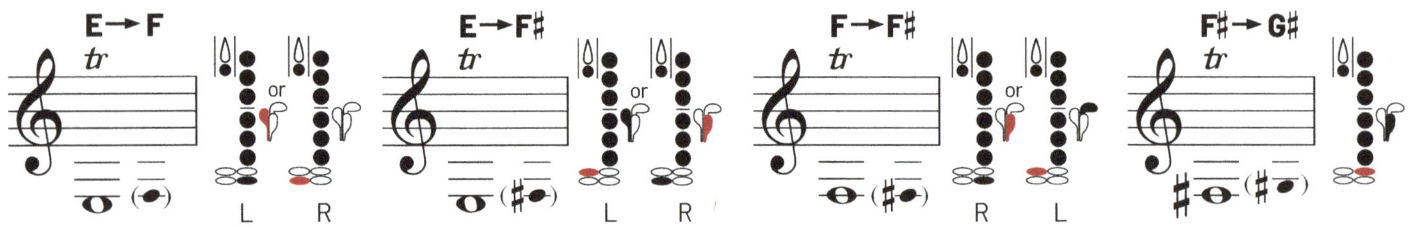

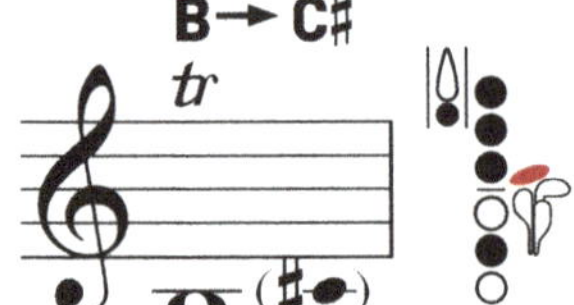

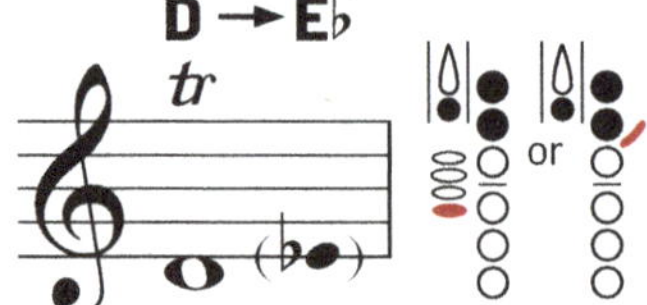

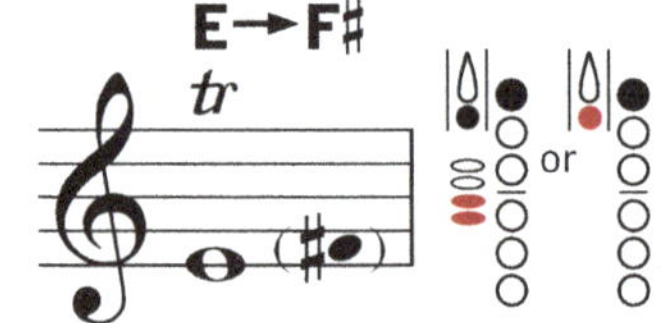

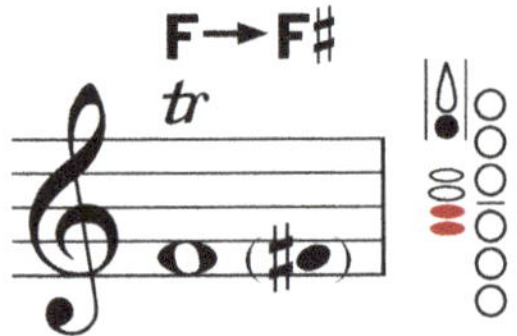

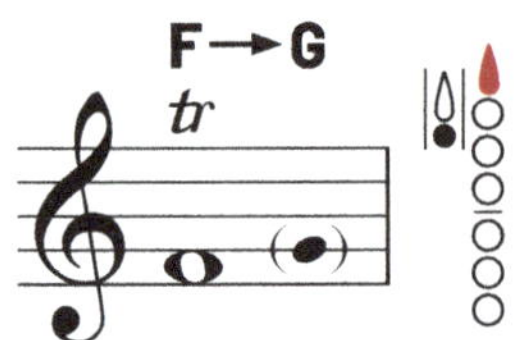

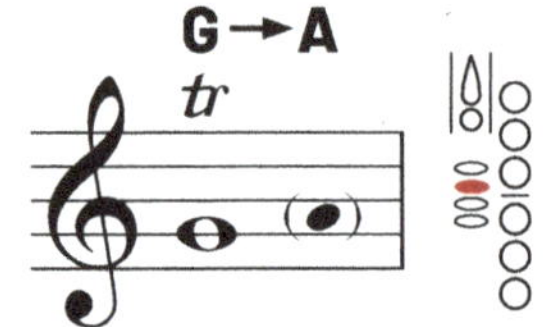

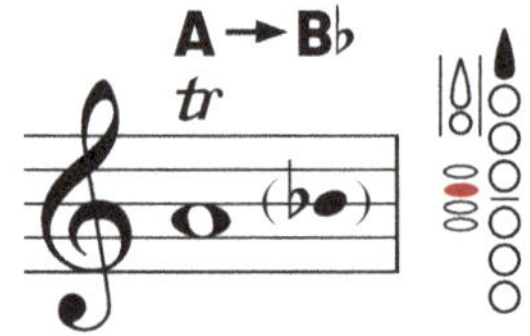

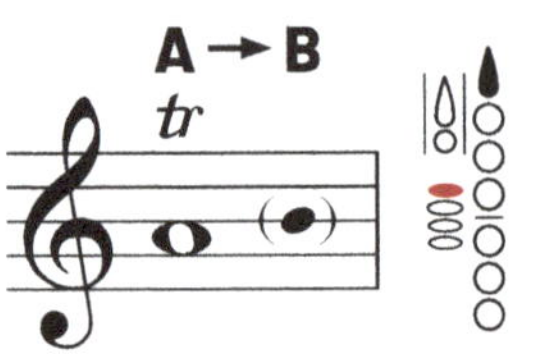

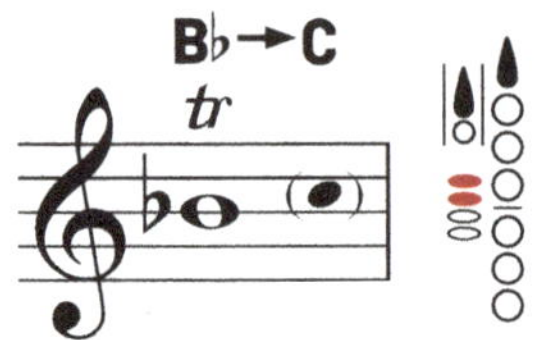

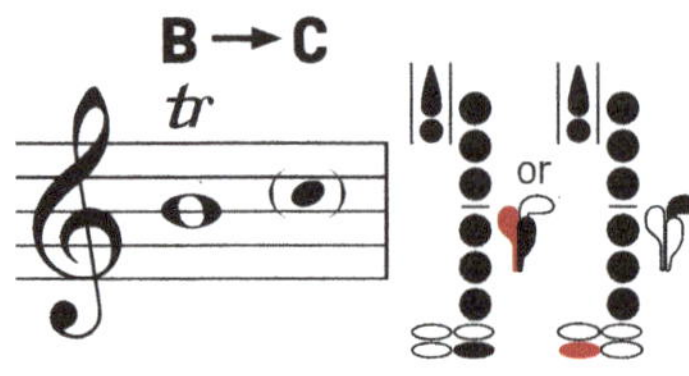

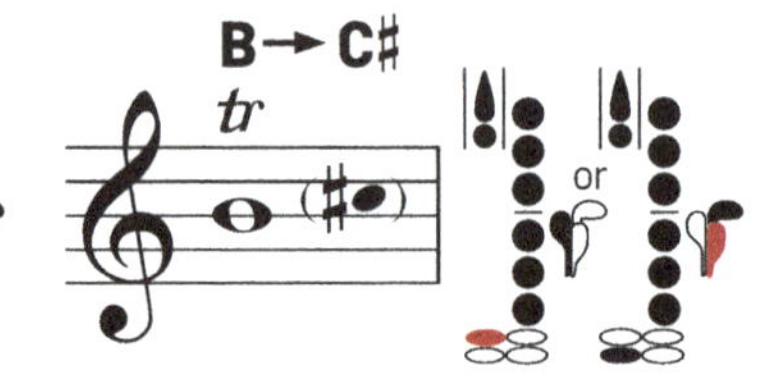

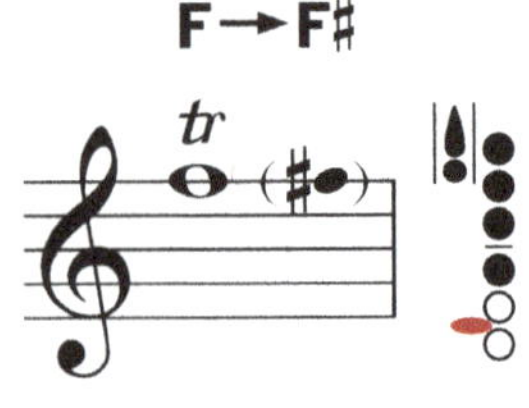

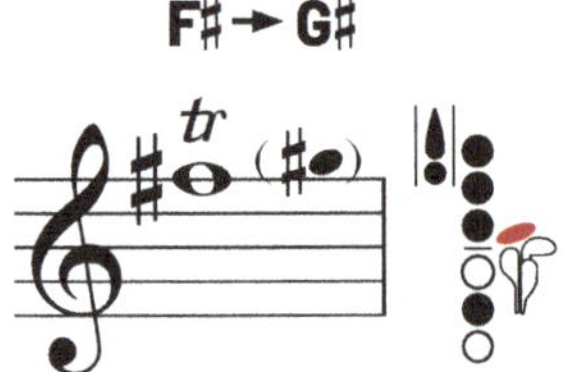

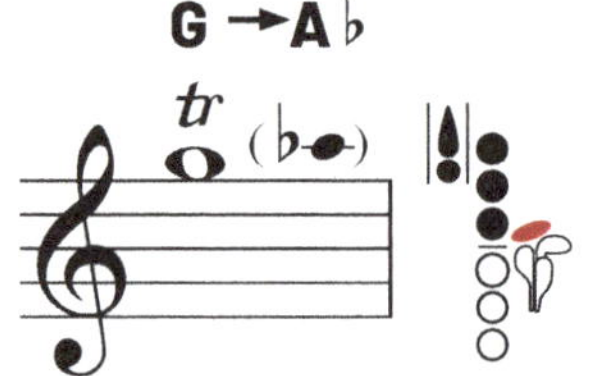

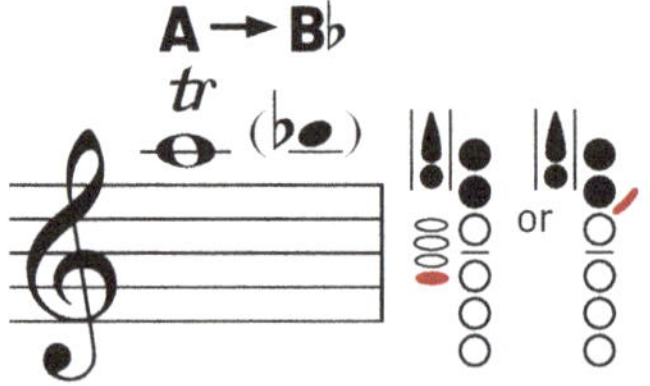

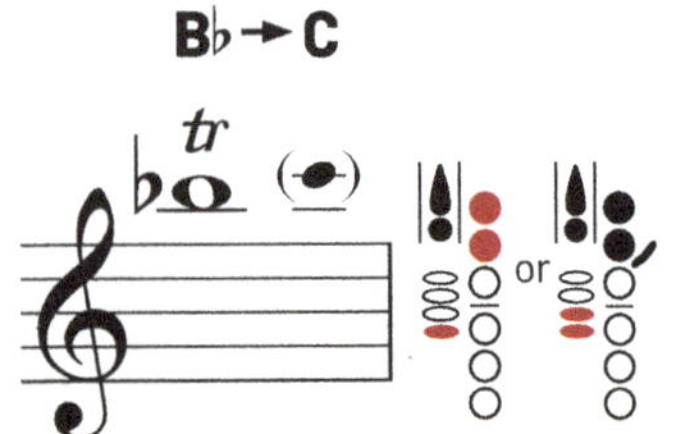

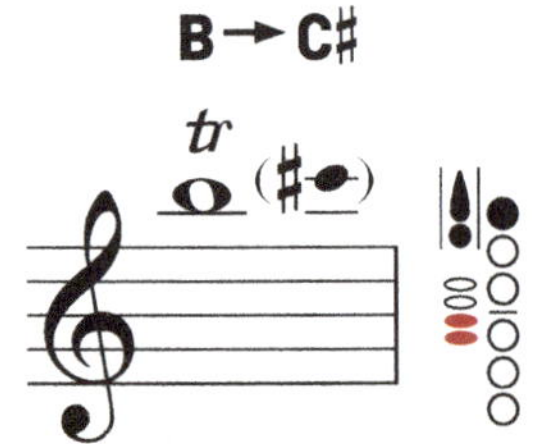

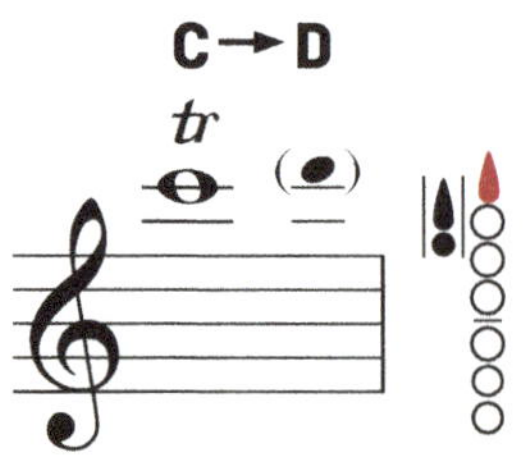

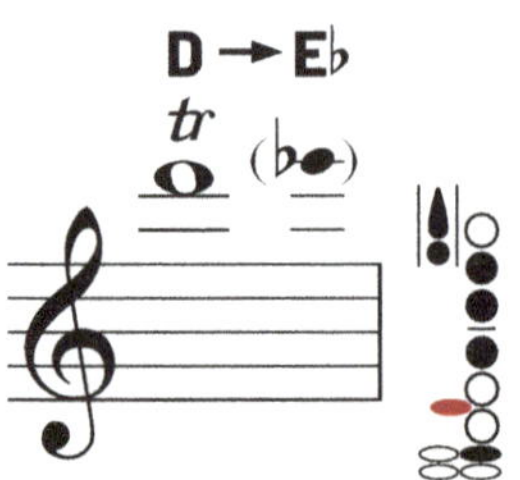

TRILL CHART

E♭ ALTO CLARINET

Here are some common trill fingerings. Trill the **red** key(s).

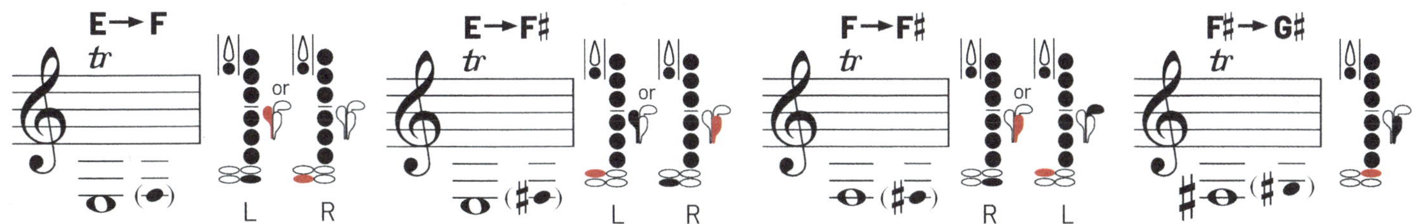

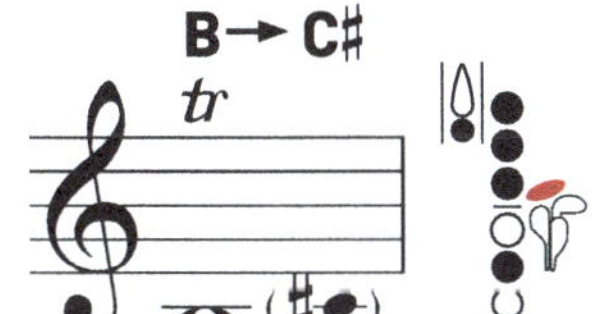

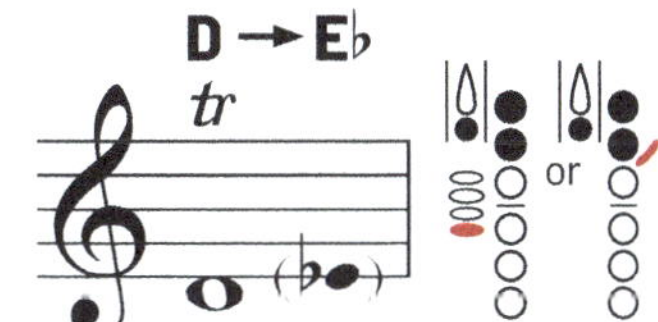

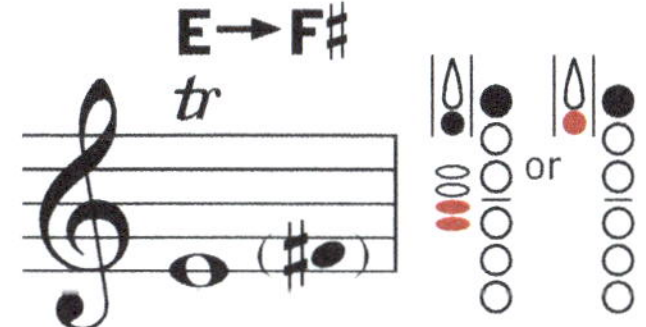

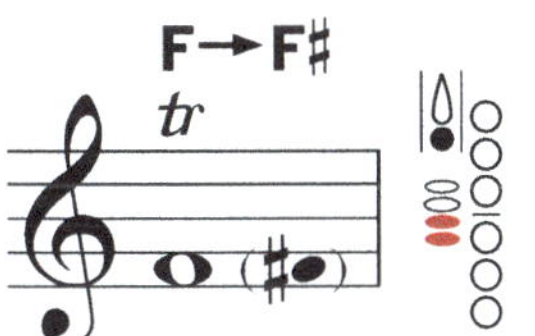

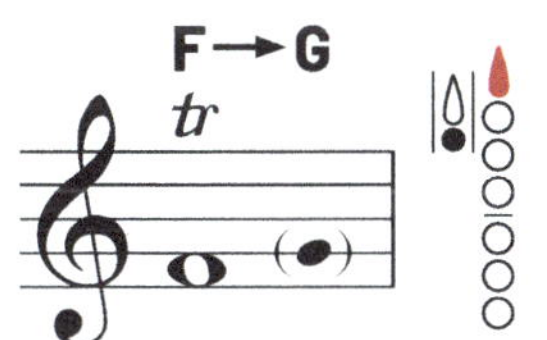

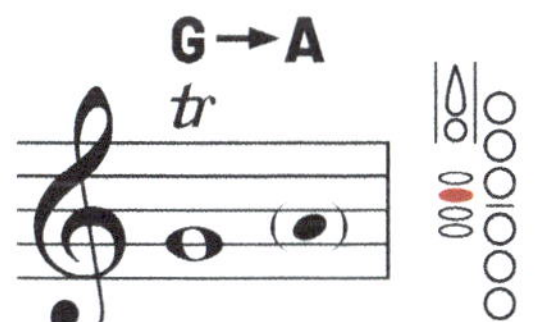

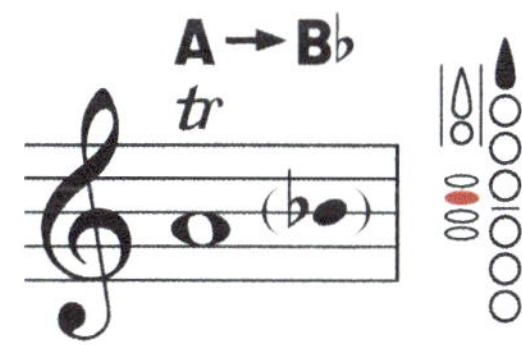

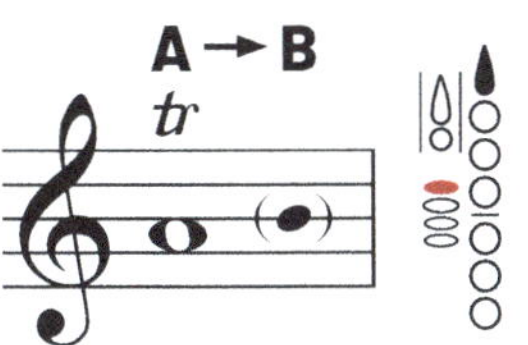

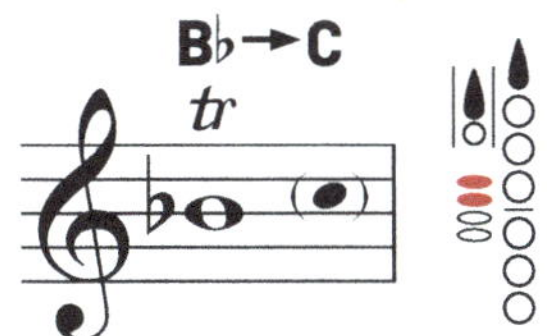

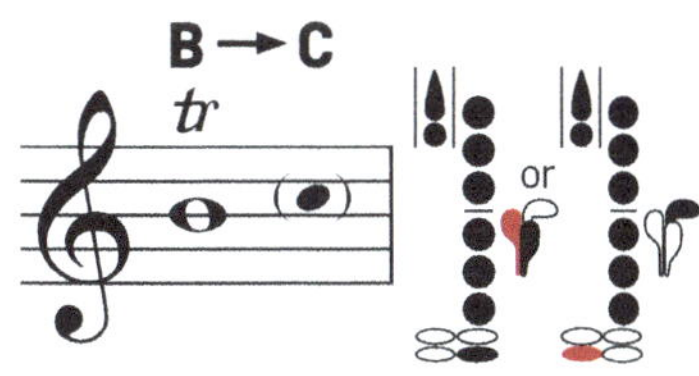

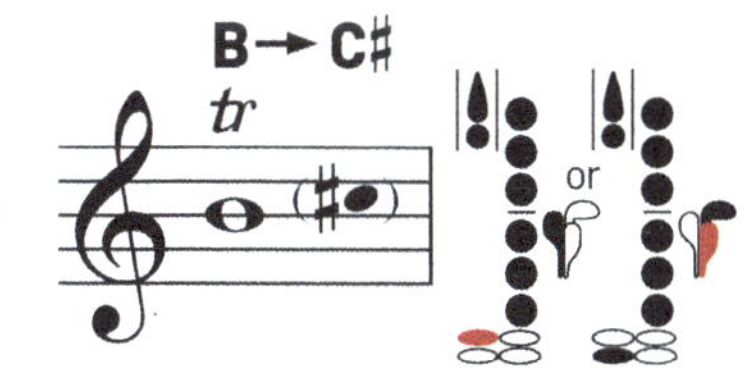

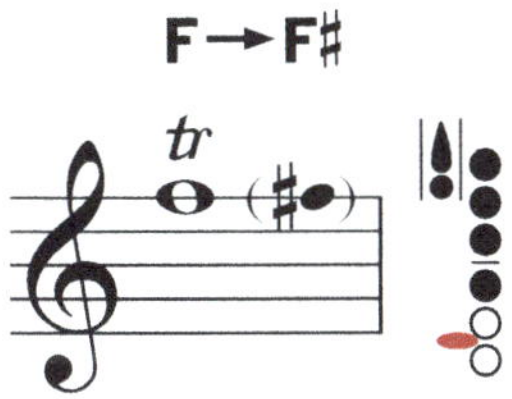

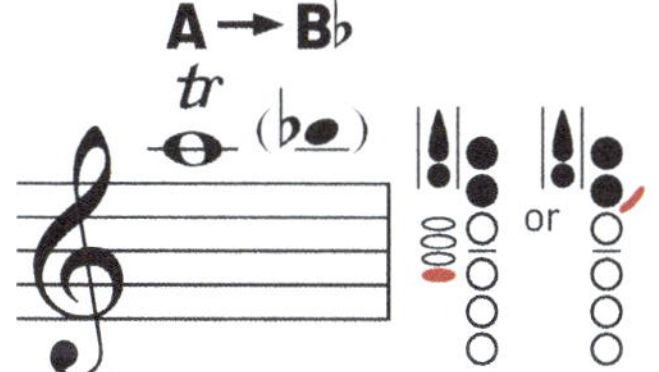

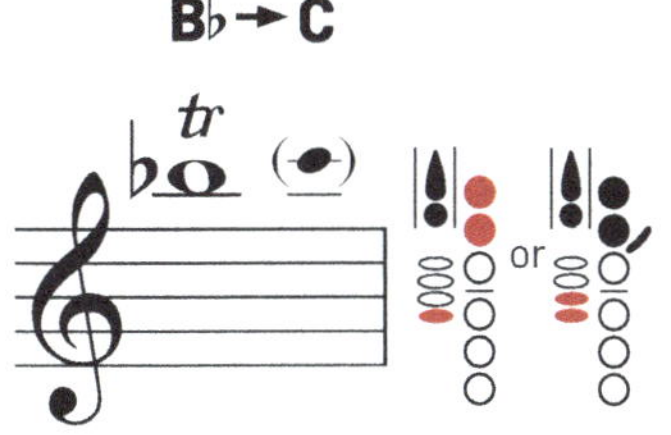

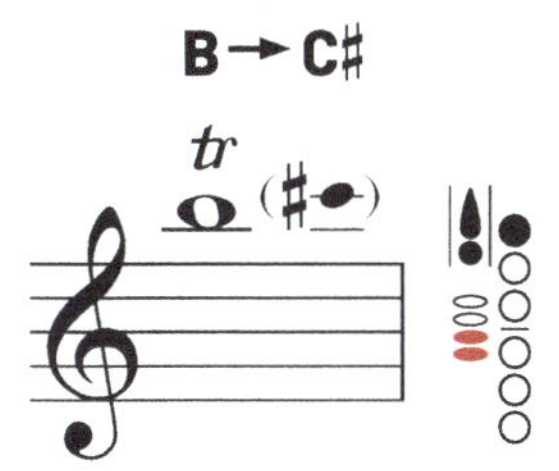

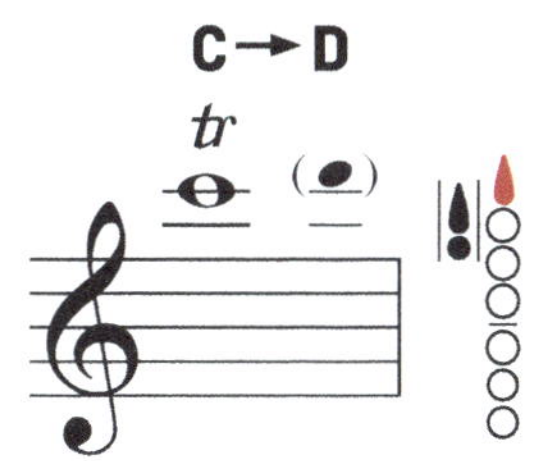

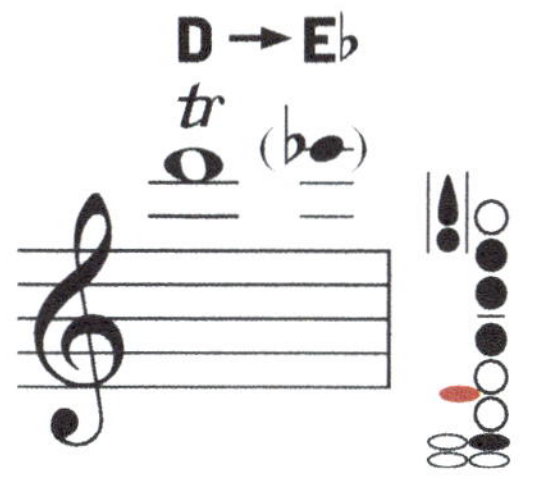

TRILL CHART

B♭ BASS CLARINET

Here are some common trill fingerings. Trill the **red** key(s).

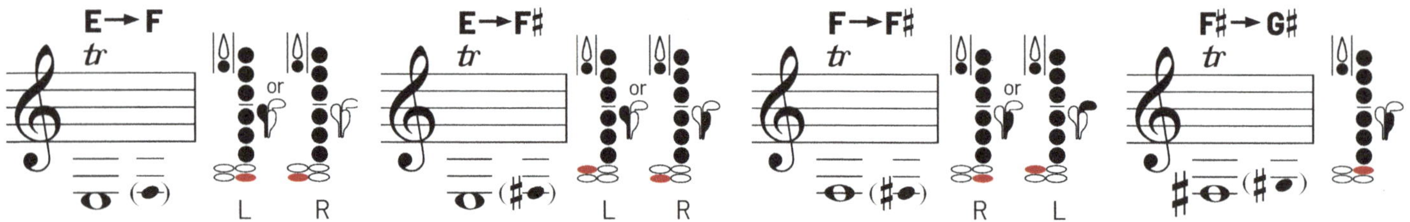

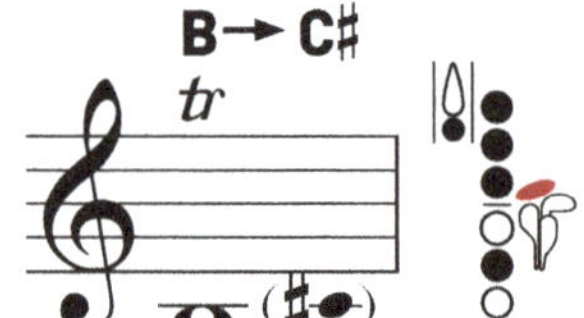

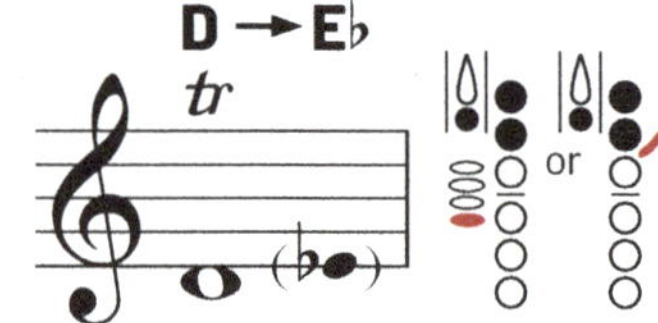

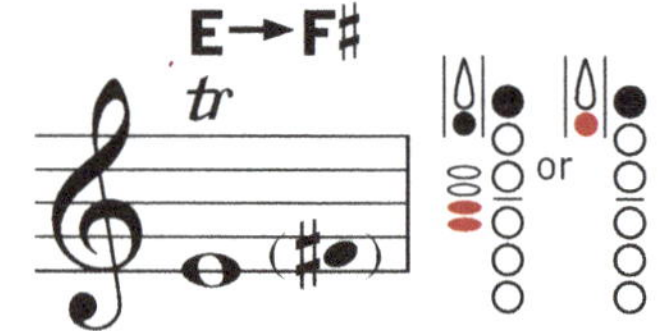

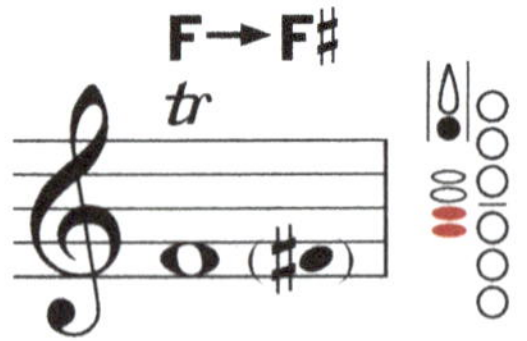

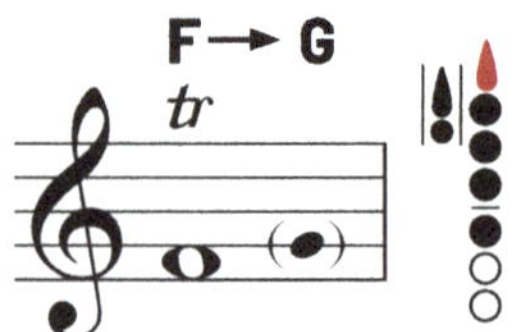

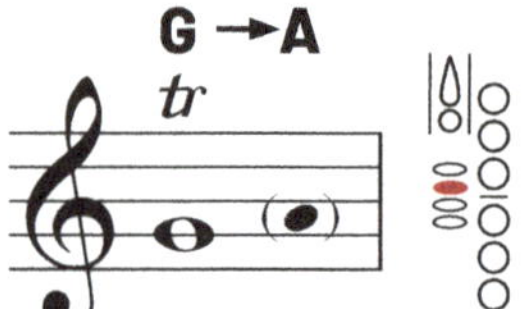

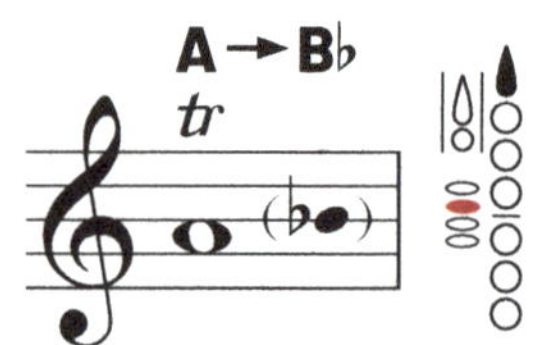

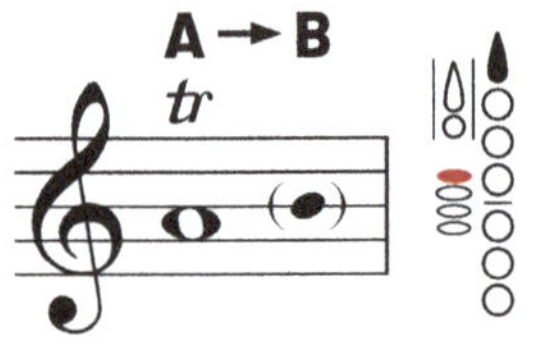

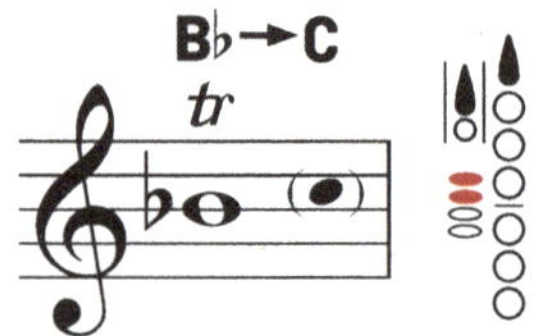

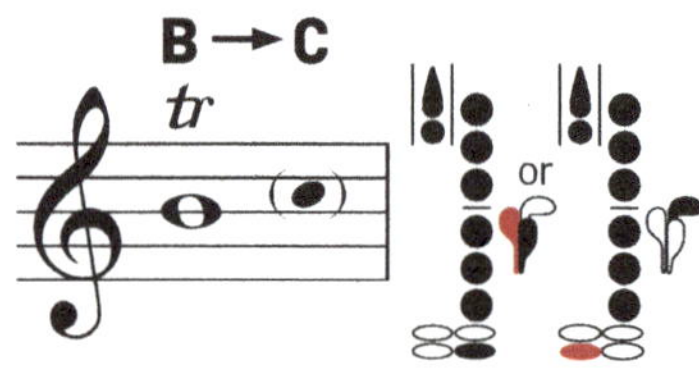

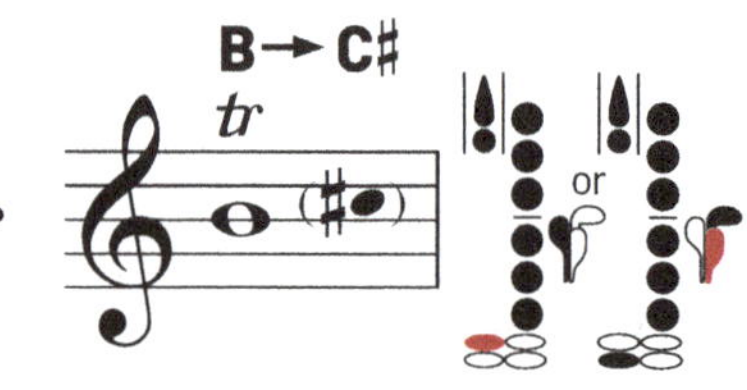

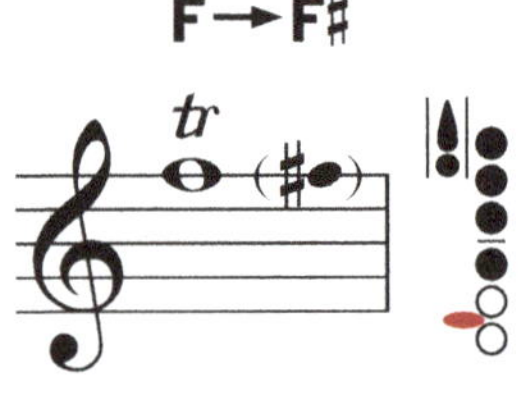

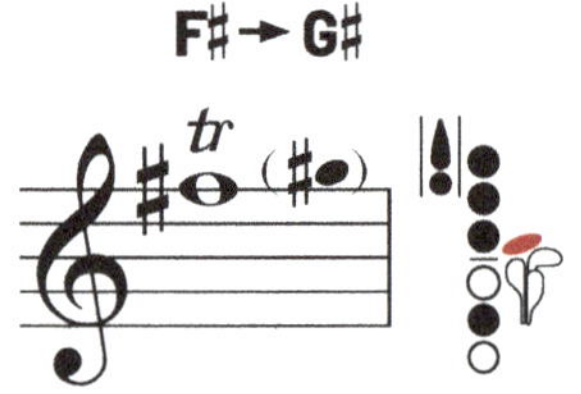

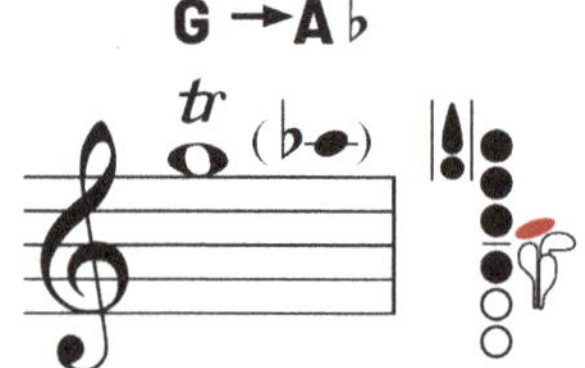

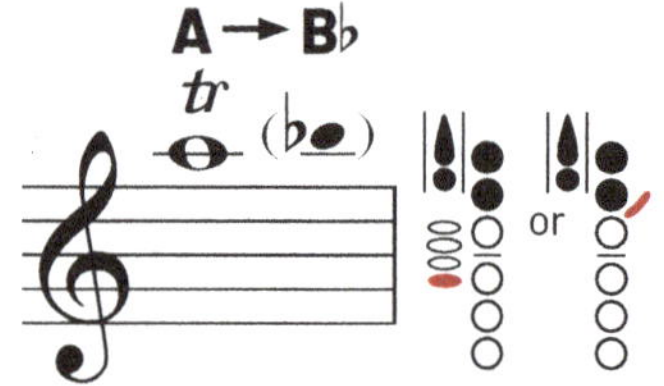

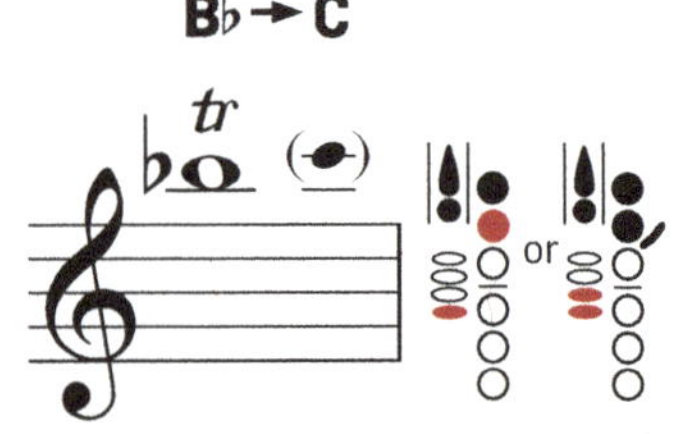

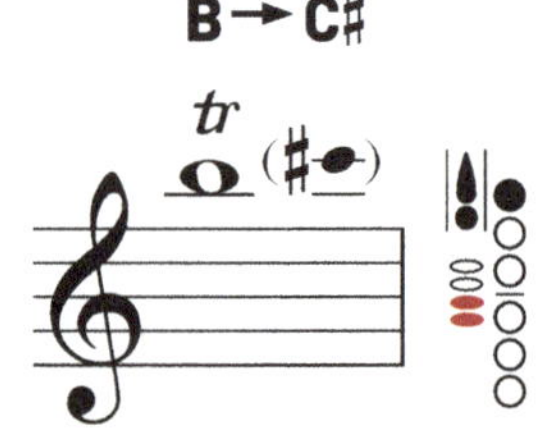

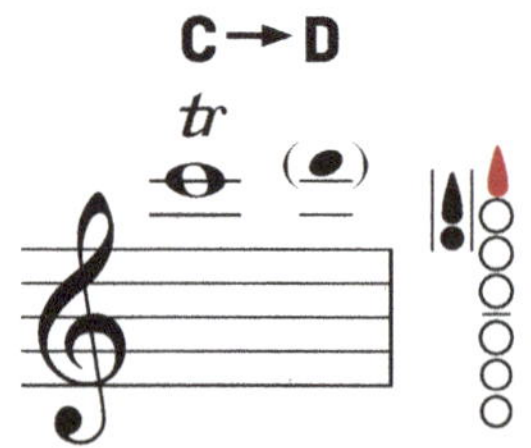

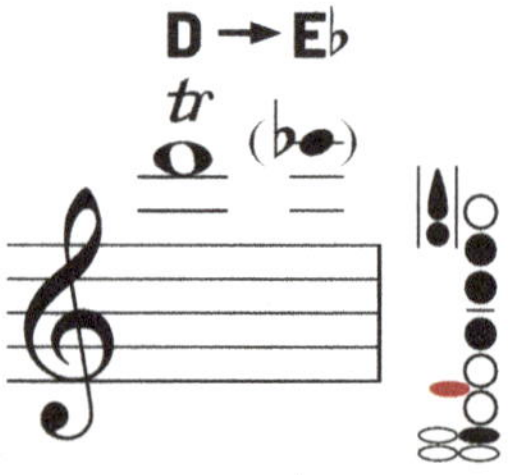

TRILL CHART

E♭ ALTO SAXOPHONE

Here are some common trill fingerings. Trill the **red** key(s).

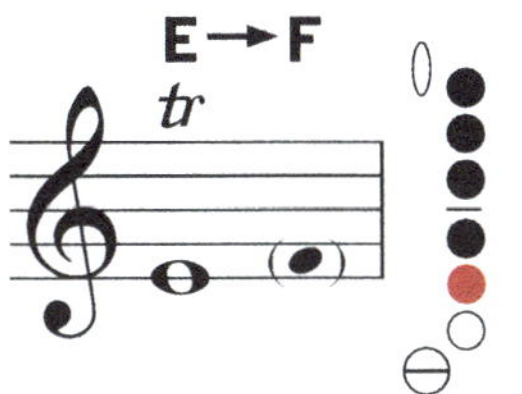

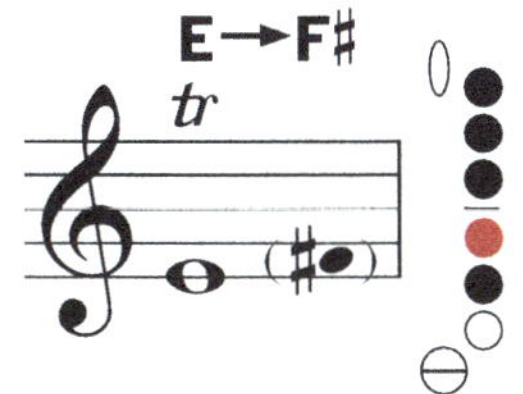

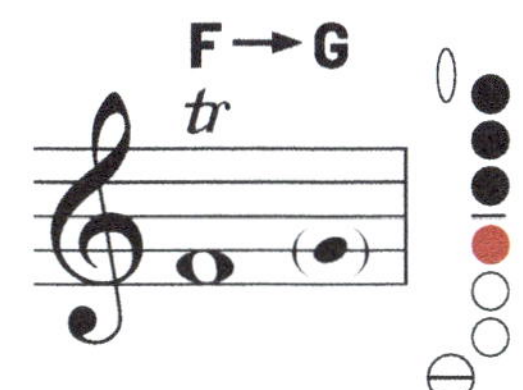

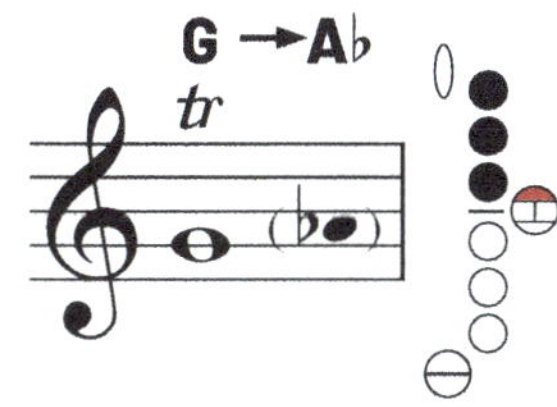

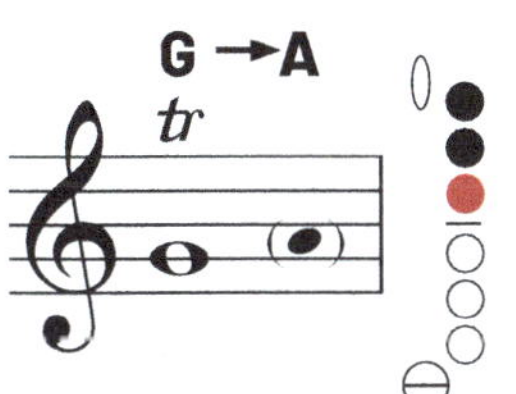

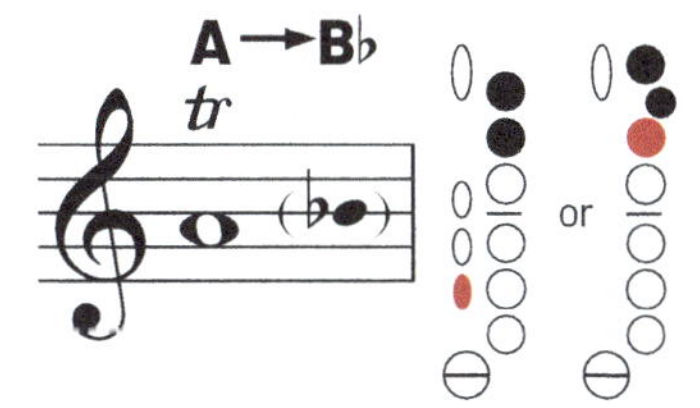

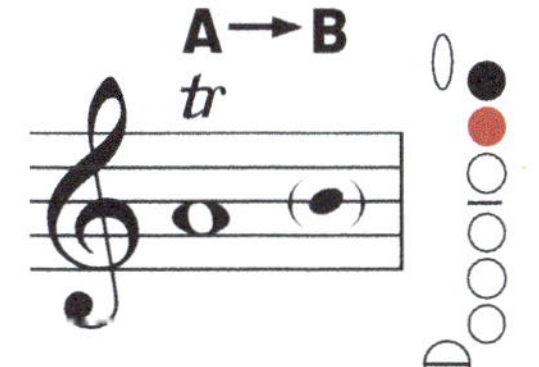

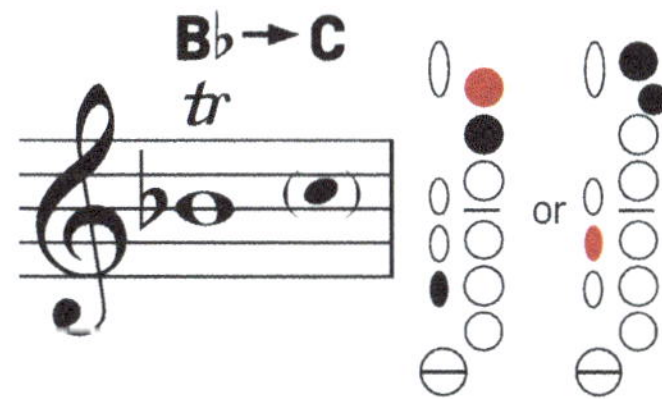

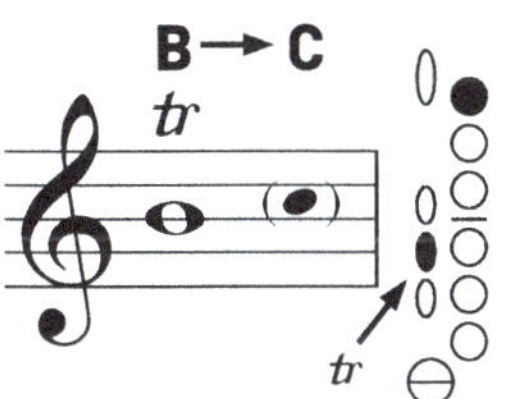

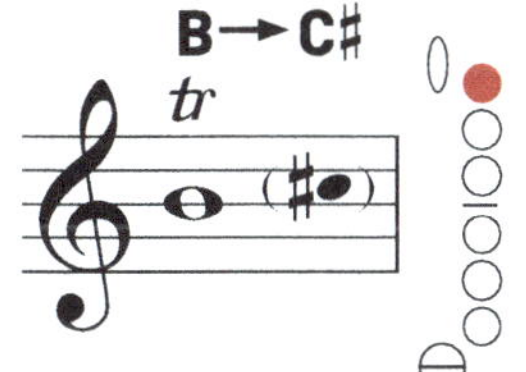

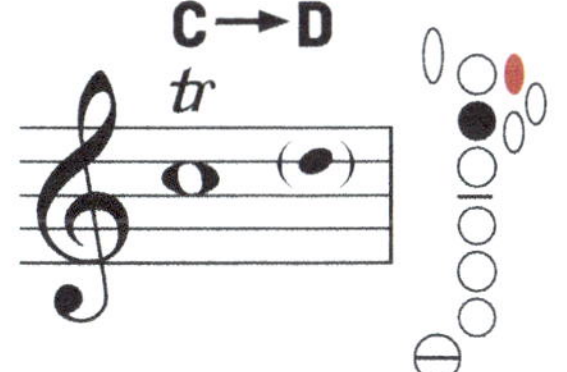

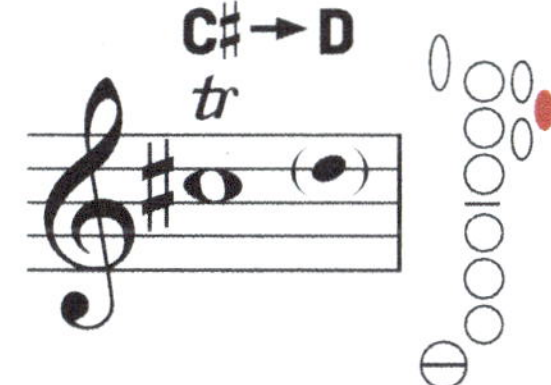

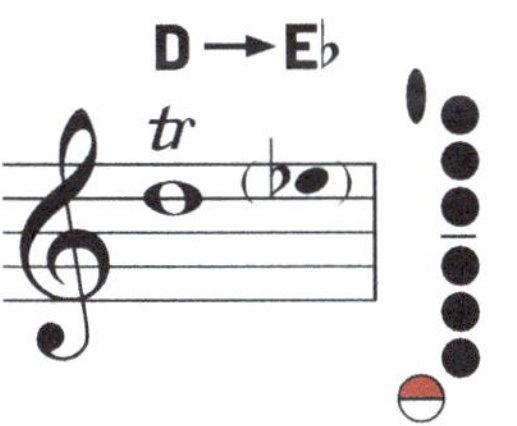

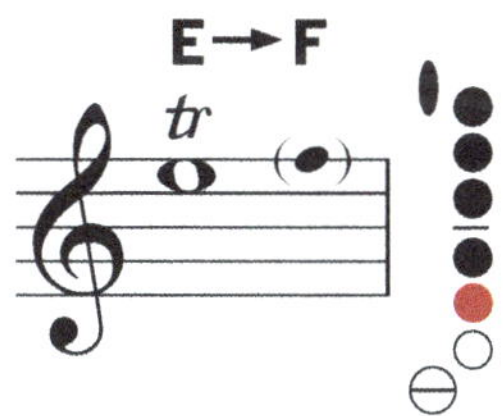

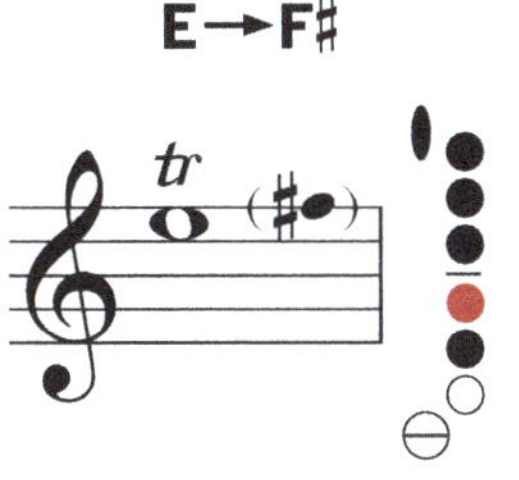

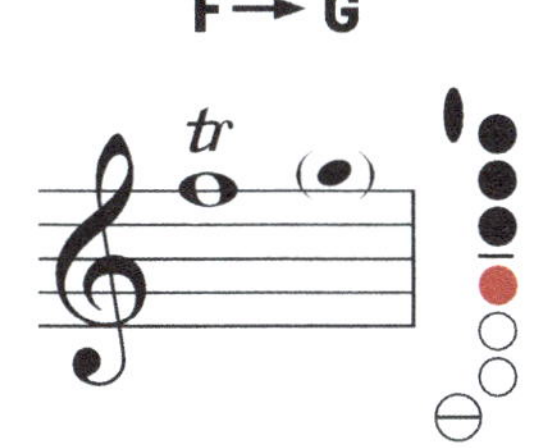

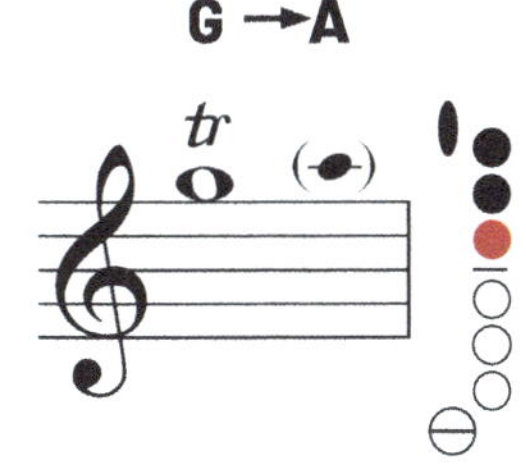

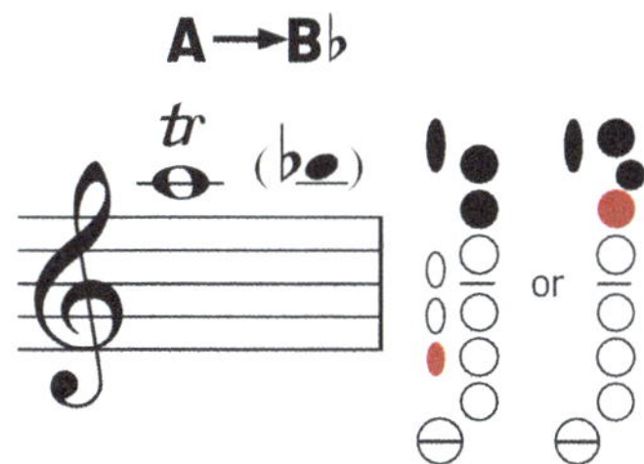

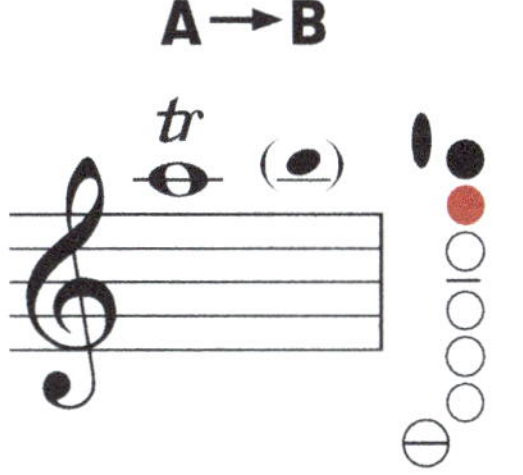

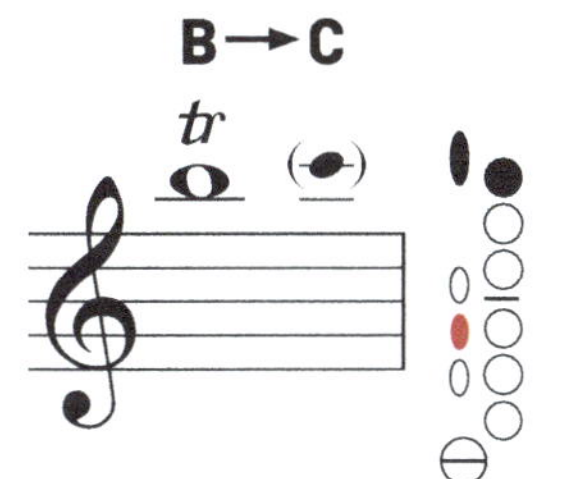

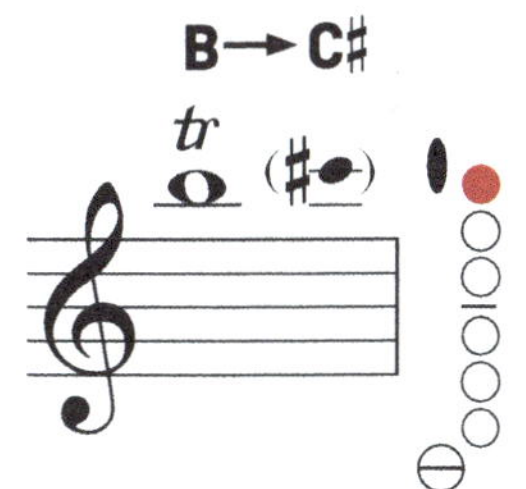

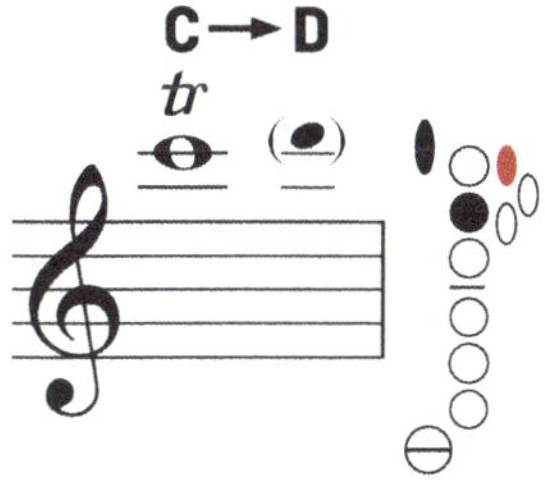

TRILL CHART

B♭ TENOR SAXOPHONE

Here are some common trill fingerings. Trill the **red** key(s).

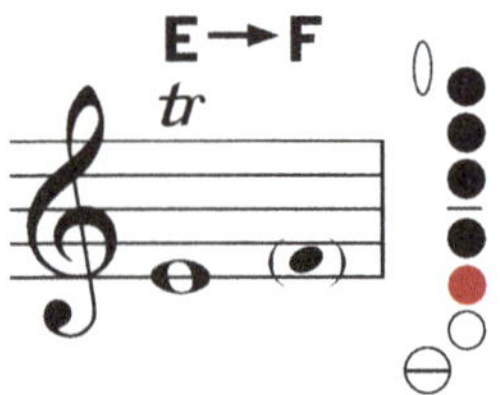

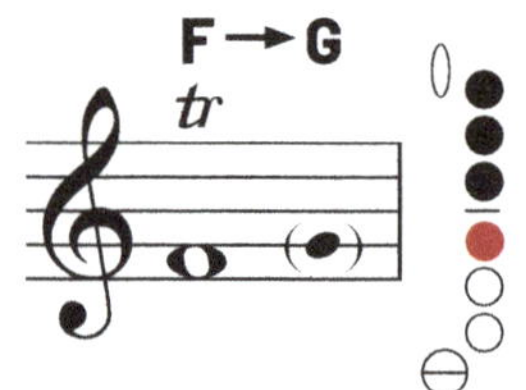

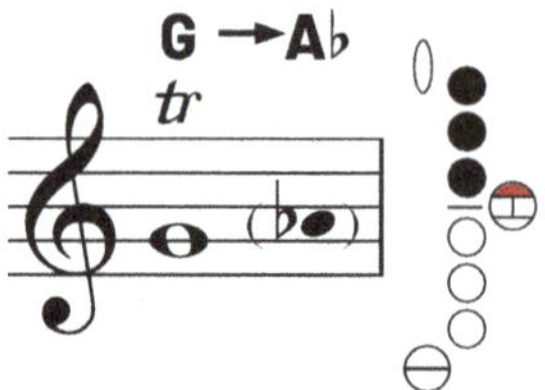

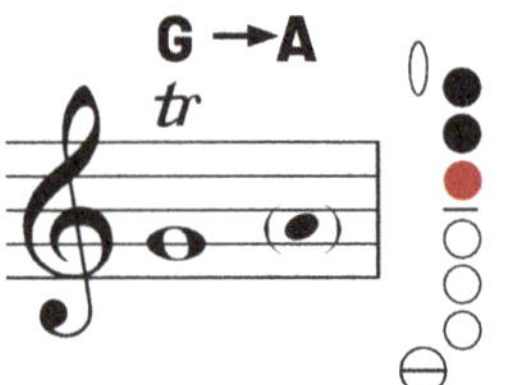

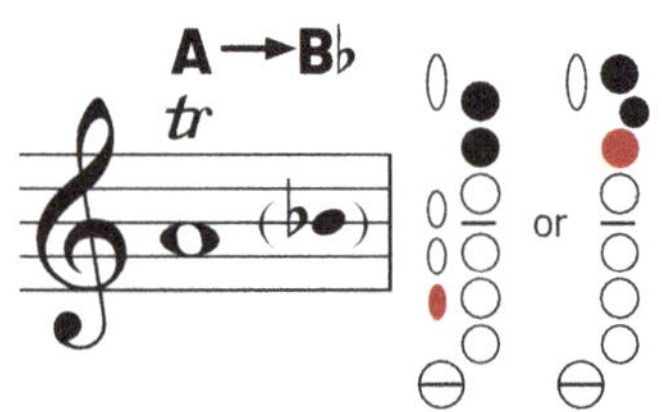

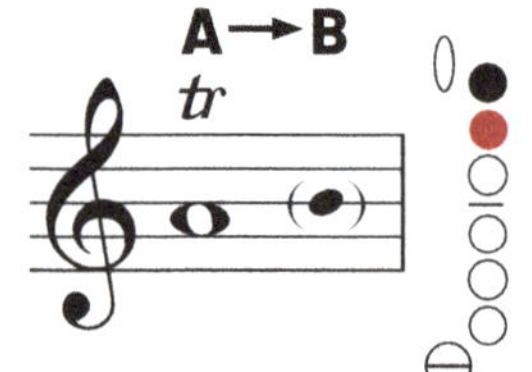

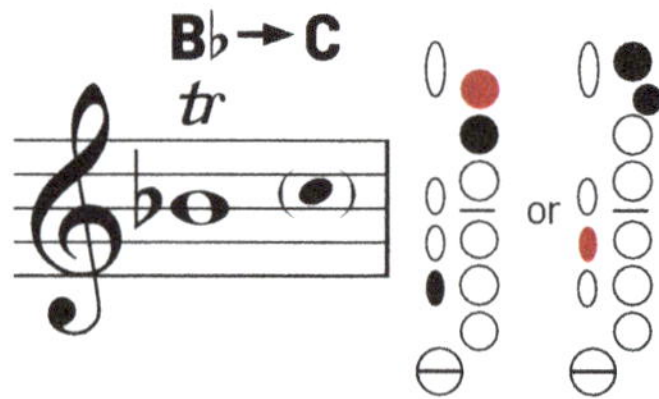

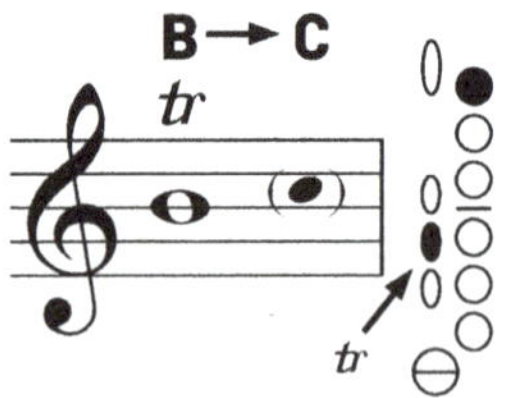

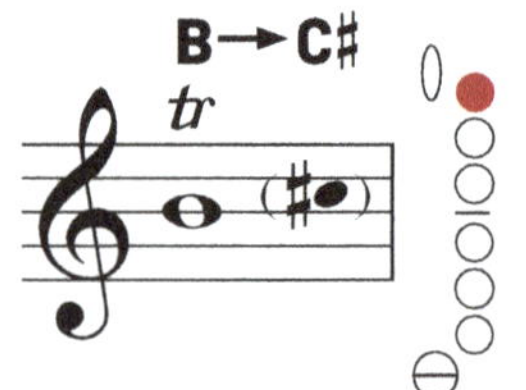

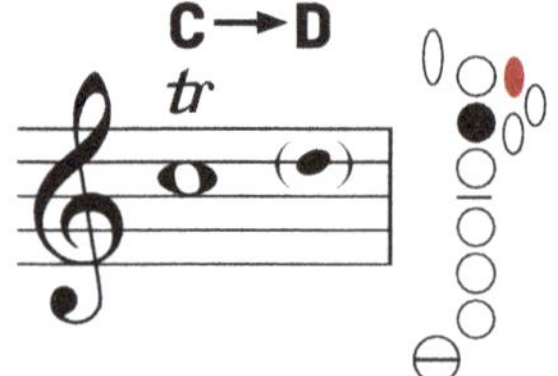

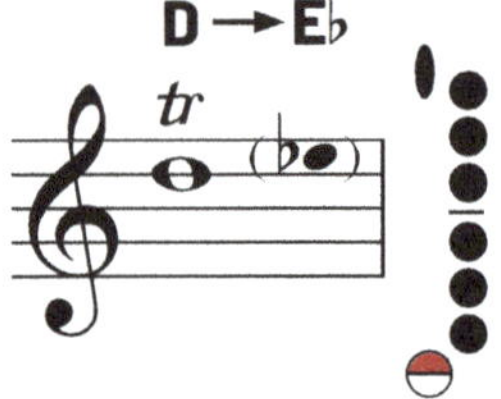

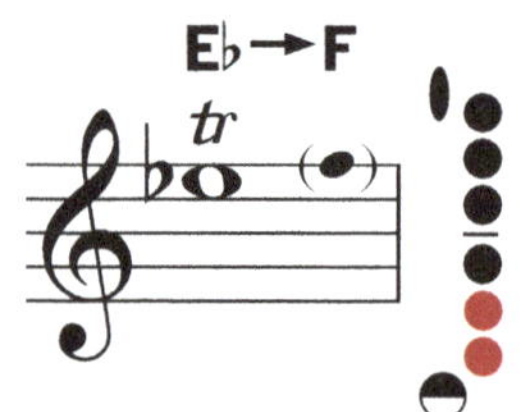

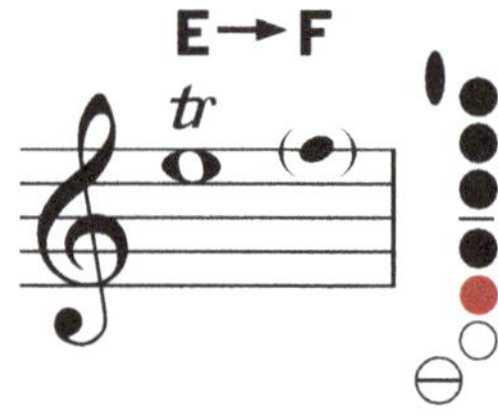

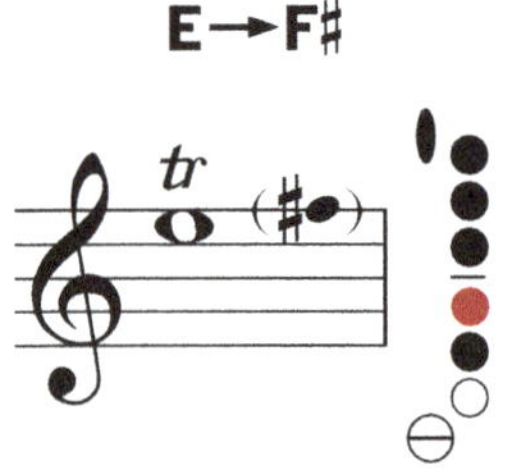

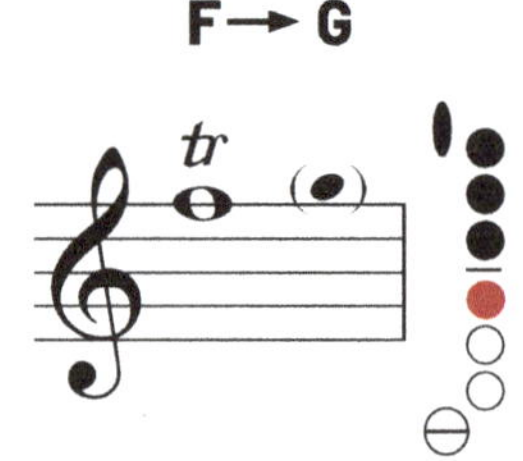

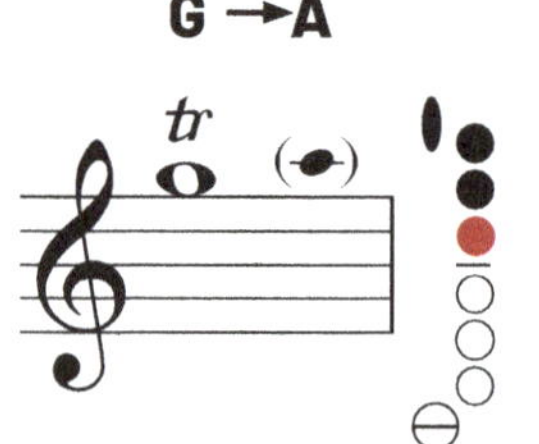

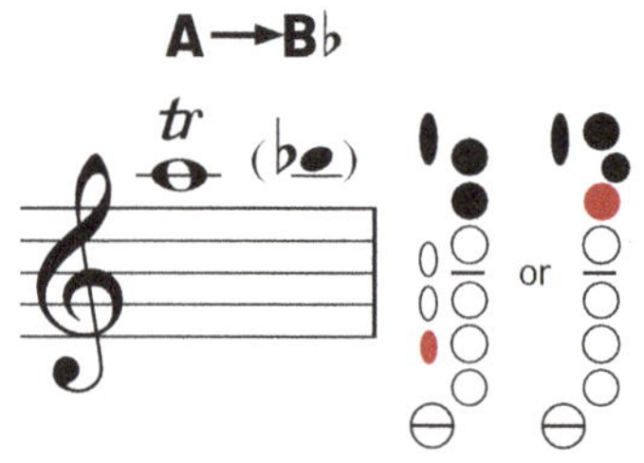

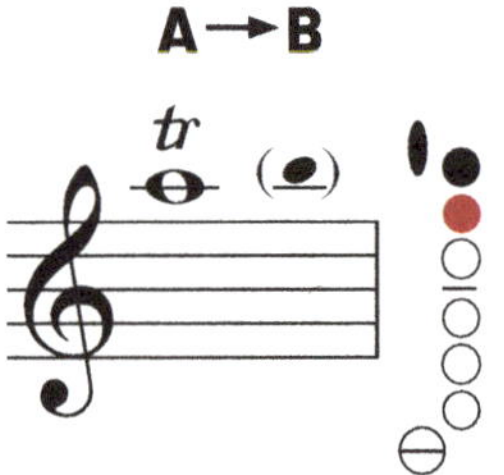

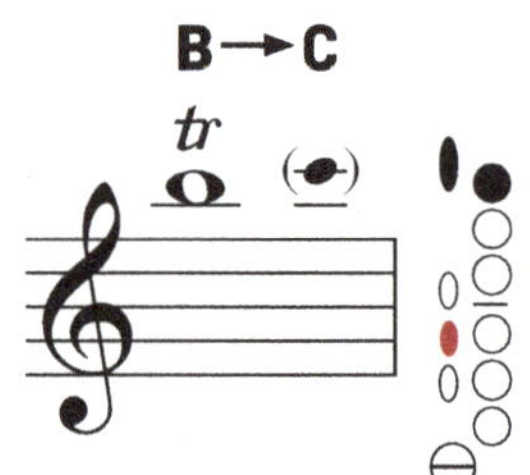

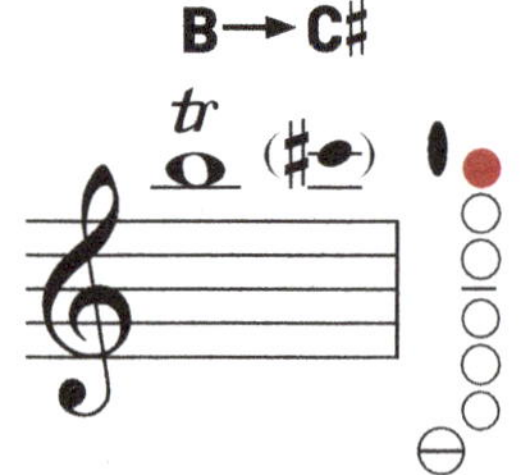

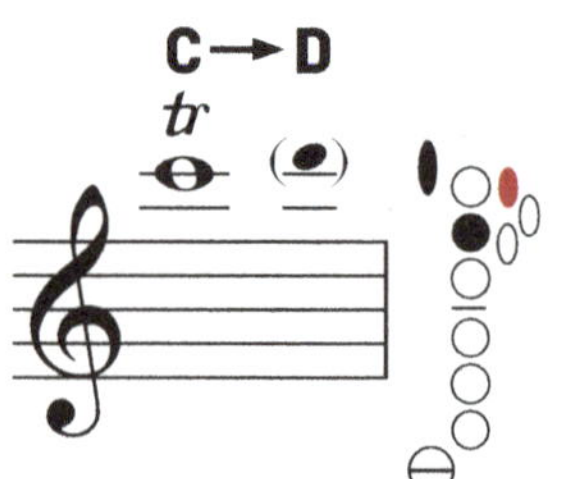

TRILL CHART

E♭ BARITONE SAXOPHONE

Here are some common trill fingerings. Trill the **red** key(s).

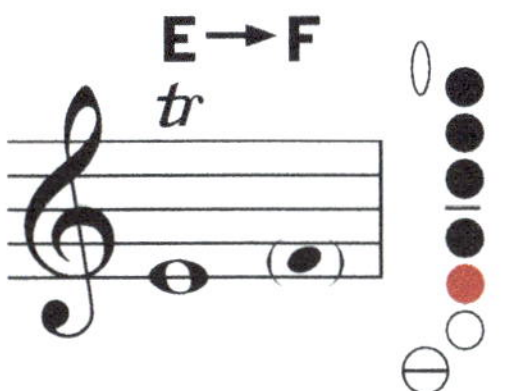

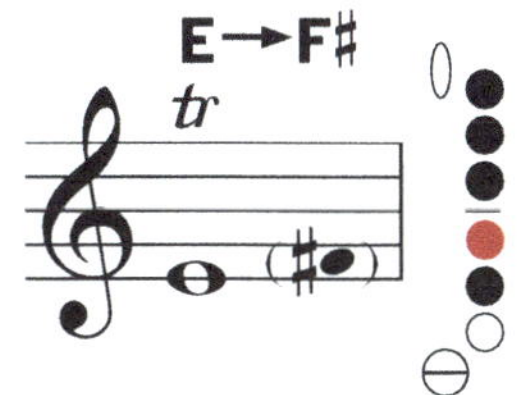

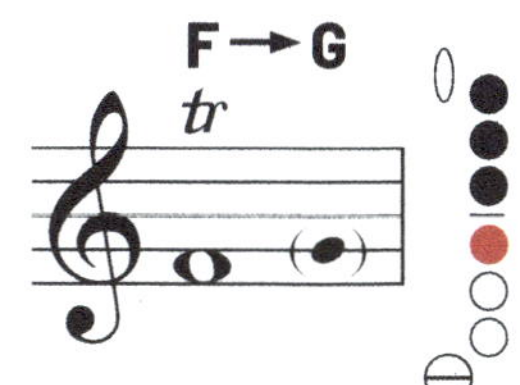

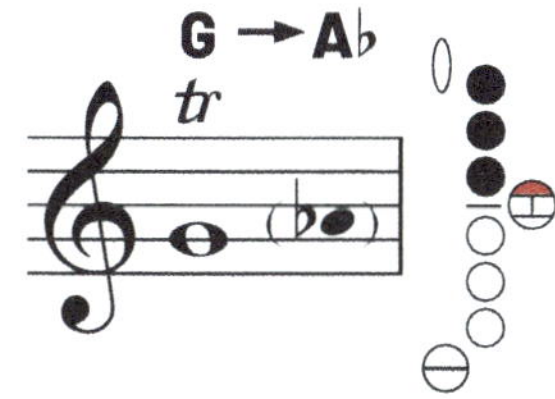

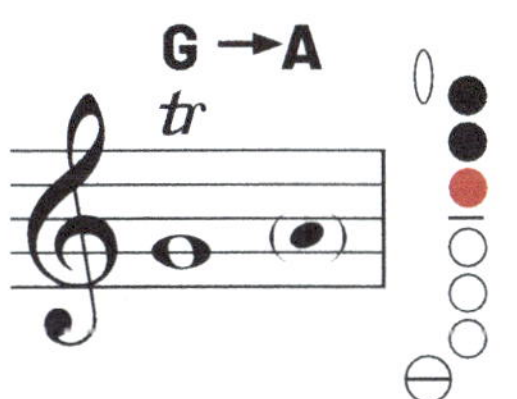

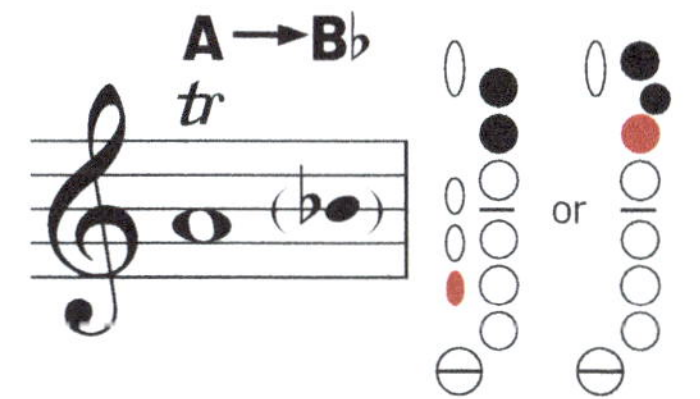

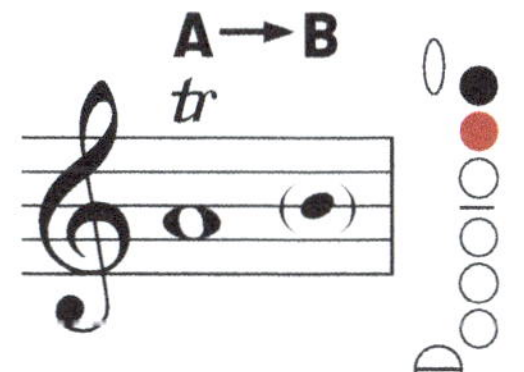

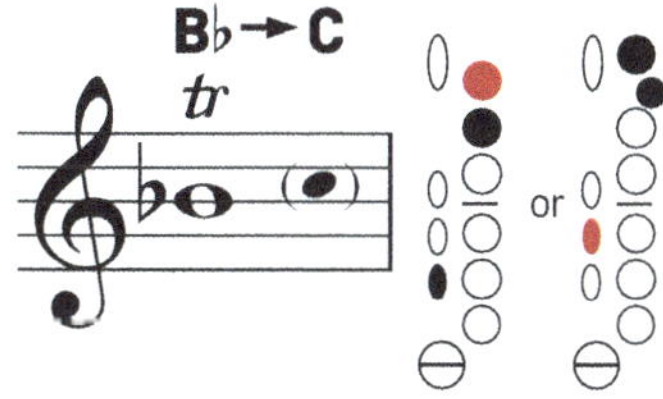

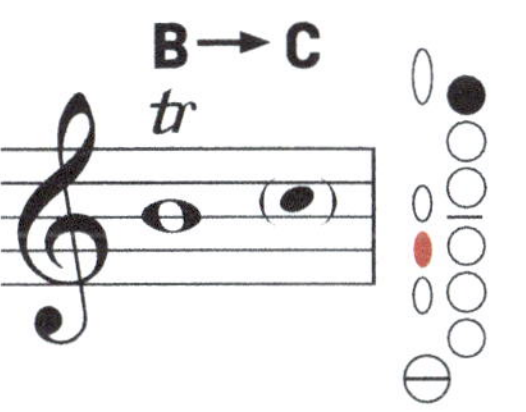

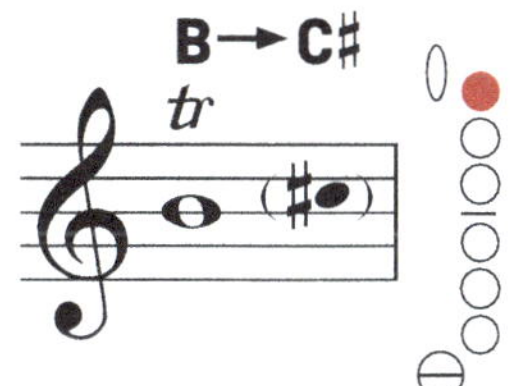

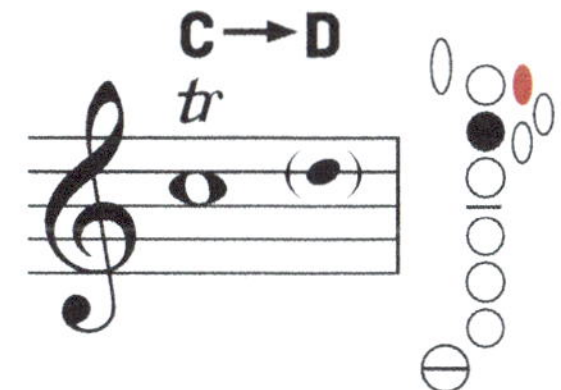

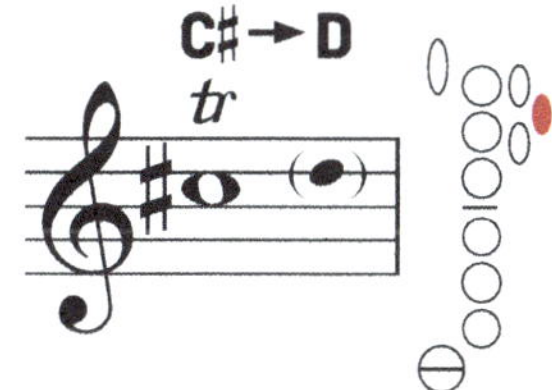

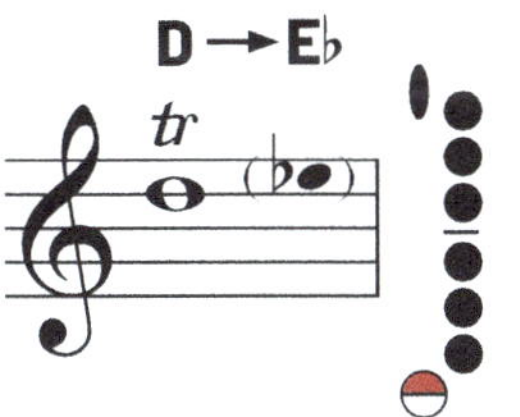

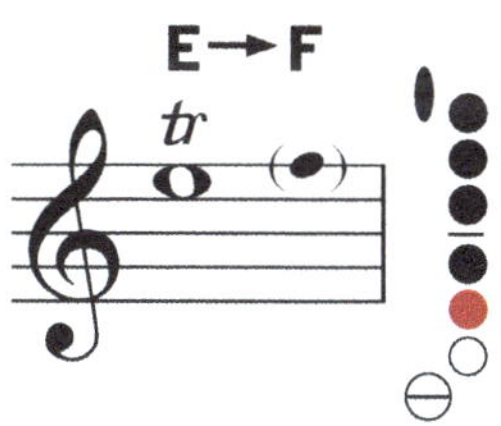

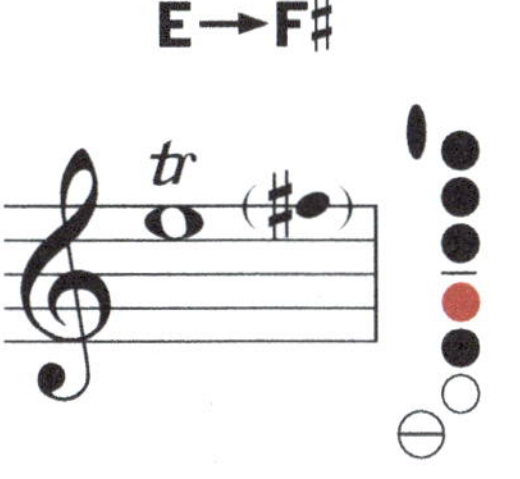

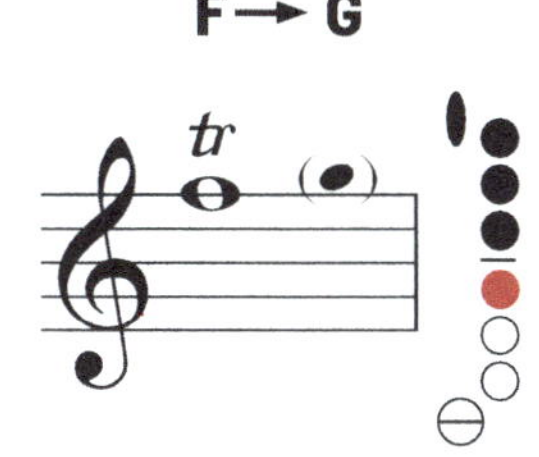

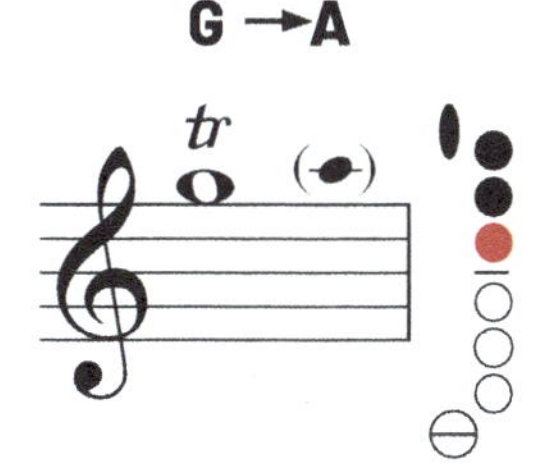

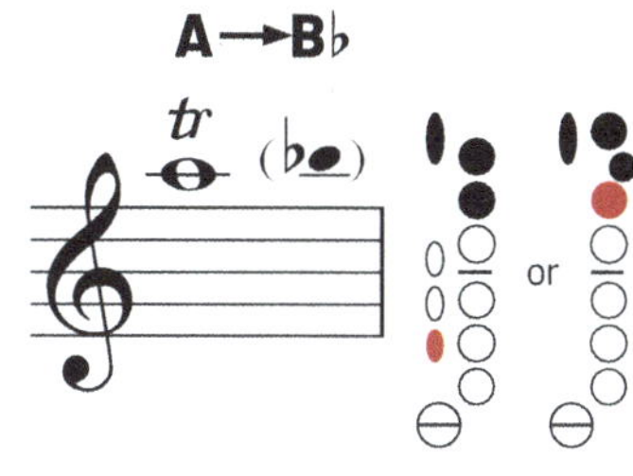

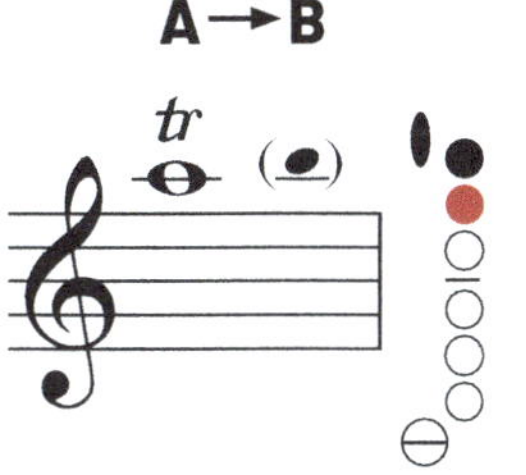

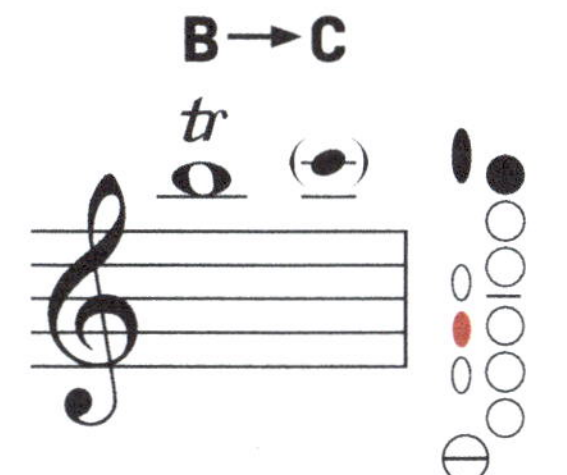

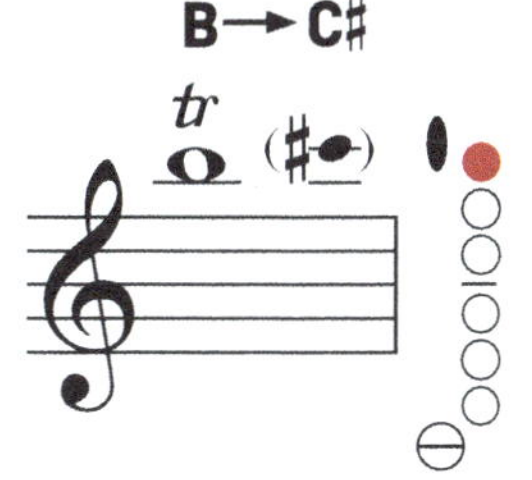

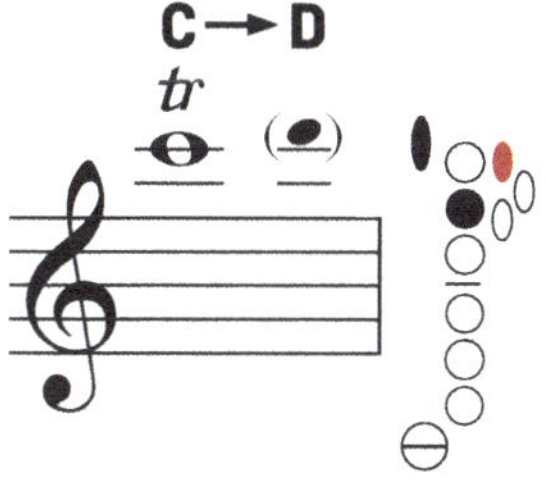

SPECIAL EXERCISES

B♭ TRUMPET

SPECIAL EXERCISES F HORN

SPECIAL EXERCISES
TROMBONE

LIP SLUR STUDY NO. 1

LIP SLUR STUDY NO. 2

FLEXIBILITY FUN

SPECIAL EXERCISES

BARITONE B.C.

LIP SLUR STUDY NO. 1

LIP SLUR STUDY NO. 2

FLEXIBILITY FUN

SPECIAL EXERCISES BARITONE T.C.

SPECIAL EXERCISES

TUBA

LIP SLUR STUDY NO. 1

LIP SLUR STUDY NO. 2

FLEXIBILITY FUN

BASS TIPS
ELECTRIC BASS

HOW TO CHANGE A STRING

If you're missing a string or your strings are old and need replacing, you'll need to know how to change them. The diagram below should help. Once you've inserted the ball-end of a string at the bridge, you need to wrap the other end around the tuning peg at the headstock. To do this, first insert the string in the posthole. Then, bend it sharply to hold it in place, and begin winding. You should allow enough slack to wrap the string around the peg 3 to 4 times; any excess can be removed with a good wire cutter.

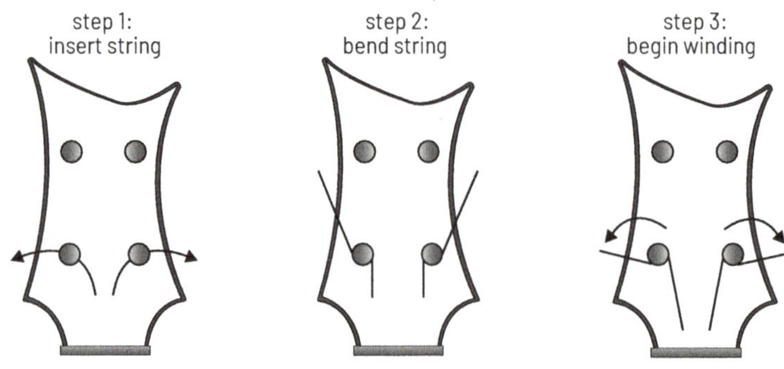

Keep in mind, new strings need to be stretched before you can expect them to hold their pitch. You can do this by playing on them awhile and tuning them up several times until each string remains in tune. (Lightly pulling on the strings one at a time, initially, can also help stretch them out.)

ADJUSTING THE BRIDGE

String height (or "action") can be adjusted by raising or lowering the bridge saddles of your bass. Some saddles require a small screwdriver, but most use a small Allen wrench, which can be purchased at a hardware store if one did not come with your bass at the time of purchase.

THE TRUSS ROD

Remember: your bass is wood (unless you purchased a graphite-neck model). With the changes of season come changes in your bass neck. Most basses have a steel rod through the neck, which can be adjusted to tighten or loosen neck tension. If you notice buzzing to be more frequent, it is a good idea to take your bass in to get the neck adjusted. If possible, watch how a professional does it so you can learn how to adjust the truss rod yourself.

SPECIAL EXERCISES

KEYBOARD PERCUSSION

INTERVALS

OCTAVES

ARPEGGIO ENCOUTER NO. 1

ARPEGGIO ENCOUNTER NO. 2

FINGERING CHART

FLUTE

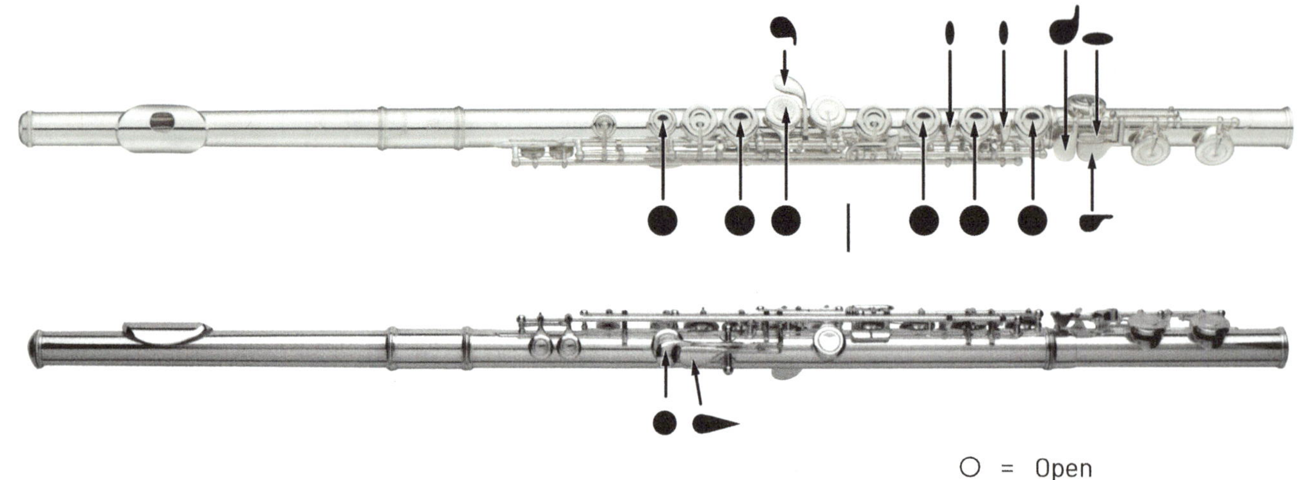

○ = Open

● = Pressed down

The most common fingering appears first when two fingerings are shown.

Instrument Care Reminders

Before putting your instrument back in its case after playing, do the following:

- Carefully remove the head joint and shake any water out.
- Put a clean soft cloth on the end of your cleaning rod and swab out the head joint.
- Twist the middle and foot joints apart and draw the cleaning rod through each joint.
- Carefully wipe the outside of each section to keep the finish clean.

Instruments and photos courtesy of Yamaha.

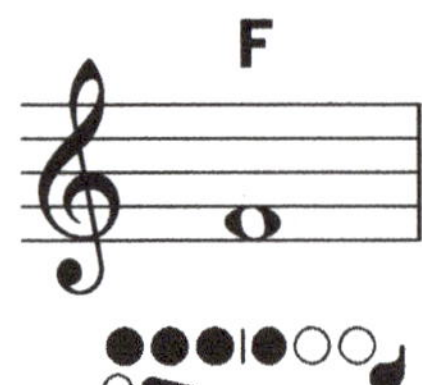

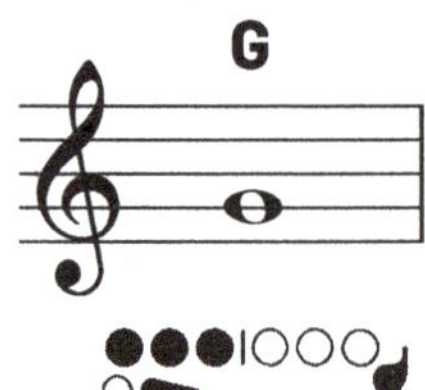

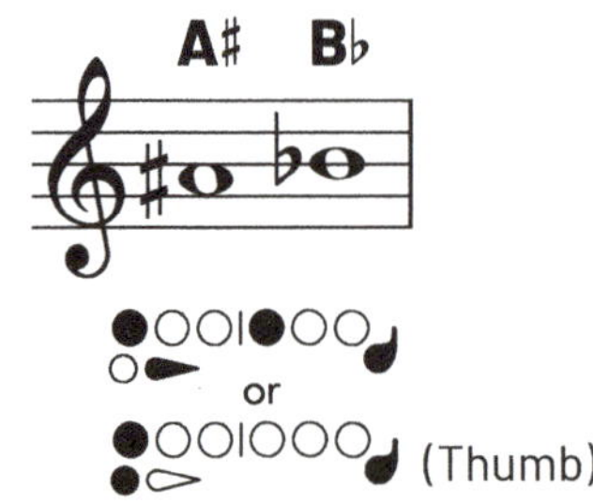

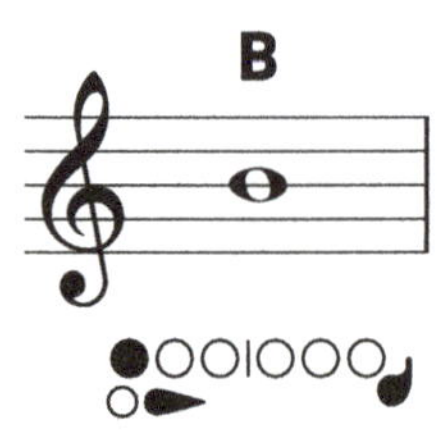

FINGERING CHART

FLUTE

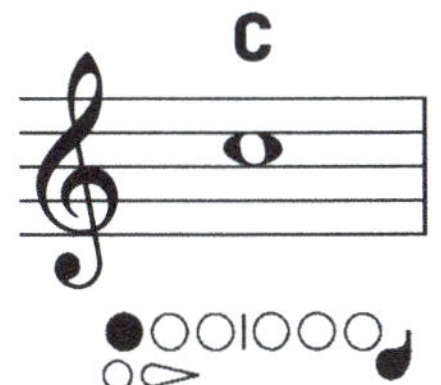

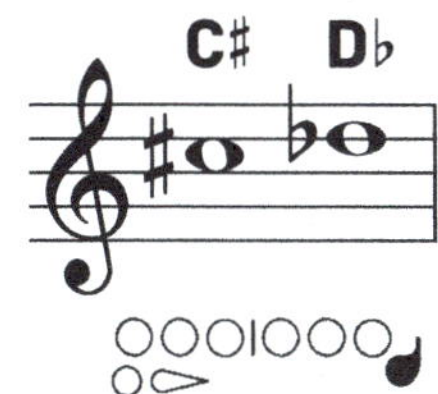

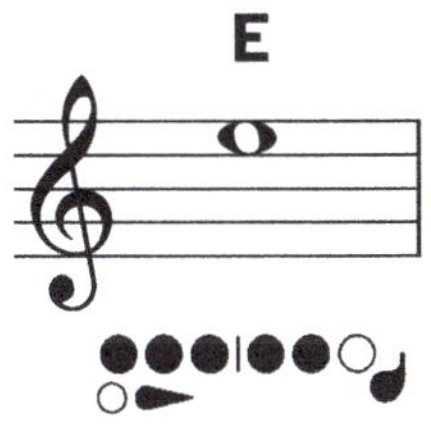

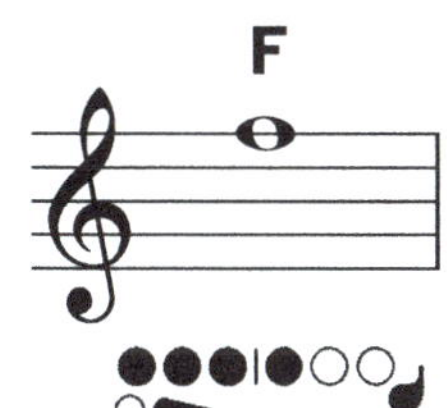

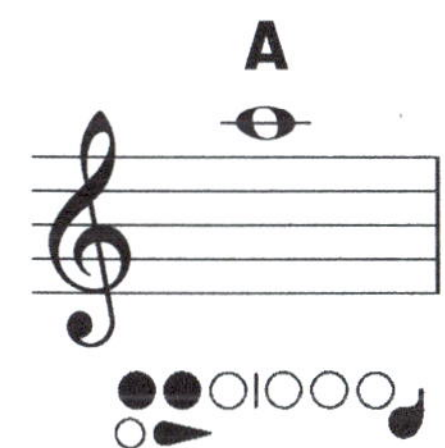

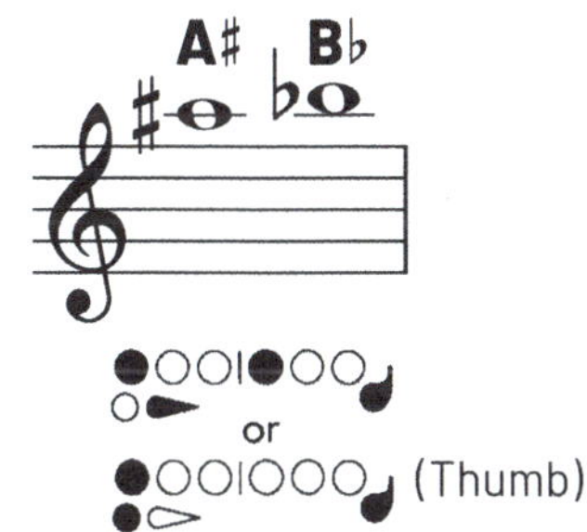

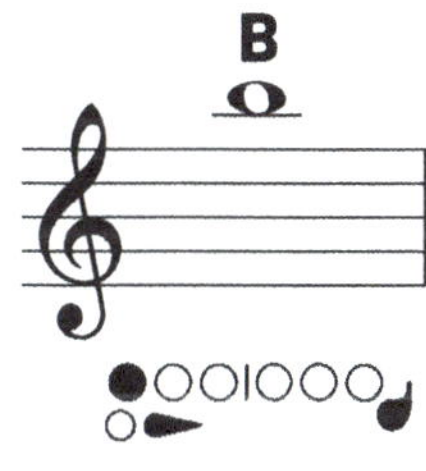

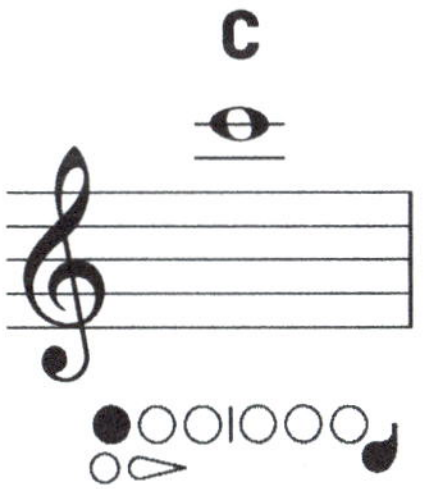

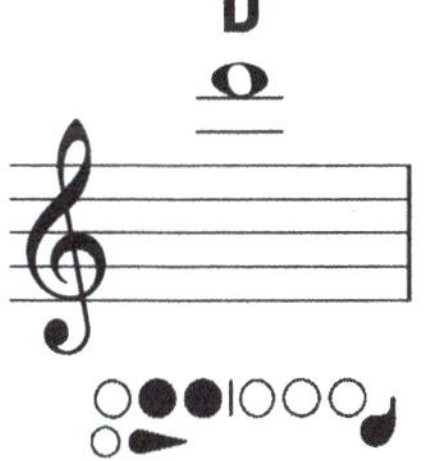

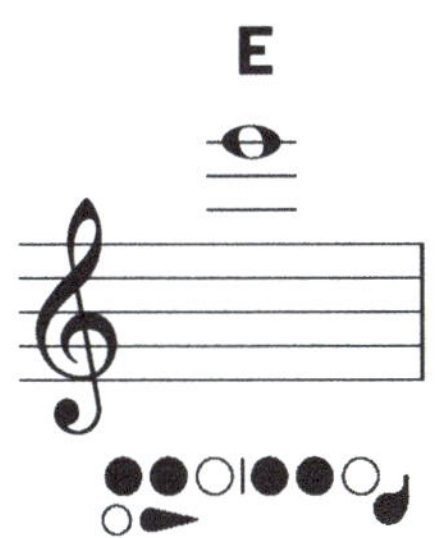

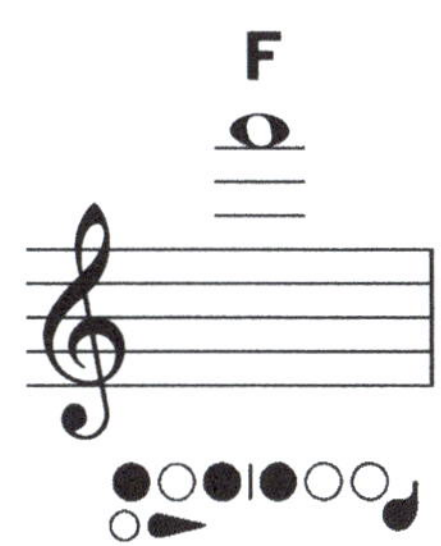

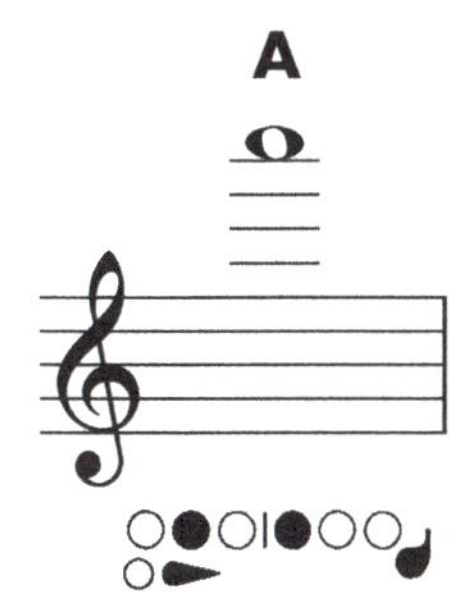

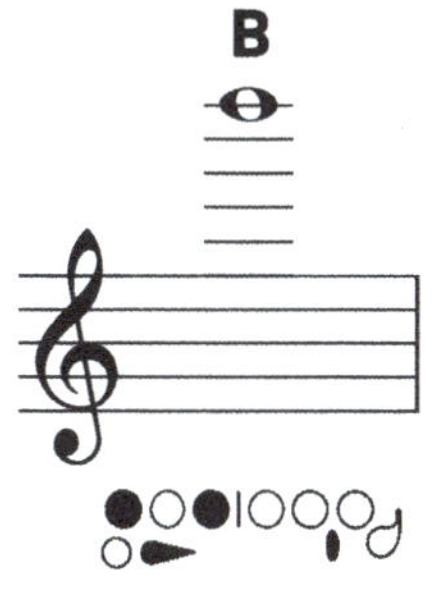

FINGERING CHART

OBOE

Instrument Care Reminders

Before putting your instrument back in its case after playing, do the following:

- Carefully remove the reed and blow air through it. Return to reed case.
- Gently twist apart the upper and lower sections. Drop a weighted swab through the lower section and pull it out the bell. Return the lower section and the bell to the case.
- Swab out the upper section or clean it with an oboe feather and return it to the case.

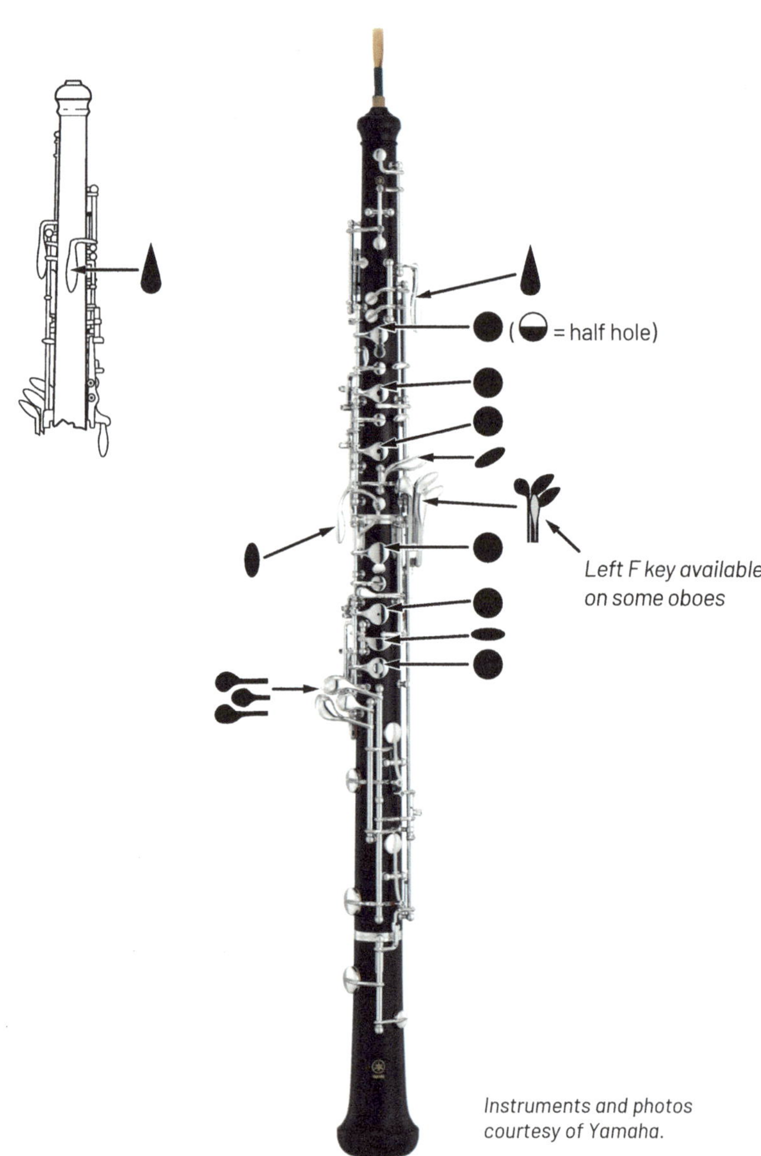

Instruments and photos courtesy of Yamaha.

○ = Open

● = Pressed down

◒ = Half hole covered

○ = Optional

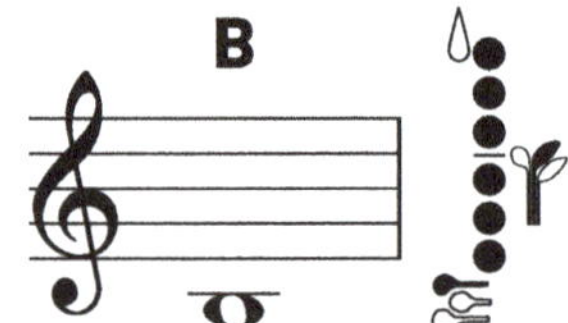

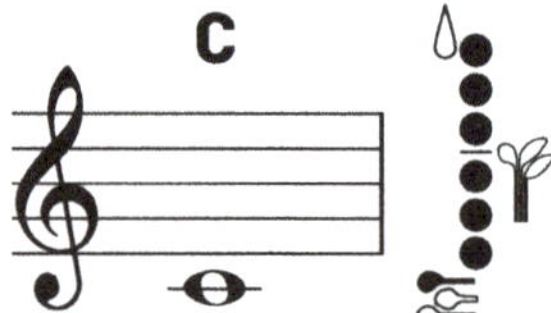

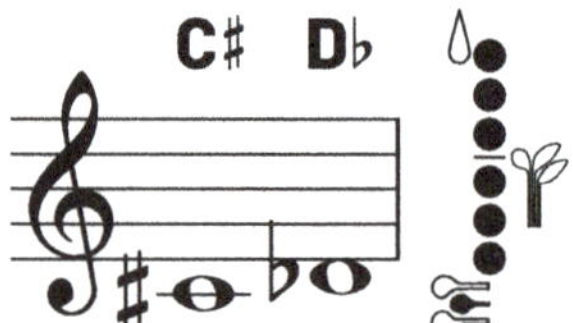

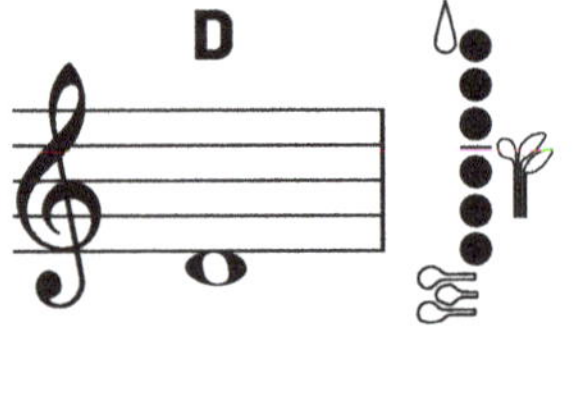

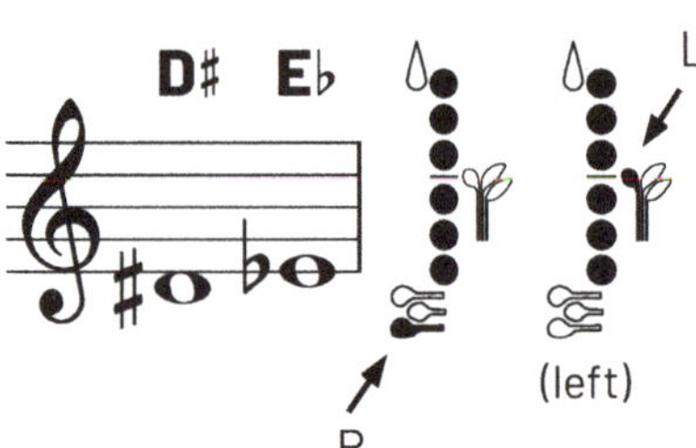

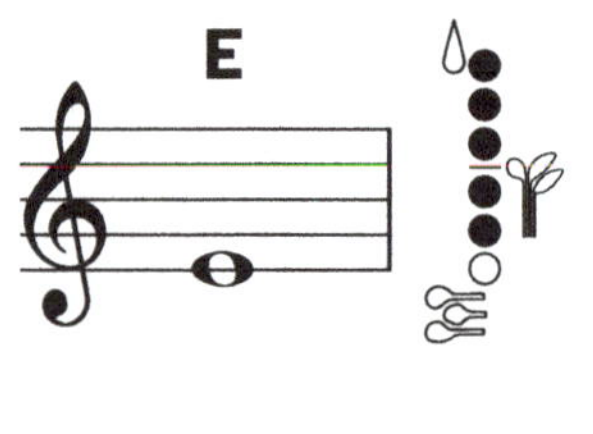

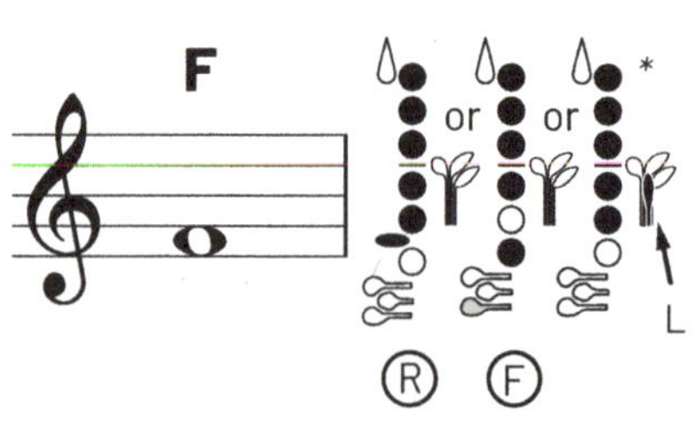

E♭ key raises pitch on Forked F. Only use if needed.

FINGERING CHART

OBOE

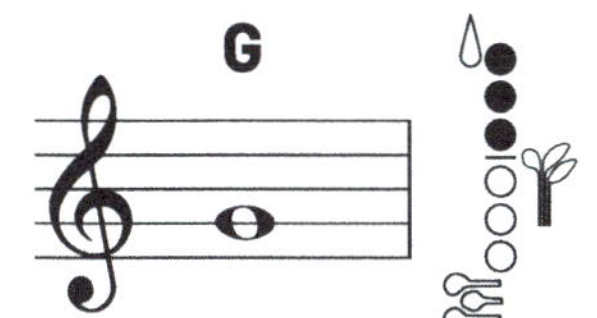

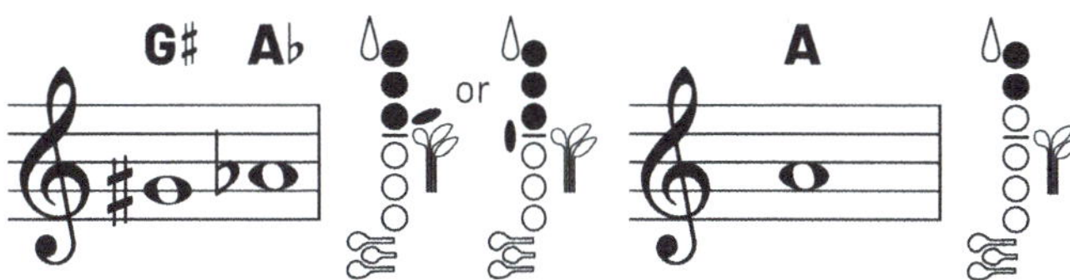

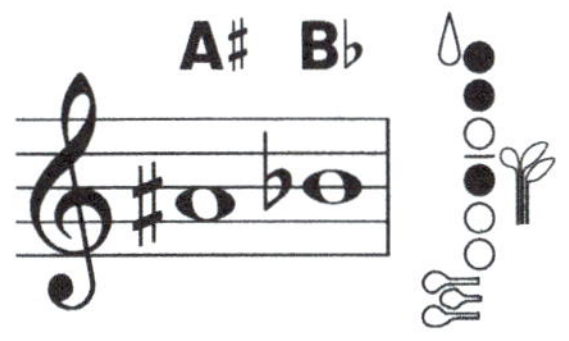

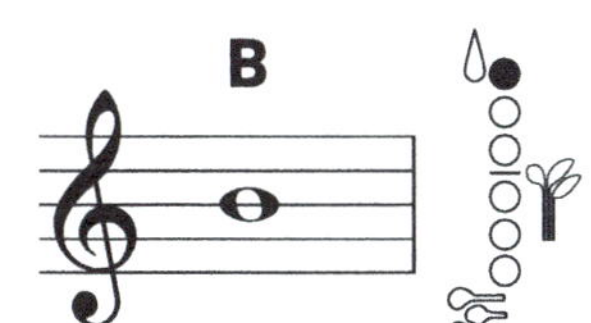

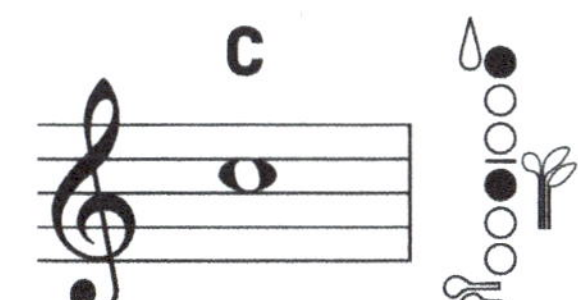

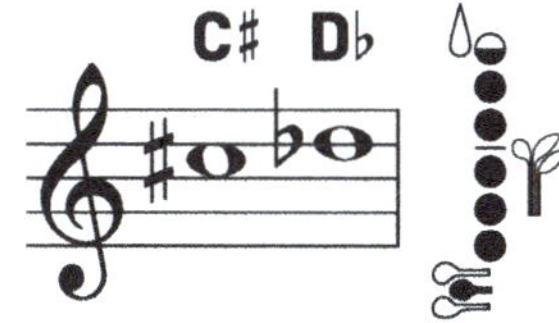

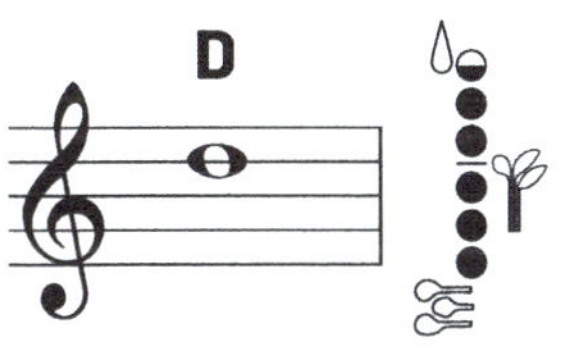

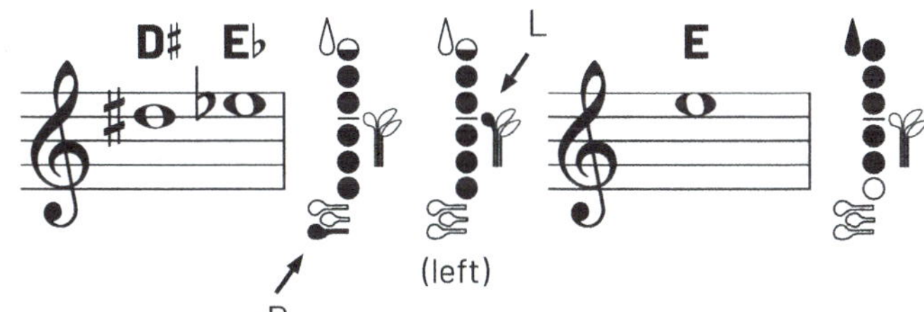

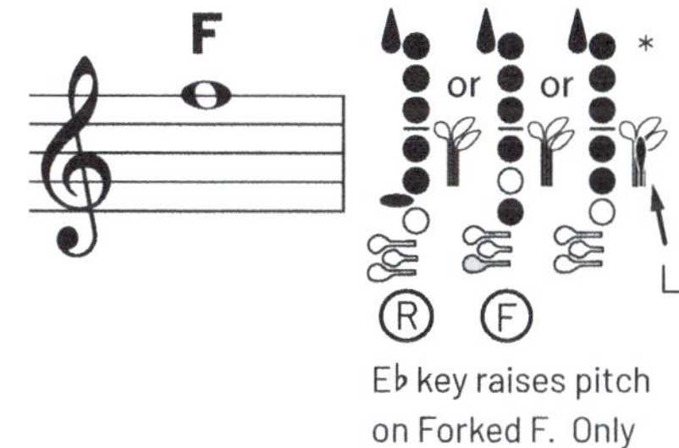

E♭ key raises pitch on Forked F. Only use if needed.

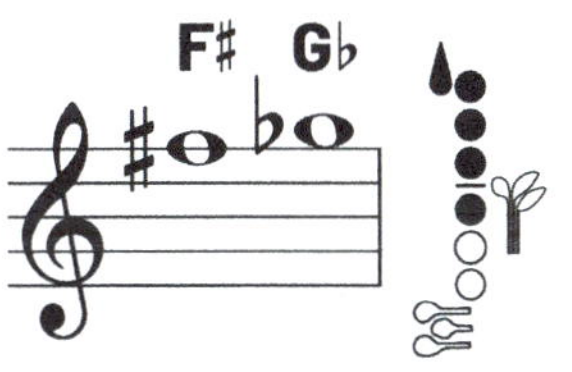

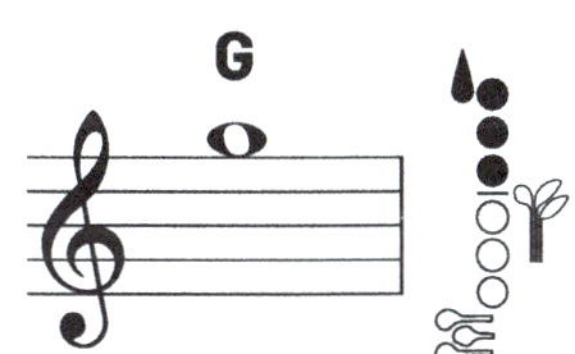

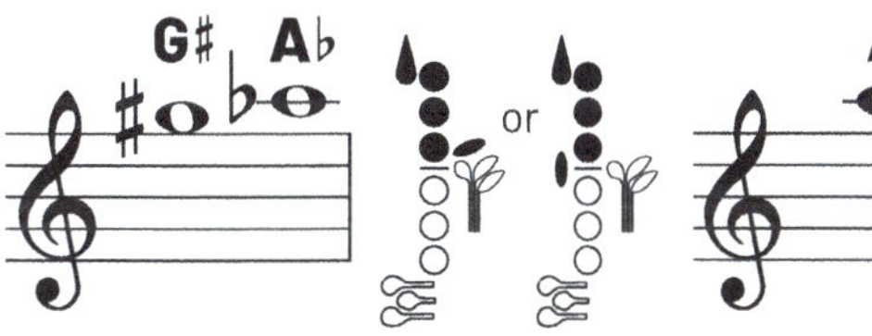

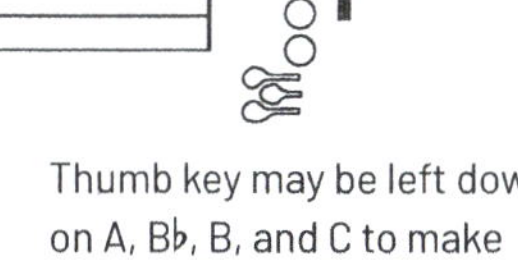

Thumb key may be left down on A, B♭, B, and C to make note changes easier.

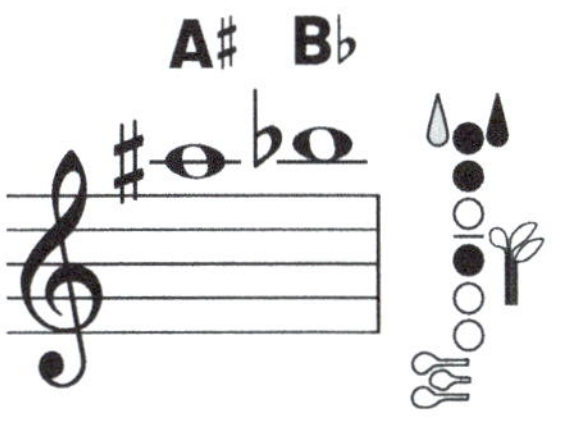

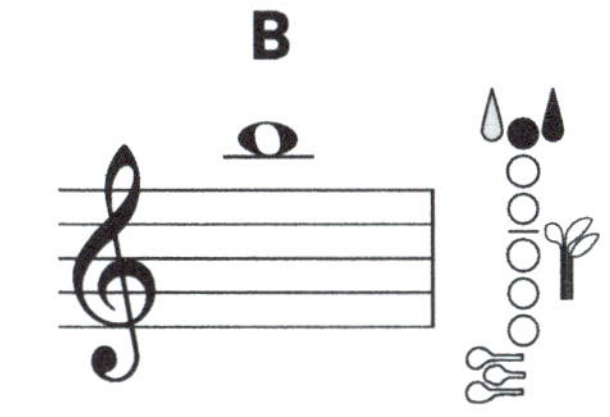

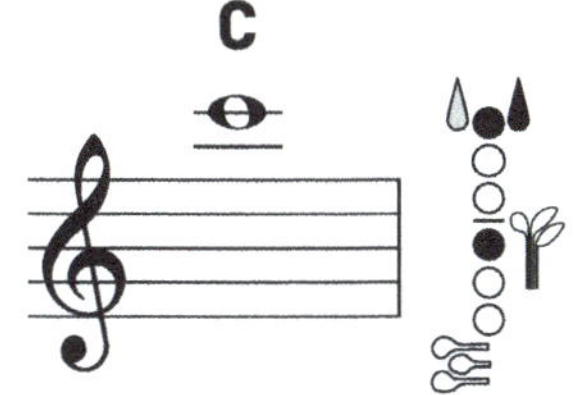

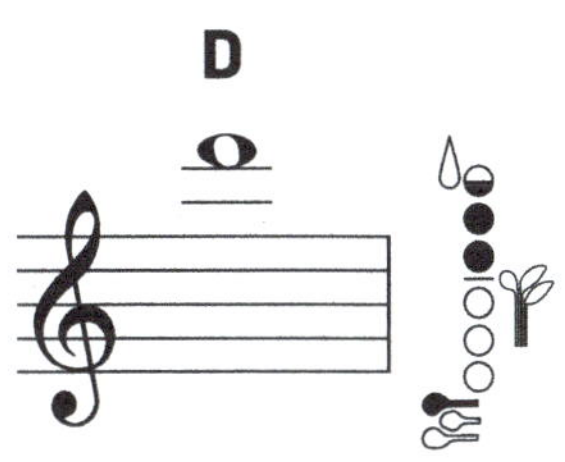

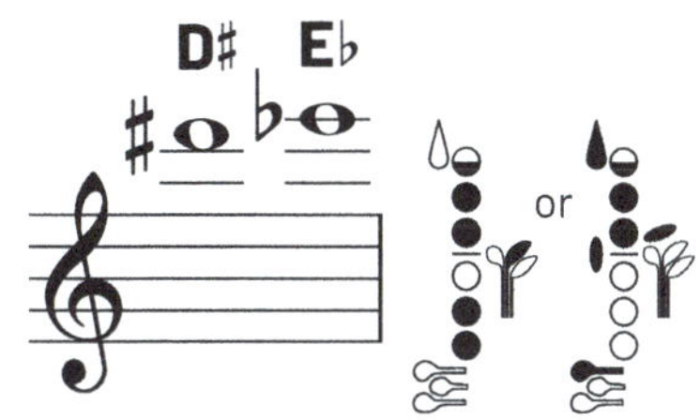

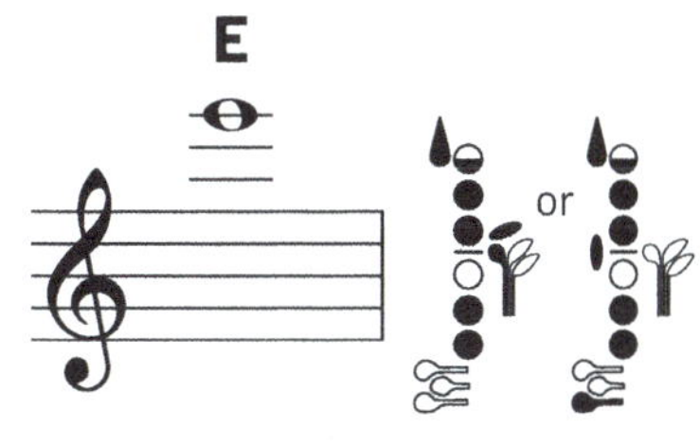

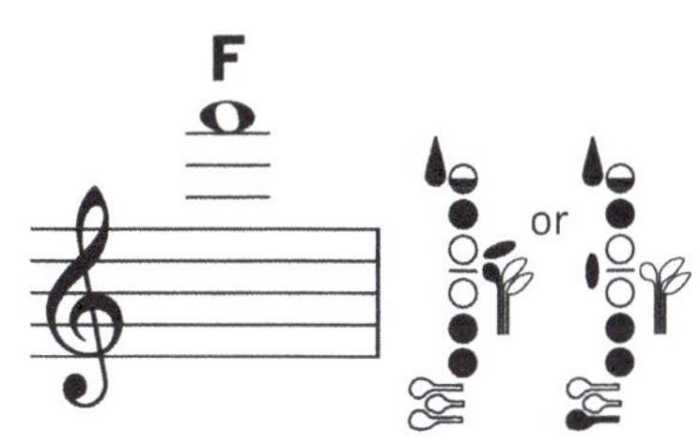

If you play an oboe with a "Left F Key," you may prefer to use the left F in place of the forked fingering.

FINGERING CHART

BASSOON

Taking Care Of Your Instrument

Before putting your instrument back in its case after playing, do the following:

- Carefully remove the reed and blow air through it. Return to reed case.
- Remove the bocal and blow air through the larger end to remove excess moisture.
- Take the instrument apart in the reverse order of assembly. Swab out each section with a cloth swab or cleaning rod. Drop the weight of the swab through each section and pull it through. Return each section to the correct spot in the case.

○ = Open

● = Pressed down

◒ = Half hole covered

● = Flicked

○ = Optional

The most common fingering appears first when two fingerings are shown.

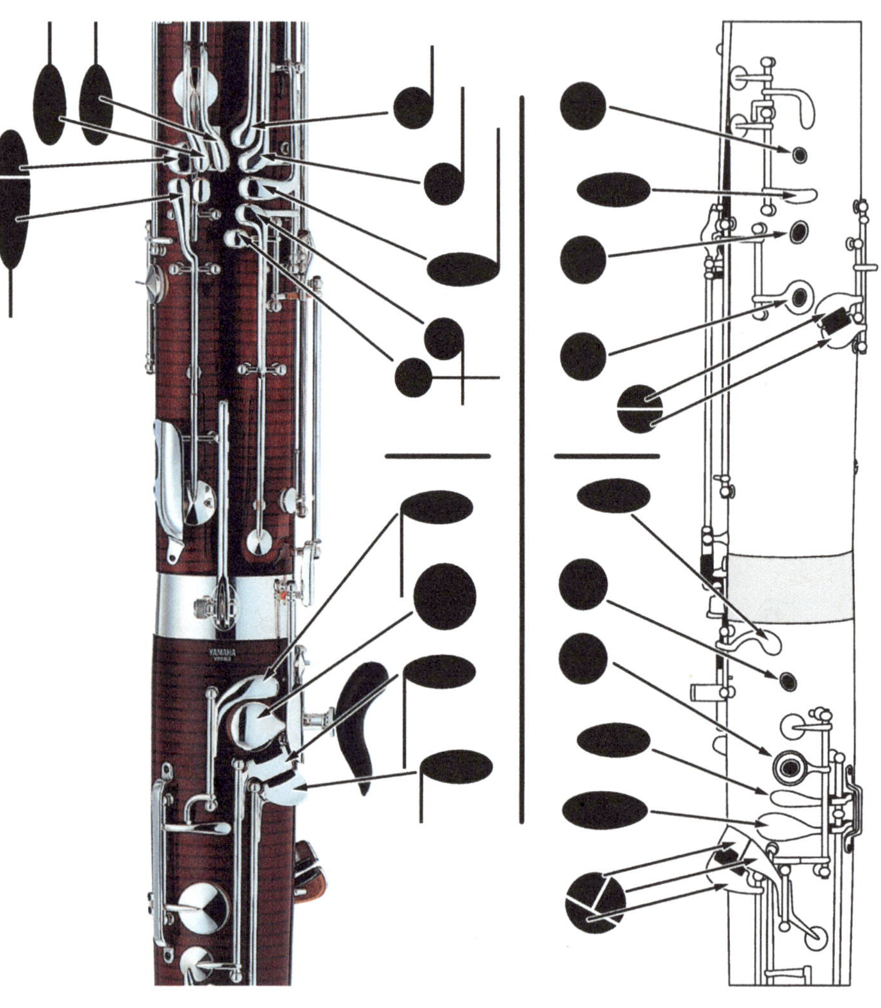

Instruments and photos courtesy of Yamaha.

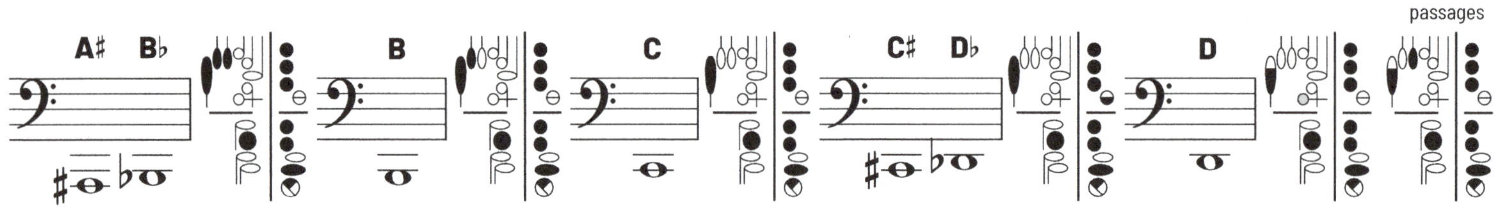

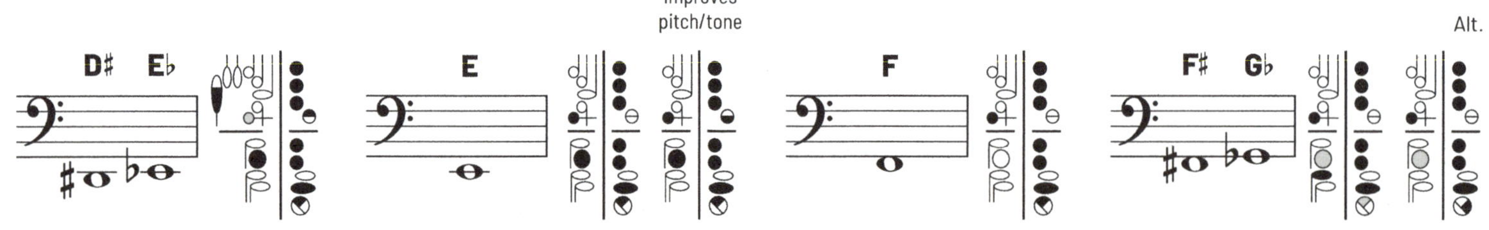

FINGERING CHART

BASSOON

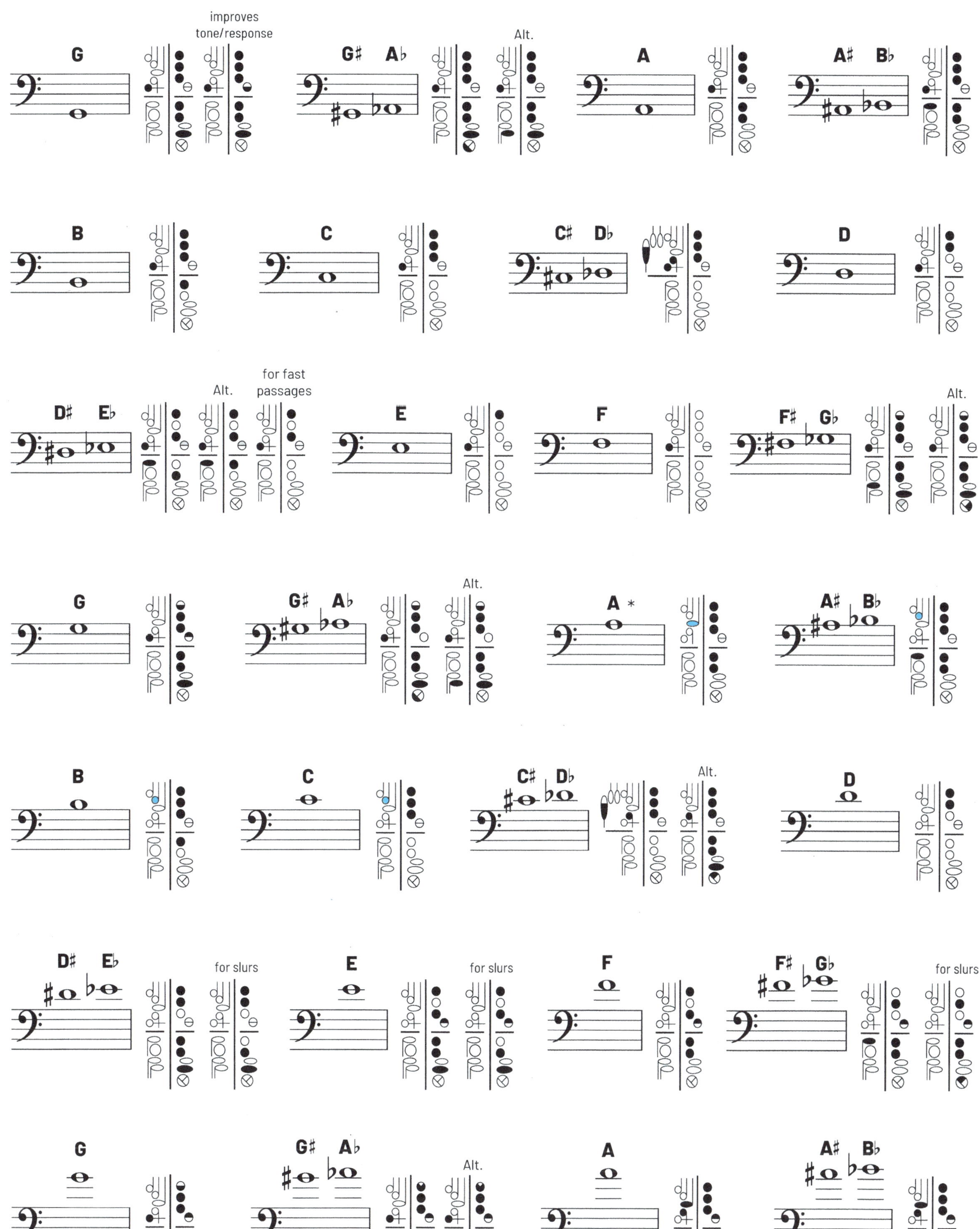

FINGERING CHART

B♭ CLARINET

Instrument Care Reminders

Before putting your instrument back in its case after playing, do the following:

- Remove the reed, wipe off excess moisture and return it to the reed case.
- Remove the mouthpiece and wipe the inside with a clean cloth. Once a week, wash the mouthpiece with warm tap water. Dry thoroughly.
- Drop a weighted chamois or cotton swab into the bell and pull it out through the barrel.
- Carefully twist off the barrel and dry off any additional moisture. Place it in the case.
- Gently twist the upper and lower sections apart, with the bell still attached. Place the upper section in the case.
- Remove the bell and place the bell and lower section back into the case.
- As you put each piece back in the case, check to be sure they are dry.
- Your case is designed to hold only specific objects. If you try to force anything else into the case, it may damage your instrument.

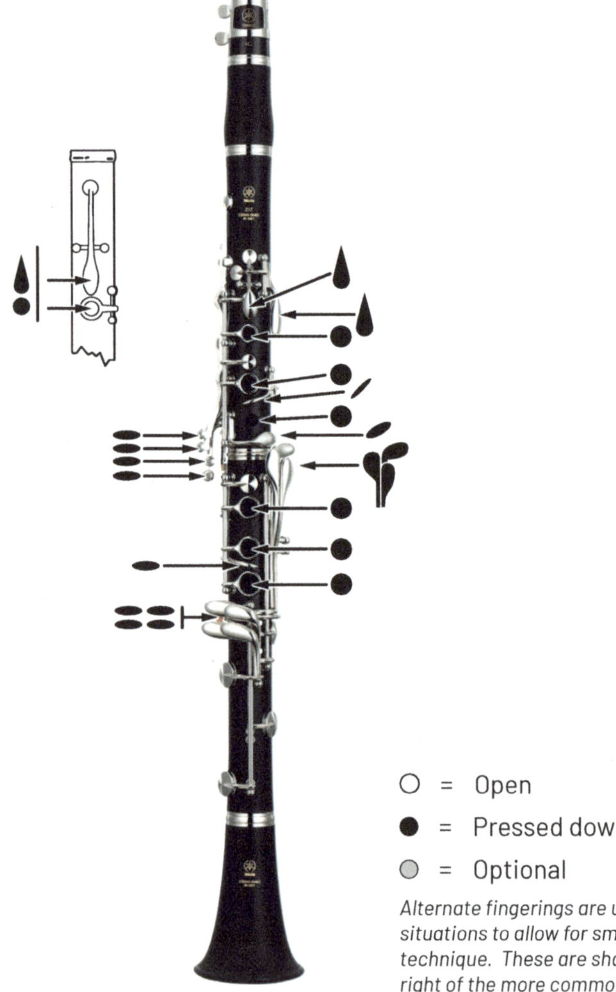

○ = Open

● = Pressed down

◐ = Optional

Alternate fingerings are used in certain situations to allow for smoother technique. These are shown to the right of the more common fingerings.

Instruments and photos courtesy of Yamaha.

1-and-1

FINGERING CHART

B♭ CLARINET

* a) Adding all or some of the gray fingers can help with note changes in various playing situations.
b) Adding different combinations of gray fingerings can also improve tone quality and intonation depending on the model of your clarinet.

FINGERING CHART

E♭ ALTO CLARINET

Instrument Care Reminders

Before putting your instrument back in its case after playing, do the following:

- Remove the reed, wipe off excess moisture and return it to the reed case.
- Remove the mouthpiece and wipe the inside with a clean cloth. Once a week, wash the mouthpiece with warm tap water. Dry thoroughly.
- Remove the neck and bell, and shake out excess moisture. Return them to the case.
- Drop a weighted chamois or cotton swab into the body of the instrument and pull it out the bottom.
- If the body of your alto clarinet has two sections, gently twist them apart. Return the body section(s) to the case.
- As you put each piece back in the case, check to be sure they are dry.
- Your case is designed to hold only specific objects. If you try to force anything else into the case, it may damage your instrument.

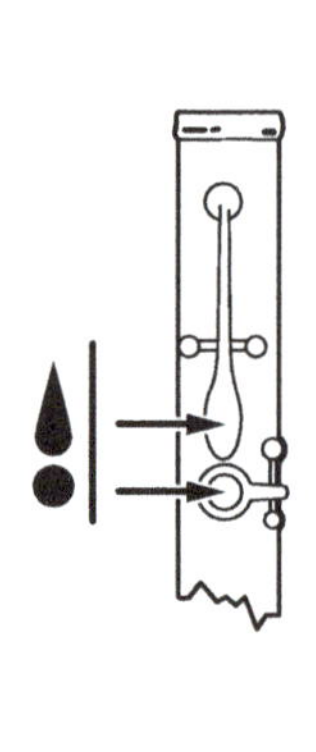

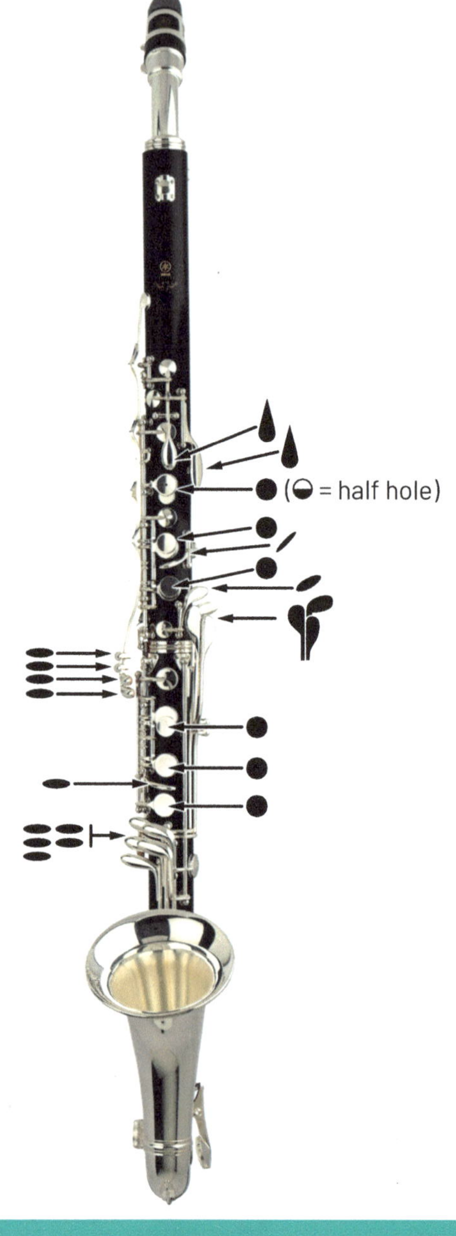

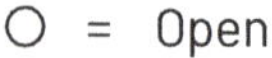

○ = Open

● = Pressed down

Alternate fingerings are used in certain situations to allow for smoother technique. These are shown to the right of the more common fingerings.

Instruments and photos courtesy of Yamaha.

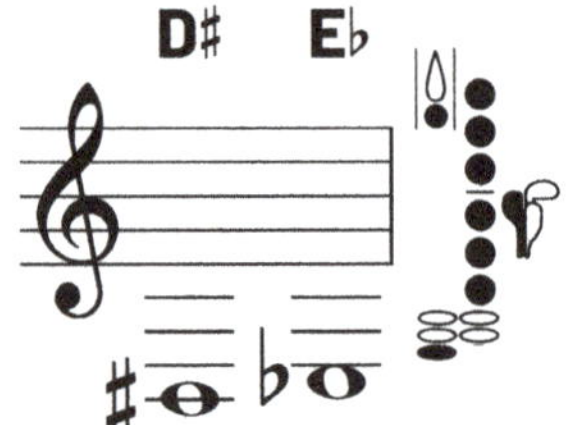

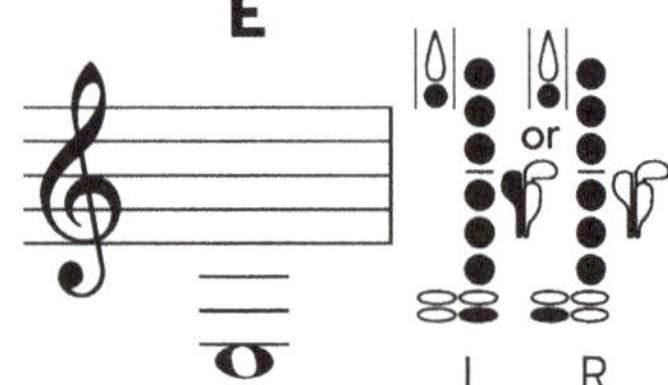

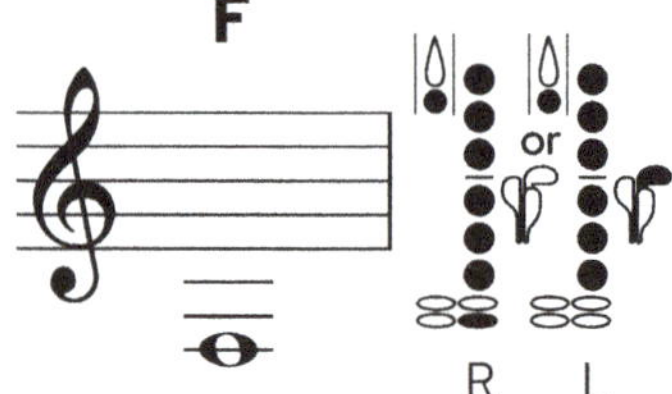

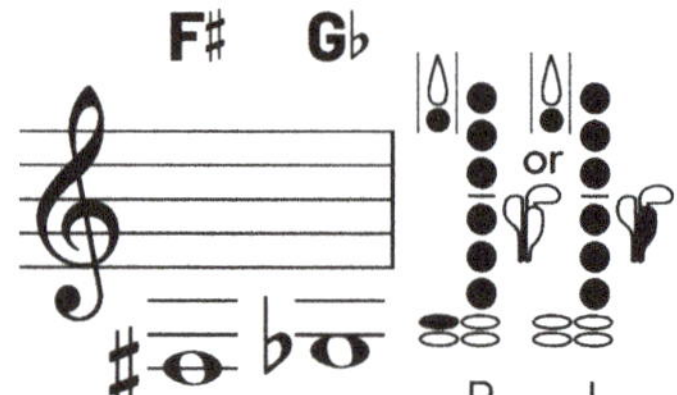

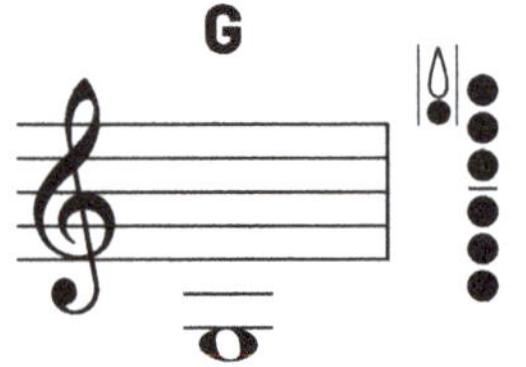

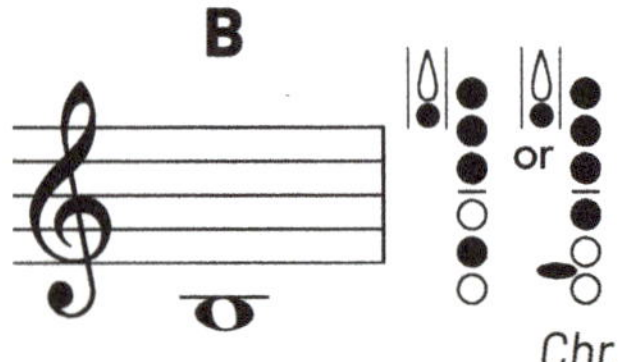

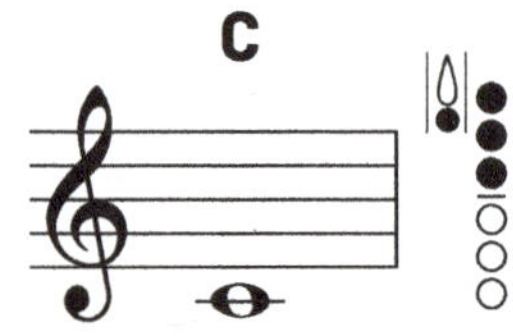

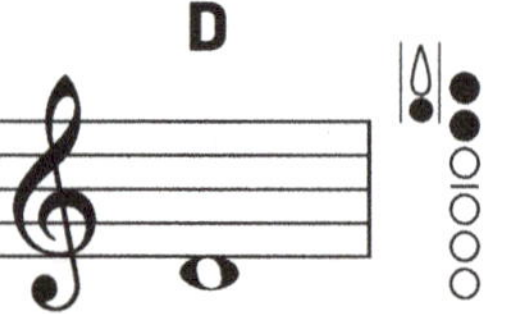

FINGERING CHART

E♭ ALTO CLARINET

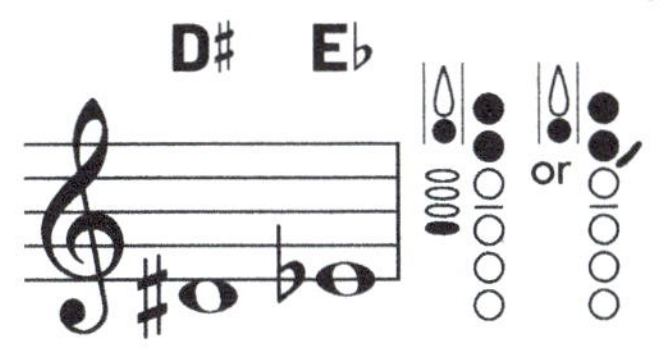

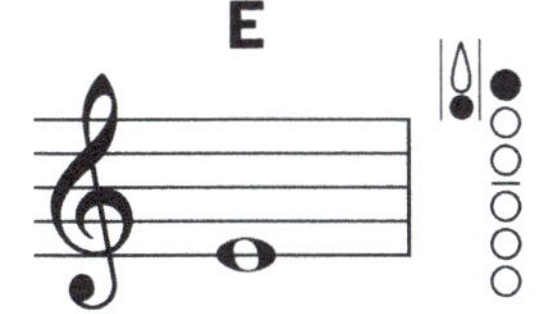

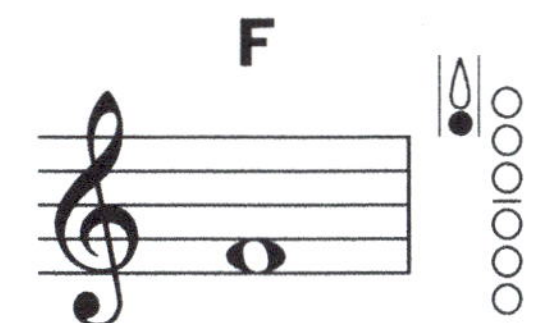

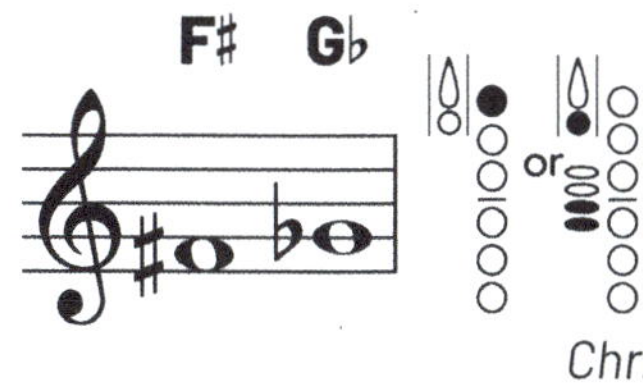

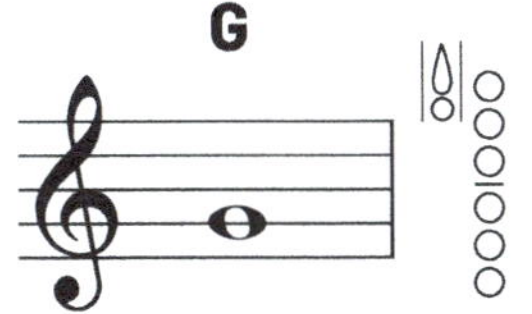

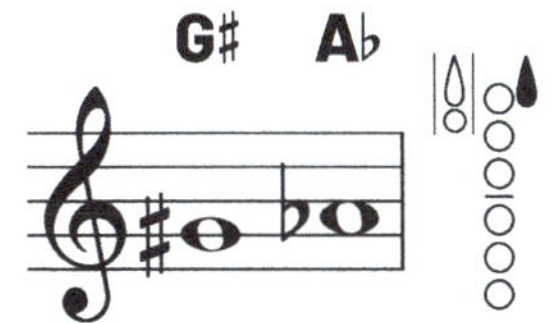

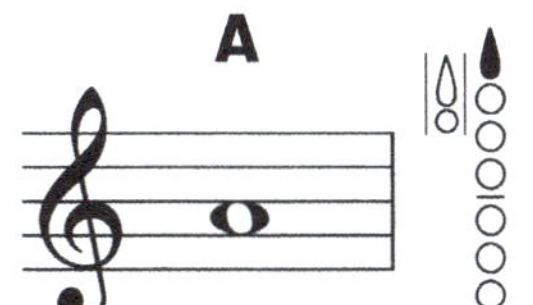

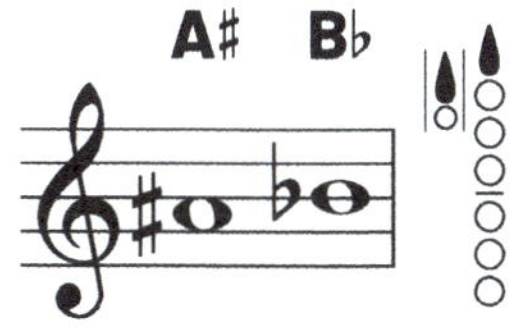

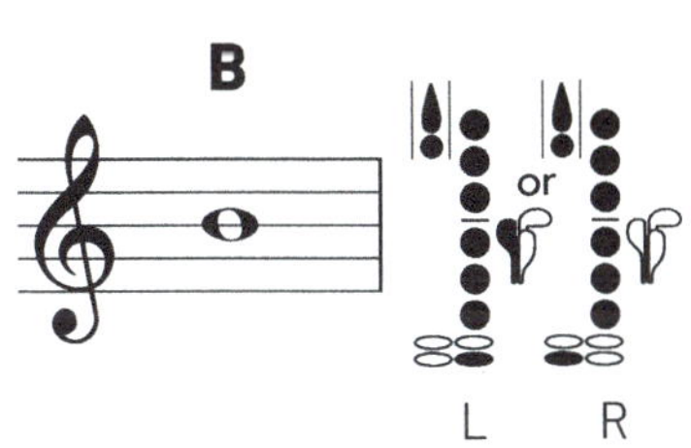

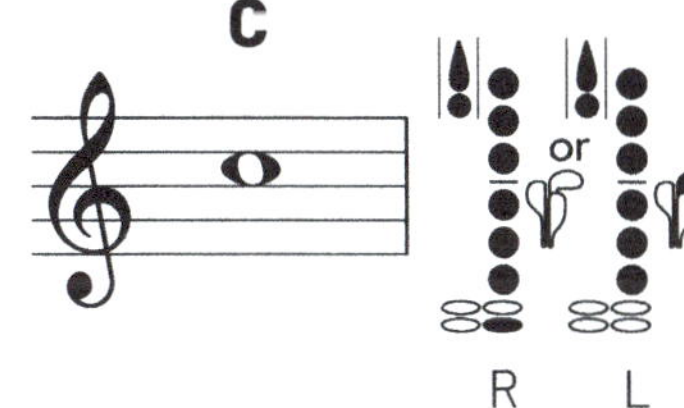

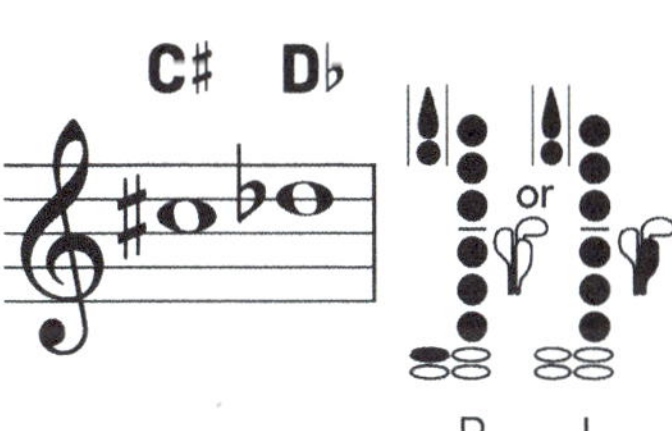

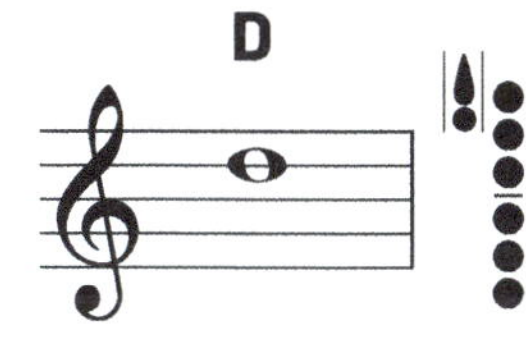

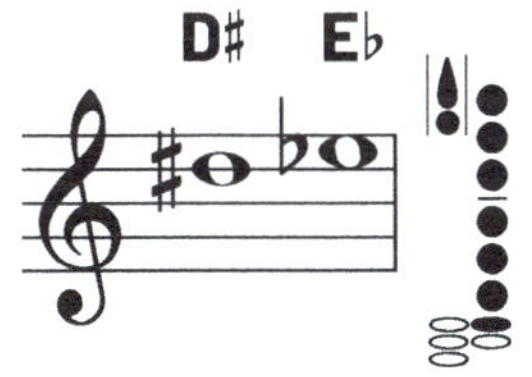

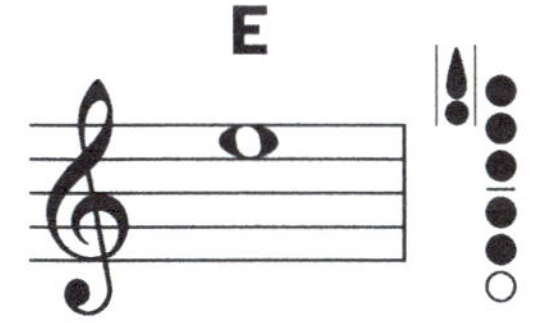

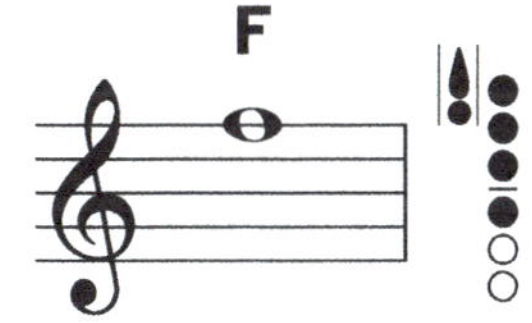

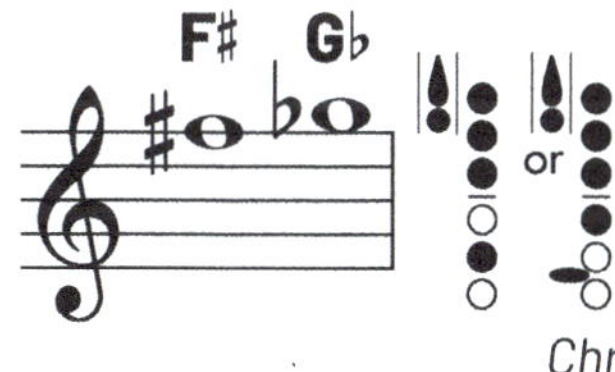

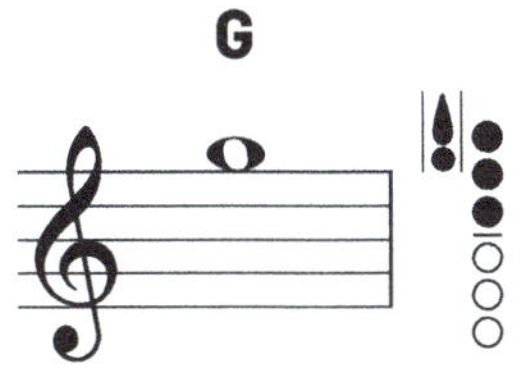

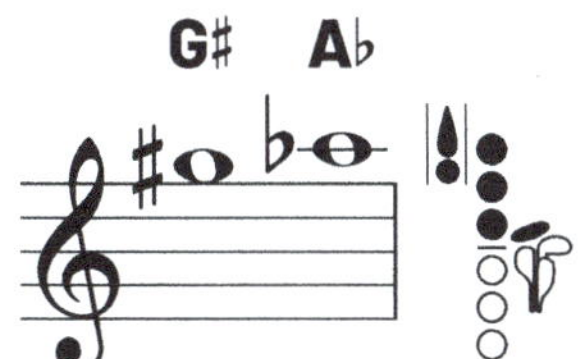

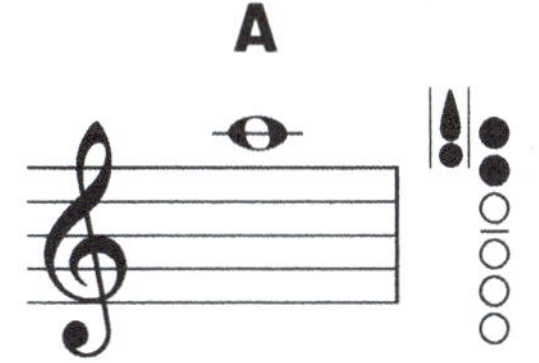

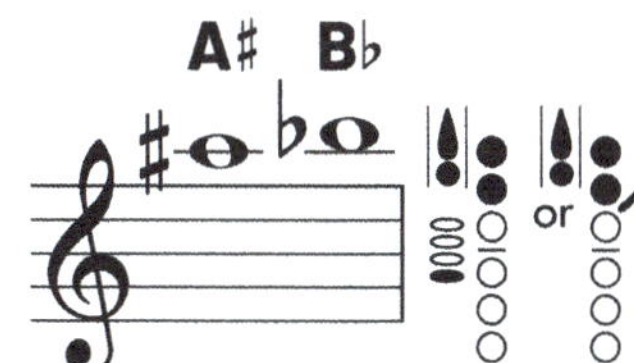

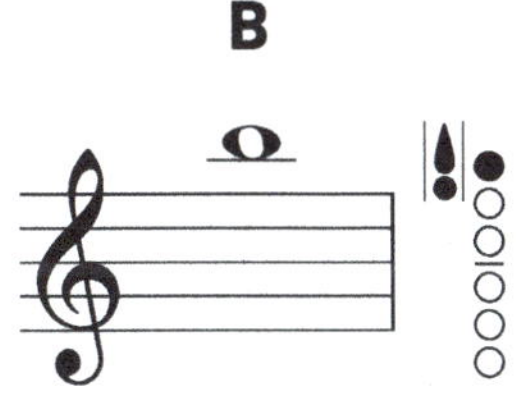

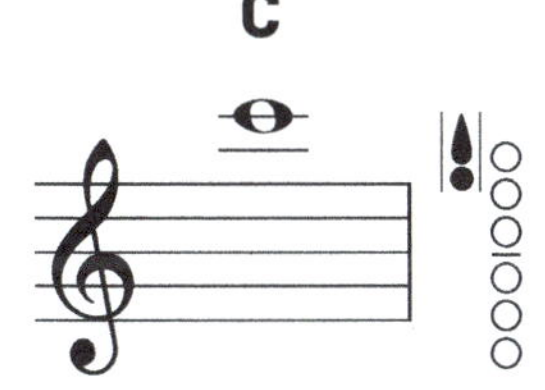

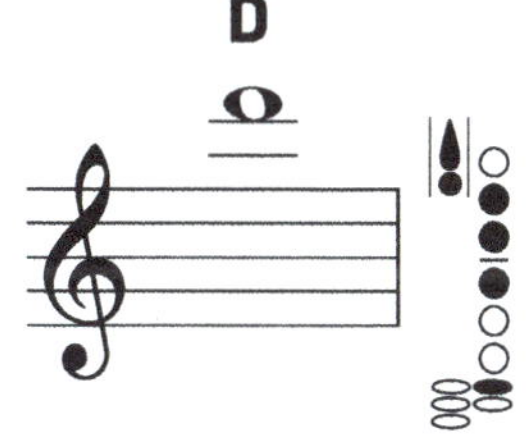

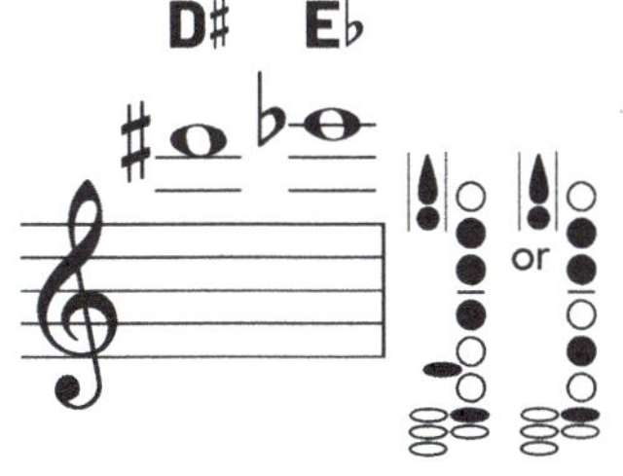

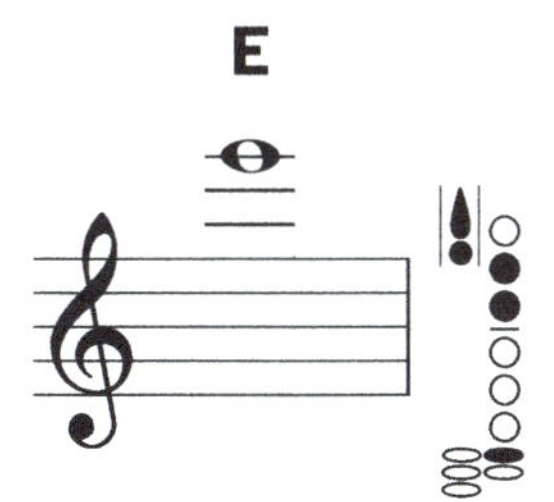

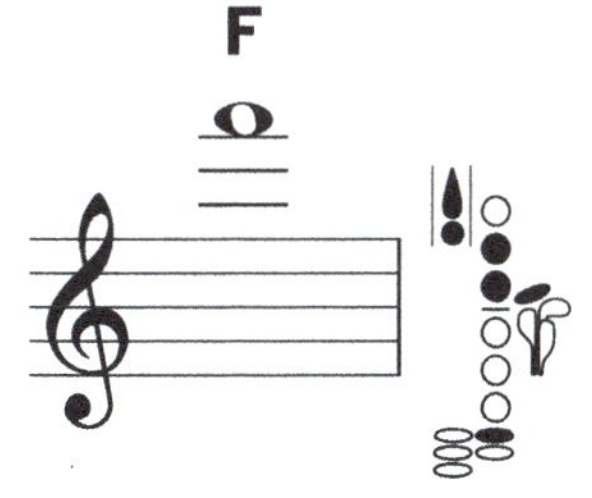

FINGERING CHART

B♭ BASS CLARINET

Instrument Care Reminders

Before putting your instrument back in its case after playing, do the following:

- Remove the reed, wipe off excess moisture and return it to the reed case.
- Remove the mouthpiece and wipe the inside with a clean cloth. Once a week, wash the mouthpiece with warm tap water. Dry thoroughly.
- Remove the neck and bell, and shake out excess moisture. Return them to the case.
- Drop a weighted chamois or cotton swab into the body of the instrument and pull it out the top end.
- If the body of your bass clarinet has two sections, gently twist them apart. Return the body section(s) to the case.
- As you put each piece back in the case, check to be sure they are dry.
- Your case is designed to hold only specific objects. If you try to force anything else into the case, it may damage your instrument.

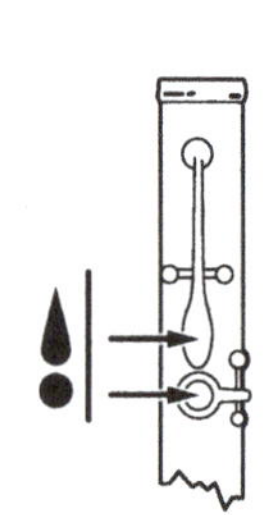

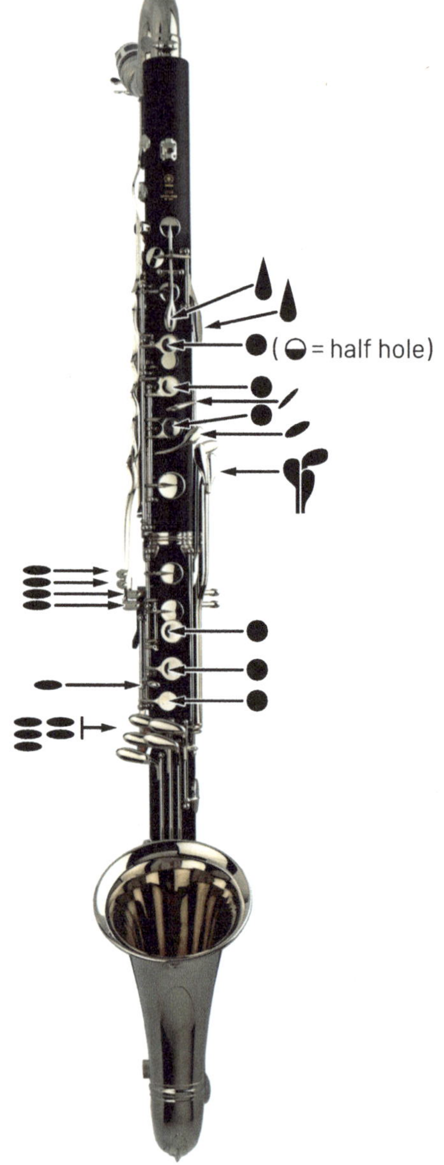

○ = Open

● = Pressed down

Alternate fingerings are used in certain situations to allow for smoother technique. These are shown to the right of the more common fingerings.

Instruments and photos courtesy of Yamaha.

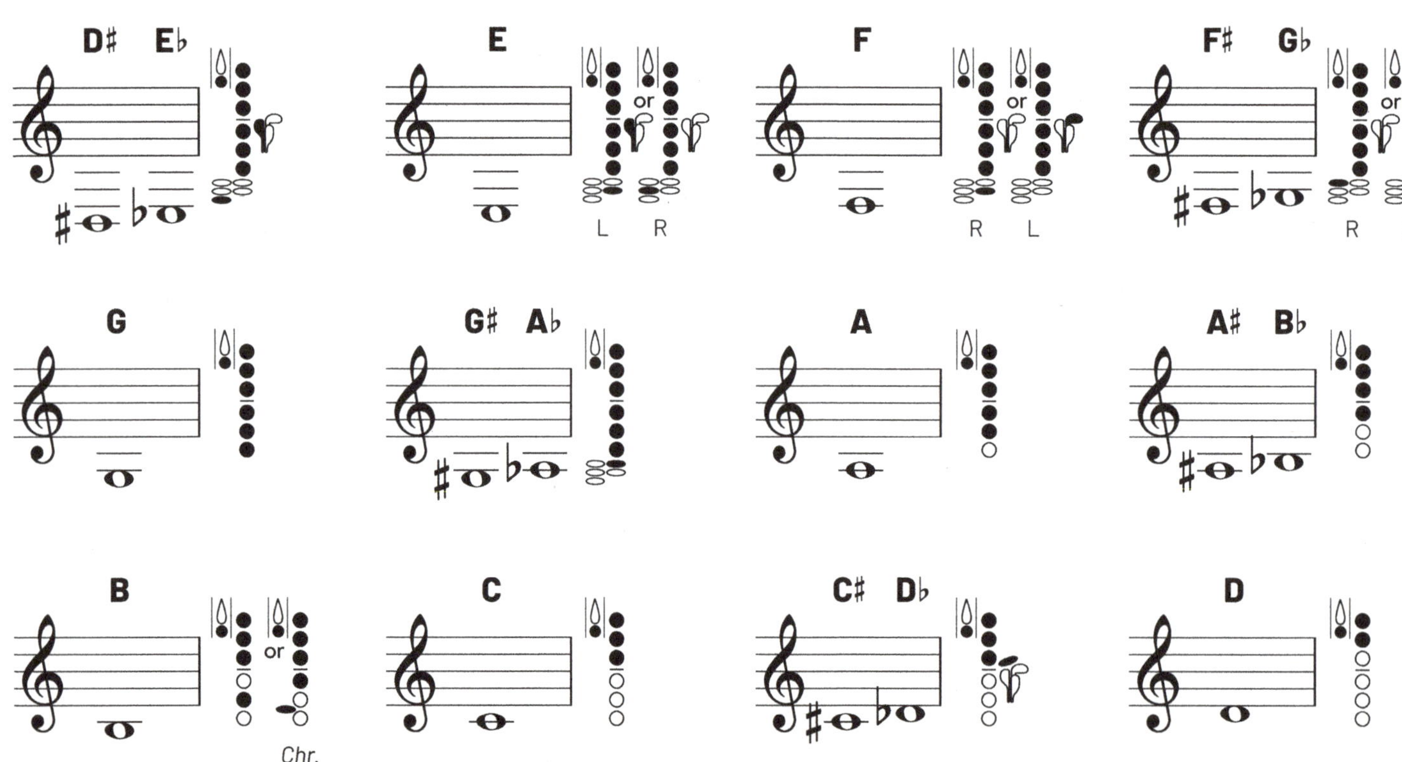

FINGERING CHART

B♭ BASS CLARINET

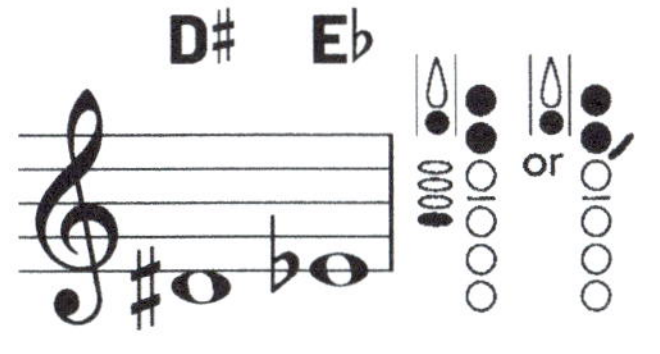

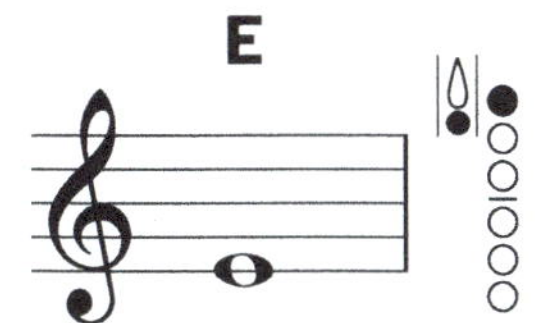

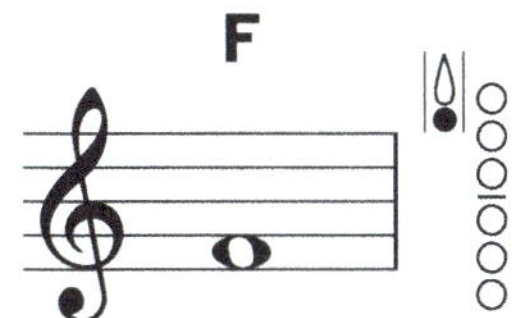

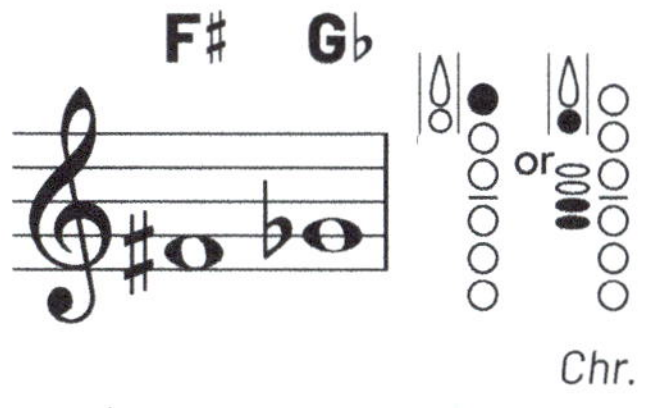

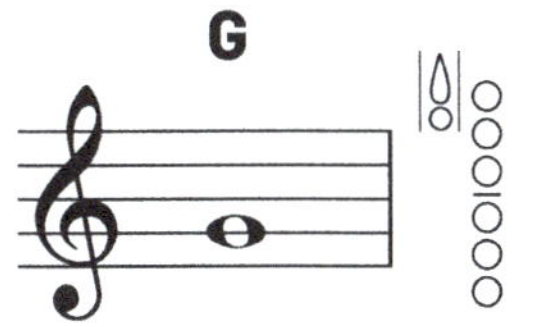

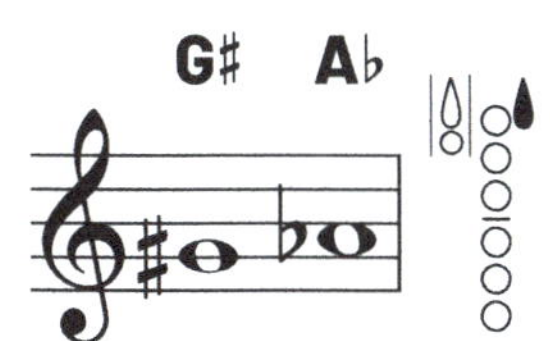

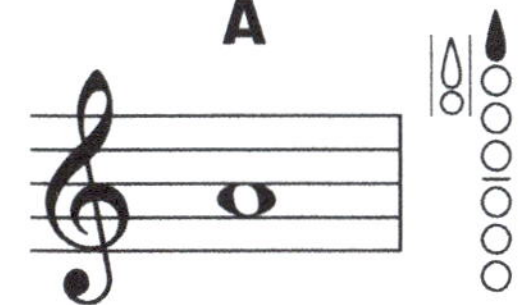

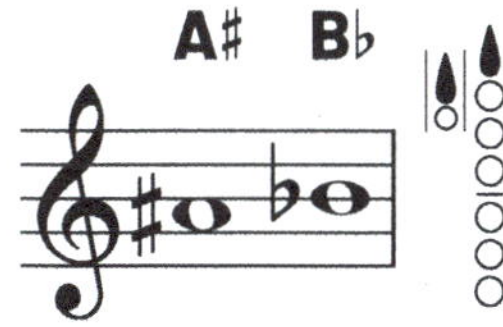

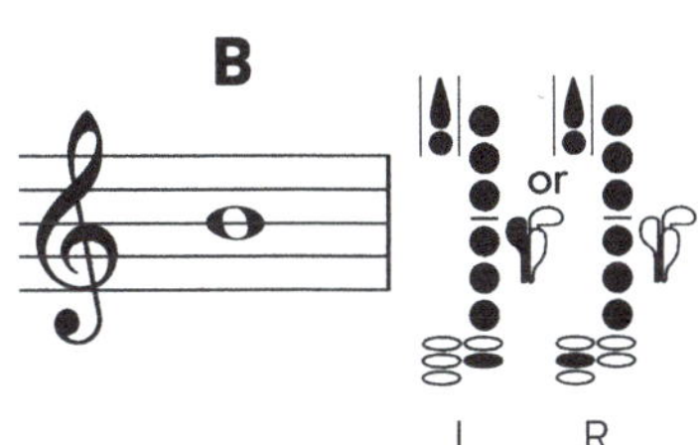

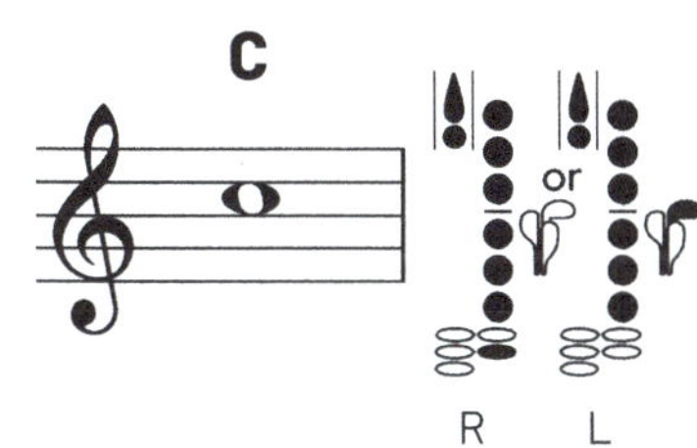

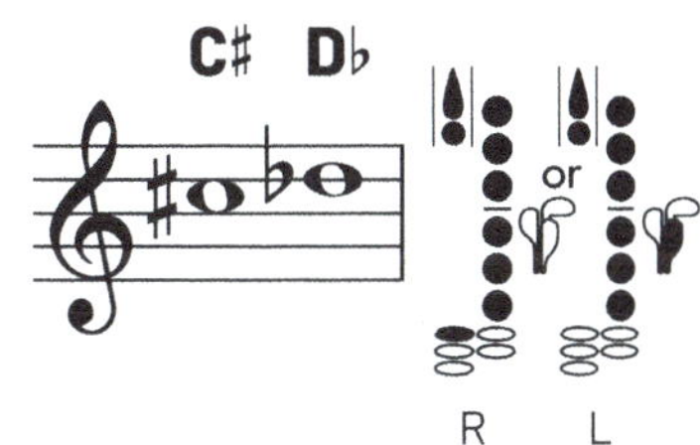

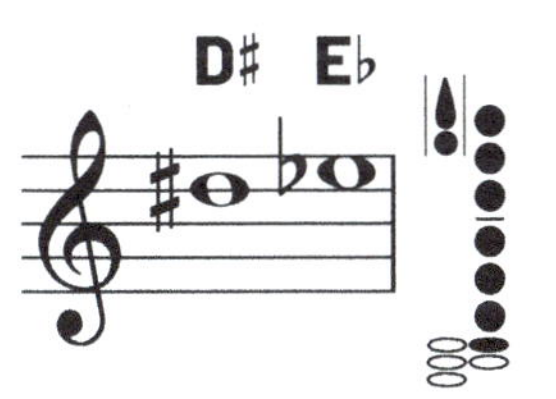

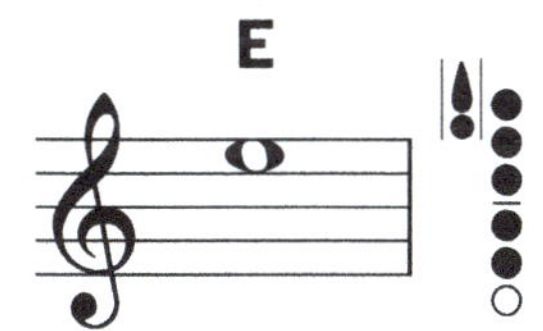

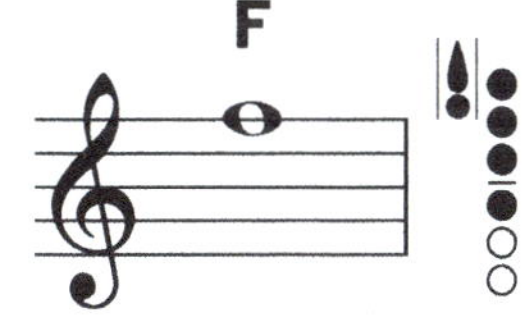

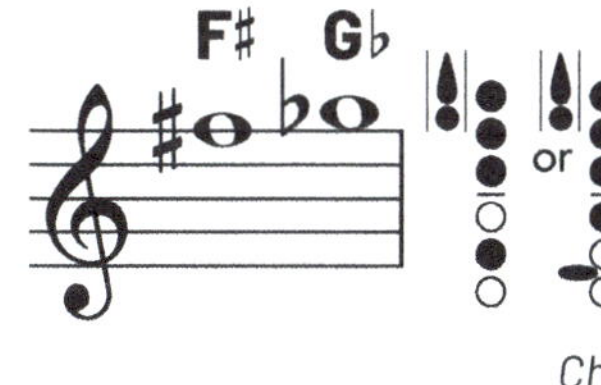

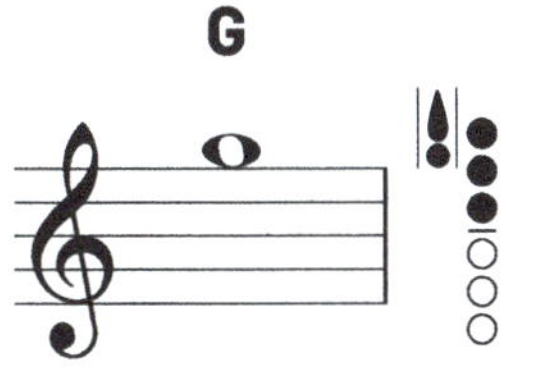

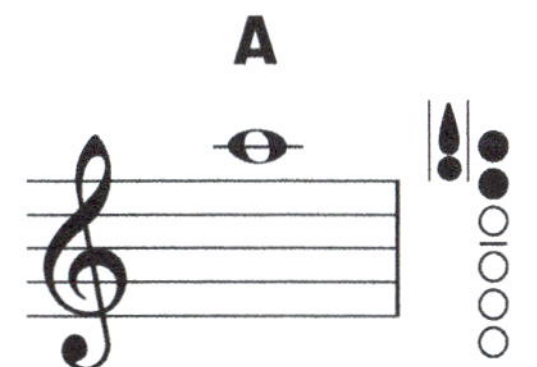

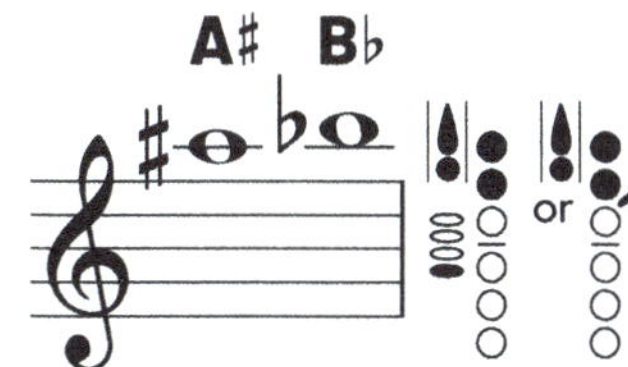

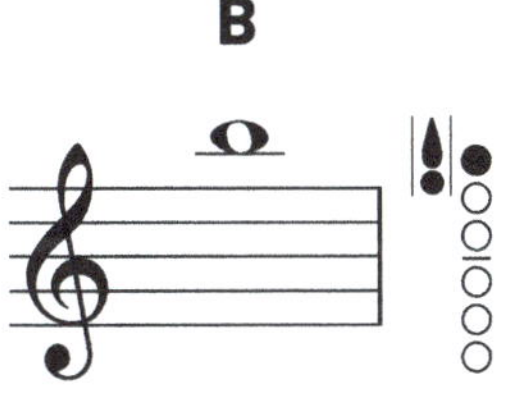

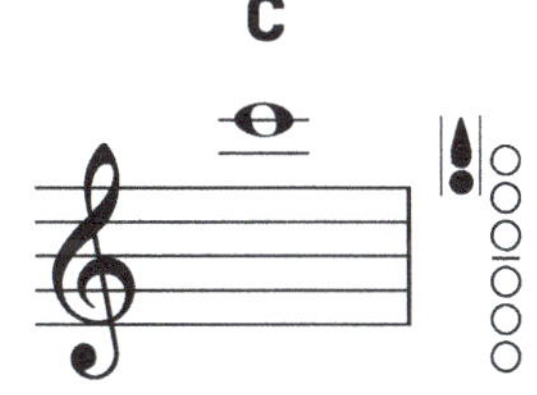

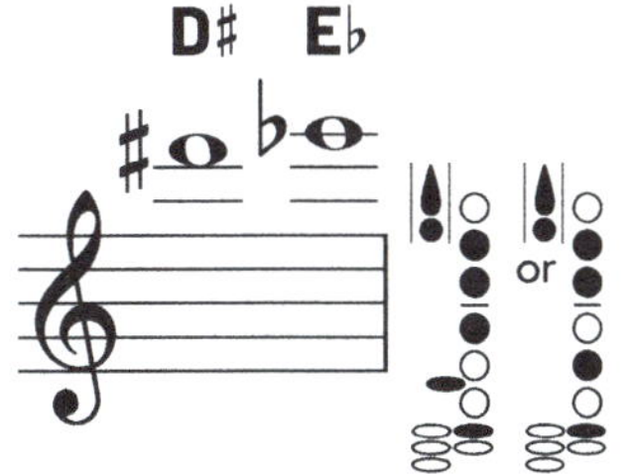

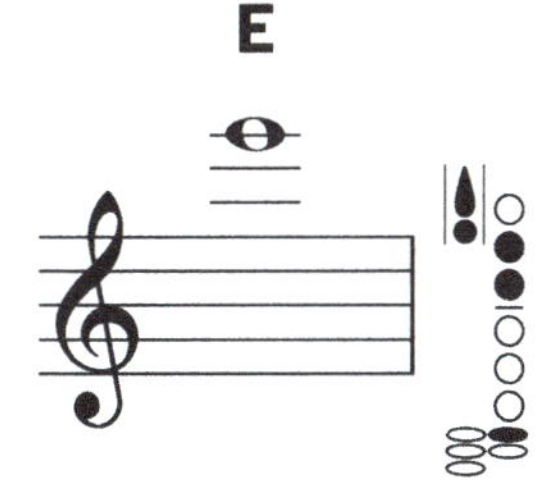

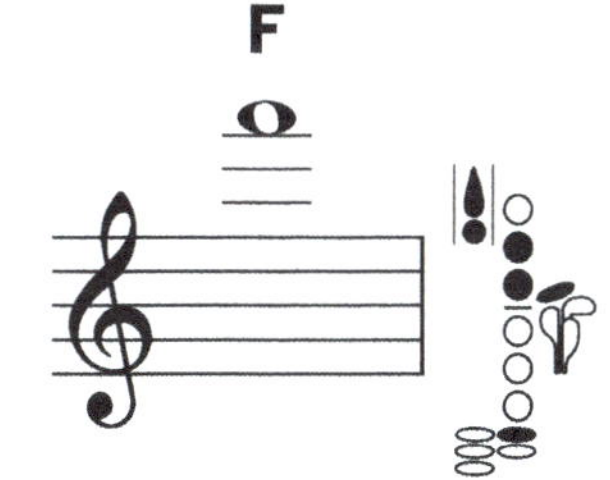

FINGERING CHART

E♭ ALTO SAXOPHONE

Instrument Care Reminders

Before putting your instrument back in its case after playing, do the following:

- Remove the reed, wipe off excess moisture and return it to the reed case.
- Remove the mouthpiece and wipe the inside with a clean cloth. Once a week, wash the mouthpiece with warm tap water. Dry thoroughly.
- Loosen the neck screw and remove the neck. Shake out excess moisture and dry the neck with a neck cleaner.
- Drop the weight of a chamois or cotton swab into the bell. Pull the swab through the body several times. Return the instrument to its case.
- Your case is designed to hold only specific objects. If you try to force anything else into the case, it may damage your instrument.

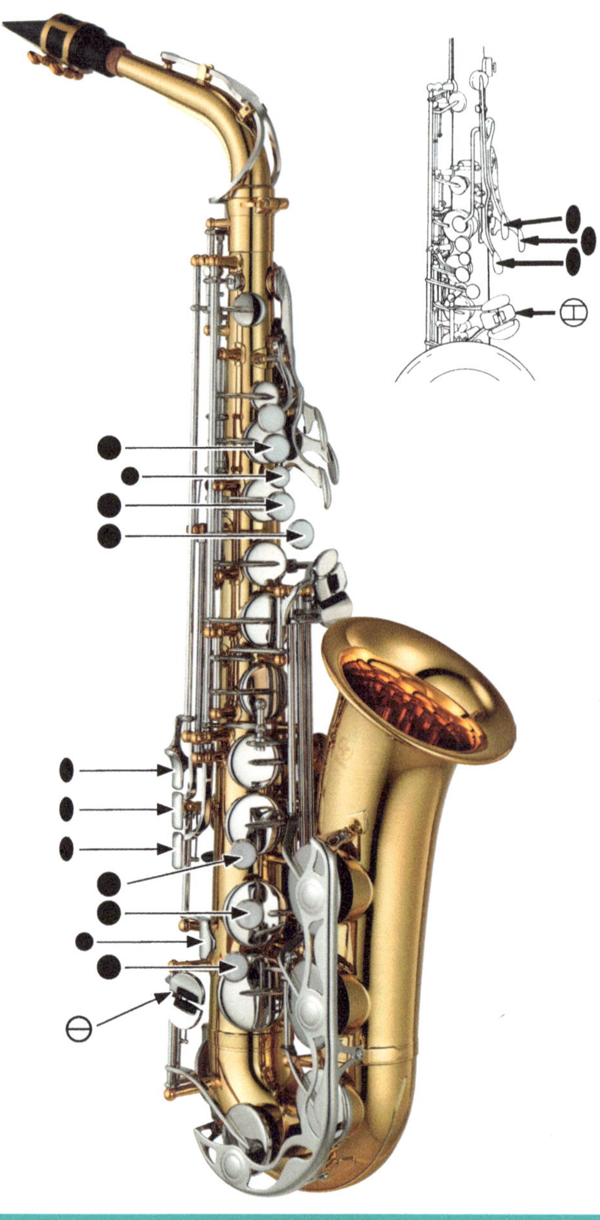

○ = Open

● = Pressed down

The most common fingering appears first when two fingerings are shown.

Instruments and photos courtesy of Yamaha.

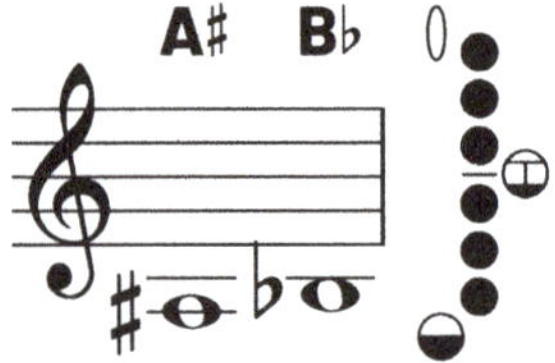

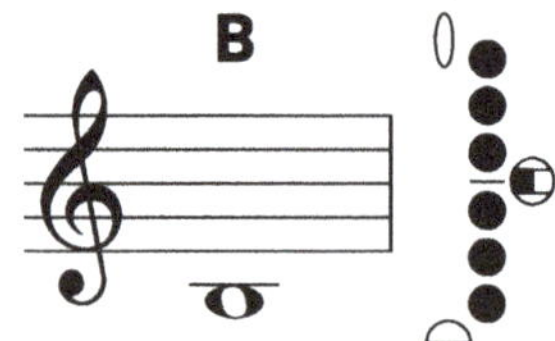

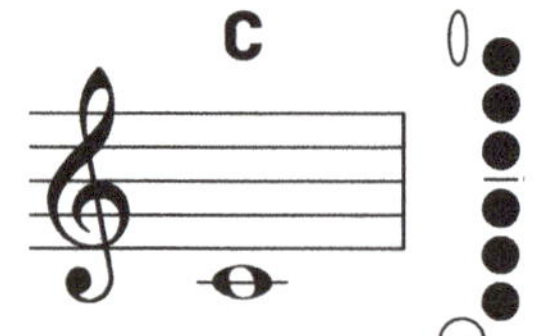

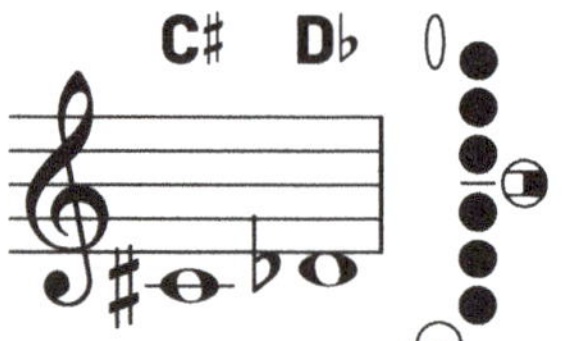

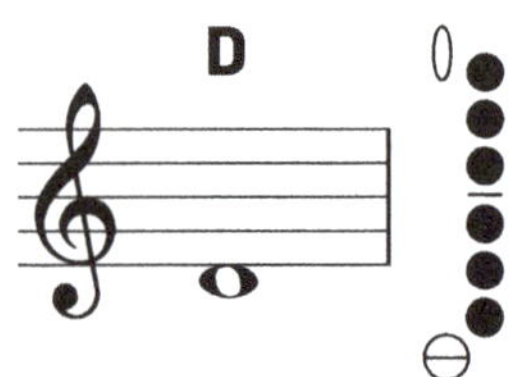

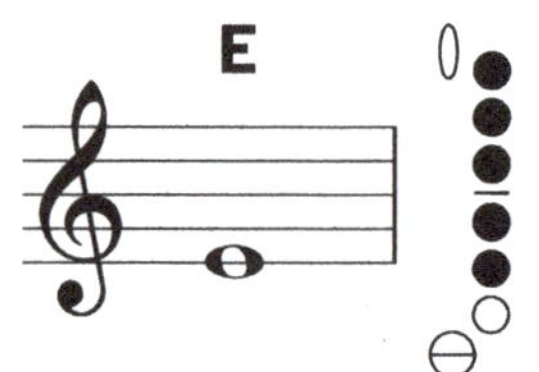

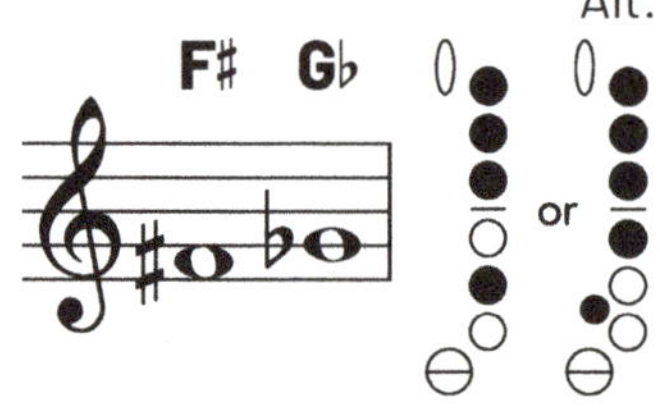

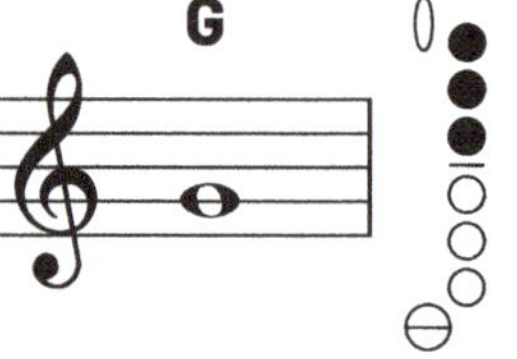

FINGERING CHART

E♭ ALTO SAXOPHONE

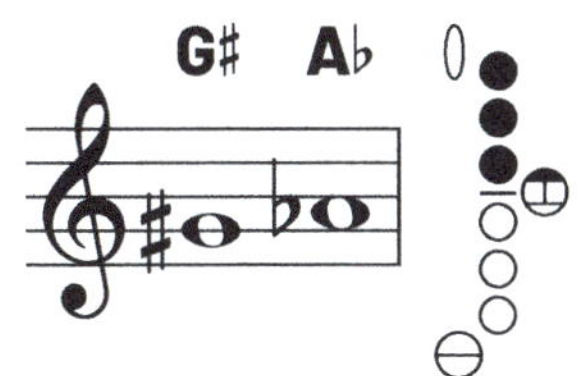

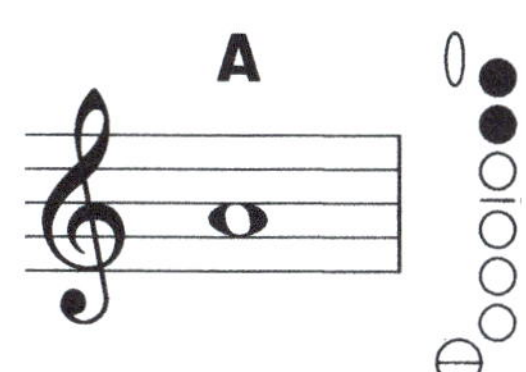

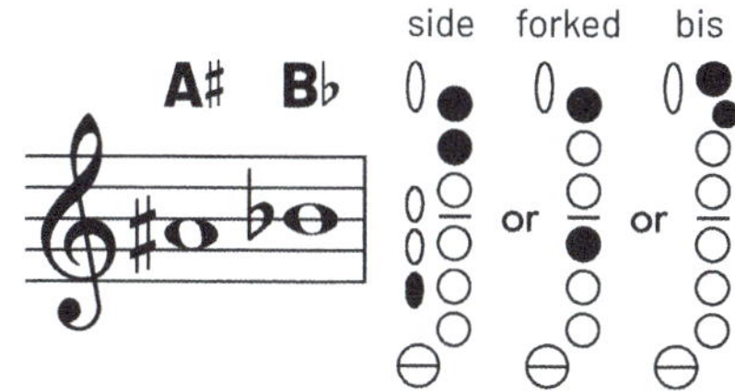

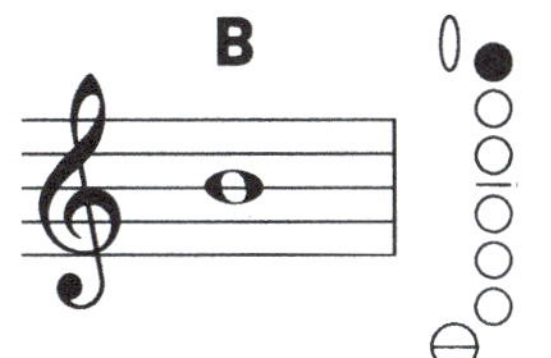

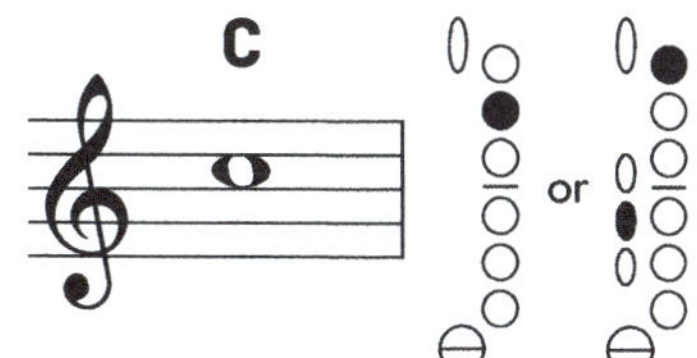

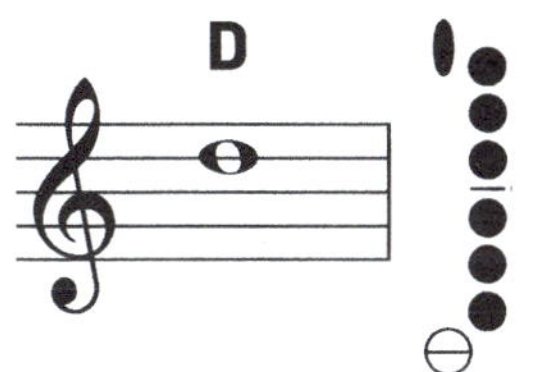

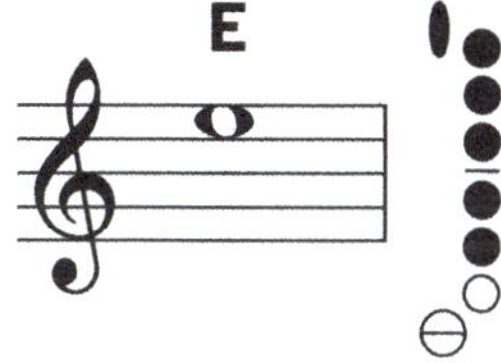

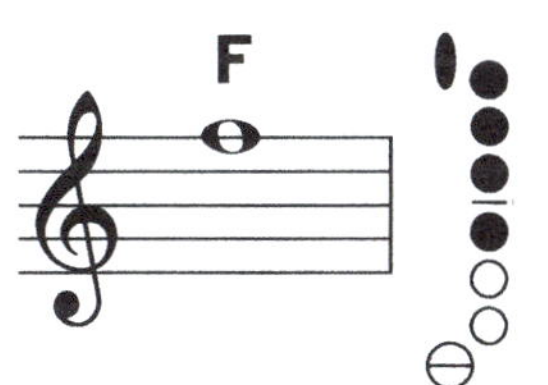

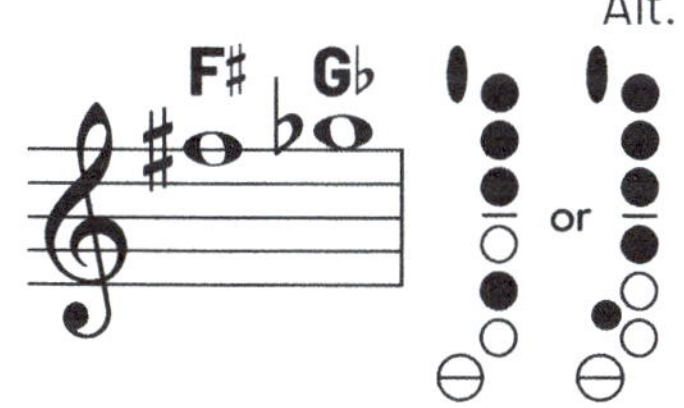

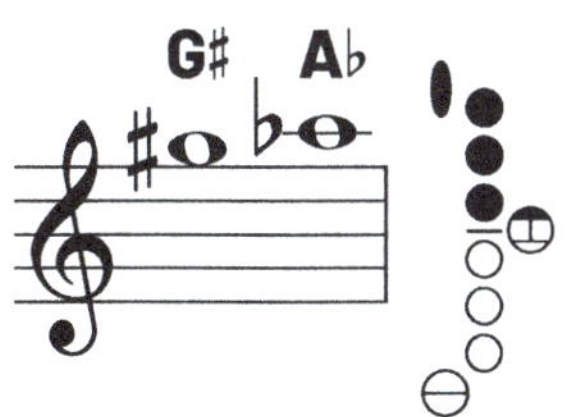

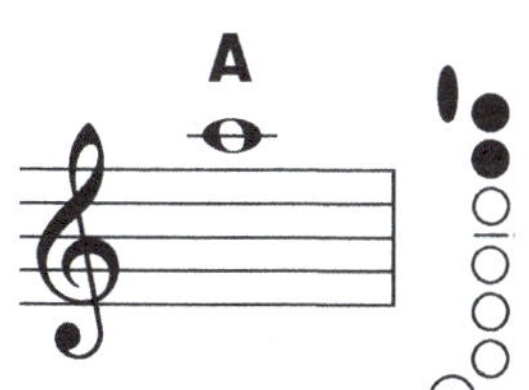

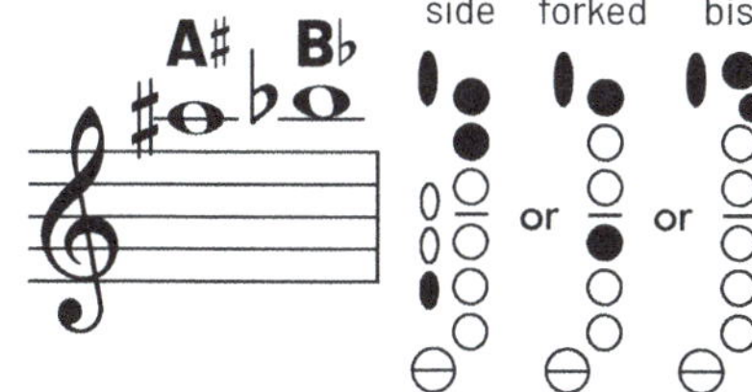

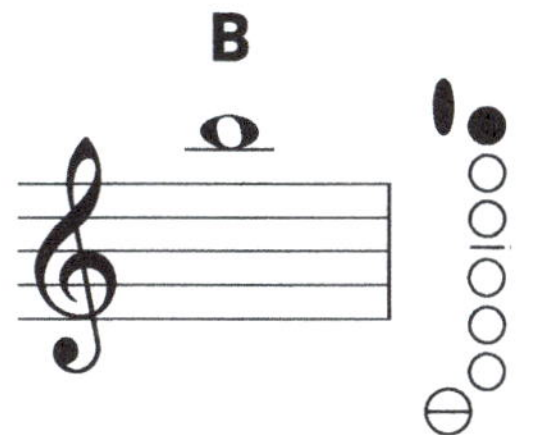

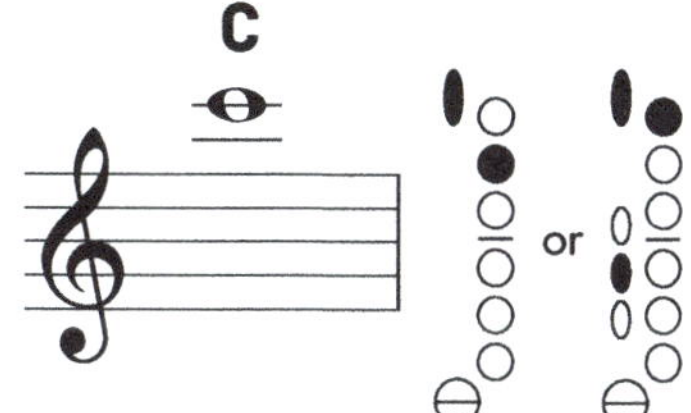

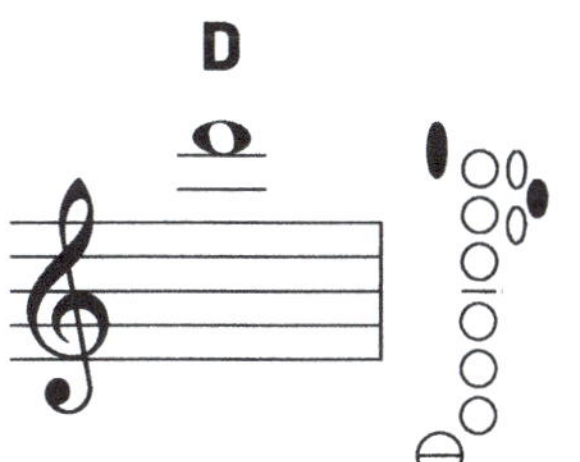

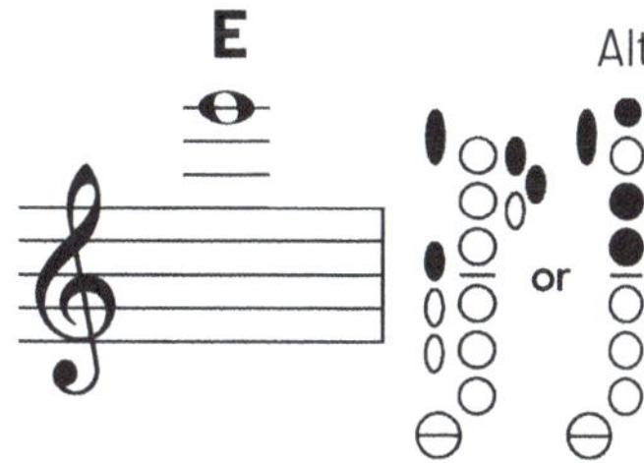

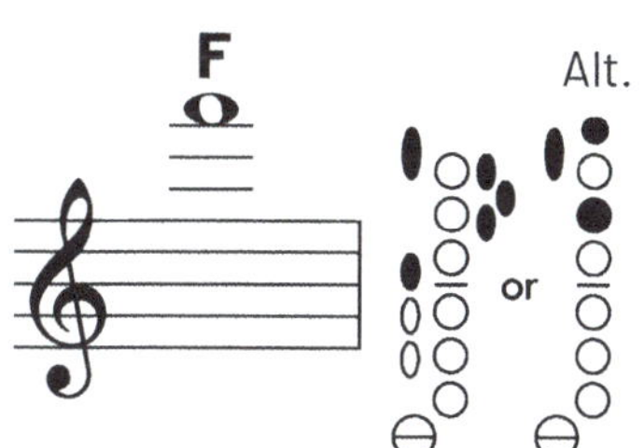

Student Book Page 46

FINGERING CHART

B♭ TENOR SAXOPHONE

Instrument Care Reminders

Before putting your instrument back in its case after playing, do the following:

- Remove the reed, wipe off excess moisture and return it to the reed case.
- Remove the mouthpiece and wipe the inside with a clean cloth. Once a week, wash the mouthpiece with warm tap water. Dry thoroughly.
- Loosen the neck screw and remove the neck. Shake out excess moisture and dry the neck with a neck cleaner.
- Drop the weight of a chamois or cotton swab into the bell. Pull the swab through the body several times. Return the instrument to its case.
- Your case is designed to hold only specific objects. If you try to force anything else into the case, it may damage your instrument.

○ = Open

● = Pressed down

The most common fingering appears first when two fingerings are shown.

Instruments and photos courtesy of Yamaha.

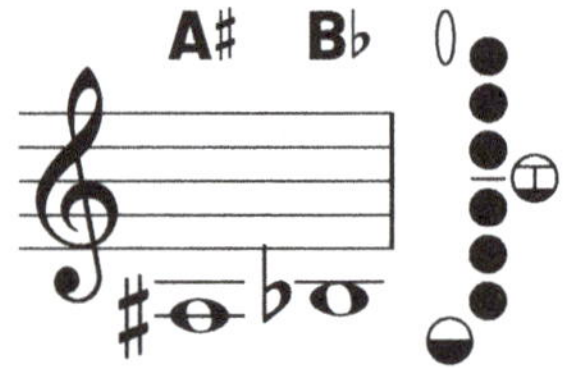

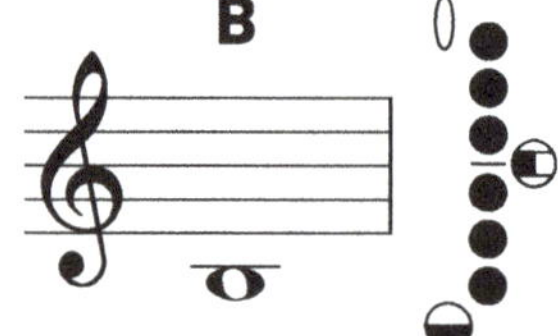

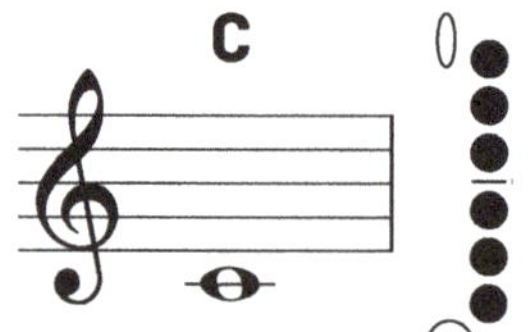

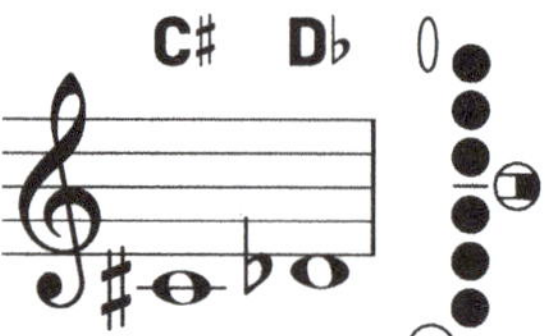

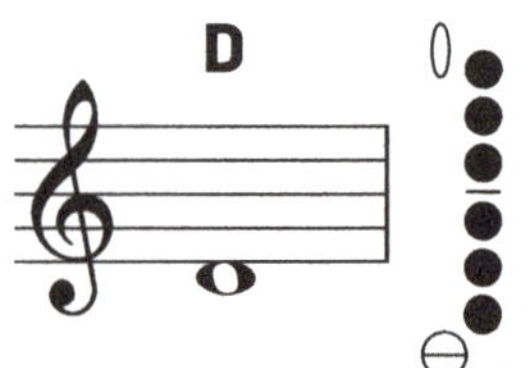

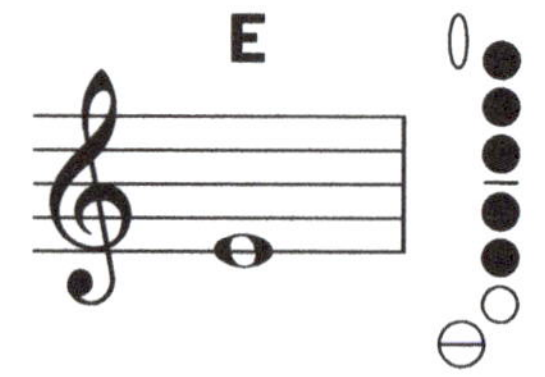

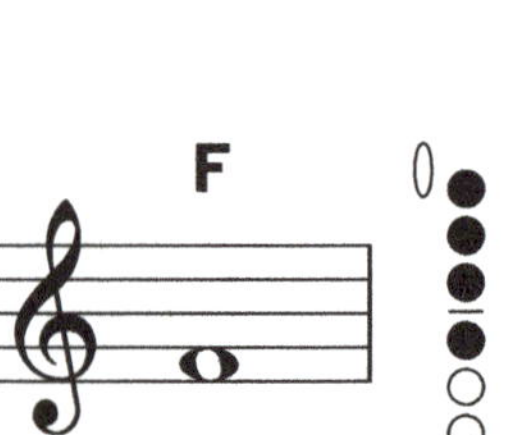

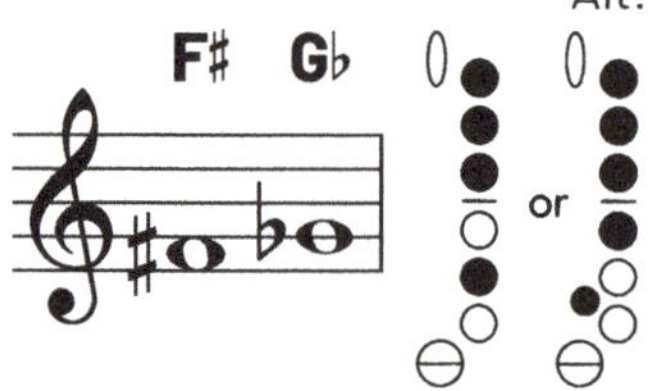

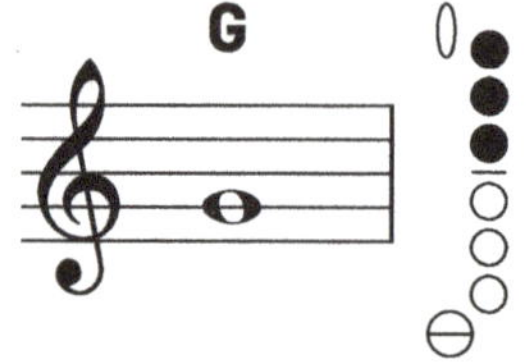

FINGERING CHART

B♭ TENOR SAXOPHONE

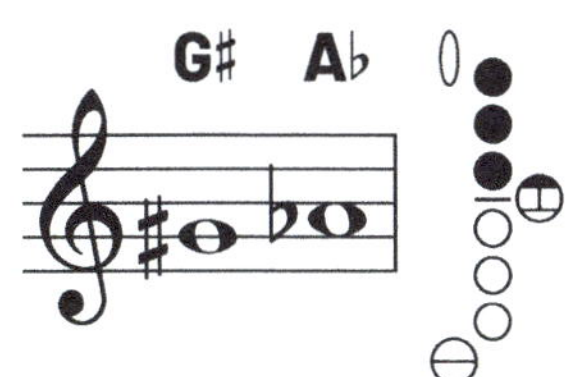

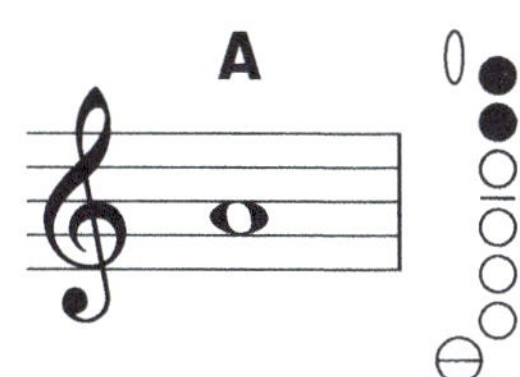

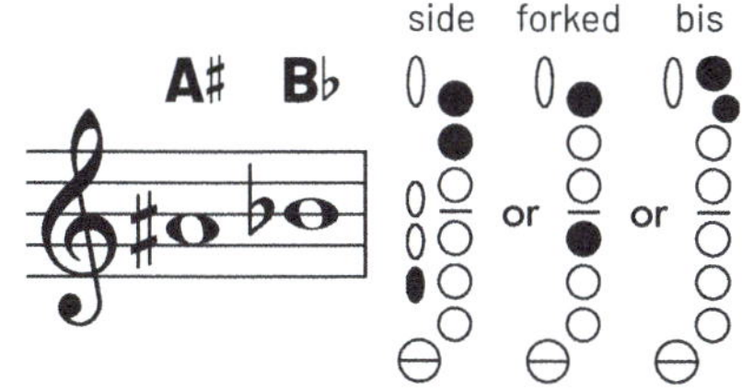

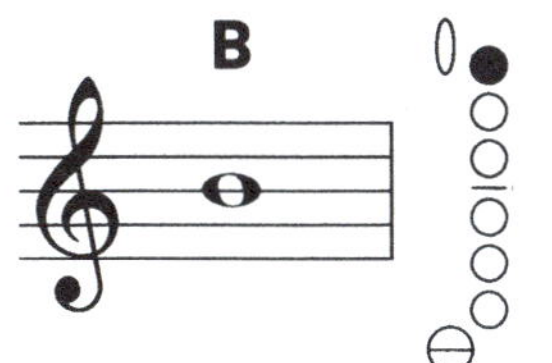

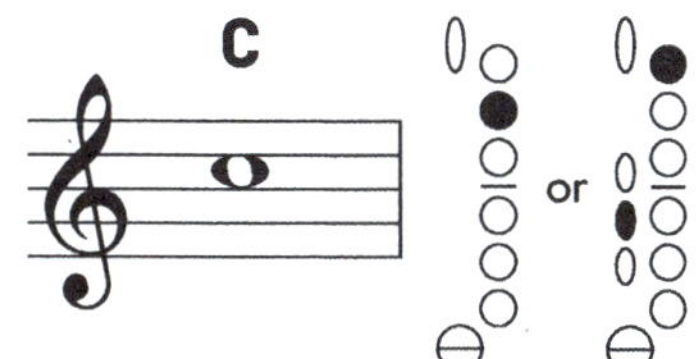

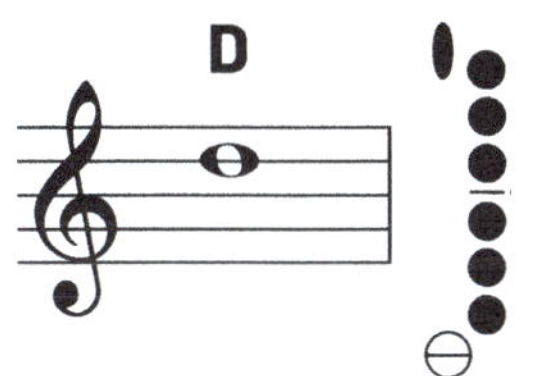

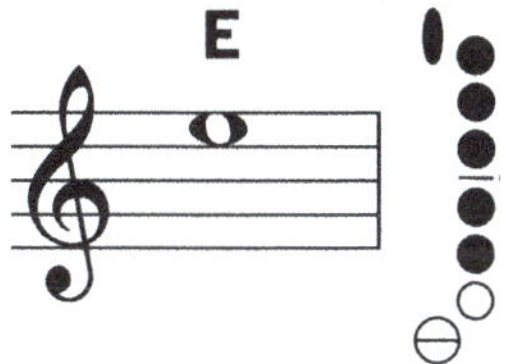

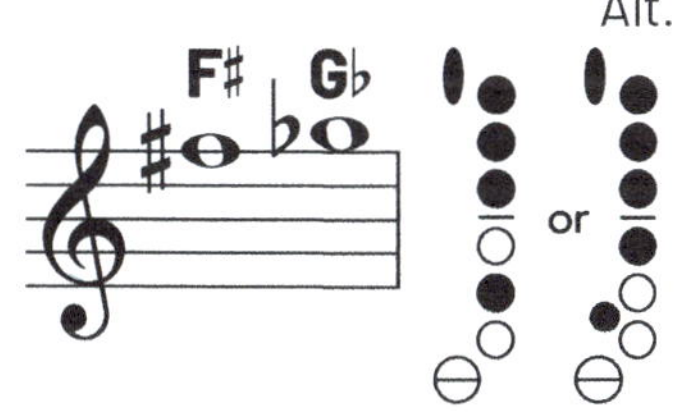

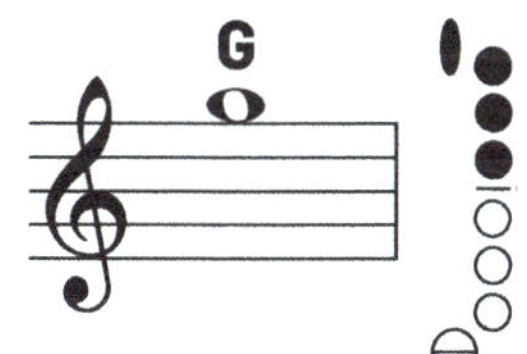

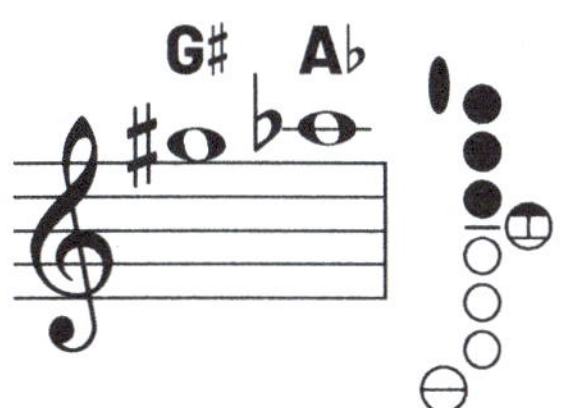

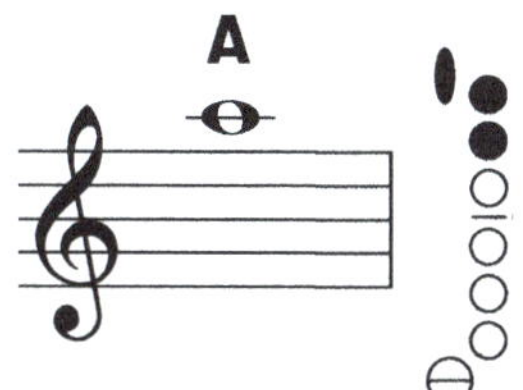

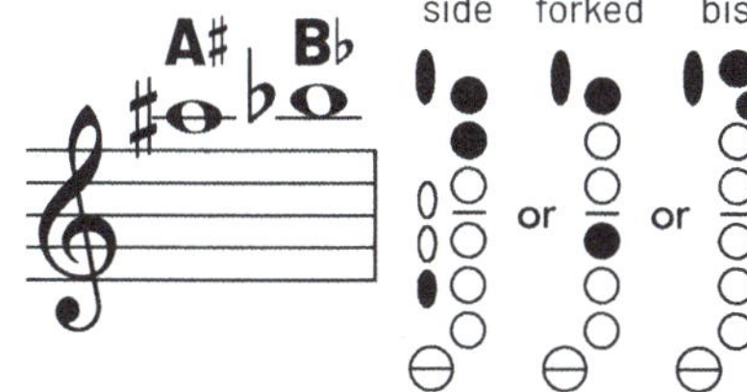

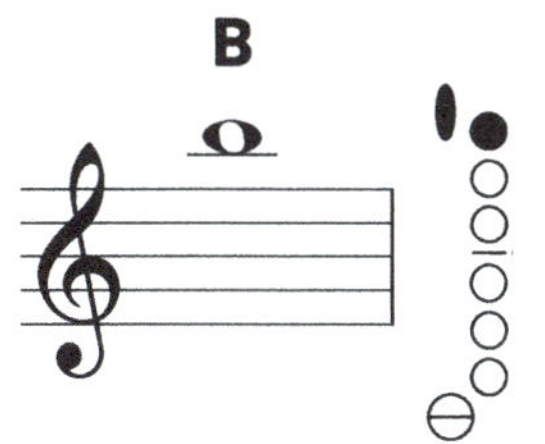

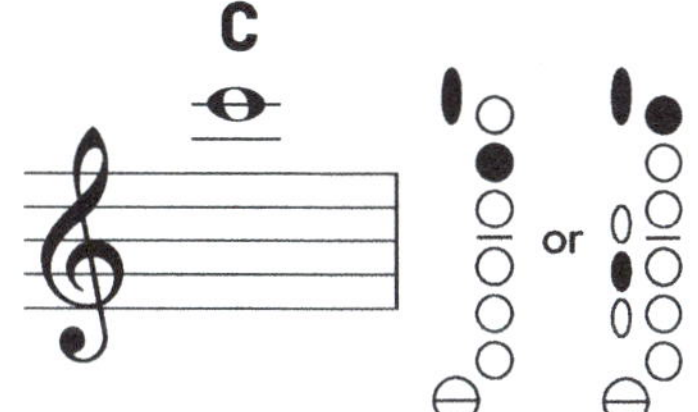

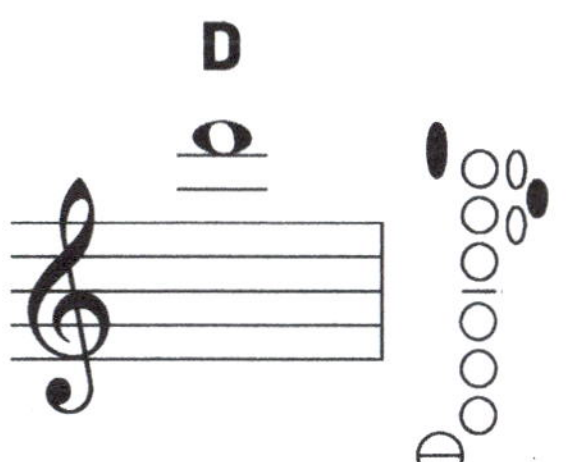

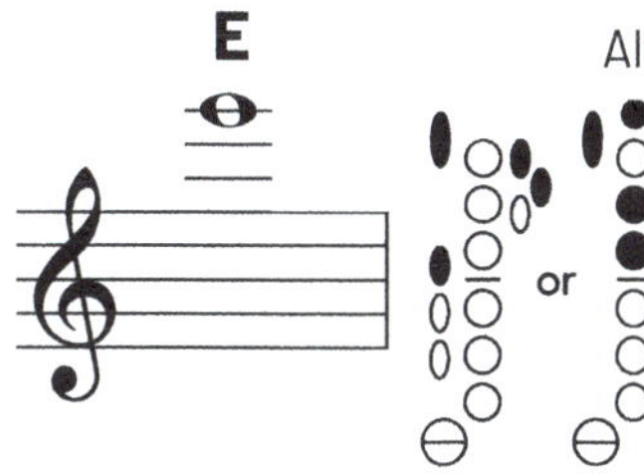

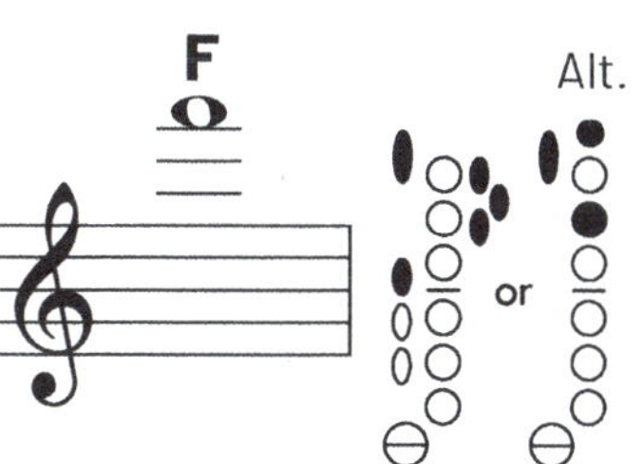

FINGERING CHART

E♭ BARITONE SAXOPHONE

Instrument Care Reminders

Before putting your instrument back in its case after playing, do the following:

- Remove the reed, wipe off excess moisture and return it to the reed case.
- Remove the mouthpiece and wipe the inside with a clean cloth. Once a week, wash the mouthpiece with warm tap water. Dry thoroughly.
- Loosen the neck screw and remove the neck. Shake out excess moisture and dry the neck with a neck cleaner.
- Use a body swab to dry the inside of your instrument. Or, drop the weight of a chamois or cotton swab into the bell. Pull the swab through the body several times. Return the instrument to its case.
- Your case is designed to hold only specific objects. If you try to force anything else into the case, it may damage your instrument.

○ = Open

● = Pressed down

The most common fingering appears first when two fingerings are shown.

Instruments and photos courtesy of Yamaha.

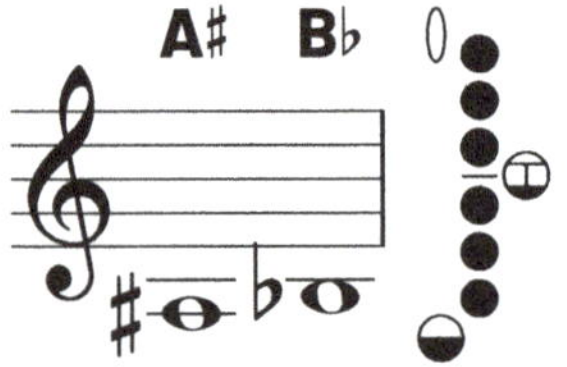

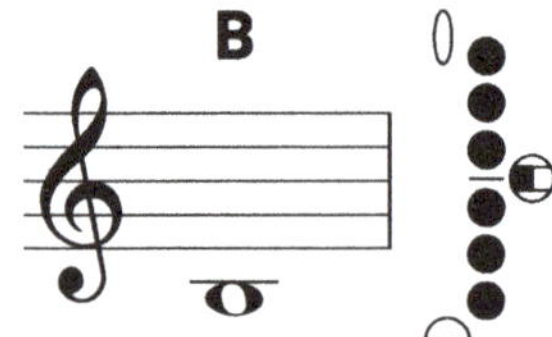

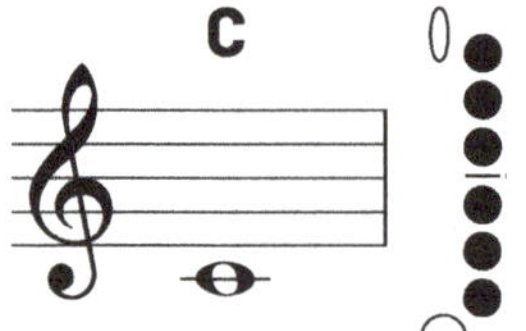

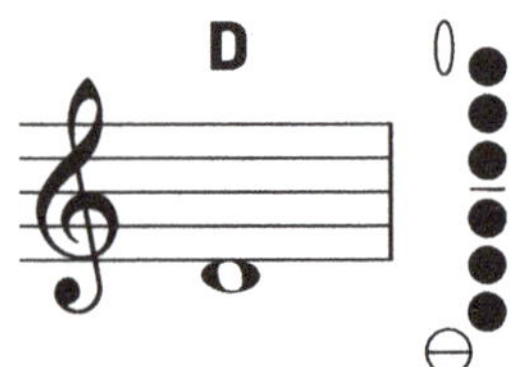

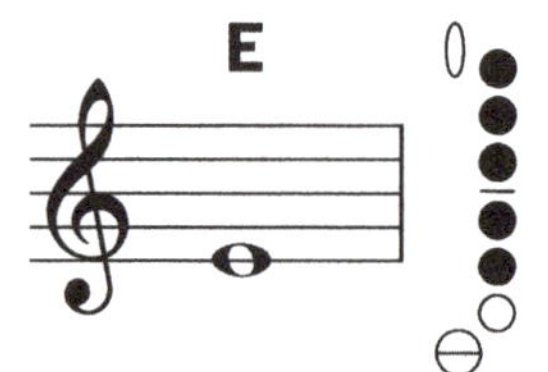

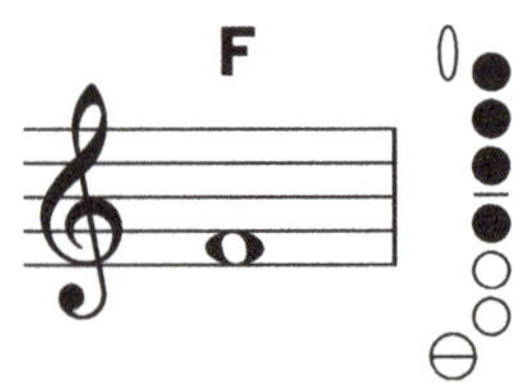

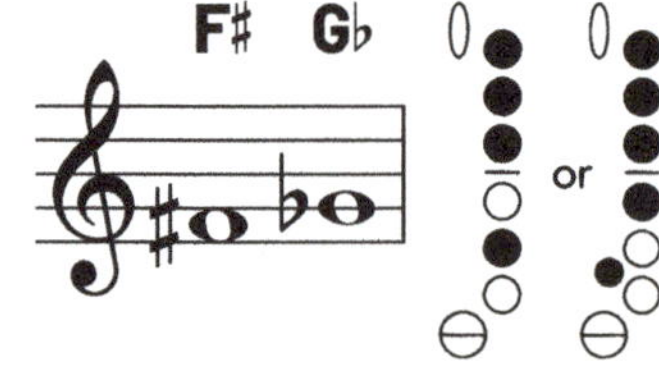

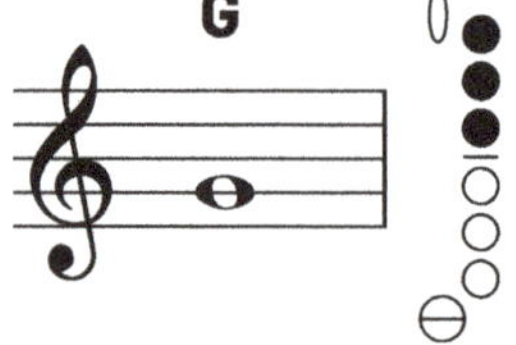

FINGERING CHART

E♭ BARITONE SAXOPHONE

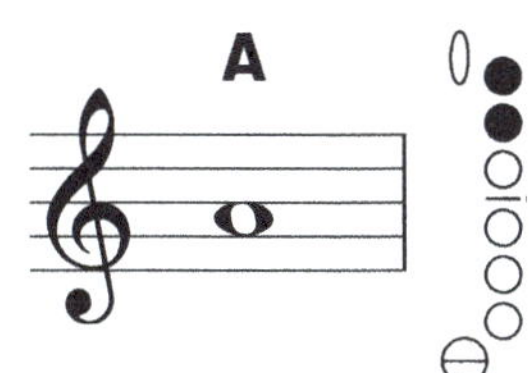

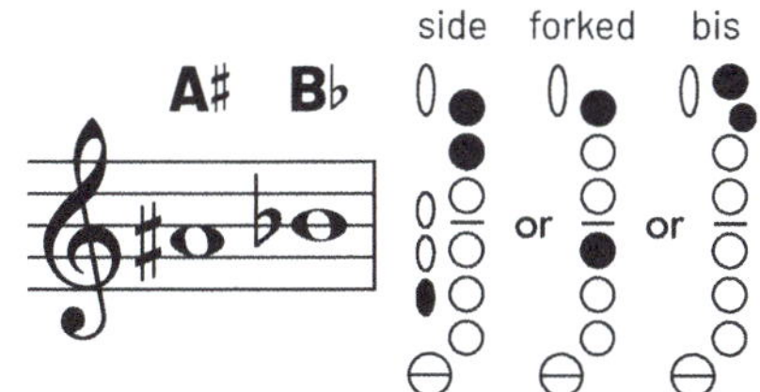

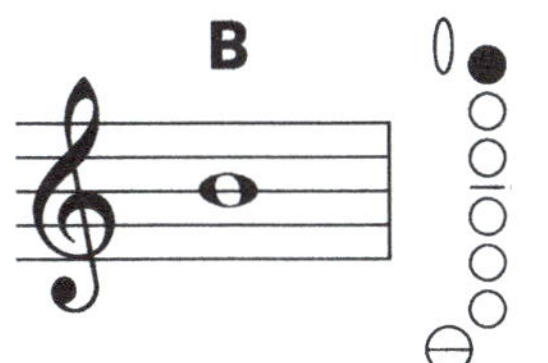

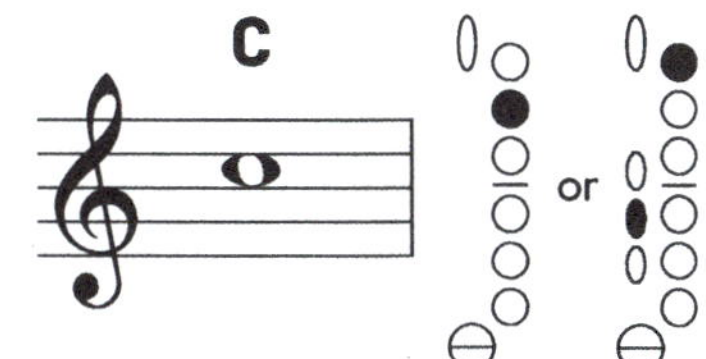

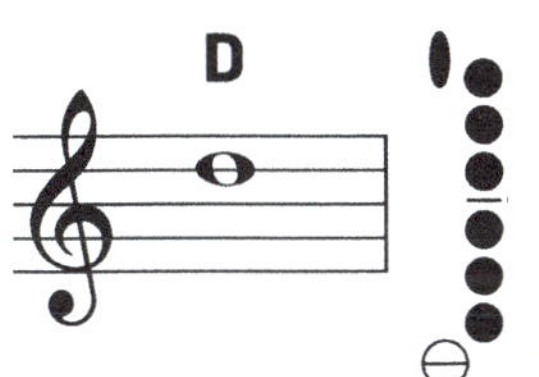

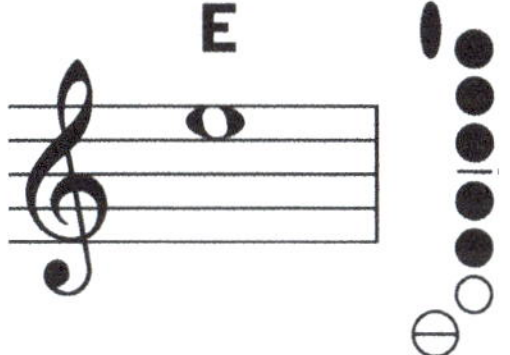

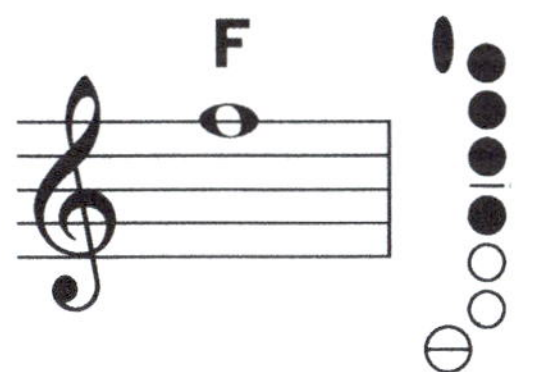

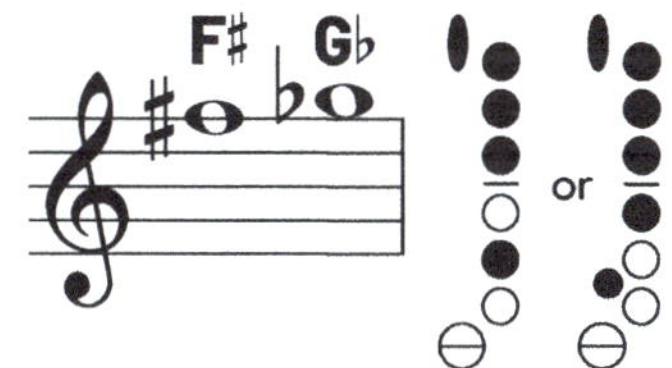

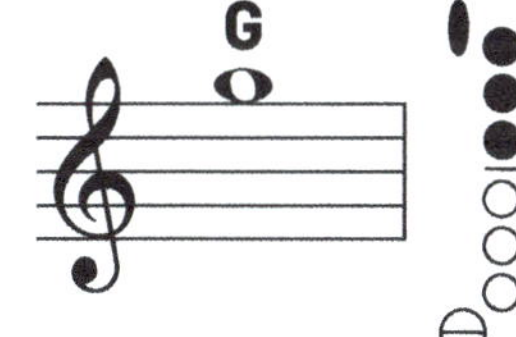

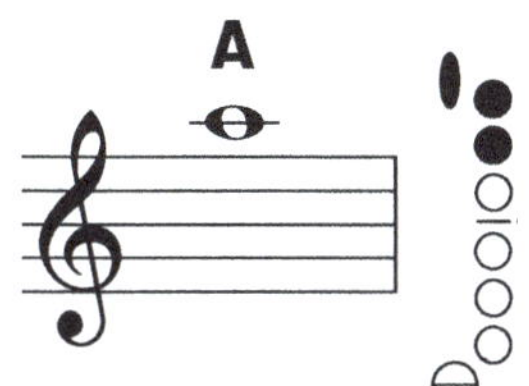

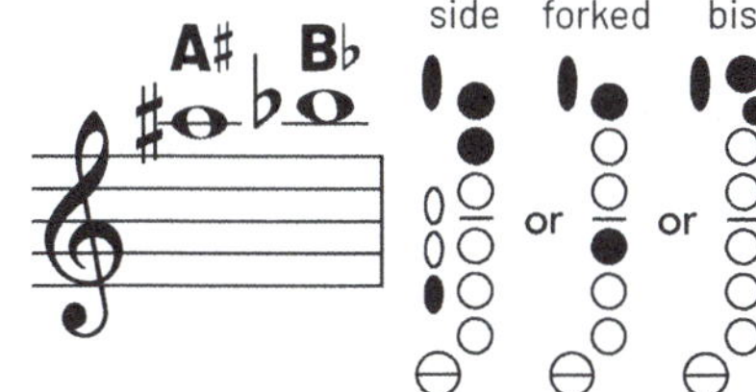

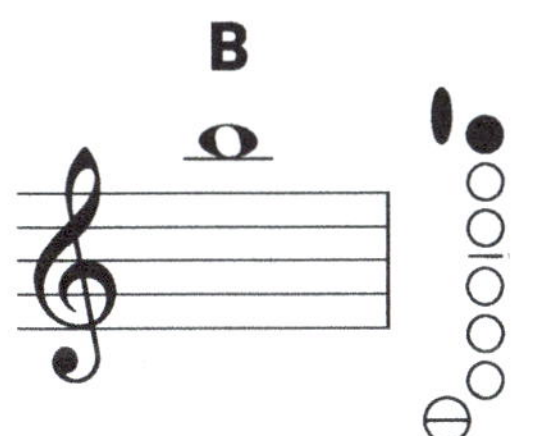

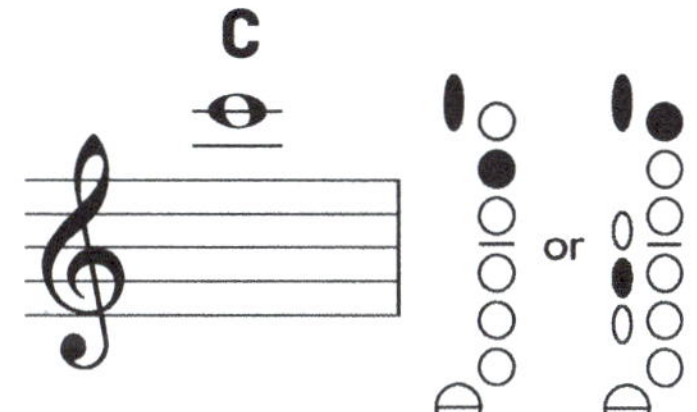

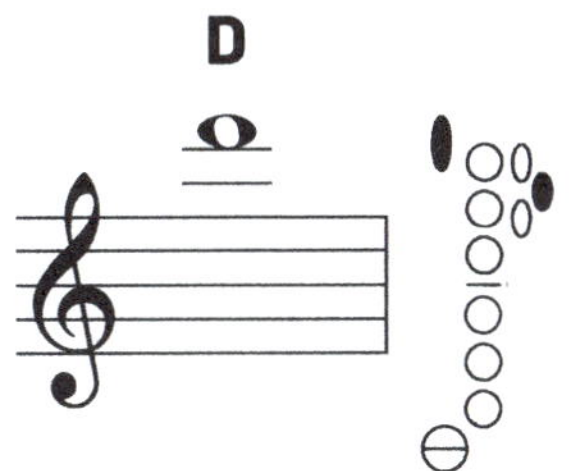

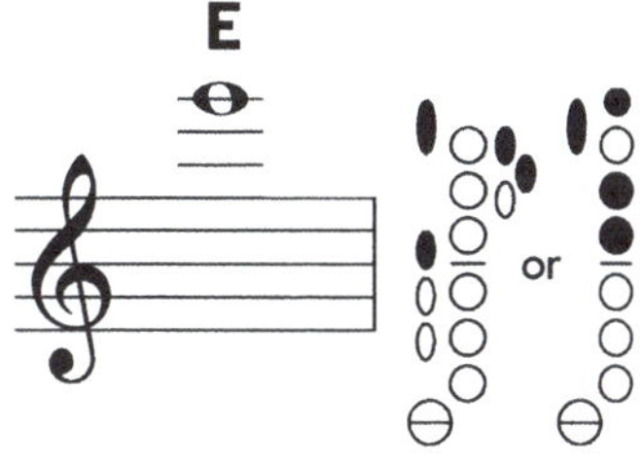

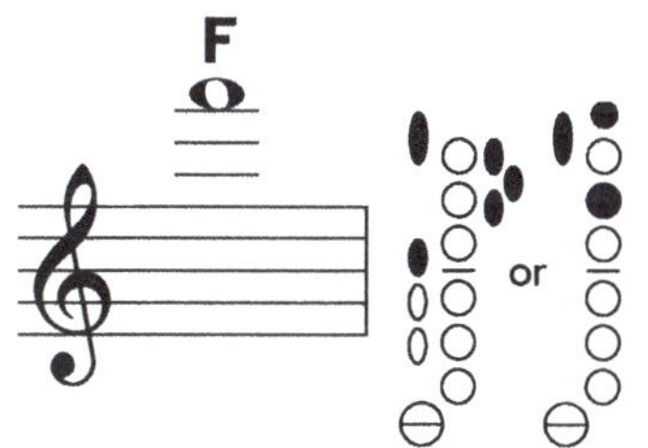

FINGERING CHART

B♭ TRUMPET / B♭ CORNET

Instrument Care Reminders

Before putting your instrument back in its case after playing, do the following:

- Use the water key to empty water from the instrument. Blow air through it.
- Remove the mouthpiece. Once a week, wash the mouthpiece with warm tap water. Dry thoroughly.
- Wipe off the instrument with a clean soft cloth. Return the instrument to its case.

Trumpet valves occasionally need oiling. To oil your trumpet valves:

- Unscrew the valve at the top of the casing.
- Lift the valve half-way out of the casing.
- Apply a few drops of special brass valve oil to the exposed valve.
- Carefully return the valve to its casing. When properly inserted, the top of the valve should easily screw back into place.

Be sure to grease the slides regularly. Your director will recommend special slide grease and valve oil, and will help you apply them when necessary.

CAUTION: If a slide, a valve or your mouthpiece becomes stuck, ask for help from your band director or music dealer. Special tools should be used to prevent damage to your instrument.

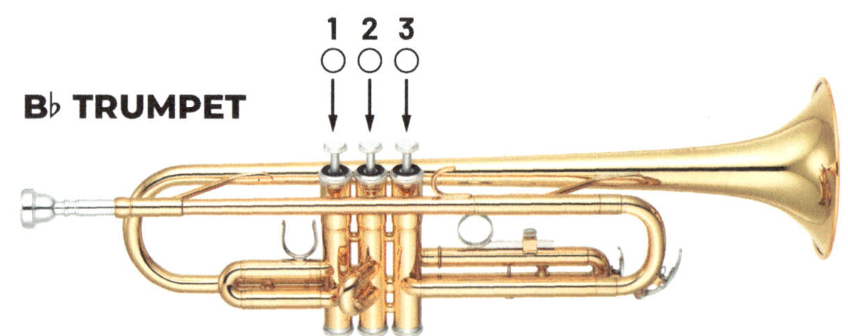

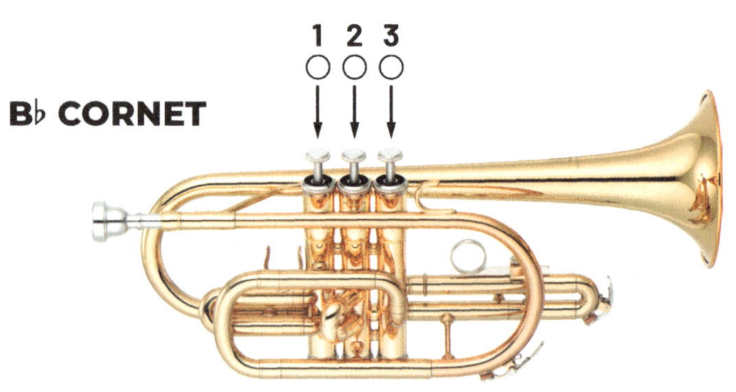

○ = Open

● = Pressed down

Instruments and photos courtesy of Yamaha.

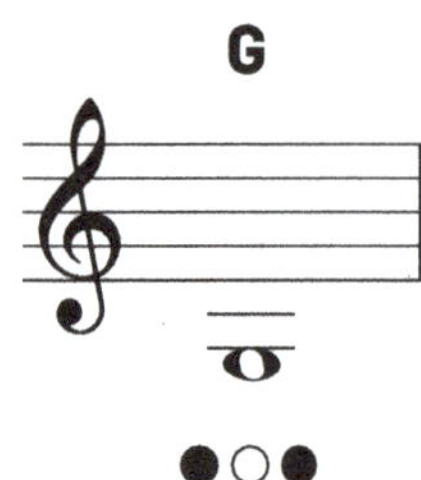

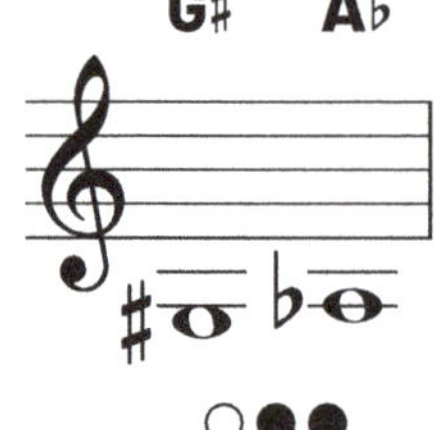

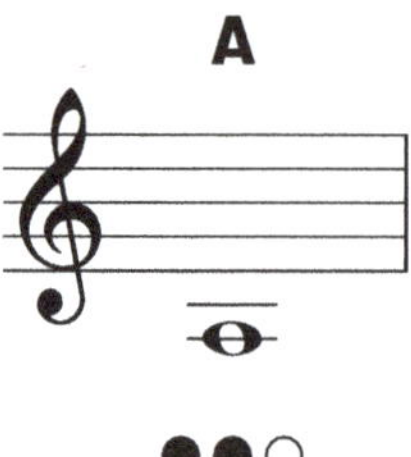

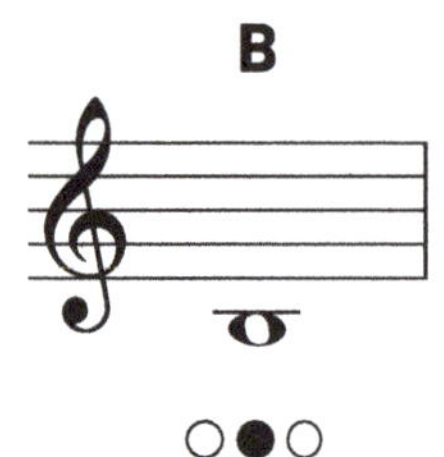

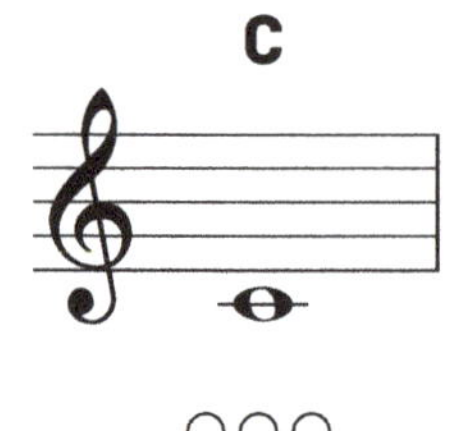

FINGERING CHART

B♭ TRUMPET / B♭ CORNET

D

D♯ E♭

E

F

F♯ G♭

G

G♯ A♭

A

A♯ B♭

B

C

C♯ D♭

D

D♯ E♭

E

F

F♯ G♭

G

G♯ A♭

A

A♯ B♭

B

C

FINGERING CHART

F HORN

Instrument Care Reminders

Before putting your instrument back in its case after playing, do the following:

- Use the water key to empty water from the instrument. Blow air through it. If your horn does not have a water key, invert the instrument.
  You may also remove the main tuning slide, invert the instrument and remove excess water.
- Remove the mouthpiece. Once a week, wash the mouthpiece with warm tap water. Dry thoroughly.
- Wipe the instrument off with a clean soft cloth. Return the instrument to its case.

Be sure to grease the slides regularly. Your director will recommend special slide grease and valve oil, and will help you apply them when necessary.

CAUTION: If a slide, a valve or your mouthpiece becomes stuck, ask for help from your band director or music dealer. Special tools should be used to prevent damage to your instrument.

Using the Correct Fingering

Single Horn Players

- F Horn players use the upper fingerings - marked "F Horn"
- B♭ Horn players use the lower fingerings - marked "B♭ Horn"
  *The trigger key (**T**) is only used on double horns.

Double Horn Players

- The trigger key (**T**) allows double horn players to switch between F and B♭ Horn
- Use the "F Horn" fingering when the trigger key is **not** pressed.
  *For notes without a "**T**" fingering, the F Horn fingering is the recommended double horn fingering for that note.
- Use the "B♭ Horn" fingering when the trigger key is pressed.
  *For notes with a "**T**" fingering, the B♭ Horn fingering is the recommended double horn fingering for that note.

○ = Open
● = Pressed down
T = Trigger (Double Horn Only)

Instruments and photos courtesy of Yamaha.

C

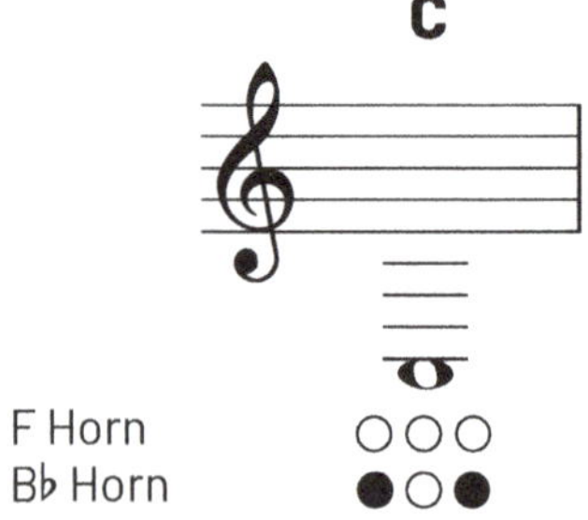

C♯ D♭

D

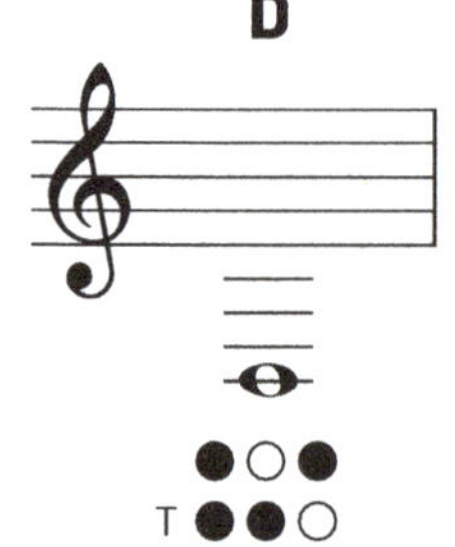

D♯ E♭

E

F Horn
B♭ Horn

F

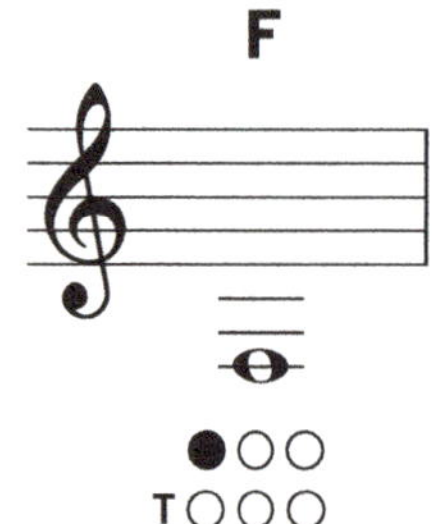

F♯ G♭

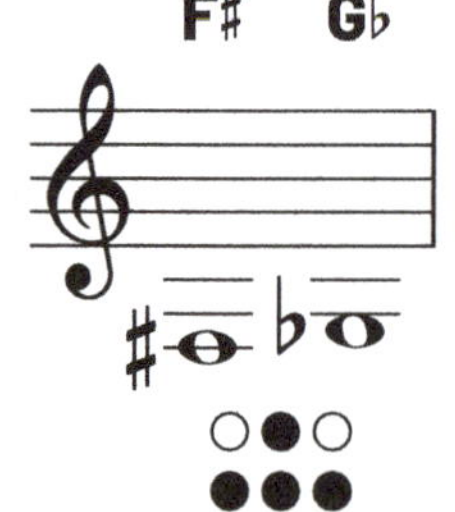

G

FINGERING CHART

F HORN

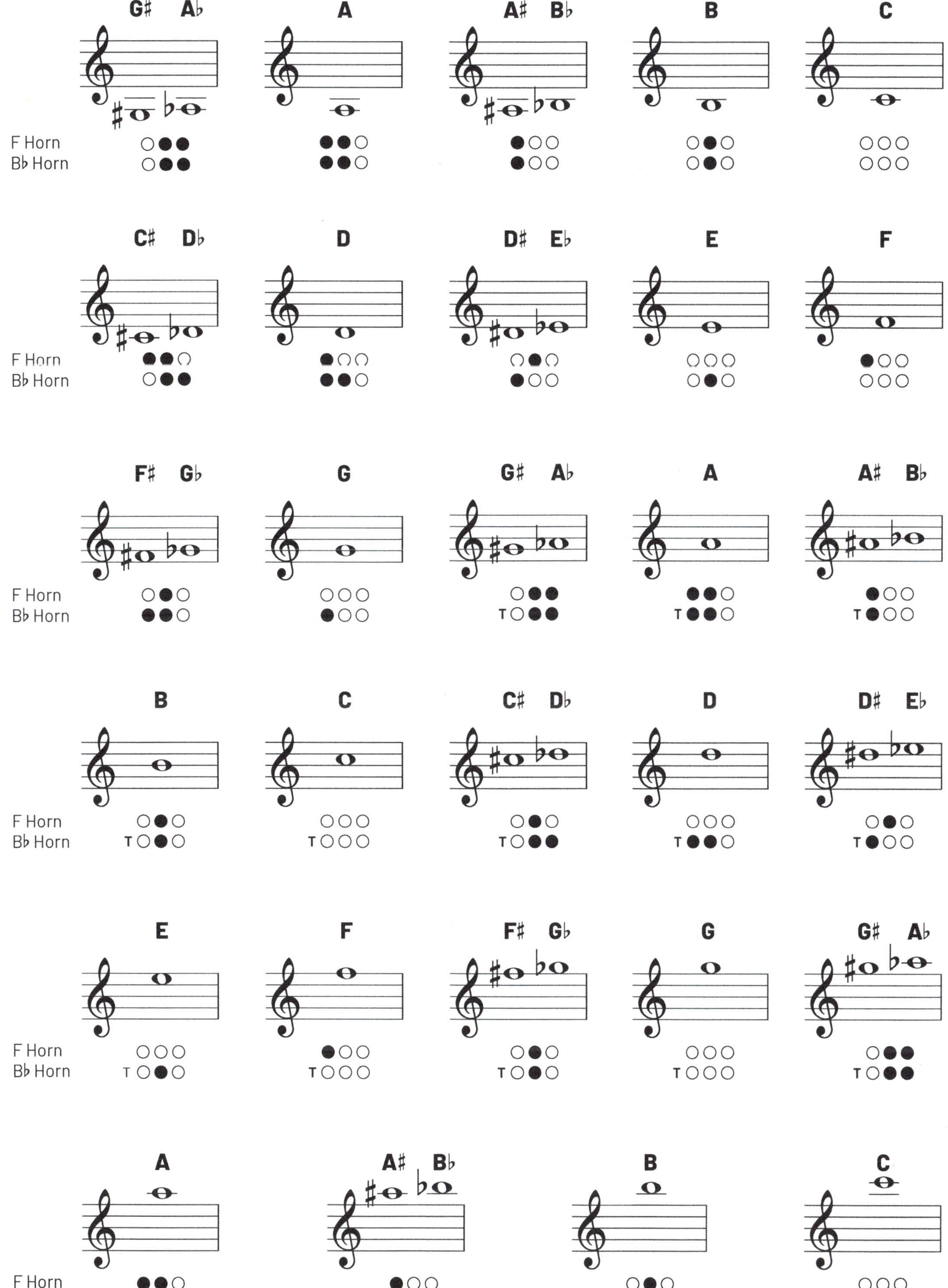

POSITION CHART

TROMBONE

Numbers below the notes = Slide positions

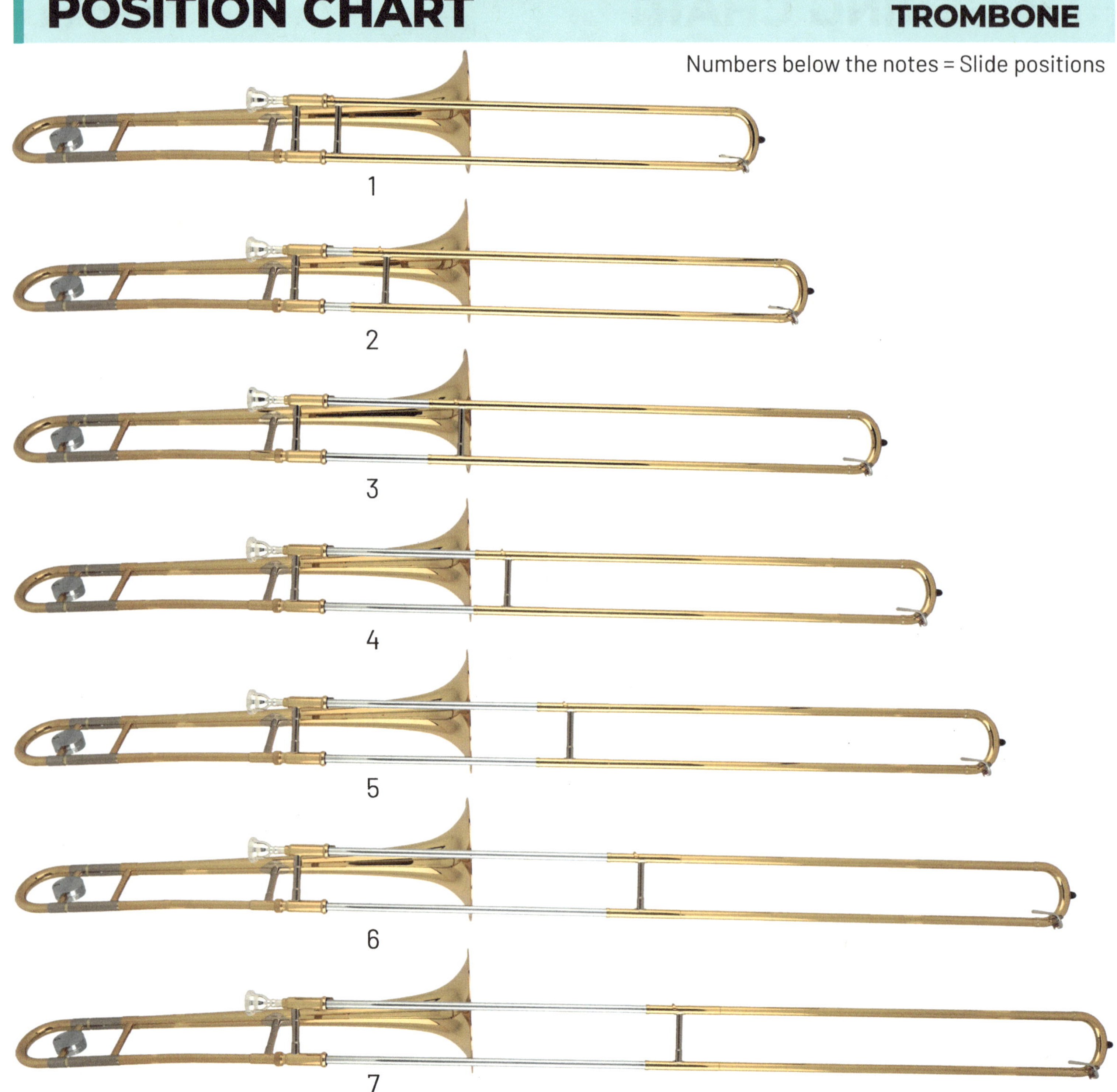

Instruments and photos courtesy of Yamaha.

Instrument Care Reminders

Before putting your instrument back in its case after playing, do the following:

- Use the water key to empty water from the instrument. Blow air through it.
- Remove the mouthpiece and slide assembly. Do not take the outer slide off the inner slide piece. Return the instrument to its case.
- Once a week, wash the mouthpiece with warm tap water. Dry thoroughly.

Trombone slides occasionally need oiling. To oil your slide, simply:

- Rest the tip of the slide on the floor and unlock the slide.
- Exposing the inner slide, put a few drops of oil on the inner slide.
- Rapidly move the slide back and forth. The oil will then lubricate the slide.
- Be sure to grease the tuning slide regularly. Your director will recommend special slide oil and grease, and will help you apply them when necessary.

CAUTION: If a slide or your mouthpiece becomes stuck, ask for help from your band director or music dealer. Special tools should be used to prevent damage to your instrument.

POSITION CHART

TROMBONE

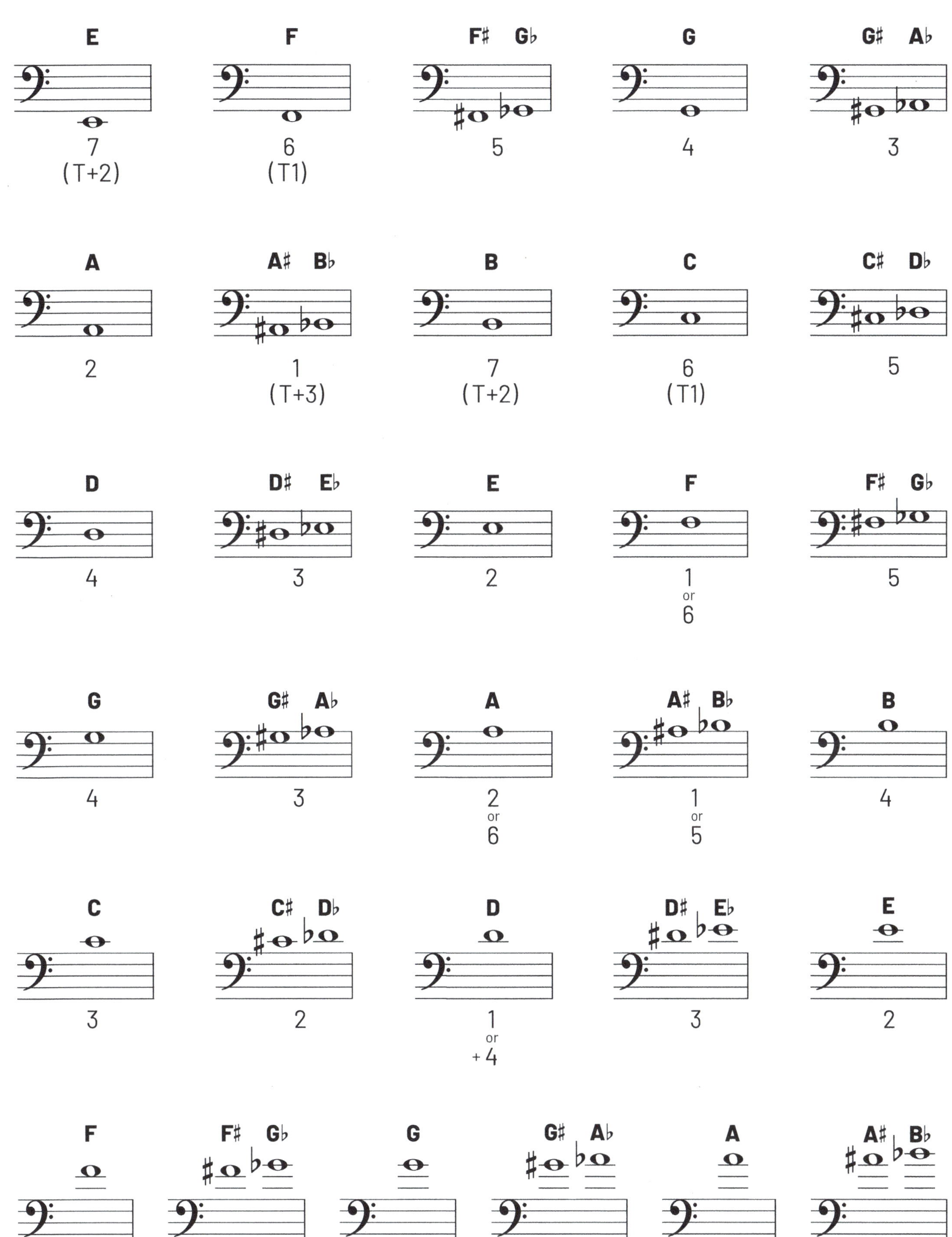

\+ = Make the slide a little longer.
− = Make the slide a little shorter.
T = F Attachment "trigger."

FINGERING CHART

BARITONE B.C.

Instrument Care Reminders

Before putting your instrument back in its case after playing, do the following:

- Use the water key to empty water from the instrument. Blow air through it.
- Remove the mouthpiece and wipe it clean. Once a week, wash the mouthpiece with warm tap water. Dry thoroughly.
- Wipe off the instrument with a clean soft cloth. Return the instrument to its case.

Baritone valves occasionally need oiling. To oil your baritone valves:

- Unscrew the valve at the top of the casing.
- Lift the valve half-way out of the casing.
- Apply a few drops of special brass valve oil to the exposed valve.
- Carefully return the valve to its casing. When properly inserted, the top of the valve should easily screw back into place.

Be sure to grease the slides regularly. Your director will recommend special slide grease and valve oil, and will help you apply them when necessary.

CAUTION: If a slide, a valve or your mouthpiece becomes stuck, ask for help from your band director or music dealer. Special tools should be used to prevent damage to your instrument.

Instruments and photos courtesy of Yamaha.

E

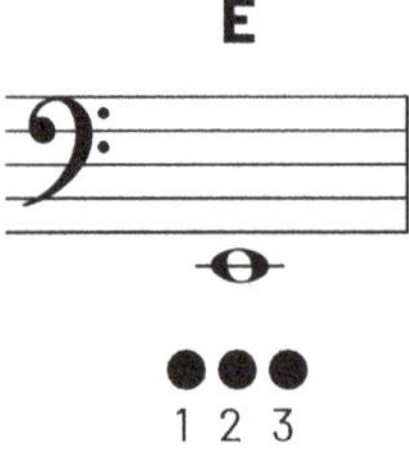

F

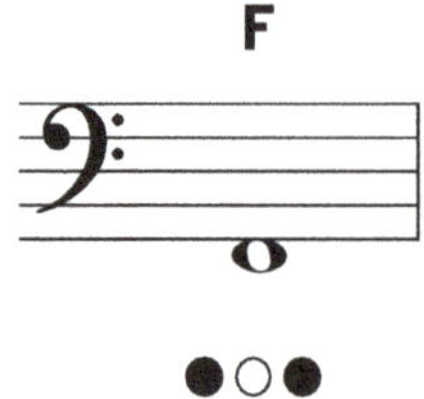

F♯ G♭

G

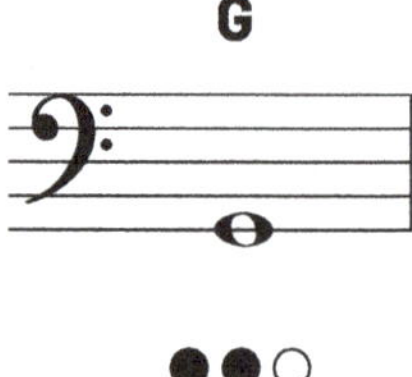

G♯ A♭

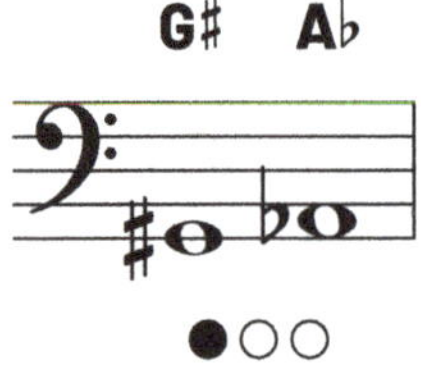

A

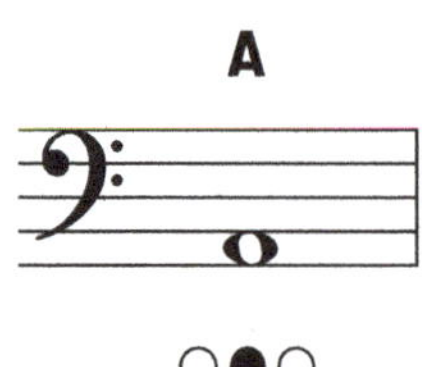

A♯ B♭

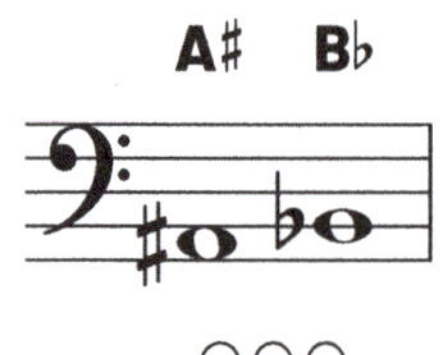

B

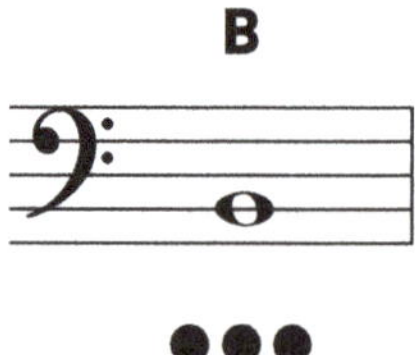

FINGERING CHART

BARITONE B.C.

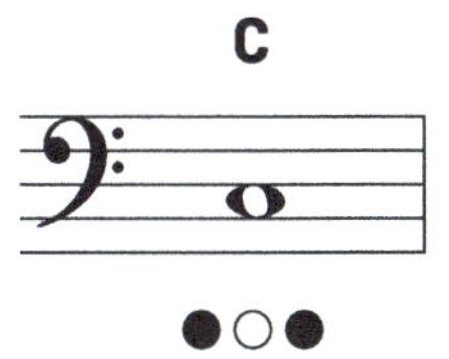

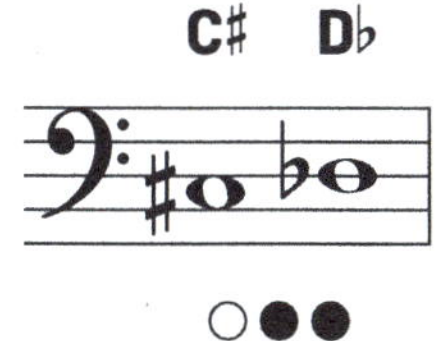

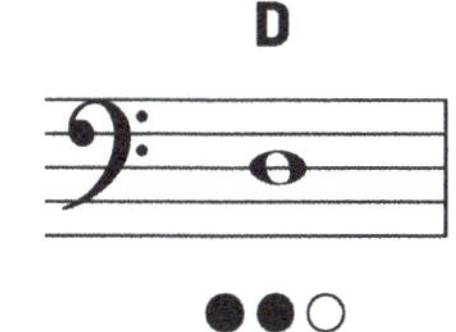

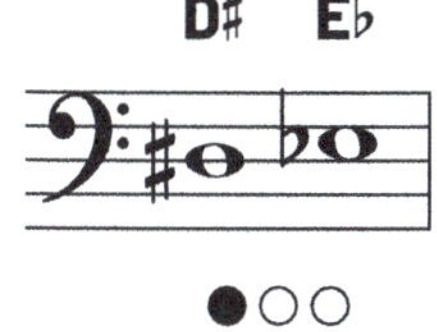

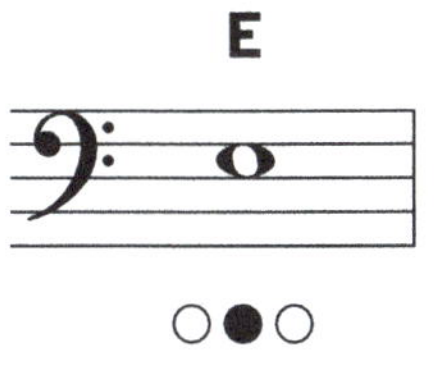

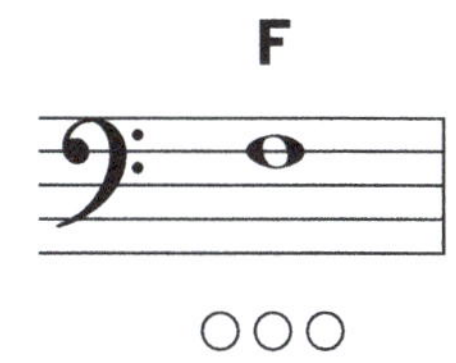

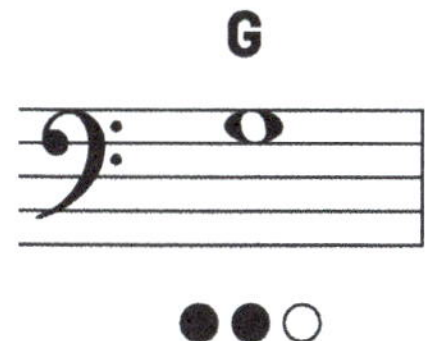

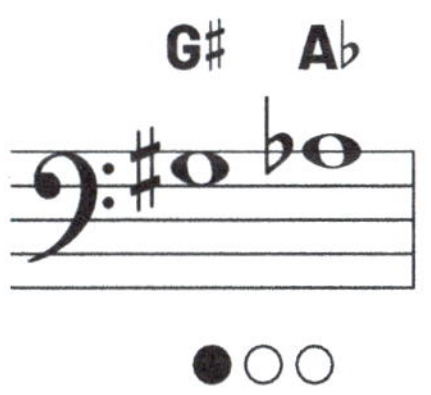

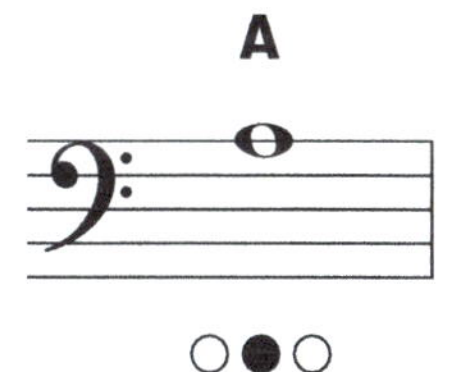

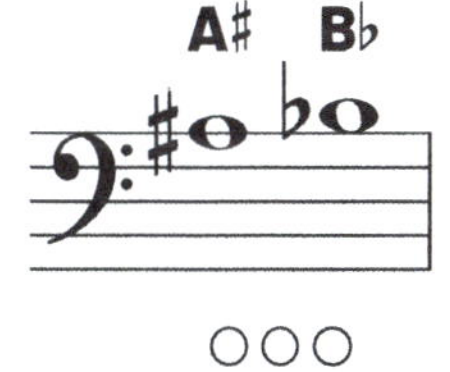

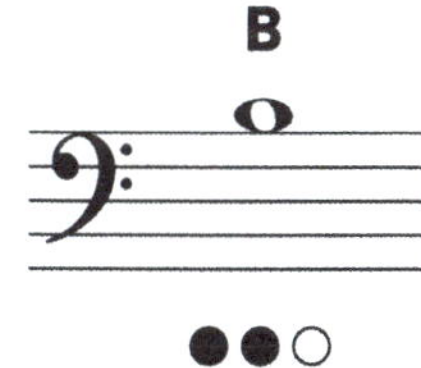

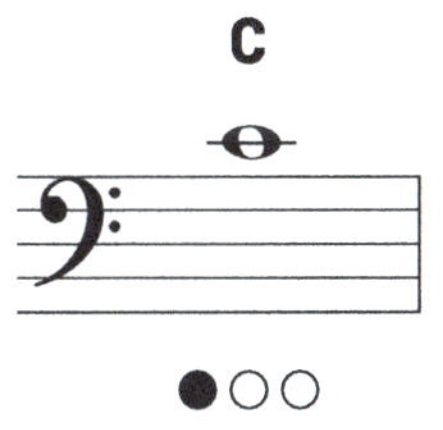

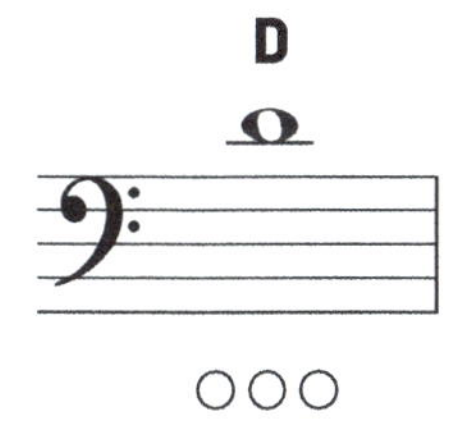

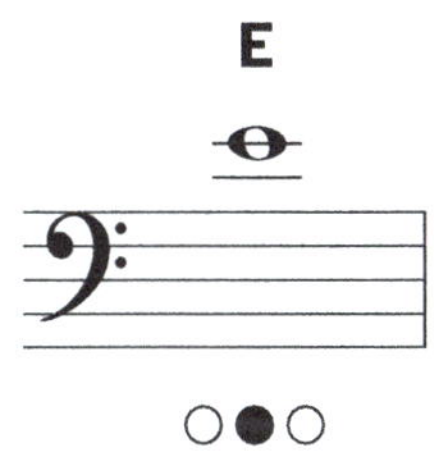

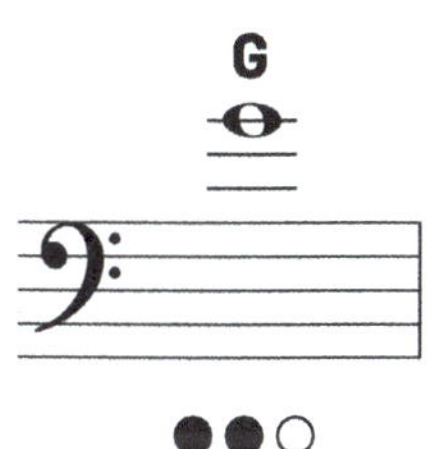

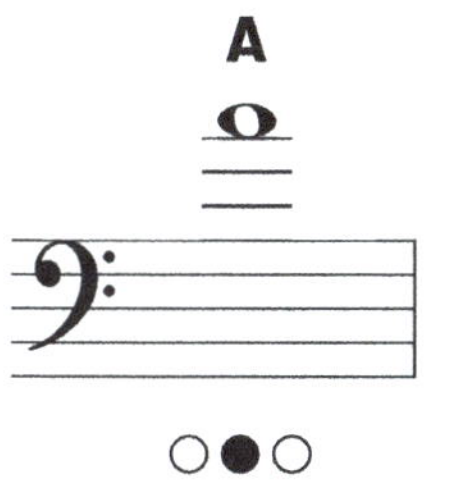

FINGERING CHART

BARITONE T.C.

Instrument Care Reminders

Before putting your instrument back in its case after playing, do the following:

- Use the water key to empty water from the instrument. Blow air through it.
- Remove the mouthpiece and wipe it clean. Once a week, wash the mouthpiece with warm tap water. Dry thoroughly.
- Wipe off the instrument with a clean soft cloth. Return the instrument to its case.

Baritone valves occasionally need oiling. To oil your baritone valves:

- Unscrew the valve at the top of the casing.
- Lift the valve half-way out of the casing.
- Apply a few drops of special brass valve oil to the exposed valve.
- Carefully return the valve to its casing. When properly inserted, the top of the valve should easily screw back into place.

Be sure to grease the slides regularly. Your director will recommend special slide grease and valve oil, and will help you apply them when necessary.

CAUTION: If a slide, a valve or your mouthpiece becomes stuck, ask for help from your band director or music dealer. Special tools should be used to prevent damage to your instrument.

Instruments and photos courtesy of Yamaha.

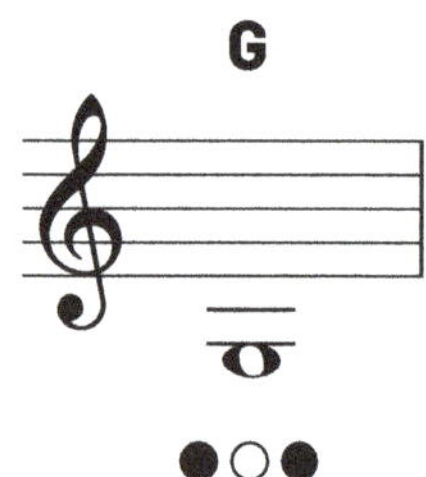

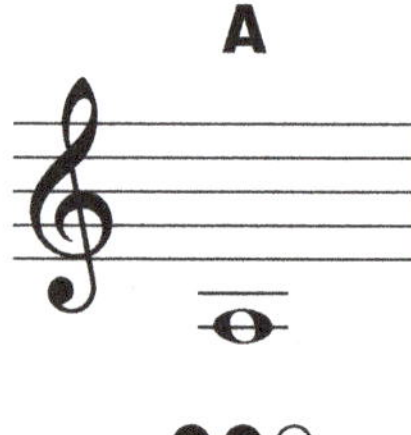

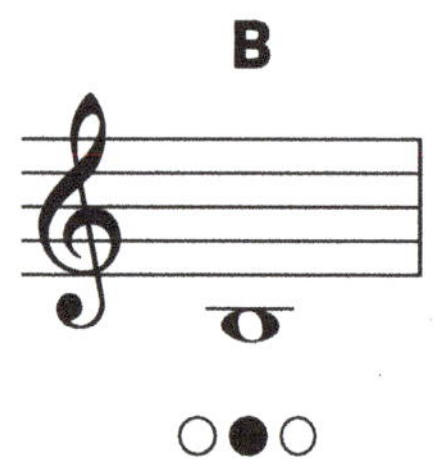

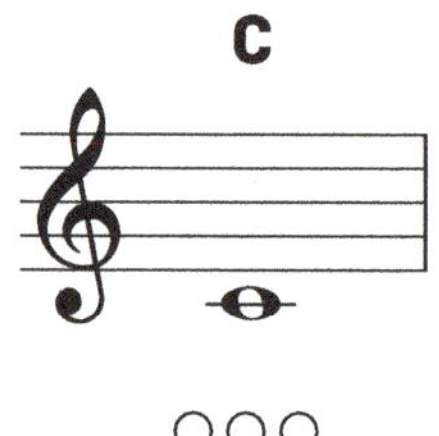

FINGERING CHART

BARITONE T.C.

D

D♯ E♭

E

F

F♯ G♭

G

G♯ A♭

A

A♯ B♭

B

C

C♯ D♭

D

D♯ E♭

E

F

F♯ G♭

G

G♯ A♭

A

A♯ B♭

B

C

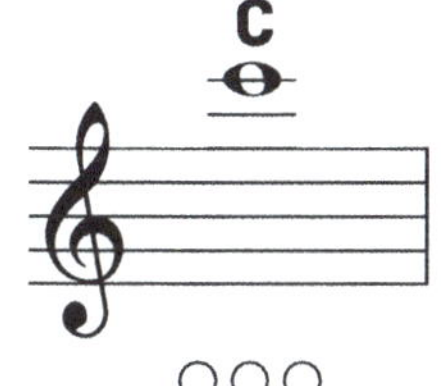

FINGERING CHART

TUBA

Instrument Care Reminders

Before putting your instrument back in its case after playing, do the following:

- Use the water key to empty water from the instrument. Blow air through it.
- Remove the mouthpiece and wipe it clean. Once a week, wash the mouthpiece with warm tap water. Dry thoroughly.
- Wipe off the instrument with a clean soft cloth. Return the instrument to its case.

Tuba valves occasionally need oiling. To oil your valves, simply:

- Unscrew the valve at the top of the casing.
- Lift the valve half-way out of the casing.
- Apply a few drops of oil to the exposed metal valve.
- Carefully return the valve to its casing. When properly inserted, the top of the valve should easily screw back into place.

Be sure to grease the slides regularly. Your director will recommend special slide grease and valve oil, and will help you apply them when necessary.

CAUTION: If a slide, a valve or your mouthpiece becomes stuck, ask for help from your band director or music dealer. Special tools should be used to prevent damage to your instrument.

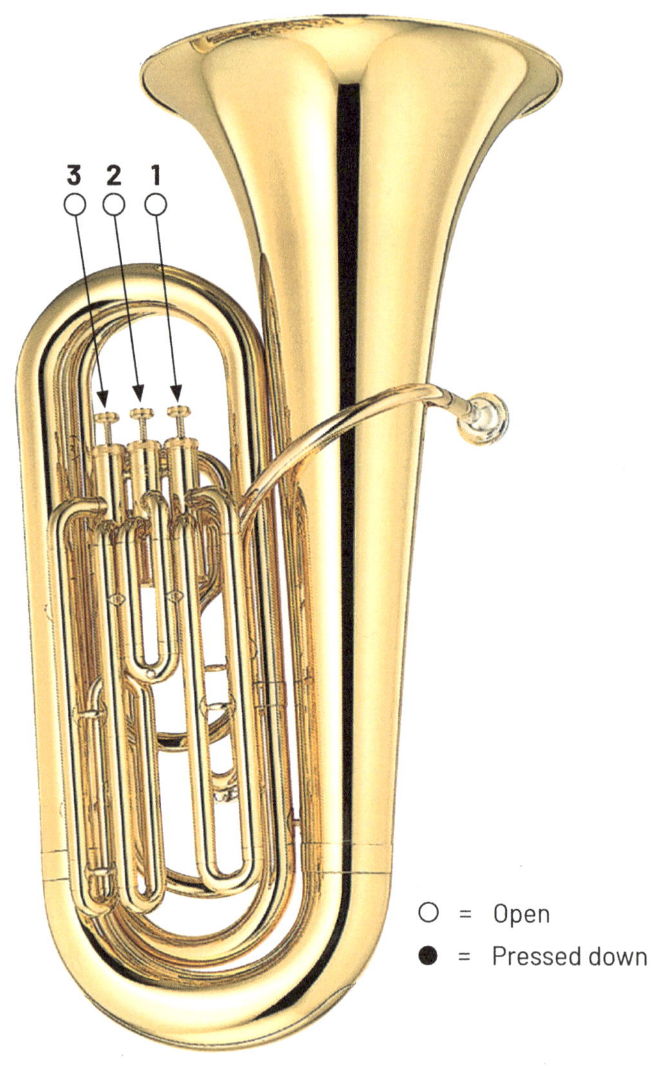

Instruments and photos courtesy of Yamaha.

E

F

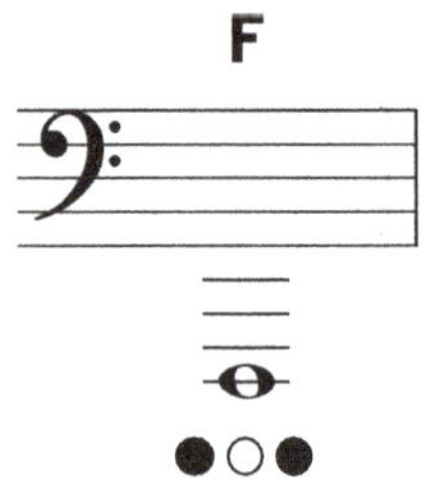

F♯ G♭

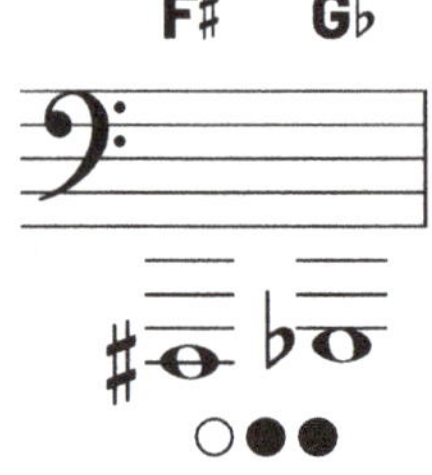

G

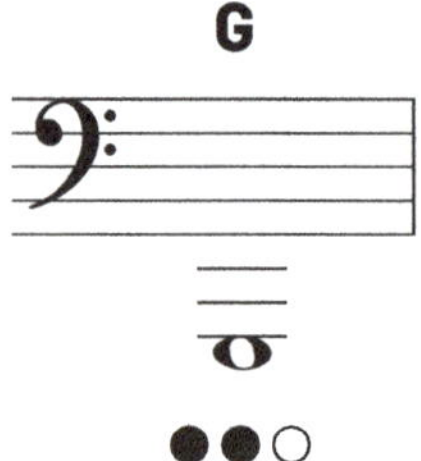

G♯ A♭

A

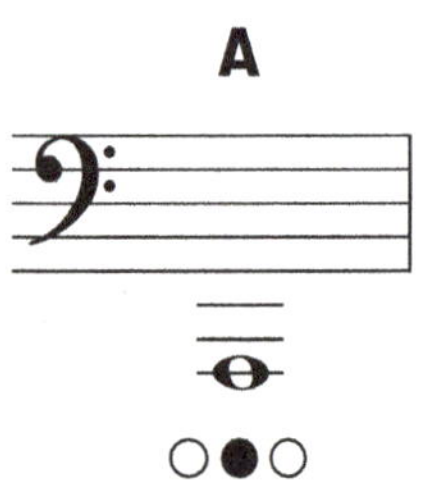

A♯ B♭

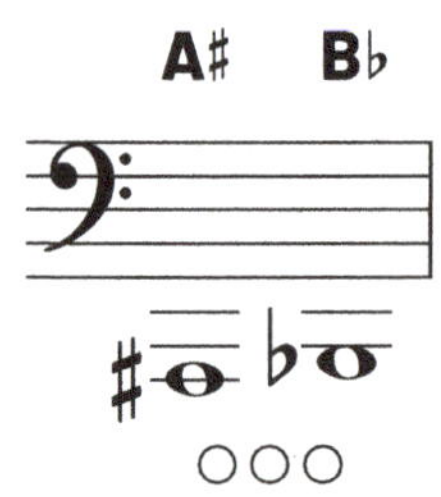

B

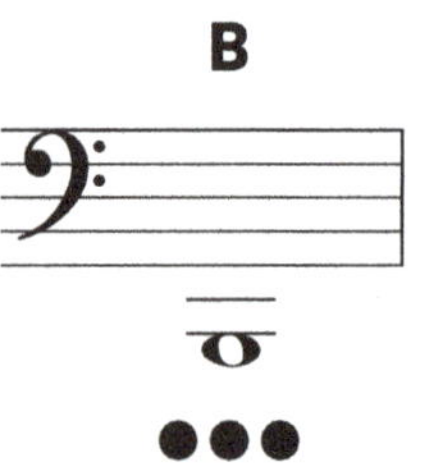

FINGERING CHART

TUBA

C

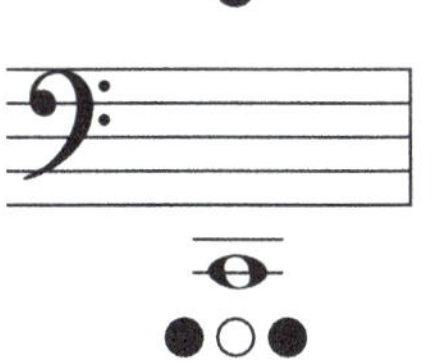

C♯ D♭

D

D♯ E♭

E

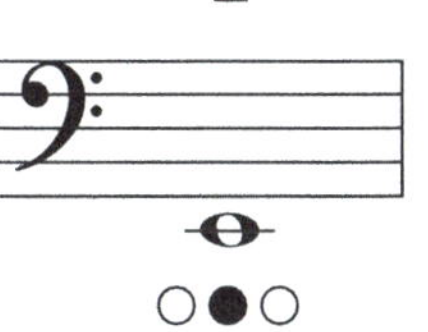

F

F♯ G♭

G

G♯ A♭

A

A♯ B♭

B

C

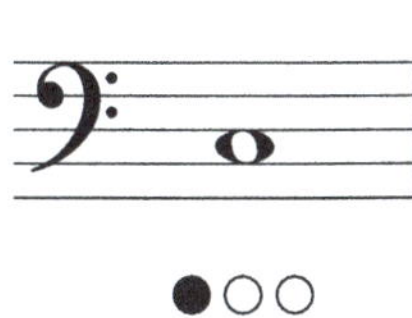

C♯ D♭

D

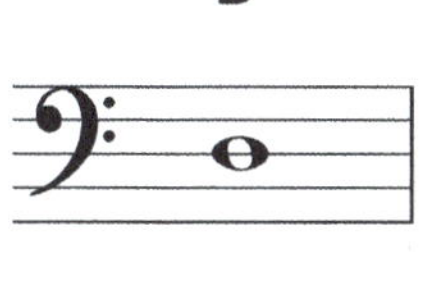

D♯ E♭

E

F

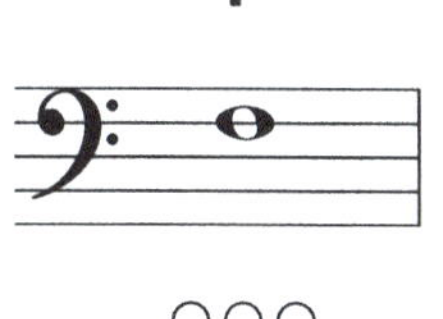

F♯ G♭

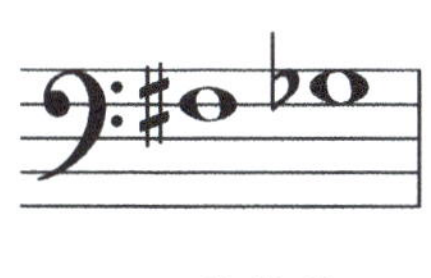

G

G♯ A♭

A

A♯ B♭

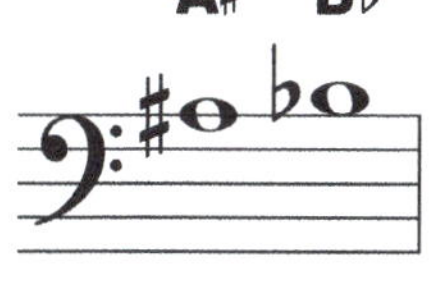

FINGERING CHART

ELECTRIC BASS

Instrument Care Reminders

- Be sure your amplifier is turned off before plugging-in or unplugging the audio cable connecting it to your instrument.
- When unplugging a cable, hold it by the plug (not by the wire).
- After playing, wipe off the instrument and strings with a clean soft cloth. Return the instrument to its case.
- Close all the latches on your case when the instrument is inside.
- Keep all 4 strings in tune (at normal tension) to prevent warping of the neck.
- Your case is designed to hold only specific objects. If you force anything else into the case, it may damage your instrument.

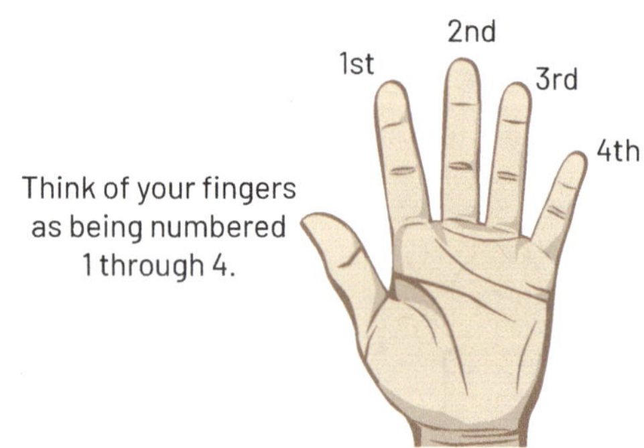

Think of your fingers as being numbered 1 through 4.

strings

4th 3rd 2nd 1st

frets

1st
2nd
3rd
4th
5th

Fingerboard diagrams show where to play the notes. Circles are drawn on the diagram to indicate the fingers to be used to play the notes.

Instruments and photos courtesy of Yamaha.

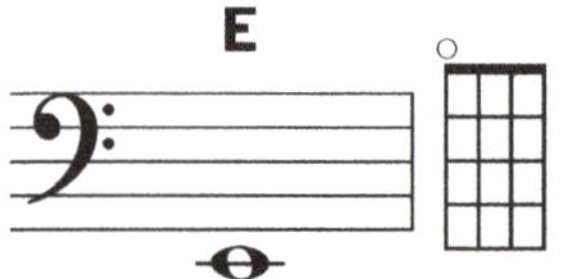

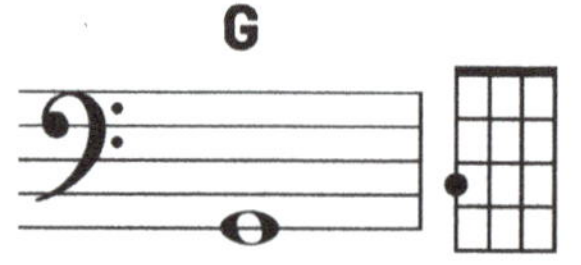

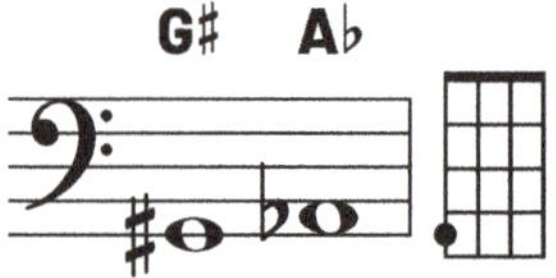

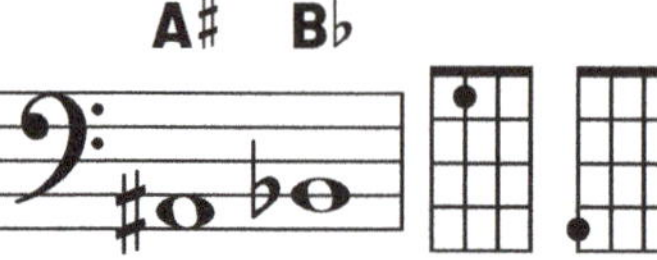

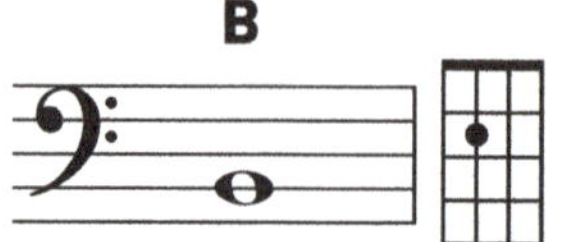

FINGERING CHART

ELECTRIC BASS

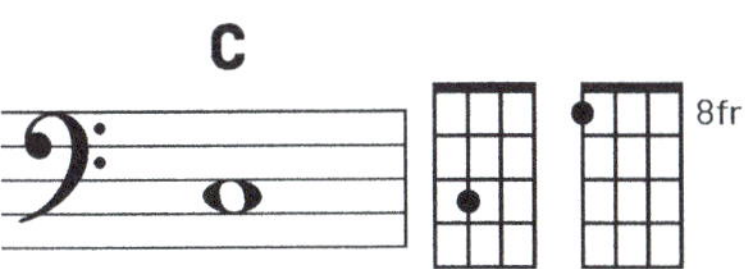

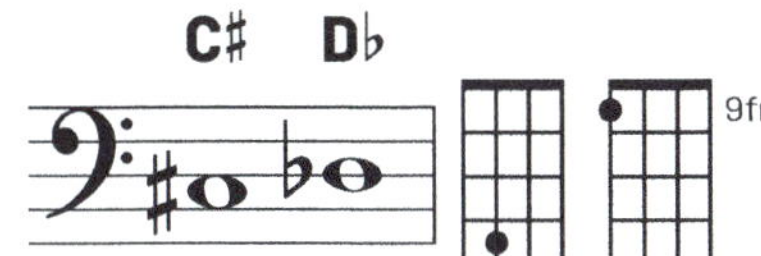

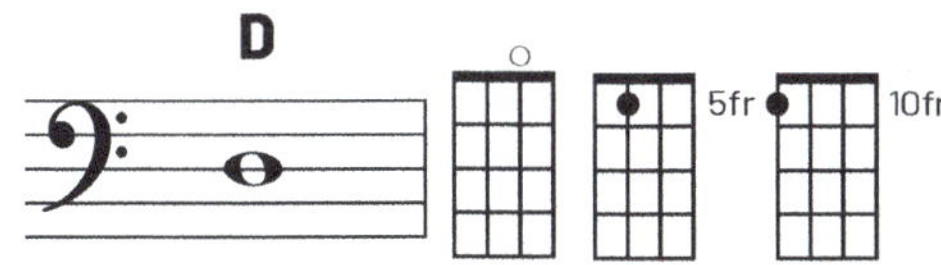

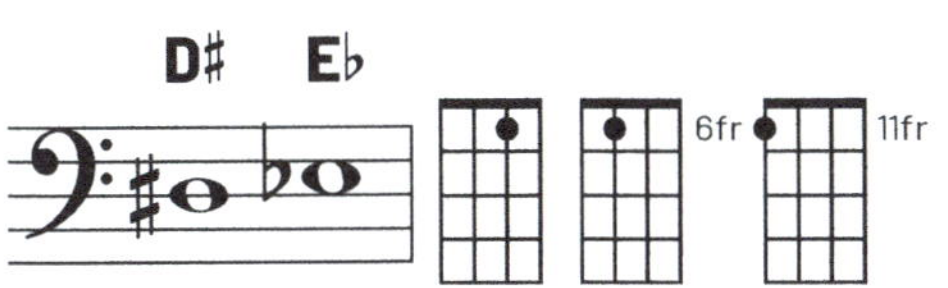

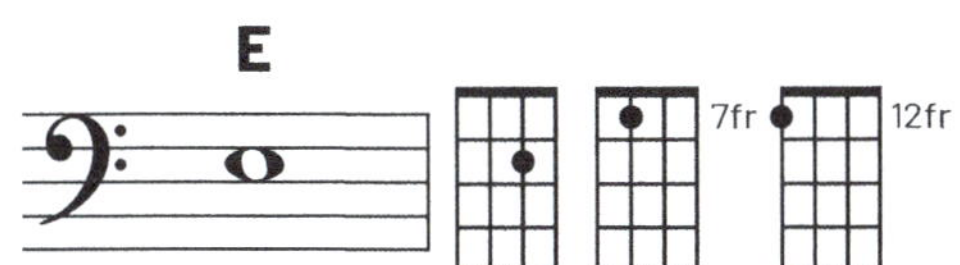

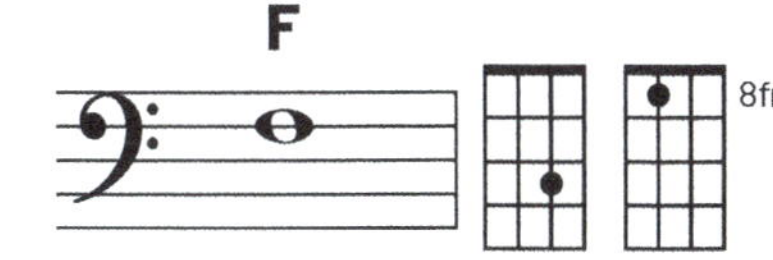

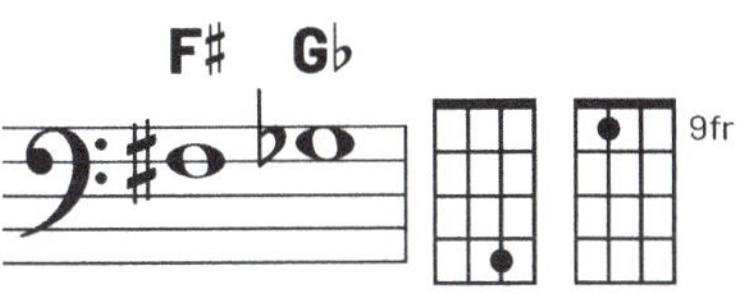

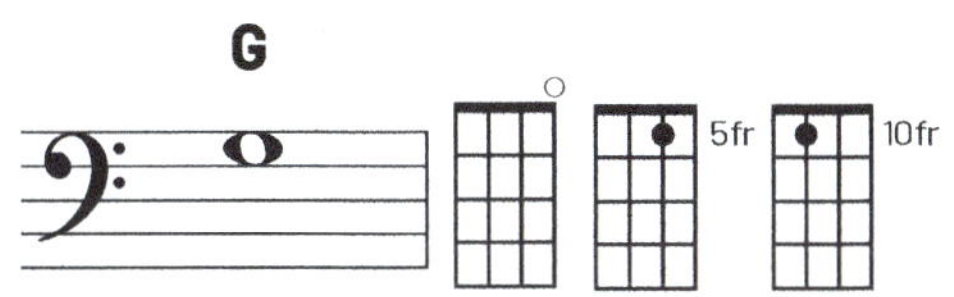

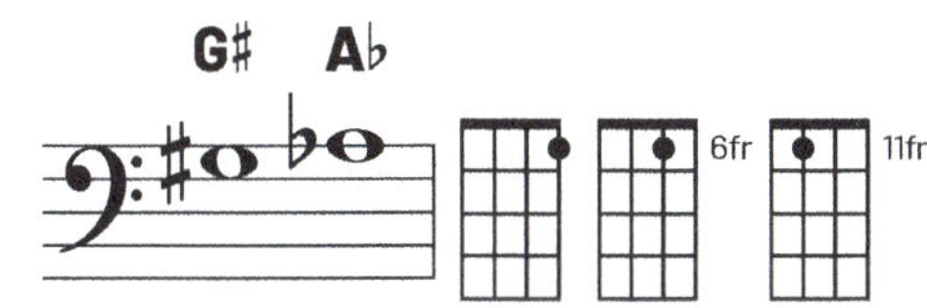

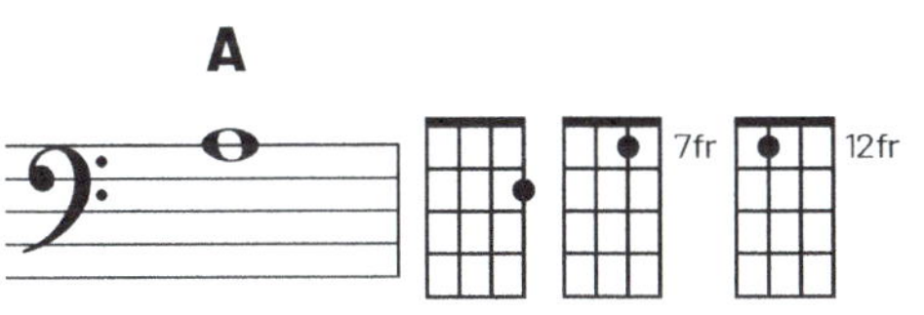

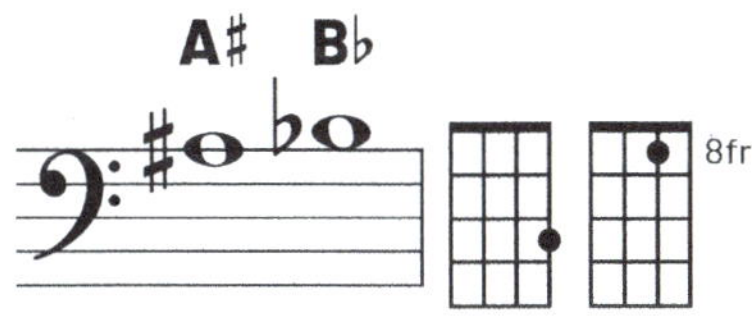

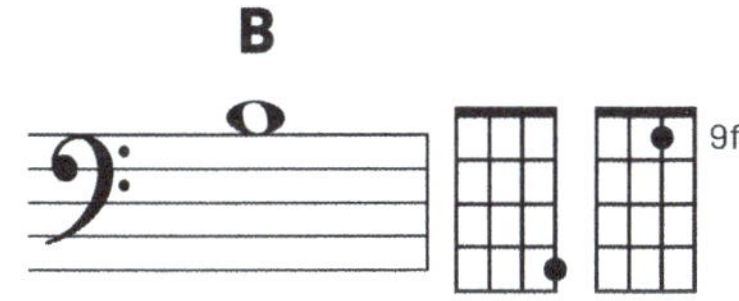

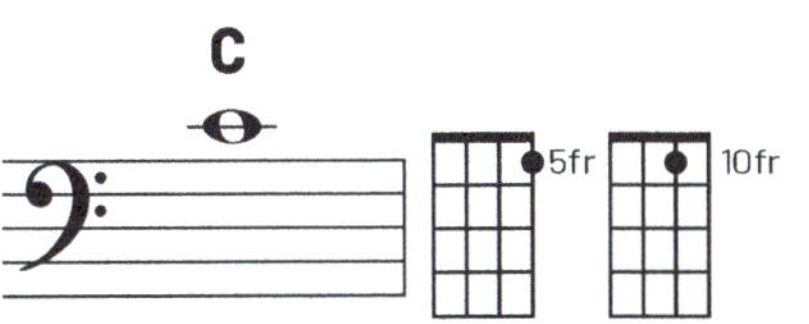

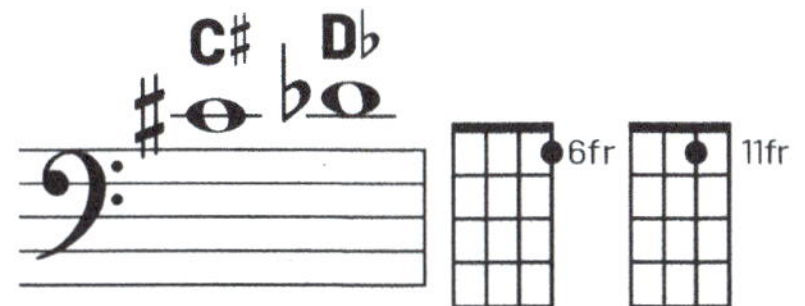

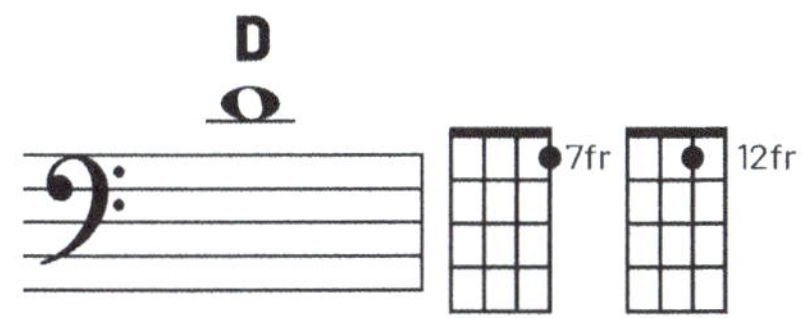

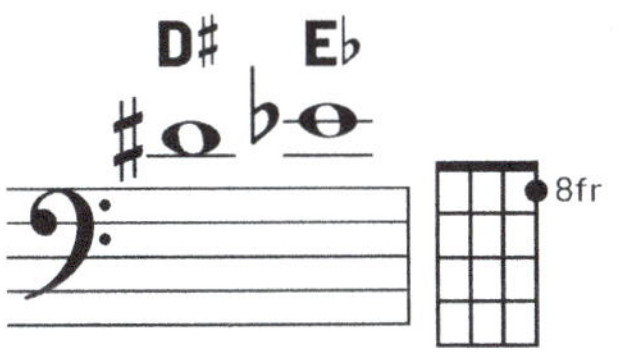

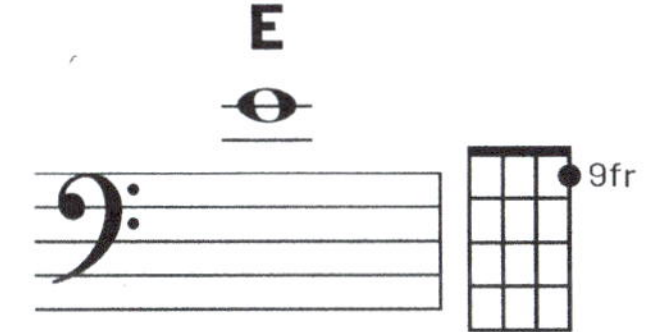

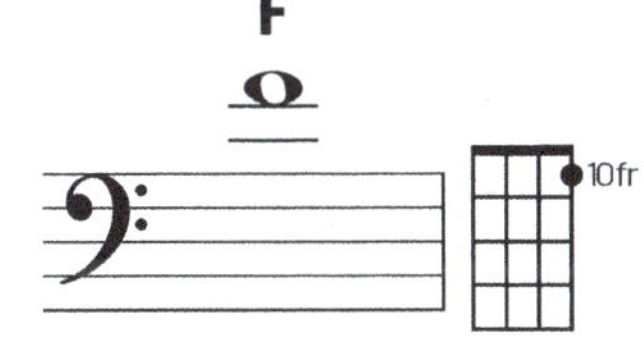

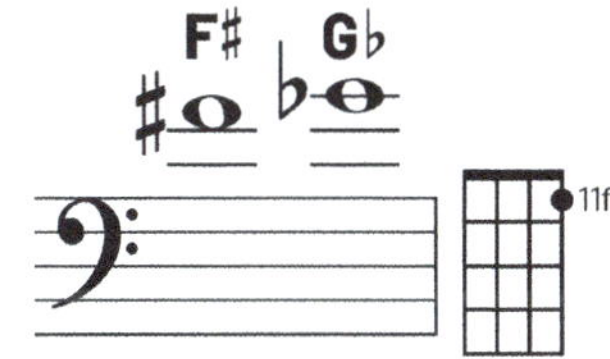

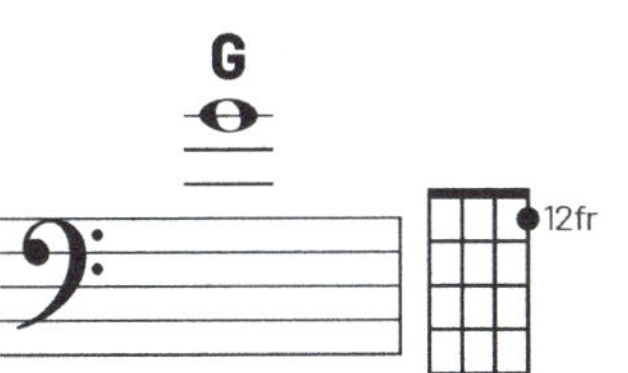

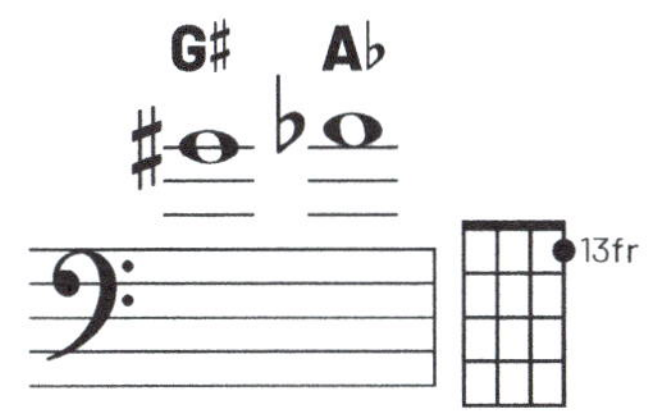

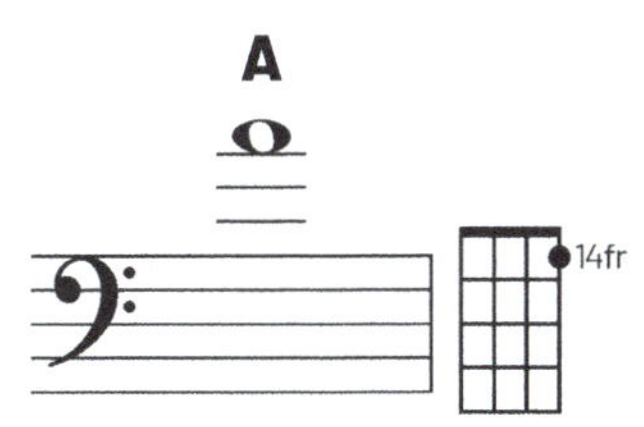

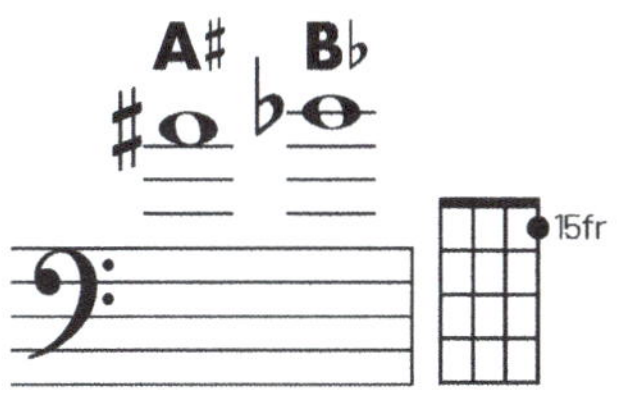

SNARE DRUM INTERNATIONAL DRUM RUDIMENTS

All rudiments should be practiced: open (slow) or close (fast) and/or at an even moderate march tempo.

Instrument Care Reminders

Snare drums occasionally need tuning. Ask your teacher to help you tighten each tension rod equally using a drum key.

- Be careful not to over-tighten the head. It will break if the tension is too tight.
- Loosen the snare strainer at the end of each rehearsal.
- Cover all percussion instruments when not in use.
- Put sticks away in a storage area. Keep the percussion section neat!
- Sticks are the only things which should be placed on the snare drum. NEVER put or allow others to put objects on any percussion instrument.

Instruments and photos courtesy of Yamaha.

I. ROLL RUDIMENTS

A. SINGLE STROKE RUDIMENTS

1. Single Stroke Roll

2. Single Stroke Four

3. Single Stroke Seven

B. MULTIPLE BOUNCE ROLL RUDIMENTS

4. Multiple Bounce Roll

5. Triple Stroke Roll

International Drum Rudiments courtesy of Percussion Arts Society

SNARE DRUM INTERNATIONAL DRUM RUDIMENTS

C. DOUBLE STROKE OPEN ROLL RUDIMENTS

6. Double Stroke Open Roll

11. Ten Stroke Roll

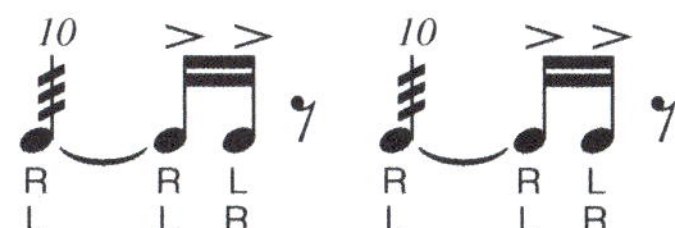

7. Five Stroke Roll

12. Eleven Stroke Roll

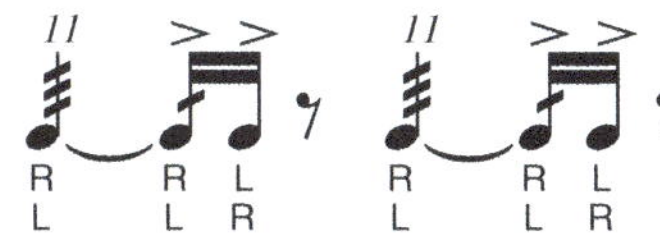

8. Six Stroke Roll

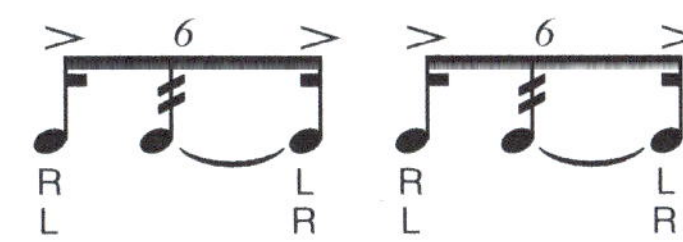

13. Thirteen Stroke Roll

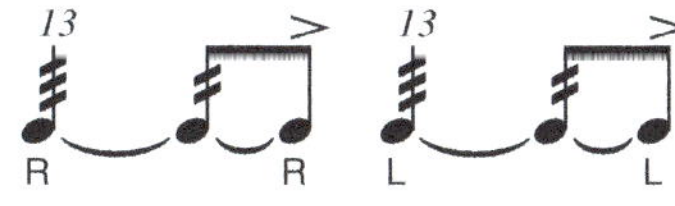

9. Seven Stroke Roll

14. Fifteen Stroke Roll

10. Nine Stroke Roll

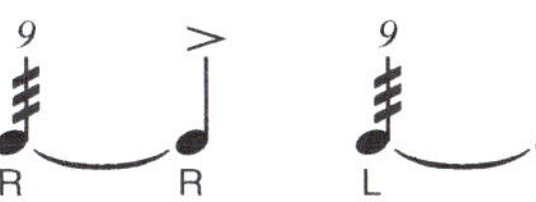

15. Seventeen Stroke Roll

II. DIDDLE RUDIMENTS

16. Single Paradiddle

18. Triple Paradiddle

17. Double Paradiddle

19. Single Paradiddle-Diddle

SNARE DRUM INTERNATIONAL DRUM RUDIMENTS

III. FLAM RUDIMENTS

20. Flam

21. Flam Accent

22. Flam Tap

23. Flamacue

24. Flam Paradiddle (Flamadiddle)

25. Single Flammed Mill

26. Flam Paradiddle-Diddle

27. Pataflafla

28. Swiss Army Triplet

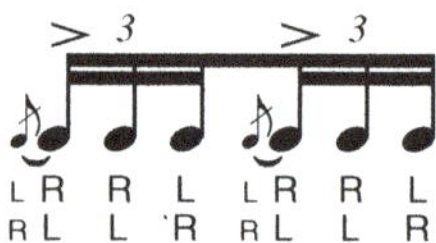

29. Inverted Flam Tap

30. Flam Drag

SNARE DRUM INTERNATIONAL DRUM RUDIMENTS

IV. DRAG RUDIMENTS

31. Drag

32. Single Drag Tap

33. Double Drag Tap

34. Lesson 25

35. Single Dragadiddle

36. Drag Paradiddle #1

37. Drag Paradiddle #2

38. Single Ratamacue

38. Double Ratamacue

40. Triple Ratamacue

KEYBOARD PERCUSSION INSTRUMENTS

Each keyboard percussion instrument has a unique sound because of the materials used to create the instrument. Ranges may differ with some models of instruments.

Instrument Care Reminders

- Cover all percussion instruments when they are not being used.
- Put mallets away in a storage area. Keep the percussion section neat!
- Mallets are the only things which should be placed on your instrument. NEVER put or allow others to put objects on any percussion instrument.

BELLS (Orchestra Bells)

- Bars - metal alloy or steel
- Mallets - lexan (hard plastic), brass or hard rubber
- Range - 2 1/2 octaves
- Sounds 2 octaves higher than written

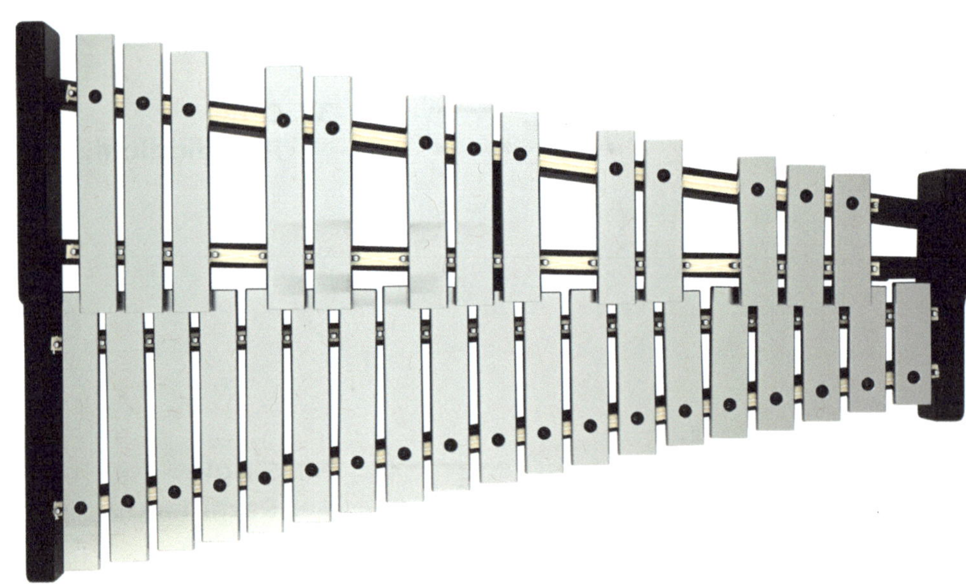

XYLOPHONE

- Bars - wooden or synthetic
- Mallets - hard rubber
- Range - 3 1/2 octaves
- Sounds 1 octave higher than written

Intruments and photos courtesy of Yamaha.

MARIMBA

- Bars – wooden (wider than xylophone bars)
  Resonating tube located below each bar
- Mallets – soft to medium rubber or yarn covered
- Range – 4 1/3 octaves (reads bass and treble clefs)
- Sounding pitch is the same as written pitch

VIBRAPHONE

- Bars – metal alloy or aluminum
  Resonating tubes located below each bar
  Adjustable electric fans in each resonator
  create "vibrato" effect
- Mallets – yarn covered
- Range – 3 octaves
- Sounding pitch is the same as written pitch

CHIMES

- Bars – metal tubes
- Mallets – plastic, rawhide or wooden
- Range – 1 1/2 octaves
- Sounding pitch is the same as written pitch

REFERENCE INDEX

Definitions (pg.)

Composers

World Music

REFERENCE INDEX FOR PERCUSSION

Definitions (pg.)

**These page numbers refer to the first section (percussion) of this book.*

Authors

DR. TIM LAUTZENHEISER
Founder, Attitude Concepts For Today, Bluffton, IN

JOHN HIGGINS
Managing Producer and Editor, Composer and Arranger, Hal Leonard Corp., Milwaukee, WI

CHARLES T. MENGHINI, D.M.A.
Director of Bands and Dean, Undergraduate Division; VanderCook College of Music, Chicago, IL

PAUL LAVENDER
Vice President – Instrumental Publications, Composer and Arranger, Hal Leonard Corp., Milwaukee, WI

TOM C. RHODES
President, RBC Music Inc., San Antonio, TX

DON BIERSCHENK
Vice President, RBC Music Inc., San Antonio, TX

Credits

Managing Editor and Producer	Paul Lavender
Production Editors	Stuart Malavsky Matt Wolf
Chorale Arrangements	John Higgins Paul Lavender
Percussion Author, Consultant, and Editor	Will Rapp
Design and Art Direction	Richard Slater Tim Bigonia Nicole Julius
Music Engraving and Typesetting	Thomas Schaller
Play-Along Tracks Arrangements and Production	Paul Lavender
Essential Elements Rhythm Section	Steve Millikan - Keyboards Steve Dokken - Bass Sandy Williams - Guitars Steve Hanna - Percussion Larry Sauer - Drums
Individual Study Accompaniment Recordings	Steve Potts - Piano
Recording and Mixing Engineers Aire Born Studios, Indianapolis, IN	Mark Aspinall John Bolt David Price Ben Vawter
Additional Recording Production	Jared Rodin Mark Aspinall
Project Supervision Aire Born Studios, Indianapolis, IN	Nanci Milam Mike Wilson Nina Hunt
Announcer	Scott Hoke

Featured Instrumental Artists

Flute	Karen Moratz Indianapolis Symphony Orchestra
Oboe	Roger Roe Indianapolis Symphony Orchestra
Bassoon	Robert Broemel Freelance performer and recording artist
Clarinet, Alto Clarinet, Bass Clarinet	Michael Borschel Indianapolis Symphony Orchestra
Alto, Tenor, and Baritone Saxophones	John Hibler Freelance performer and recording artist
Trumpet	John Rummel Professor of Trumpet, Indiana University, IN
F Horn	Gerald Montgomery Indianapolis Symphony Orchestra
Trombone, Baritone	K. Blake Schlabach Indianapolis Symphony Orchestra
Tuba	Anthony Kniffen Principal, Indianapolis Symphony Orchestra
Electric Bass	Steve Dokken Freelance performer and recording artist
Percussion	Will Rapp, D.M.A. Director of Bands and Applied Percussion, Kutztown University, PA

The authors wish to give special thanks to Herman Knoll, Vice President of Product Development, for his dedication, leadership, and expertise in the creation of the Essential Elements educational program.